99 BEST CLOSED-END FUNDS TO OWN NOW

Frank Cappiello & Peter Madlem

International Publishing Corporation
Chicago, Illinois

©1994 by International Publishing Corporation, Inc. All rights reserved. This publication may not be reproduced in whole or in part by any means without prior written consent. Requests for permission should be sent to:

Permissions Department
International Publishing Corporation
625 N. Michigan Avenue, Suite 1920
Chicago, IL 60611

Library of Congress Catalog Number: 94-78599

ISBN Number: 0-942641-59-0

The data in this book were gathered from company releases. This publication is designed to provide accurate and authoritative information in regard to the subject matter covered. However, it is sold with the understanding that the publisher is not engaged in rendering legal or professional investment services. If legal advice or other expert assistance is required, a competent professional should be retained.

Table of Contents

Preface .... *vii*

Chapter 1: Closed-End Funds: An Overview 1
    Definition 1
    Major Attractions 1
        Professional Investment Management 1
        Diversification 2
        Marketability 2
        Regulation 2
        Discounts 3
    A Modern Approach 4
    Tracking the Discount or Premium 7

Chapter 2: Recent Developments 11
    Soaring Assets, Narrowing Discounts 11
    Why the Discount? 12
    The Industry Tackles the Discount 13
    The Hybrid Funds 13
    Options on Closed-End Funds 13
    New Ways to Analyze a Fund 14
    Where Are the Bargains Now? 14
        Equities 15
        Beans or Bonds? 16
    Changes for Foreign Investing 17
    Rights Offerings 18

Chapter 3: Closed-End Fund Characteristics 21
    Investment Objective 21
    Distributions and Dividends 21
        Dividends 22
        Capital Gains 22
    To Reinvest or Not to Reinvest 24

Taxes 25
"Backup Withholding" 26
Reinvestment and Taxes 26
Complications 27
How to Buy a Tax 27
Minimizing the Tax Bite 27
Non-Taxable Dividends 28
Costs and Fees 28
Understanding Shareholder Reports 28
Board of Directors 30

Chapter 4: Closed-End Fund Categories 31

Overview 31
Bond Funds 31
    Corporate Bond Funds—Investment Grade 32
    Flexible Portfolio Bond Funds 32
    U.S. Government Bond Funds 32
    High Yield Corporate (Junk) Bond Funds 33
    International Bond Funds 33
    Multi Sector/Strategic Bond Funds 33
    Single State Tax-Free Bond Funds 34
    Federal Tax-Free Bond Funds 34
    Term Trust Bond Funds 34
Equity Funds 35
    Convertible (Bond and Equity) Funds 35
    Domestic and Specialized Equity Funds 36
    Dual Purpose Equity Funds 36
    Global and Multi Country Equity Funds 37
    Single Country Equity Funds 37

Chapter 5: Closed-End Fund Portfolios 39

Before You Invest 39
Beta 40
Average Maturities 41
Portfolio Risk Levels 42
    Low Risk 42
    Medium Risk 42
    Medium to High Risk 42
Model Portfolio Frameworks 43
Income Portfolios 44
    Taxable Portfolio 44
    Income Tax-Free Portfolio 44

Equity Fund Portfolios 45
    Balanced Portfolio (Growth and Income) Average Beta .. 45
    Global Growth Average Beta 45
Trading in the Closed-End Fund Market 45
Trading Opportunities 46
Market Timing 47
Some Pointers 48
Keeping up 48

Chapter 6: Reading the Fund Summaries 51

Shareholder Report Information 51
Statistics 52
    Stock Price 52
    NAV 53

Chapter 7: Summaries of the 99 Best Closed-End Funds to Own Now 55

Domestic Equity Funds 57
Single Country Funds 77
Multi County Funds 117
Single State —Tax Free Funds 131
Municipal Bond Funds—Leveraged 153
Municipal Bond Funds—Non-Leveraged 177
High Yield (Junk) Bond Funds 187
Convertible Bond Funds 197
Investment Grade Corporate Bond Funds 205
U.S. Government Bond Funds 219
Term Trust Bond Funds 229
International Bond Funds 241
Multi Sector Bond Funds 257

Appendix: Sources of Additional Information 281

Index of Funds 285

Preface

LESS IS MORE

This book represents a departure from our normal *The Complete Guide to Closed-End Funds: Finding Value in Today's Stock Market*. Rather than remain as part of an evolving problem, we decided to offer a solution.

And just what is the problem we endeavor to solve? It is the ever-increasing and overwhelming barrage of facts and figures threatening to smother all of us—particularly investors.

Encyclopedic data presentation for closed-end funds is available by subscription to either our monthly newsletter publication, *Frank Cappiello's Closed-End Fund Digest*, or through the on-line services of Unilink, which is updated weekly. Other sources include Standard & Poor's, Morningstar, and Thomas Herzfeld. Refer to the Appendix for further sources.

What is not available is a concise presentation of what to buy now, and why. So, we did all the work, crunched the numbers, considered economic data, spoke to management, looked at premiums and discounts, noted expenses, investigated the yields, discussed portfolio strategies, and after copious research, came up with a list of 99 closed-end funds to buy now.

The 99 closed-end funds presented in this book offer attractive buying opportunities for investors seeking either global diversification, a balanced portfolio, high current income, or tax-free income. All offer liquidity as they are traded on either the New York Stock Exchange (NYSE) or the American Stock Exchange (AMEX). Approximately 33% of these funds are equity; 67% bond. Of the 99 funds covered in this book, 6 trade on the AMEX and 93 trade on the NYSE.

This book offers the results of our research staff in selecting what we consider to be the best opportunities for investors for the remainder of 1994 and the first half of 1995. It begins in Chapter 1 with a definition of closed-end funds including their major attractions, methods of tracking the discount or premium, and a list of sources that supply regular net asset value and share prices. Chapter 2 discusses recent developments and how these new changes are affecting the closed-end fund market. Chapter 3 provides a description of various fund characteristics, including investment objectives, dividend distributions, tax considerations, services, costs, fees, shareholder reports, and other special considerations. Chapter 4 breaks down both equity and bond funds into various fund categories. Chapter 5 presents guidelines for creating any one of four recommended model portfolios: Global Growth; Balanced; Income; and, Tax-Free Income. Chapter 6 will assist you in reading the fund summaries contained in this book.

Once you have become familiar with closed-end funds, their characteristics, and how to structure a portfolio, move on to Chapter 7. Here we present our list of selections chosen from the following groups: Domestic Equity Funds; Single Country Funds; Multi-Country Funds, Single State Tax-Free Funds; Leveraged Municipal Funds; Non-leveraged Municipal Funds; High Yield (Junk) Funds; Convertible Bond Funds; Investment Grade Corporate Bond Funds; U.S. Government Bonds Funds; Term Trusts; International Bond Funds; and, Multi-Sector Bond Funds.

Should you need more information about any fund than is available in this book, write or call the fund to obtain a copy of its prospectus and latest annual report. In fact, it's always best to study a fund's prospectus and annual report before investing in it. The Appendix also offers additional sources of information. Carefully review this information, keeping in mind what you have learned in this book before making any investment decisions.

1
Closed-End Funds: An Overview

DEFINITION

Closed-end investment company, publicly traded fund, investment trust, and publicly traded investment fund are all terms applied to the closed-end fund. Similar to open-end funds, a closed-end fund is created when investors pool their money for a shared investment goal. This collective buying power affords an opportunity to participate in a well-diversified, professionally managed investment portfolio.

Closed-end funds differ from open-end funds in one very distinct way. While the shares of an open-end fund can be continually issued or redeemed on demand at net asset value (NAV), shares of a closed-end fund cannot. For the most part, the capitalization of a closed-end fund is fixed. New shares may be created for dividend or capital gains distributions and rights offerings, but unlike open-end funds, there is no continual offering of new shares. Sometimes a closed-end fund may choose to repurchase some of its outstanding shares on the open market. However, this is not a regular requirement for the benefit of shareholders wishing to sell. Usually, the only way a closed-end fund can redeem its shares at NAV is when it open-ends, is liquidated, or when a tender offer is made.

Investors who wish to sell their shares must "find" a buyer (like any other publicly-traded stock) on one of the major stock exchanges. The share price is determined independently of NAV by factors of supply and demand, general market sentiment, portfolio composition, yield, fees, liquidity, and extraneous factors such as year-end tax selling or unrealized capital gains.

MAJOR ATTRACTIONS

Closed-end funds are an attractive investment alternative because they offer professional investment management, a portfolio of diversified securities, and the opportunity to purchase these assets at a discount.

Professional Investment Management

Most of us lack the time, temperament, or training necessary to manage our investments on a full-time basis. We also can't afford to hire a full-time professional investment manager to do it for us. Pooling our investment dollars in a closed-end fund allows us to hire a professional manager and share the cost of the management fee. The manager decides what and when to buy or sell, what and when to hold, and when it may be more advisable to own dollars instead of stocks or bonds.

This is also true of open-end funds, with one important difference. Because of the fixed capitalization structure of closed-end funds, managers are not hampered by continuous buying and selling of fund shares in order to accommodate new investors and redemptions. This responsibility of open-end funds frequently conflicts with ideal market timing. A well-managed closed-end fund can generally buy and sell on more favorable terms and thus maintain a more consistent investment philosophy.

Diversification

Diversification reduces risk by spreading investments over a broad spectrum of holdings. A closed-end fund can take pooled assets to the market and make many purchases. This combined purchasing power allows for diversification in many different companies, industries, and countries. The closed-end fund arena includes aggressive, balanced, conservative, taxable income, tax-free income, precious metals, bullion, global, and international funds.

There are two basic types of closed-end funds: diversified and non-diversified. Diversified funds generally offer greater stability and lower risk because of the broader base and resulting higher liquidity of holdings. Non-diversified funds only invest in one type of security although they can own many different issues. An example of a non-diversified fund would be a precious metal fund or a single state municipal bond fund. The opening statement of every fund prospectus discloses the degree of portfolio diversification. (This information is also available in the fund summaries covered in this book.)

Marketability

Shares of closed-end funds are afforded a high degree of liquidity because they are traded on the major exchanges. Shares may be purchased from either a full-service securities broker or a discount broker.

Closed-end funds may be purchased in an Initial Public Offering (IPO) or in the aftermarket. As a rule of thumb, unless a fund offers something unique, such as an opportunity to invest in foreign or restricted markets (Chile, Mexico, Korea), it should be bought in the aftermarket when the chance exists for purchase at a discount to NAV.

Regulation

Closed-end funds are regulated by the Securities and Exchange Commission (SEC), the Securities Act of 1933, the Securities Exchange Act of 1934, and the Investment Company Act of 1940. The statutes require that full disclosure of all relevant fund characteristics be made available to potential investors through the issuance of a prospectus. They also mandate that shareholders be kept informed of fund activities and developments through quarterly, semiannual, or annual reports. Normally, these reports contain a message from management regarding fund performance, the outlook for the economy, portfolio composition, expenses incurred to operate the fund, and other information specific to the operation and performance of the fund.

Discounts

The Efficient Market Theory holds that at any given time stocks are accurately priced because they always reflect current market information. The major implication of this theory is that no one, except by sheer luck, can consistently beat the market. Closed-end funds could still present an exception to this theory.

Shares of equity closed-end funds have historically traded at discounts to their underlying NAV. (For a more complete discussion of the discount see Chapter 2.) Discounts generally deepen during uncertain economic times and shrink, or move to a premium, during upward-moving markets. Actual trends can be determined by reviewing various closed-end fund resources listed in the Appendix.

In the past, this characteristic of closed-end funds presented some rather interesting possibilities for both profit and loss. For example, assume that unfavorable and depressed market conditions have forced the shares of the ABC closed-end fund with a $10 per share NAV to sell for only $8, i.e., at a 20% discount. Now assume that a bull rally doubles the fund's NAV to $20 per share. While this occurs, the market drives the shares up from a 20% discount to a 20% premium above the new $20 NAV, or to $24. The end result is that the fund's NAV increased just 100% (from $10 to $20), while the share price increased 200% (from $8 to $24). This not-so-imaginary example illustrates how closed-end funds can easily double the performance of market averages in both directions. However, the recent increase in closed-end fund investors in the market has resulted in a considerable narrowing of both average discounts and discount swings.

In the past, this characteristic of closed-end funds presented some rather interesting possibilities for both profit and loss. For example, assume that unfavorable and depressed market conditions have forced the shares of the ABC closed-end fund with a $10 per share NAV to sell for only $8, i.e., at a 20% discount. Now assume that a bull rally doubles the fund's NAV to $20 per share. While this occurs, the market drives the shares up from a 20% discount to a 20% premium above the new $20 NAV, or to $24. The end result is that the fund's NAV increased just 100% (from $10 to $20), while the share price increased 200% (from $8 to $24). This not-so-imaginary example illustrates how closed-end funds can easily double the performance of market averages in both directions. However, the recent increase in closed-end fund investors in the market has resulted in a considerable narrowing of both average discounts and discount swings.

Despite increasing investor awareness, it is still possible to profit by buying closed-end funds at a discount and then selling them when the discount shrinks. Such a strategy is not merely theoretical but has actually been shown to work. As an Assistant Professor at the University of Alabama, Seth Copeland Anderson studied eight different closed-end fund trading strategies and then compared their investment results. Each of the trading systems required purchasing funds at specific discounts from NAV and later selling the shares when the discounts narrowed to a predetermined and smaller percentage. This study, published in the Fall 1986 issue of *The Journal of Portfolio Management*, used the weekly stock price, NAV, and distribution data for 17 diversified and specialized closed-end funds over three independent time periods:

- July 1965 to December 1969
- January 1970 to December 1976
- January 1977 to August 1984

At the time of the study, the selected funds represented approximately 85% of the total assets of all the closed-end funds.

Each portfolio consisted of $100,000, equally divided among those funds that met the criteria for each of the eight investment strategies. If four funds under Strategy 2 were selling at discounts of more than 10%, equal dollar amounts of $25,000 were invested in each. The funds were then held until the discount dropped to 5%. As shares were sold, or if a new fund met the criteria for inclusion in the portfolio, the dollar amounts were readjusted to always allow an equal amount to be invested in each fund. The results produced a perfect record with every one of the trading systems beating the performance of the Standard & Poor's Index of 500 common stocks (S&P 500). The most successful strategy was to buy those funds selling at a 20% discount and then sell them when the discount narrowed to 15%. On a compounded basis, this purely mechanical technique produced an astounding return of nearly 3,000% over the combined 20-year test period. Professor Anderson found that investors could do just as well over these three periods even when they didn't actively trade. The funds were simply bought at the beginning of each period and sold at the end.

The study results provide possible trading strategies that could enable investors to earn excess rates of return and demonstrate that the inefficiencies of the market for closed-end fund shares do offer potential for profit. Table 1.1 presents the results of this study.

The evolutionary changes that have taken place in the closed-end fund market since the original Anderson study have greatly affected overall discounts. For a number of reasons, specified in Chapter 2 of this book, discounts for nearly all closed-end funds have considerably narrowed. Recent studies have shown that the strategy and methods utilized by the Anderson study remain valid. However, the discount ranges must be adjusted to reflect the new environment. In addition, new strategies for trading closed-end funds are emerging with the changing market.

A MODERN APPROACH

When utilizing closed-end funds, the investor has at his or her disposal a unique set of two different criteria for measuring value and performance, the share price

Table 1.1: Study Results of Eight Trading Strategies (Seth Copeland Anderson)

Strategies		Average Performance (%)		
Discount From NAV for:		July 1965 to	Jan. 1970 to	Jan. 1977 to
Buy (%)	Sell (%)	Dec. 1969	Dec. 1976	Aug. 1984
5	0	+114	+105	+260
10	5	+129	+110	+262
15	10	+147	+104	+334
20	10	+136	+83	+387
20	15	+135	+126	+448
25	10	+171	+61	+404
25	15	+123	+86	+387
30	15	+49	+98	+344
Buy and Hold (No Trading)		+86	+51	+273
Standard & Poor's 500 Index		+24	+49	+126

Adapted from *The Journal of Portfolio Management*, Fall 1986, with permission.

as reflected on the stock exchange and the net asset value (NAV) as computed by the fund on a daily or weekly basis. A traditional equity share, such as IBM, certainly has a share price, but not a NAV. Meanwhile an open-ended mutual fund has a NAV that exactly matches its share price. Only a closed-end fund has a share price and a NAV that are generally not the same and may in fact be 20% to 30% different. In the case of such a difference, the investor might ask: What is the value of my investment—the share price or NAV? The answer is both.

If the investment must be sold within a short period of time, say the next several days, then the share price will govern. After all, this represents the amount that other investors are willing to pay for the shares. But the real value of these shares is always represented by the NAV. Here's a brief example. On April 1, 1994, the closing price of the Central Securities Fund (CET) was $15.00, yet the actual NAV was $17.08. Put differently, shares actually worth $17.08 were selling at a 12.2% discount, that is, for $15.00.

If the shares of Central Securities always sold at a 12% discount, then this fact would be of little value, but this is not the case. Over the past 12 months, the fund has traded at an average discount of 3.7%. In this case, a 12% discount is very significant and may well represent an excellent buying opportunity. There are, however, two other factors that must be taken into consideration. Does Central Securities represent a good investment value, and has the NAV been increasing or decreasing over time?

A little fundamental analysis reveals that Central Securities contains a solid portfolio of domestic stocks, and its performance over time has been excellent. Having decided that we would like to add it to our own investment portfolio how do we do this in the most auspicious manner? Step number one involves an analysis of the fund's recent NAV performance and expected future performance. One might expect, that if the prospects looked excellent, then the stock would be trading at a small discount or even a premium. If the fund is trading at a premium, you are in much the same position as buying a corporate issue at a high P/E (price earnings) ratio. By so doing, you are "over paying" now in order to attain an exceptional return in the future. An acceptable but risky decision.

Fortunately, it is often possible to buy a quality fund like Central Securities at a discount. Logic suggests that if you can buy a quality closed-end fund at a discount you will be paying less today (thereby reducing risk) with the expectation of an excellent return tomorrow. This is the crux of closed-end fund investing. If you find a fund with good prospects that is selling at a discount, and you buy at a discount, then you have purchased exceptional value.

Let's agree that the portfolio of CET is well constructed and that we therefore expect the NAV to perform well. Now we can determine what the stock price could rise to in order to return to its normal 3.7% discount. In our example, the NAV is now worth $17.08. Based upon the average discount of 3.7% we would expect the fund to trade at $16.50 per share. As NAV improves, the stock price should move rather smartly. Should the fund perform to our expectations then two things will happen. The NAV of the fund will increase, and the discount will narrow as more people realize the potential of the investment. Should the fund do exceptionally well, there is every reason to expect that its share price might actually rise to a premium to its NAV.

Why, do you ask, will people pay more for something than it is really worth? Before we attempt to answer the question, it is helpful to point out that this happens on a regular basis, so obviously it's possible. A few examples and their 12-month average premiums come to mind: Bergstrom Capital 9.9%, Source Capital 7%, Zweig Fund 17%, and the Gabelli Trust 4.3%.

Although many rationales have been offered for why funds are purchased at a premium, they all rest on the premise that the anticipated profit will more than offset the initial premium. As the funds just mentioned point out, paying a premium loses much of its significance if the premium holds constant over the period of your investment, or if it increases.

In the authors' opinions, a closed-end fund investor should be primarily focused on the NAV performance of the fund. If the NAV is decreasing, it is of little significance that the premium may be increasing. The premium or discount should be viewed as nothing more than the bridge that connects the NAV to the stock price. The nature of closed-end fund price structure suggests that share price and NAV will seldom be equal, and in their differences premiums and discounts are created. These differences are important, but are only important in the way that they relate to the underlying NAV movements.

As a diagnostic aid, premium/discounts can provide a useful indication of the fund's health and investment value. The first and most basic approach is to find situations where the NAV is increasing while the share price is decreasing. On a weekly basis, this phenomena can be found on the pages of T*he Wall Street Journal* or *Barron's,* and it represents the basic motivator for reducing discounts. Obviously, increasing value and decreasing price is an attractive proposition.

The next situation involves a case where NAV is increasing while price is increasing, but NAV is increasing more rapidly. This is also an attractive opportunity. Bear in mind that an open-end fund buyer will always be paying full NAV and cannot take advantage of share price/NAV discrepancies.

Now consider the case where share price is advancing more rapidly than NAV. This is typical of a "fad" or overheated situation, where too many investors are chasing a limited number of shares. As the discount narrows or perhaps goes to a premium, you are put on notice that a fundamental change in share price value is taking place. As the price is rising, you are getting less and less NAV with each dollar invested even though this entire process may take place within a discounted price structure. The important fact here is that you are in a position to know what is going on and can make your investment decisions accordingly. If this were an open-end mutual fund, the fund would simply issue more shares and there would be no indication that an "overheated" situation might be building.

Herein we see yet another interpretation of the discount/premium structure. One may choose to view discounts and premiums as an indicator of the market's reaction to the funds performance and expectations. Conceptually, it's a little like an audience applause meter. Note that we are speaking of the market's perception, not the actual performance of the fund. The fund can be doing quite well, but the audience may not be enthused and a discounted price structure may result. In other cases, performance can be mediocre resulting in relatively flat NAV but the public will bid up the price thereby narrowing the discount or even creating a premium.

The case for closed-end funds remains compelling. With their discounts, low fees, and coherent management, they lend themselves to asset allocation and multifund investing.

TRACKING THE DISCOUNT OR PREMIUM

Closed-end fund share discounts or premiums are determined by comparing the NAV with the market price. The NAV is calculated by totaling the market value of all securities in the fund's portfolio, adding all other assets such as cash or cash equivalents, deducting all liabilities, and then dividing by the number of shares outstanding. When the market price of a share is above its NAV, it is said to be selling at a premium. When the market price is below its NAV, it's selling at a discount. The formula used to determine the actual premium or discount is:

$$\frac{(\text{Stock Price} - \text{Price})}{\text{NAV}}$$

A number of publications report the share premium or discount of closed-end funds in addition to other information. Equity fund figures for Friday are supplied by the Monday edition of *The Wall Street Journal* under the heading "Publicly Traded Funds". The table provides a fund's NAV, market price, and premium/discount for the preceding Friday. Figure 1.1 is an example of a *Journal* listing for a closed-end fund.

Figure 1.1: An Example of a Closed-End Fund Quotation

Fund Name	Stock Exchange	N.A. Value	Stock Price	% Difference
Diversified Common Stock Funds				
Adams Express	NYSE	19.50	17-3/8	-10.90

Source: *The Wall Street Journal,* March 28, 1994.

In this example from March 28, 1994, the *Journal* reported that the Adams Expressdiversified common stock fund, which is traded on the New York Stock Exchange, had a NAV of $19.50 per share, a market price of 17-3/8 per share ($17.38), and was selling at a 10.90% discount to NAV. Any footnotes regarding the reporting date, currency exchange rates, and whether the prices reflect dividend or tax payments are shown at the bottom of each chart. The same information can be found every Monday in *Barron's*. The *Barron's* tables also include the bond funds, and these figures are also based on closing figures from the previous Friday. These same bond figures also appear in the Wednesday edition of the *Journal*.

A moving average of individual fund premium/discount figures is available in the monthly newsletter, *Frank Cappiello's Closed-End Fund Digest* (see Figure 1.2 on page 9). Value Line and Morningstar also publish summations for closed-end funds.

Annual premium/discount figures, along with pertinent information found only in a fund's annual report, are supplied in the tables of each selected fund summary included in this book. Investors who are familiar with closed-end fund investing can go directly to Chapter 7, where we list those funds from which you may select and build your own portfolio. Individuals who require more information about closed-end fund characteristics, how categories are defined, and how to interpret the fund summaries should review Chapters 2 through 5.

Figure 1.2: Equity Fund Statistics

Fund	Sym	As of 7/29/94- Stk Pr	NAV	Cur Pr/Dsc	Avg p/d	-7/30/93- Stk Pr	NAV	12 Mo Dist	-12 Mo TR- Stk Pr	NAV	Portfolio	Digest Recom
Domestic Equity Funds—Diversified												
Adams Express	ADX	17.38	19.31	(10.02%)	(9.36%)	20.38	20.65	1.630	(6.72%)	1.40%	Consmr 26%, Utils 16%, Fin.17%, Engy 10%,	SB
Allmon Trust	GSO	9.62	10.36	(7.09%)	(5.35%)	10.00	10.56	0.000	(3.74%)	(1.89%)	Mine 5%, Telecom 2%, BanKg 2%, Ins 2%, Util 2%	SB
Baker Fentress	BKF	16.50	19.37	(14.81%)	(16.68%)	18.38	21.78	2.240	1.98%	(0.78%)	Technology 13%, Cap Gds 10%, Fin'l Svcs 10%	OP
Bergstrom Cap	BEM	86.50	94.60	(8.56%)	(0.79%)	92.00	88.52	2.000	(3.80%)	9.12%	Biotech 21%, Invest Co 9.5%, Telephone 6%	SB
Blue Chip Value	BLU	6.75	7.51	(10.11%)	(0.42%)	8.25	7.82	0.460	(12.60%)	1.91%	Elec Cos 4%, Oil 6%, Rtl Stores 4.%, Misc 8%	SB
CenFd Canada	CEF	5.38	4.96	8.35%	7.68%	5.38	4.90	0.000	0.00%	1.22%	Gold 58.1, Silver 41.2%	
Central Sec	CET	17.12	18.41	(6.97%)	(8.32%)	14.88	16.29	1.650	26.21%	23.14%	Electrn 15%, Com 11%, Bus Svcs 11%, Ins 12%	OP
Couns Tandem	CTF	12.75	15.32	(16.77%)	(15.11%)	16.00	18.00	0.000	(20.31%)	(14.88%)	Util-Elec 37%, Telecom 13%, Gas 8, Other 43%	SB
Delaware Gr Div	DDF	13.62	13.33	2.21%	(0.08%)	14.25	14.56	1.080	3.19%	(1.03%)	Util 50%, Fin 28%, Hlth 6%	
Engex Inc	EGX	7.50	9.90	(24.24%)	(21.46%)	9.38	11.65	0.000	(20.00%)	(15.02%)	Biotech 16%, Mec Tech 15%, Comm 9%	
Gabelli Trust	GAB	11.12	10.75	3.48%	3.67%	10.50	11.48	1.110	16.52%	3.31%	Tele 12%, Broadcasting 8%, Ind Prods 8%	SB
Gen'l Am Inv	GAM	20.88	23.21	(10.06%)	(10.00%)	23.25	24.79	2.090	(1.22%)	2.05%	Hlth 26%, Rtl 20%, Cnsmr 22%, Fin'ins 14%	SB
Inefficient Mkt Fd	IMF	9.62	11.90	(19.11%)	(14.79%)	9.62	11.34	0.000	0.00%	4.93%	Eq 95%, Cash 10%, Conv 4%	
Jundt Growth Fund	JF	12.88	14.17	(9.13%)	(7.19%)	14.50	14.74	0.890	(5.06%)	2.17%	Comp. Svcs 18%, Comm 22.6%, Rtl 20%	SB
Liberty All-Star	USA	10.12	9.78	3.52%	4.11%	11.00	10.47	1.050	1.59%	3.43%	Drugs/Hlth 10%, Ins 8%, Cmptr 8%, Oil/Gas 7%	
MG Sm Cap	MGC	9.50	10.96	(13.32%)	(11.21%)	10.50	11.62	1.137	1.30%	4.10%	Cnsmr 35%, Tech 17%, Energy 12%	SB
Patriot Global Div	PGD	12.00	12.31	(2.51%)	(0.33%)	14.88	15.26	1.134	(11.70%)	(11.89%)	Utils 33%, Fin'l 18%	SB
Patriot Prfd Div	PPF	12.12	12.18	(0.45%)	0.56%	15.00	14.01	0.963	(12.75%)	(6.19%)	Utils 25%, Fin'l 22%	
Patriot Prem Div	PDF	8.50	8.24	3.15%	1.02%	11.00	11.13	1.250	(11.36%)	(14.73%)	Utils 66%, Fin Svcs 11%	
Patriot Prem Div II	PDT	10.12	10.28	(1.50%)	(2.63%)	12.62	13.65	1.100	(11.08%)	(16.63%)	Utils 66%, Fin'l 1%, Treasures 3%	SB
Patriot Sel Div Tr	DIV	13.12	13.43	(2.27%)	2.28%	18.50	17.47	1.637	(20.20%)	(13.75%)	Utils 67%, Fin'l 10%, Treasuries 3%	SB
Pfd Inc Mgt	PEM	12.75	13.20	(3.40%)	0.02%	14.75	14.29	1.316	(4.63%)	1.58%	Pfd Stk 97% — LEV	
Pfd Inc Opp Fd	PFO	11.38	11.76	(3.27%)	1.68%	—	—	1.577	—	—	Pfd Stk 95% — LEV	
Pfd Income Fd	PFD	15.75	15.88	(0.81%)	(1.19%)	—	—	2.821	—	—	Adj Rate Pfd 65%, Pfd Stk 35% — LEV	
Putnam Div Inc	PDI	10.00	10.99	(9.00%)	(1.73%)	12.00	12.51	1.417	(4.85%)	(0.82%)	Pfd 35%, Pfd Srvers 28%, ARP 25%, Com 8%	OP
Royce Micro Cap	OTCM	7.00	7.45	(6.04%)	—	—	—	0.000	—	—	Ind cyclicals 20%, Tech 16%, Consmr Dur 15%	SB
Royce Value Tr	RVT	12.38	13.29	(6.88%)	(5.10%)	13.25	13.58	1.150	2.07%	6.33%	Ind Prod 24%, Fnan. Inter. 20%, Ind Ser 17%	OP
Salomon Bros Fd	SBF	12.38	14.34	(13.70%)	(10.55%)	13.38	15.64	1.830	6.20%	3.38%	Basic Ind 16%, Fin 15%, Energy 11%	SB
Source Cap	SOR	40.62	36.92	10.03%	6.95%	40.62	39.32	3.600	8.86%	3.05%	Svcs 20, Hlth 20%, Ind Cyclicals 19%, Fin 12%	SB
Tri-Continental	TY	22.88	26.58	(15.82%)	(14.64%)	24.75	27.98	2.600	0.90%	4.28%	Fin/In 9%, UST 8%, Engry 8%, Csmr gds/svc 9%	SB
Zweig Fund	ZF	12.00	10.44	14.94%	14.11%	12.88	11.38	0.860	(0.11%)	(0.70%)	Tech 11%, Oil 6%, Retail 3%, Banks 3%	
Group Average				(5.49%)	(2.90%)					(0.81%)		

Reprinted with permission from *Frank Cappiello's Closed-End Fund Digest*, August 1994, Madent Publishing Co., Inc.

2

Recent Developments

In less than ten years closed-end mutual funds have emerged as vibrant and viable investment vehicles. Since 1986, the number of closed-end funds has grown five-fold to over 525 funds.

After falling out of favor with the Crash of 1929, closed-end funds regained popularity after the Crash of 1987. A plethora of new funds have come to market. Capital flooded into new issue single country funds and, most notably, tax-free municipal funds. In fact, John Nuveen & Co. is the current reigning king of closed-end funds, with nearly 20% of the $120 billion market under management. The rapid expansion of the closed-end fund realm should continue to accelerate now that topics unique to the vehicle have drawn the attention of industry groups and the SEC. At the top of the list are two items: 1. the question of the discount to net asset value and 2. how to bring more flexibility to the funds. In mid-1991, SEC and industry responses to these questions resulted in a revolutionary change, aspects of which are discussed below.

SOARING ASSETS, NARROWING DISCOUNTS

1994 continued the patterns begun in 1993. Capital influx continued to rise, as did NAVs and share prices. The most active segment of the market was the single country funds. Emerging markets became the darling of investors as stock prices soared and premiums swelled. But the most significant change continued to be the shrinkage of the discount. Since 1979, the average discount for domestic equity funds has narrowed from around a negative 29% to about minus 4%. Year-end discounts on all categories of closed-end funds were indicative of the changing environment. On the equity side, where larger discounts were the historic norm, only the equity side of the Dual-Purpose funds continued to trade at substantial discounts. Elsewhere, Multi Country funds moved from an average minus 6.9% in 1993 to a premium of 2% at year end 1994; Single Country funds fell from a discount of 7.9% to a premium of 6.7%, and Convertible funds traded at a 3.5% discount, up from a 7.6% discount in 1993. With three exceptions, the Bond Income funds saw their premiums move back to discounts in 1994. The exceptions were the U.S. Government Bond funds, the High Yield (Junk) Bond funds, and the Flexible Bond funds all of which cotinued to trade at premium levels. The Leveraged Tax-Free group ended the year at a 4% discount, Unleveraged Federal Tax-Free funds traded at an average discount of 1%, and Investment Grade Corporates traded at 1.2% premium. This presents a problem for value hunters because it is difficult to justify paying a premium for a fund.

One of the historical appeals of closed-end fund investing has been the ability to purchase funds at a discount. (See Seth Anderson's Study on pages 3-5.) While it is still prudent to avoid significant premiums, it is even more important to recognize that narrow discounts are not reasons to avoid specific funds. Investors can no longer move to the sidelines and wait out shrinking discount cycles.

Bargains can still be found by comparing average discounts to NAV. Recent studies continue to support the strategy of buying a fund when it trades at a discount that is 5 percentage points lower than its own average discount. In addition, that fund must also trade at a wider discount than that of similar funds.

For example, if a fund that normally trades with a 5% discount to NAV can be purchased at a 10% discount, it is a buy only if similar funds are not trading at a 15% or wider discount.

WHY THE DISCOUNT?

Most closed-end funds have always traded at discounts to their NAV. There have been many theories put forth as to why. For instance, some commentators feel that discounts exist primarily because investors have not been able to redeem their shares on demand at NAV. Unlike open-end funds that continually issue and redeem shares at NAV, closed-end funds have a fixed number of shares that trade on a stock exchange. The result is that supply and demand determine share price.

Another theory states that the cause of the discount has been the lack of promotion for closed-end funds by the brokerage community. It's ironic that the only time such promotion occurs is during a fund's initial public offering. That's the worst time to purchase a closed-end fund because offering fees and commissions built into the initial share price can nip the investor out of seven cents of every dollar. After the fund is brought to market, the once hot sales topic all but disappears.

High expense ratios are another reason put forth to explain why closed-end funds can trade at a discount. Sometimes it's just not worth a 2% or 3% management fee to assemble a portfolio.

Tax liability can also lead to discounts. For example, suppose a mature fund had purchased shares of Apple computer and Xerox during their formative stages at very low prices. Further, suppose that the fund now has a NAV of $12, of which $5 is unrealized gain on the value of those judiciously purchased shares. When the fund sells out those positions they will have $12 in cash and will distribute the $5 as a capital gains distribution. The investor will have to pay a tax on that $5 gain even if his or her funds did not earn it. However, a fund that trades at a wide discount as a result of unrealized capital gains shouldn't be overlooked. It's still an excellent candidate for IRA and pension accounts where the tax liability is deferred. Check the annual and/or quarterly reports for portfolio information. And, call the fund with any questions you may have.

Discounts can also be the result of illiquidity. This can be a problem with funds that have restricted securities or invest in small or foreign markets. Poor performance can be another factor. Some funds have stringent anti-takeover provisions that can protect poor management. Currency risks can also cause discounts in funds that invest abroad. Any one or a combination of these issues can result in a closed-end fund that trades at a discount to NAV.

THE INDUSTRY TACKLES THE DISCOUNT

In 1991, the industry began to seriously address several of the factors affecting the discount. The end result has resulted in our current era of narrow discounts. This is not to be viewed as a brief occurrence, it is an evolutionary event. There are a handful of basic reasons behind this phenomenon. The easiest explanation lies in the recognition of the industry's rapid growth and increased investor awareness. More and more brokerage firms, investment advisers, and individuals are trading closed-ends. Many newsletters are springing up to track the market. The consequence has been an increase in the general knowledge and activity in the market, and the shrinkage of the discount.

Secondly, many new funds have introduced innovative mechanisms in their charters specifically designed to narrow the discount. Among the first devices to occur several years ago were the pay-out policies adopted by many equity funds. Share tender option features were also introduced, and some funds inaugurated open-ending provisions. As the trend extended, discounts continued to narrow.

Once it is understood, on a broader scale, that these devices are now in place and expanding, new opportunities will be found to trade closed-end funds with small discounts. Presently, it is safe to say that certain closed-end funds can be purchased at discounts that are narrower than historical averages.

THE HYBRID FUNDS

The authors feel that one of the most important reasons for the discount is the inability to exit a fund at NAV. In May of 1991, the SEC proposed the concept of a hybrid fund that would combine the features of both open-end and closed-end funds. SEC chairman Richard C. Breeden told leaders at the Investment Company Institute conference that the SEC is considering "increasing flexibility of choice" for investors by the creation of a third category of mutual fund, the Hybrid fund. These funds would be similar in all aspects to closed-end funds, but investors will be able to redeem shares periodically at NAV.

Shareholders of existing closed-end funds would be able to vote on whether or not to adopt this new format. While exact details describing the nature of the proposed fund have yet to be determined, the key feature of hybrid funds is this redemption right. Such a right would allow shareholders to redeem shares at NAV as often as once a month or perhaps every quarter.

Even if the right occurred only once a quarter it could effectively eliminate the tendency of equity funds to trade at discounts while allowing managers to go about the business of investing without worrying about skittish investors. Plus, once it's possible to get out of a fund at, or even near NAV, it becomes prudent to buy funds previously considered to be trading at too narrow a discount.

It's interesting to note that nothing has been heard on the topic since the 1991 conference. Even if these proposed SEC changes were enacted, there is no certainty that existing fund management would bring the issue to a shareholder vote. Don't forget, a shrinking asset pool due to redemptions or buybacks leads to a shrinking management fee.

OPTIONS ON CLOSED-END FUNDS

Starting October 27, 1993, both the American Stock Exchange and the Chicago Board Options Exchange began options trading on three international funds: Growth Fund of Spain (GSP); Asia Pacific Fund (APB); and, Templeton Emerging Markets Fund (EMF). ASA Fund (ASA); Salomon Brothers Fund (SBF); and, Tricontinental (TY) have since been added to the list. Options allow investors to buy or sell stock within a specified period for an agreed-upon price. Options allow an investor to hedge their holdings or to speculate on expected market moves with little out-of-pocket cash while controlling risk. This is a very positive trend for the industry and it is hoped that the list will expand to include a larger array of issues.

NEW WAYS TO ANALYZE A FUND

When trying to determine the merits of a particular closed-end fund the investor should run through the following checklist:

1. What is the discount/premium? Discount analysis still remains the most important consideration for an investor.
2. Is the fund's discount wider than average? Is it wider than other funds in its category? Is the fund at a premium?
3. Should the fund be a candidate for shorting? Many municipal funds fall into this category if one can borrow the shares and is willing to take on the responsibility for paying the dividend.
4. What is the expense ratio? Is it higher or lower than other funds in the same category?
5. What is the dividend ratio? Look in the latest quarterly reports. Is it comparable to other similar funds?
6. What has been the historical performance for the fund? While important, performance can be the most misleading of all the variables. Most investors will pay more for a fund or manager with a good performance history. However, remember that past performance cannot guarantee future results. The Gabelli Equity Fund is a case in point. For many years Mario Gabelli was a top-performing asset manager. When he brought out his Gabelli Equity Fund, investors rushed to pay a premium for his historic results and justifiable reputation. However, the fund languished and underperformed the market. Another problem with buying performance can arise when a stellar performing fund may have had its portfolio concentrated in an industry with strong relative strength. When the cycle changes the fund will

underperform the market. Of course, a good reverse indicator may be to buy closed-end funds that are invested in areas of weak relative strength at a wide discount. That way when the leadership rotates into that segment the discount will narrow and the fund will have strong performance.
7. How large is the fund? The larger funds can usually afford greater liquidity.

WHERE ARE THE BARGAINS NOW?

Equities

All eyes continue to be on the Federal Reserve and its policy of tightening. With three Federal Fund rate increases climaxed by the recent Discount Rate increase, there is a growing view that the Federal Reserve may have ended its tightening of monetary policy with its objective of removing excess stimulus from the economy; the result of interest rates being set too low for too long. These higher rates will have an immediate effect on housing demand and have already resulted in business optimism being more guarded and cautious. This could spell a slower economy and a Federal Reserve policy of neutrality, allowing rates to stabilize at these levels.

Stabilization in the Dow Utility Average and in Treasury bonds would be a positive base for a bottoming of the stock market. Currently it seems the Dow Utility Average has very good support in the 170-180 area. As to the 30-year Treasury bond, major yield resistance is at the 7-3/4% to 8% yield level.

As of this writing, the correction has lasted for nearly four months and to date the downturn qualifies as a normal correction with the S&P 500 down about 8%. The most recent corrections in Bull Markets have been in 1985 and 1986 and these corrections were over in two months or so.

Accordingly, while the length of this correction is worrisome, we still maintain our belief that this is a correction and not a bear market.

There are now some attractive valuations in utility stocks—particularly the electrics. The Dow Utility Average is off more than 30%—an extraordinary event that has been equaled only twice before and each time the utility average has bottomed out and moved up from these depressed levels.

Accordingly we believe that investors should include at least one closed-end fund with exposure to utilities in their portfolio.

Some of the brighter economic news is coming from abroad. For example, U.S. exports to Mexico were reported at $11.9 billion for the first quarter. This represents an annualized 448 billion for the year; a 15% increase over last year. Mexico is now rivaling Japan as our second largest trading partner (Canada is first at $100 billion a year). This reinforces our view that the North American Free Trade Agreement is making a real difference in U.S.-Mexico trade. We continue to believe that the Mexican stock market, battered by political events, represents good long-term value.

Europe makes up 25% to 30% of the entire capitalization of the world's stock markets with Britain, the largest, and Germany the second largest market in

Europe. Germany is now beginning to stimulate their economy with successive cuts in their key interest rates. This should begin to energize the long delayed stimulus to the German economy and stock market.

Beans or Bonds?

Recent data indicate that the economy is expanding at a solid clip. Despite adverse weather conditions and natural disasters that held down construction activity and personal spending, GDP growth in the first quarter advanced 3%. To slow economic recovery before it triggers a new outburst of inflation, the Federal Reserve Board implemented a fourth round of rate increases, one of its steepest four-month rate hikes in the postwar period. In doing so the Federal Reserve has shifted monetary policy and assumed a "neutral" stance, at the same time that government spending has been reduced. As a result of the recent tax hike, the Treasury posted a $17.5 billion surplus in April, twice last year's level, while government spending remained the same.

According to the White House, the budget deficit in 1992 was $290.7 billion, was $254.7 billion in 1993, and is projected to approximate $220-230 billion in 1994, and $165 billion in 1995. Higher taxes and the shrinking federal deficit means that we now have a restrictive fiscal policy and the absence of an accommodative or neutral policy on the part of the Federal Reserve.

Despite the fact that inflation is still nowhere to be seen, the bond market and the dollar failed to experience a sustained rally following the Fed's May 17 hikes. A weakening dollar is of concern, because of the inflationary implications, and could cause the Fed to tighten again. Sharply higher commodity prices are also pressuring the U.S. financial markets.

On May 23, the Commodity Research Bureau Index reached its highest level since October 1990; 238.36, up 4.67 (its biggest single-day gain since July 6, 1993). The CRB index is up 5% since the first of the year, and is considered a key inflationary indicator. A 10% increase in the CRB index, in the past has caused a 1% increase in the Consumer Price Index.

Economists disagree whether the economy will slow down as a result of higher interest rates. However, when one considers the fact that during the past year, 80% of the economic growth was in interest sensitive sectors, namely consumer durables, housing, and business equipment, a slowdown in the second half of the year can be anticipated. The evidence is mixed, although there has been some decline in home sales due to rising mortgage rates, a leveling off of car sales in April, and declining consumer confidence.

Investors unsure of which camp to believe should not sit on cash. Current long-term positions should be retained while new purchases should take into consideration the current status of the Treasury yield curve, the benchmark for interest rates. See Figure 2.1.

A normal curve typically has a positive slope, with short-term rates yielding less than longer-term rates. A positive yield curve will compensate the investor for various risks inherent in long-term commitments, such as loss of purchasing power due to inflation, and greater volatility and market risk due to fluctuation

Figure 2.1: U.S. Treasury Yield Curve

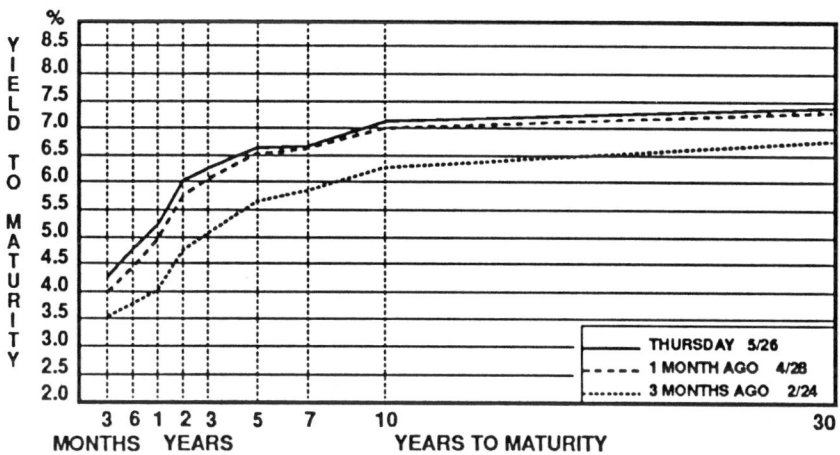

THE YIELD CURVE PROVIDES A PICTURE OF CREDIT MARKET CONDITIONS. IT DEPICTS THE AVAILABLE TRADE-OFF BETWEEN YIELD AND MATURITY. THE CHART SHOWN HERE COMPARES THE YIELD CURVES FOR THE PRIOR DAY, MONTH, AND QUARTER.

in interest rates. In this case, the investor has an incentive for extending maturities.

Historically, the average spread between 1-year and 10-year Treasury securities has averaged 120 basis points. During a period between 1992 and 1993, the spread exceeded 350 basis points. Currently it is about 190 basis points. Based upon the current slope of the yield curve it is difficult to make a case for investors extending maturities beyond ten years. For this reason we have given careful consideration to the average length of the portfolio of the closed-end funds summarized in this book.

CHANGES FOR FOREIGN INVESTING

Closed-end and open-end mutual fund investors have been laboring under rules and regulations dating back to 1940. In a world of global economic reality and the potential for 24-hour trading, old ways of doing business are unravelling under the strain. U.S. markets are no longer the only places to invest. Opportunities exist all over the world. The American investor is faced with a uniquely modern problem. How can one invest in these foreign markets? American Depositary Receipts (ADRs) have been the traditional method whereby, instead of buying shares of foreign-based companies in overseas markets, Americans can buy shares in the U.S. in the form of an ADR. These receipts for the shares of foreign-based corporations are held in the vault of a U.S. bank. The holder of an ADR is entitled to all dividends and captial gains. ADRs are available for hundreds of stocks from numerous countries.

For the small investor desiring broad overseas diversification, ADRs are not a good choice. Diversity would be possible for U.S. investors if they were allowed to purchase shares of foreign mutual funds. But none are available. Current SEC regulations stipulate that foreign investment companies be governed by the same standards and provide the same safeguards as U.S. mutual funds. The former absence of U.S. demand for foreign mutual funds negated any need for these assurances to be provided.

As a result, no foreign mutual fund has ever been cleared for sale in the U.S. and won't until the SEC standards are changed and/or updated. That's exactly what the SEC is trying to accomplish. Officials are attempting to develop guidelines that will continue to protect American investors while allowing them to buy overseas funds. Whether current SEC regulations will be relaxed, or if those foreign funds desiring entrance to U.S. markets will provide comparable safeguards remains to be seen.

Publicly traded investment funds will transform and remain as excellent vehicles for participating in international market sectors. One important development will be the continuing expansion into other market spheres, most notably international real estate. As economic perceptions change so will the potential for new profits both here and abroad. Good fortune to all and stay tuned.

RIGHTS OFFERINGS

With the staggering growth of the closed-end fund industry has come the rights offering. The first closed-end rights offering took place in 1990. The following year 4 more occurred, while 17 took place in 1992. 1993 was a watershed year, with 32 rights offerings. The trend continues in 1994 with 13 offerings through the end of April.

Unlike open-end mutual funds, which can continuously offer new shares, closed-end funds must use the rights offering in order to raise new money for the pool. Managers like the concept because they don't have to sell out exisiting, perhaps promising positions, in order to make new purchases. They also have a ready supply of potential investors in the existing shareholder pool. Investors are attracted to the rights offering because they can purchase new shares at a discount to market value, and because of the increase in assets, the expense ratio can conceivably decline.

In a rights offering, the company offers to sell to existing stockholders additional shares of company stock on a pro-rata basis at a price usually below the current market. Each shareholder is issued rights evidenced by a certificate known as a subscription warrant, which can be exercised before the expiration date. The right may or may not be transferable. If non-transferable, the rights may only be exercised by the shareholder to whom they have been issued. If transferable, the rights not exercised by the shareholder may be sold prior to their expiration. During the period when the rights are issued and outstanding, transferable rights will trade separately, while the shares of the original security will trade "ex-rights". The number of shares to be sold will determine the ratio at which shareholders may subscribe. For example, if a company has an existing capitalization of 1 million shares and wishes to sell an additional 500,000 shares, the ratio of the number of rights required to purchase one share of stock would be two for one. Two rights are necessary to subscribe for each additional share. The price at which the shareholder purchases the additional share is the "subscription price". The subscription period is limited. The value of a transferable right is determined by subtracting the subscription price from the market value and dividing by the number of rights required to purchase one share plus one.

$$\text{Value of 1 Right} = \frac{\text{Market Price} - \text{Subscription Price}}{\text{Number of Rights} + 1}$$

Rights offerings are a way of increasing capital available for investment, without disturbing existing stock positions and incurring any capital gains or losses, in order to take advantages of any new perceived investment opportunities. Rights offerings are advantageous to the investor because they are able to increase their equity position in the fund directly through the corporation, without incurring any commission expense, and usually at favorable prices or a discount. If the stock is already trading at a discount, the rights offering would permit the investor to acquire shares at an extremely favorable price.

Rights offerings increase the number of shares outstanding and thus the fund's liquidity. If the shareholder is unable or unwilling to exercise his rights, and the shares are transferable, the sale of the rights will reduce the investor's overall interest in the fund. However, the sale of the rights will result in additional income to the investor and will result in a capital gain or loss. Usually rights offerings are conducted during periods of market strength, a time when investor enthusiasm is high. Therefore investors are making additional purchases and the fund manager is investing the new funds during periods of excessive valuations. The sale of rights may result in dilution. For example, suppose a 10 million share fund with total assets of $150 million (NAV $15.00) wishes to sell an additional 5 million shares at $14.00 per share, a 7% discount to the NAV. After the rights offering, the fund has $220 million in assets which, when divided by 15 million shares outstanding, has a NAV after the rights offering of $14.66, resulting in a dilution of 2.3%.

3

Closed-End Fund Characteristics

All closed-end funds are registered investment companies and, as such, share several characteristics. All have stated investment objectives, dividend distribution policies, shareholder services, costs, fees, a Board of Directors, and all must provide shareholder reports.

INVESTMENT OBJECTIVE

Each investor is unique in attitude toward investments and in specific financial needs. There are many different financial goals.

Though investors may be willing to pool dollar resources to start an investment program, it is not likely that all investors will continue to share the same risk tolerance or have the same constant objectives. Fortunately, there are numerous types of closed-end funds through which investors can pool dollars with other investors sharing the same objectives.

Basically, all closed-end funds fall into one of the following general categories: income, growth, balanced (income and growth), convertible, and specialty. Within these categories are numerous alternatives and variations. For example, specialty funds may include international funds, emerging growth funds, single country funds, and specific sector funds. The large number of fund types and objectives allows for a great degree of flexibility. As investment needs change and grow, it is helpful to have a wide variety of cost-effective, liquid investment options.

The specific objectives of each fund are disclosed in the prospectus. This book also presents brief outlines of the investment objectives for each selected fund.

DISTRIBUTIONS AND DIVIDENDS

Investment companies allow more flexibility for the payment of spendable funds than any other investment medium. Although there are many choices available, the typical investment company makes only two kinds of payments to its shareholders: income dividends and distributions from capital gains.

Suppose you have decided to begin receiving a check each month. Your monthly checks will result from one or more of four sources. These are:

1. Dividends
2. Realized capital gains
3. Unrealized capital gains
4. Return of principal

If the amount you requested the fund to send each month is more than the dividends the fund is earning, the second source of income would be your realized capital gains, the profits the fund has made by buying and selling stocks. If your withdrawal is more than these two, they will need to use some of your unrealized gains. (This occurs when the fund has bought a stock, and it has increased in value, but they have not yet sold it. Thus the gain is unrealized.) If the amount per month you have requested is greater than these three, you will then start using a portion of your original investment, which amounts to a return of principal. This isn't all bad. After all, you have saved it for this purpose. Your primary concern should be to make your savings last as long as you want them to.

Monthly income can be an excellent way to use your accumulation in an orderly fashion while keeping the remainder at work in a diversified, continuously managed portfolio of common stocks.

Dividends

As a company prospers, profits are periodically distributed to shareholders. The amount of these earnings distributions, called dividends, is determined by the company's board of directors and is usually paid quarterly. Dividends paid by closed-end funds represent the net earnings of the fund's investment portfolio after operating expenses are deducted. Unlike other dividend paying companies, such as utilities or mature industrial companies, tax laws compel closed-end funds to pay out essentially all net income to their shareholders. They do not hold back or retain earnings.

Investment company dividend payments can be made monthly, quarterly, semi-annually, or annually and are taxable to the shareholder as ordinary income. Typically, the investment company is not subject to any federal tax on investment income. Any tax liability is passed directly through to the shareholder in direct ratio to his or her proportionate share of the securities owned by the fund.

Naturally, fund income dividends can be expected to fluctuate from year to year. This results from variations in prevalent corporate dividend payments and changes in fund investment policy. However, the broad diversity that underlies investment company dividends may result in a higher and more stable income stream than is obtainable from individual corporations.

The relationship between the dividend and the market price of a share is the dividend yield. To find the approximate dividend yield, total all dividend payments made by the investment company for the preceding 12 months, then divide that number by the current offering price (ask price) of the share. The resulting percentage is the dividend yield or "estimated return" per share. Do not include any capital gains distributions made during that period, and you may have to adjust the share price by the amount of any reinvested capital gain. Average yields for all 99 closed-end funds covered are available in the data pages.

Capital Gains

The difference between the purchase and sale price of an asset is known as the capital gain (or loss). In the course of normal operations, investment companies sell securities. Capital gains distributions occur when the profit from these sales is distributed to the shareholders. Capital gains distributions are naturally irregular. In fact, there is no guarantee that there will be any at all. However, many companies have managed to continuously pay out capital gains for many years.

Under our present tax law, all capital gains, whether short-term or long-term, are treated as ordinary income and are taxable to the shareholder at ordinary tax rates which may not exceed 28%. Even if you are in a 33% tax bracket, the rate on capital gains cannot exceed 28%.

Most investment companies follow a policy of paying out all capital gains to the shareholders. This greatly simplifies tax reporting for the investor. However, sometimes an investment company will retain the realized gains and pay the applicable tax on behalf of the shareholder. Dual-purpose funds normally fall into this category. In such a case, the shareholder will take his or her proportionate share of the tax paid on his or her behalf as a credit. The per-share amount of the gain is included on Schedule D of the individual's personal tax return. The investor will have to report the original cost of the shares in order to reveal the percentage of retained capital gains remaining after the tax paid by the company.

Capital gains distributions can distort the dividend yield computation, particularly if the distribution is substantial. Therefore, it is necessary to compensate for the fact that the price of the share will reflect the distribution, but the dividend will not.

Assume that for the previous 12 months, a $10 per share fund paid out a total of $0.85 in dividends. If it then paid out a year-end capital gain distribution of $1 (10%) a justifiable yield figure would be obtained by attributing only 90% of the previous 12 months' income dividends ($ 0.85) to the year-end price.

```
Price-per-share of the fund ............................ $10
less $1 capital gains distribution ........................ $9
12 months' dividend ................................ 0.85
x  90 % ......................................... 0.765
Dividend Yield (0.765 ÷ $9) .......................... 8.5%
```

However, it's easier to adjust the price instead of the dividend and merely add back the capital gains distribution.

```
Price-per-share of the fund ............................ $10
less $1 capital gains distribution ........................ $9
12 months' dividend ................................ 0.85
Dividend Yield [0.85 ÷ ($9 + $1)] ..................... 8.5%
```

If price or NAV performance figures are to be determined, then adjustments for capital gains distributions are also necessary. A general rule of thumb is to consider the distribution as having been reinvested if the period in question is over a year. If performance figures for less than a year are being computed, it is sufficient to add the amount of the distribution to the price or NAV at the end of the period.

Since shareholders usually have the option of receiving capital gains distributions in either additional shares (at NAV) or in cash, it's helpful to explore the benefits and drawbacks of both alternatives.

TO REINVEST OR NOT TO REINVEST

If an investor chooses to spend a portion of his or her principal and recognizes that in so doing the earning capabilities of the assets will decline, then capital gains should be taken in shares. Since principal is being diminished, the receipt of additional shares is essentially a return of capital.

The payment of a capital gains distribution by an investment company automatically causes the per-share NAV to decline by the same amount. For example, if the NAV of a share of XYZ Fund is $9.50 and a 50¢ capital gain is paid out, then the new share price will fall 50¢ to $9.00. Because the value of the earning assets has been decreased, future per-share income will be less than if the distribution had not been made. Furthermore, all future gains or losses in per-share NAV will be less than if the fund had not paid out the capital gains.

Depending upon the choice either to take the capital gains distribution in additional shares or in cash, the long-term effects on investment income can be substantial. Figure 3.1 compares the results. The white ribbon shows the actual dividends paid over a ten year period when all capital gains distributions were taken in cash. The dark ribbon shows the adjusted dividends obtained as a result of reinvesting all capital gains distributions over the same period.

Figure 3.1: Long-Term Effects of Reinvested Capital Gains

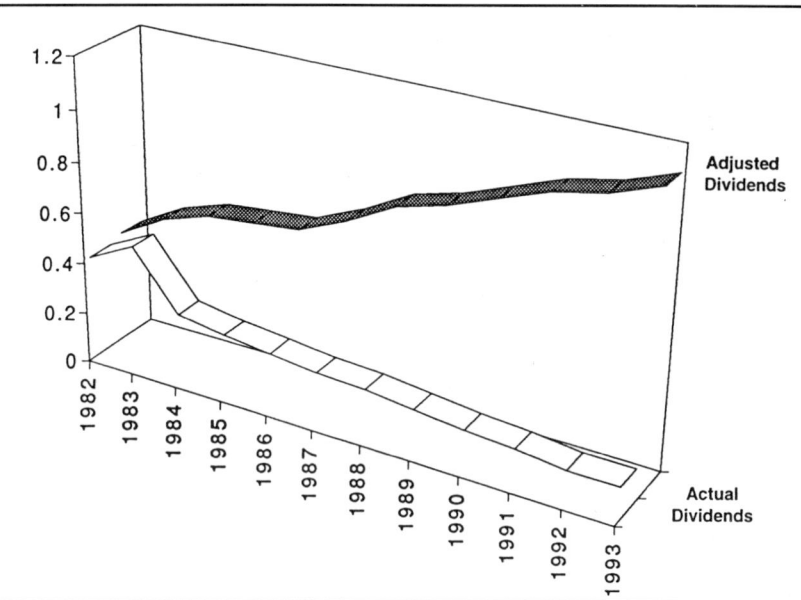

Nothing is simple in our relative world. Despite the previous argument, some investors prefer to take all distributions in cash and then reinvest in other funds for greater diversity. This is a good strategy when the shares are held in a tax-sheltered account such as an IRA. There are also circumstances when spending a portion or even all the capital gains may be the judicious choice. Investor needs vary and so do the demands for spendable cash. There is nothing sacred about principal. Periodic withdrawals can be an excellent way to take advantage of your savings in an orderly fashion while maintaining the balance at work in a diversified, professionally managed portfolio. The key concern is how long the assets will last.

Figure 3.2 will help determine just how long principal will last when capital is used at a higher rate than it earns.

Figure 3.2: How Long Will Your Money Last?

		\multicolumn{9}{c}{Percent Earnings of Investment}
		1%	2%	3%	4%	5%	6%	8%	8%	9%
	1%									
	2%	69								
Payout	3%	40	55							
Rate	4%	28	35	46						
Percent	5%	22	25	30	41					
	6%	18	20	23	28	36				
	7%	15	16	18	21	25	33			
	8%	13	14	15	17	20	23	30		
	9%	11	12	13	14	16	18	22	28	
	10%	10	11	12	13	14	15	17	20	26

Number of Years Money Will Last

Based upon the table, if you are using capital at the rate of 8% each year, but the investment is earning 7%, it will take 30 years to deplete the account. If you start at age 65, you will be 95 when the funds are exhausted.

TAXES

There are no tax benefits for an investor who chooses to invest in a closed-end fund rather than directly in individual securities. However, fund investing does offer the benefit of simplifying tax reporting. It's much easier to determine income, gains, and losses held in a pooled investment vehicle than it is to list and compute data from an extended list of stocks and bonds.

In the first quarter of each year, all closed-end funds are required to send their shareholders detailed copies of the returns it supplied to the I.R.S. If the securities are held in street name then the brokerage house must consolidate and forward this data to the investor. The returns show the total of all distributions, whether qualified or non-qualified, including capital gains, and any distributions which may have been non-taxable. If the fund retained capital gains and paid the tax for the shareholder, all necessary information is supplied. The figures can then be transferred to the investor's tax form.

As previously described, all distributions of ordinary income and capital gains are taxable and are reported by the funds to the I.R.S. It doesn't matter whether the investor received the amounts in cash or in additional shares. If the investor reinvested all ordinary income and capital gains he or she must pay any required taxes from other sources.

"BACKUP WITHHOLDING"

All investment companies are subject to I.R.S. backup withholding provisions. This means that every time the company makes a dividend or interest payment to a shareholder it must deduct and withhold 20% of the payment if:

1. the investor failed to furnish his or her taxpayer identification number to the investment company; or
2. the I.R.S. has notified the fund that the taxpayer identification number furnished by the shareholder is incorrect; or
3. the investor under-reports interest and dividends received; or
4. the shareholder fails to report if he or she is subject to backup withholding.

REINVESTMENT AND TAXES

Over time the taxes that are paid on reinvested dollars (dividends and capital gains distributions) increase the tax cost of the investor's holdings. When the fund shares are redeemed, capital gains or losses must be computed. The tax cost utilized for this determination is the original purchase price paid for the shares plus all the dividends and capital gains distributions used to obtain additional shares.

For example, an investor purchased $10,000 worth of Big Income Growth Fund (BIG) 8 years ago. All dividends ($4,250) and distributions ($7,500) were reinvested in additional shares. Today the total account is worth $28,500 and the investor redeems all shares. Despite the fact that the account has increased by $18,500, the investor is only liable for taxes on $6,750.

Original cost of investment	$10,000
Income dividends reinvested	$4,250
Capital gains in additional shares	$7,500
Total tax cost	$21,750
Proceeds from liquidation	$28,500
Taxable long-term gain	$6,750

Be sure to keep careful records of all costs. Even though many funds do provide complete computerized records of all transactions, as do the brokerage firms where trades initiate, investors should also maintain their own records.

COMPLICATIONS

Tax cost computations become much more complicated when partial share redemption takes place. This is particularly true if the shares were accumulated over a period of time. Under a partial redemption, I.R.S. rules present the investor with two choices for determining the tax cost of his or her shares: 1. the price paid for the earliest shares purchased; or 2. using shares specifically "identified" and acquired at different times. Consult with a tax specialist for the best option.

HOW TO BUY A TAX

If the investment strategy of a fund has been successful and there has been a terrific advance in overall stock prices held in the portfolio, the fund will show a substantial unrealized gain. Because closed-end funds are allowed to employ a consistent management strategy without the intrusion of untimely calls for redemption, they usually exhibit the highest proportion of unrealized profits.

It's possible that this considerable unrealized appreciation in the fund's portfolio will obligate a new purchaser to be held responsible for payment of a capital gains tax on profits that were earned before he became a shareholder. However, the real question is whether or not the new investor believes that the fund will suddenly liquidate all, or a large portion, of its entire portfolio. This has rarely ever happened. Even during periods of rapidly rising stock prices, capital gains distributions rarely exceed 9% to 10% of the fund's NAV.

Don't think of taxes on capital gains as an additional burden. It all works out in the end. Since tax payments are paid periodically, there will be less taxes due, or greater losses to use elsewhere, when the shares are finally sold. In fact, the tax liability will usually be about the same as if no gains had ever been paid out by the fund.

MINIMIZING THE TAX BITE

The easiest way to avoid unnecessary taxes on fund investments is to avoid purchasing shares of any fund just before the record date of a large distribution. Up until the record date, the amount of the distribution is included in the share price. Wait until after the record date and avoid paying tax on income or capital gains which your funds did not earn. Better yet, purchase the shares immediately after the pay date when the cost of the shares has fallen back. Another easy way to minimize taxes on investment income is to invest in funds whose primary objective is long-term growth. These funds invest for maximum growth, not income, and it is very possible that fund expenses will exceed any income obtained. For example, if the management fee is less than the yield, the investor will certainly not have a capital gain. The equity shares of a dual-purpose fund will also generally have a higher management fee than distribution yield.

NON-TAXABLE DIVIDENDS

Closed-end municipal bond funds present an excellent avenue for obtaining current income that is exempt from federal income taxes. A number of municipal bond funds are also exempt from individual state taxes. See Chapter 4 for a description of municipal bond funds.

COSTS AND FEES

Closed-end funds charge management and administrative fees before any income is distributed to shareholders. These fees generally run from 1/2 of 1% to 1-1/2 of 1% of the net assets of the fund. Plus, there is a normal brokerage commission to buy or sell fund shares.

UNDERSTANDING SHAREHOLDER REPORTS

All of the funds are required by law to supply shareholders with accurate, up-to-date reports. The fund will send quarterly, semi-annual, and annual reports describing the fund's performance, holdings, and expenses. Annual reports are essentially audited financial statements. Quarterly reports are interim bulletins that update shareholders about any material changes in the portfolio or the affairs of the company. Since they are required to present comparative data, they are often more informative than the annual reports.

The annual report typically begins with a letter to the shareholders that chronicles the fund's performance for the year, followed by an economic review, and ending with a projection of what management sees for the future. Next is the Statement of Assets and Liabilities which also shows the current portfolio (see Figure 3.3). This is followed by the Statement of Operations, which breaks down all the expenses incurred by the fund. The largest expense is normally the investment management fee, followed by the custodial, directors, and professional fees.

Closed-end funds differ from other companies listed on the open market in that their assets are almost exclusively in the form of cash, receivables, and securities. Therefore, most investors should be looking at where and in what percentages the fund's assets are allocated and invested. What percentage of assets are in bonds, convertibles, straight equity, or cash? Actual holdings are not as important because they often change between reports. But the percentages allocated to particular industry groups may indicate how the fund will perform in differing market environments.

Subsequently, a determination of the relative accomplishment of the fund management can be learned by studying the data in Table 2 of the 99 fund summaries (see Figure 3.4 for an example).

Figure 3.3: Example of a Statement of Assets and Liabilities

March 31, 1994

ASSETS
  Investments, at value (note 1a)
    General portfolio securities (cost $336,411,943) $513,283,138
    Corporate discount notes (cost $11,186,993)   11,186,993
                                                            524,470,131
    Investment in controlled affiliate (note 1b) 228,129

  Cash, Receivables and other assets
    Cash $162,018
    Receivable for securities sold 1,462,243
    Dividends, interest and other receivables 2,418,542
    Other 1,131,984
                                                             5,174,787
    Total Assets 521,937,856

LIABILITIES
  Payable for securities purchased 5,410,160
  Accrued expenses and other liabilities 2,391,546
  Total Liabilities 7,801,708

NET ASSETS $521,937,856

NET ASSET VALUE PER SHARE $23.32

Source: General American Investors, 1994 Quarterly Report. Statement of Assets and Liabilities

Figure 3.4: General American Investors Five-Year Statistical History

	5 Year Performance				
Fiscal Year Ending 12/31	1993	1992	1991	1990	1989
Net Assets ($mil)	553.90	586.50	587.20	382.20	381.90
Net Income Distribution ($)	0.06	0.03	0.10	0.21	0.25
Capital Gains Distribution ($)	2.98	3.06	2.14	1.91	1.73
Total Distributions ($)	3.04	3.09	2.24	2.12	1.98
Yield from Distributions	10.13	10.66	13.18	11.70	14.80
Expense Ratio	1.16	1.16	1.02	1.07	1.04
Portfolio Turnover (%)	19.50	14.42	23.13	18.77	26.91
NAV per Share ($)	24.75	28.56	30.60	20.60	21.41
Market Price per Share ($)	22.25	30.00	29.00	17.00	18.13
Premium (Discount) (%)	-10.10	-18.91	-22.07	-22.50	-21.41
Total Return, Stock Price (%)	-15.70	14.10	83.76	5.46	48.60

For example, from this chart (previous page) the following can be extracted:

```
Net Asset Value 12/31/92 .......................... $28.56
Net Asset Value 12/31/93 .......................... $24.75
Capital Gains Distribution ......................... $3.04
Dividend, Net Income .............................. 0.06
Total Return (NAV) 1992 (%) ...................... (2.69)
Net Asset Value 12/31/89 .......................... $21.41
Net Asset Value 12/31/93 .......................... $24.75
Capital Gains Distribution, 5-Years ................ $11.26
Dividend Income Distribution, 5-Years .............. $0.65
Total Return (NAV), 5-Years (%) ................... 71.18
```

These results may be compared with unmanaged indexes, such as the S&P 500 or the Dow Jones Industrial Average (DJIA) to determine how the fund has performed. "Special Considerations" included in the annual report should be read carefully to discern if any restrictions would prevent a fund from being open-ended or taken over. Many funds now offer provisions to convert to open-end status, or to liquidate the fund after a predetermined number of years or if the discount becomes excessive. These provisions offer a degree of protection for shareholders since any discount will be regained after the fund open-ends or liquidates.

BOARD OF DIRECTORS

Each fund has a Board of Directors elected by the shareholders and empowered to carry out certain tasks determined by the fund's "Articles of Incorporation". These powers include the appointment of fund management and the declaration of dividends.

Before investing it is important that you read the prospectus and recent annual and quarterly reports to assure that the fund meets your investment objectives.

4

Closed-End Fund Categories

OVERVIEW

There are two basic classifications of closed-end funds: Bond funds and Equity funds. In order to clarify the characteristics of the bond and equity funds, they have been separated into eight categories of bond funds and five categories of equity funds as listed below.

Bond Funds
1. Corporate, Investment Grade
2. Flexible Portfolio
3. Government (U.S.)
4. High Yield Corporate (Junk)
5. International
6. Multi-Sector/Strategic
7. Single State Tax-Free
8. Federal Tax-Free

Equity Funds
1. Convertible (Bond and Equity)
2. Domestic and Specialized
3. Dual Purpose
4. Global and Multi Country
5. Single Country

BOND FUNDS

Five to ten years ago, all closed-end bond funds were basically the same. They would invest primarily in high-grade corporate and some Government securities.

However, modern bond portfolios have expanded to include tax-free, international, high-yield, and convertible securities. As fund managers strive for higher current yields and better returns, portfolio strategies have become more complex.

Fund managers are now able to use financial futures and options on U.S. Government bonds. This, coupled with the growth and accessibility of foreign markets, has allowed managers to increase portfolio returns. To simplify the review process, the bond funds covered in this book have been grouped by common characteristics. The following discussions highlight the common elements found within the groups of funds. Look for consistent or increasing current yield along with a stable NAV. Also, remember that as interest rates rise, bond prices decline and vice versa. Any portfolio principally invested in fixed income securities tends to increase in asset value when interest rates decline and decrease when interest rates rise. Prices of longer-term securities generally increase or decrease more sharply than those of shorter-term securities in response to interest changes. Global funds and those funds that invest in foreign bonds, have the added risk of exposure to currency fluctuations, which can also affect the NAV of the fund.

Corporate Bond Funds—Investment Grade

Most of the funds in this group have been in operation for years and therefore have long-term track records. The portfolios consist primarily of investment grade bonds, those rated BBB/Baa or better by Standard and Poor's or Moody's rating services. Quite a few of the fund managers are insurance companies or banks, with long histories of managing corporate bonds.

The returns on these funds may not be as high as the newer U.S. Government and high-yield (junk) bond funds, but their safety factor makes them more appealing to the conservative investor. The majority of these funds pay quarterly rather than monthly dividends, which lowers costs. However, this may not be as appealing to investors who are accustomed to receiving monthly payments.

The NAVs of corporate high-grade bond funds tend to fluctuate more than government, international, multi-sector, and high yield (junk) funds, because they don't use enhancements and hedging strategies as extensively. These funds are the "pure vanilla" variety. What you see is what you get!

Flexible Portfolio Bond Funds

The objective of flexible or total return bond funds is to produce total return comprised of current income along with capital appreciation. Under normal circumstances, a high percentage of these portfolios will be invested in fixed income securities. However, total return funds do have the ability to invest varying degrees in income producing common stocks or convertible securities. Some of the flexible funds can invest up to 75% in common stocks when market conditions warrant it. These funds offer a flexibility similar to the open-end growth and income funds.

Be sure to carefully read the fund's latest report and prospectus. Total return funds perform well under most market conditions due to their flexibility. However, the manager's ability and experience are very important.

U.S. Government Bond Funds

The portfolios of this group are predominantly invested in U.S. Government bonds. Most are able to invest a limited percentage of their assets in foreign and corporate bonds. Many of the funds use the options and futures markets to enhance income and to hedge the portfolio. By using the options and futures markets, managers are able to moderate fluctuations normally affecting bonds during unstable interest rate periods. Most of this sector is now selling at high premiums which makes them unattractive investments. Many of them have or will be cutting their distributions to reflect the lower interest rates on U.S. Government bonds. Government bond funds are actively managed by some of the country's most experienced management companies. For additional information, contact your broker or obtain a copy of the prospectus or a recent report directly from the fund.

High Yield Corporate (Junk) Bond Funds

Also known as junk bond funds, the assets of this category are invested primarily in corporate debt of domestic corporations that are rated BBB, Baa, or lower. The significant credit risk involved for investors in this sector was evidenced by dismal performance figures from 1989 through 1990. Most of the fund managers reduced payouts and upgraded portfolio holdings as much as possible to better weather the storm. Total returns for 1993 averaged 23.9% on stock price and 24.5% on NAV.

These are still high-risk investments and should be closely monitored. The performance of junk bond funds rests with the economic recovery. If the recovery continues, the deeper discounted funds may still have more upside potential.

International Bond Funds

This group of funds requires great expertise and astuteness on the part of the manager. Not only are fund managers required to seek high current yield, but they also must work diligently to protect the portfolios from the adverse effects of currency fluctuations. The long-term potential of this group of funds, if managed well, could prove to be the best of all the bond funds. Currency and bond trading can produce substantial short-term profits, or losses.

A few of these funds may be invested in the markets of a single country. This strategy makes these funds less flexible, and investors should monitor the country's currency on an ongoing basis. Most of the funds in this group can and will shift assets between various foreign and U.S. markets to reflect long-term currency trends. They will also use investment hedges such as options, futures, and foreign currency transactions to protect the portfolio. These hedging strategies can enhance distributions.

The diversity available through these funds makes them much less risky than investing in foreign markets directly.

Multi-Sector/Strategic Bond Funds

This group of funds invests for high current income with a secondary focus on capital appreciation. Volatility is controlled by diversification into three basic bond market sectors: U.S. Government bonds, corporate bonds (usually high yield), and foreign Government bonds. The percent exposure to each sector is determined by the fund manager who is also free to employ almost any of the hedging and enhancement strategies available with options and futures. Most of these bond funds are aggressively managed to maximize returns, with frequent shifts of assets between the various sectors. The greater flexibility afforded by these funds allows higher current yields with less risk.

When determining whether or not to invest in a multi-sector fund, be sure to monitor the NAV of the selected fund in order to compare how it performs relative to its peers. The potential for this very flexible type of fund should be superior to those that are more limited; but remember, the manager's expertise is crucial.

Single State Tax-Free Bond Funds

As states raised taxes in an attempt to offset deficits, many new Single State funds came to market in 1993. Look at the portfolio information carefully before investing. Choose only those funds with 100% investment-grade bonds.

Federal Tax-Free Bond Funds

This remains the fastest growing category in the closed-end fund universe. From only 6 funds in early 1986, the field grew to over 200 funds at the end of 1993. For greater clarity, municipal bond funds are divided into two categories, Federal Tax-Free, and Single State Tax-Free. In their quest for tax-free income from a managed portfolio, investors since 1992 have driven up the prices of muni bond funds to premiums. The interest rate hikes at the end of 1993 and into 1994 caused the muni funds to fall in tandem with Treasuries and corporates. But the reality of higher tax rates, fewer new issues, and high rates have brought many buyers back to the market.

Most muni bond funds have leveraged capital structures, which, given the current yield curve, has enabled them to increase their net income per share above what a non-leveraged mutual fund or unit trust would provide. As the previous paragraph stated, any rise in short-term rates can adversely affect a leveraged fund. Beware.

Don't consider these funds to be safe havens. Many of the portfolios are leveraged with auction-rate preferreds, which allows the fund to borrow at current low short-term rates and invest in the long end of the market where the returns are higher. Given the current yield curve, current returns have ranged between 7% and 8%, which is well above what a mutual fund or unit trust pays. As long as an investor feels that short-term rates will remain low and that the covered municipalities are fiscally sound, then all would appear well. But if the yield curve flattens or if interest rates rise or if defaults start becoming a factor, one can expect a very adverse effect on net income per share. Be cautious with this group.

Term Trust Bond Funds

Initially introduced to the investment community in 1989, this type of closed-end fund did not receive popular acceptance until recently. There are currently 29 such funds outstanding, with the majority having been offered in 1992. The stated objective of the Term Trust is to provide a high level of current income consistent with the investment objectives of the particular trust and to terminate the trust at a pre-determined time, distributing all of the assets to shareholders. The goal is generally to return the original offering price of shares of the trust to investors on or about the termination date. Of course there is no guarantee that this objective will be accomplished.

Most of the Term Trusts use leverage to offer an attractive yield in order to compete with bond funds that have longer term objectives. Leverage is also used by Term Trusts to pay management fees and the initial offering expenses. The use of leverage may have an adverse effect on the fund's NAV under certain circumstances.

EQUITY FUNDS

This section is divided into five groups: Convertible, Domestic and Specialized, Dual Purpose, Global and Multi Country, and Single Country. In all equity funds, with the exception of the Dual Purpose funds, yield from distributions, the yield an investor would receive if shares were purchased at the beginning of the 12-month period is included in Table 1 of the 99 fund summaries.

Domestic and Specialized equity funds are quite diverse. Some emphasize investments in highly capitalized (blue chip) stocks, while others invest primarily in smaller capitalized or emerging growth stocks.

Global and Multi Country and Single Country equity funds are exposed to currency risks present in foreign markets, such as changes in the foreign currency exchange rates. Exchange rates will affect the U.S. dollar value of the fund's assets and yield. The managers of these funds, some of the nation's and the world's top money managers, will often use hedging techniques to minimize this risk. Global and Multi Country equity funds offer a more flexible portfolio, as they can invest just about anywhere in the world. The summaries for both of these groups of funds, especially the single country equity funds, should be read carefully, and a prospectus should be obtained from the fund before investing. With all of the new single country funds that have recently come to market, closed-end equity funds truly offer "a world of investment choice."

Convertible (Bond and Equity) Funds

This is one of the smallest categories of closed-end funds. Their popularity grew in 1993. Although the group average continued to sell at a discount, the figure narrowed sufficiently to allow the single state munis and international bond funds to surpass them and sell at higher discounts.

Convertible funds offer an investment opportunity of current income with an equity kicker. The portfolios consist of bonds and preferred stocks that are convertible into the common stock of corporations.

Although current yields from this group are usually 2% to 3% less than straight bond funds, total returns make them extremely attractive, particularly near the latter part of bull markets.

Domestic and Specialized Equity Funds

There are two classifications of Domestic Equity funds: non-diversified and diversified.

At the time of the fund's initial public offering, a non-diversified fund will state in its prospectus that its investment objective is to have the ability to limit the scope of investment choices both as to industry and as to a particular investment. The primary characteristic of these funds is their concentration in specific areas such as financial services, health care, precious metals, petroleum/natural resources, and utilities. Non-diversified funds are best used as part of a diversified or limited-term portfolio because of their very specialized nature. Within this group, specialized or sector equity funds are included. A diversified equity closed-end fund has as its stated investment objective (defined in its prospectus) limitations as to the quality of securities held, the percentage of securities that may be held in each sector as well as a percentage limitation on individual issues. Diversified funds by definition fulfill one of the basic investment objectives of "spreading" investment risk and were initially the norm. Some funds have been in existence since 1929. Others have been around for only a few years. The investment objectives range from investment in small capitalized or emerging growth stocks to emphasis on highly capitalized blue chip portfolios. The fund managers' objectives should correspond with each investor's goals.

Dual Purpose Equity Funds

The Dual Purpose concept was originally conceived to serve two types of investors: the income investor and the growth oriented investor. It is during the early life of this type of fund that the income investor is best served.

A Dual Purpose equity fund has two classes of shares: capital shares and preferred or income shares. The capital shares are entitled to all the capital gains and growth over the life of the fund, usually 10 to 12 years. The preferred or income shares are entitled to all the income from the entire portfolio in addition to a guaranteed repayment of the original investment, less the underwriting fees. The preferred shares also have a cumulative dividend, set at the time of the original offer, that is guaranteed to be paid from the total assets of the fund.

If the portfolio underperforms, the NAV of the capital shares diminishes in order to pay the preferred shares' principal and any unpaid cumulative dividends.

Dual Purpose funds make a very attractive short- or long-term trading vehicle if bought at the right time. The best time to buy the capital shares is when the discounts are steep and a bull market is in its early stage. Though it is not easy to tell when a bull market begins, it is obvious when a big discount is available. Often these events will coincide. The income shares should be bought on the initial public offering or in the early life of the fund when the shares are selling at or near the NAV. The distributions usually will increase as the fund matures, which will often cause the income shares to sell at a substantial premium. As the income shares approach the maturity date of the fund, the premium will disappear. Check the prospectus and the following summaries to determine the number of years left before the fund is open-ended. The capital shares are appropriate for cost averaging in an aggressive investment portfolio.

Global and Multi Country Equity Funds

These funds truly offer, "a world of investment choice." They allow worldwide investing on a more diversified basis than the single country funds. That's because Multi Country funds may invest regionally as well as in the securities of specific countries.

The fast pace of global economic and social change has focused a lot of interest on this group. Most of the truly attractive discounts reside in the country funds. 1993 brought one new fund to market: The Schroeder Asia Fund. But 1994 has so far seen seven new funds: The Emerging Markets Infrastructure Fund, The Templeton Emerging Markets Appreciation Fund, TCW/DW Fund, The GT Global Development Fund, The Asia Tigers Fund, The Emerging Tigers Fund, and the Fidelity Emerging Asia Fund.

These funds can be volatile and many of the markets are relatively illiquid. Country funds, both Multi and Single, are best used as trading vehicles. Their share prices can be affected by natural disasters, political upheavals, rumors, court decisions, and press releases. It's often best to buy these funds on bad news and exit on good news. Study this arena carefully before taking the plunge. Check the Appendix, "Sources of Additional Information," at the end of this book.

Single Country Equity Funds

Most of the world's stock markets are represented by Single Country equity funds. During 1993, attention was again focused on emerging markets. Two new country funds were introduced; the Korea Equity Fund, and the Pakistan Fund. So far in 1994, six new funds have come to market; three South Africa funds and three India funds.

After a tremendous run throughout 1993, there are once again many discount-driven bargains in this group. Because political and economic conditions can create more volatility than exists in domestic markets, it is best to include these funds as part of a diversified portfolio of five or six different countries. In addition, currency fluctuations can have a powerful effect on investment results.

Although Single Country equity funds offer the astute investor interesting and potentially rewarding investment opportunities, tread carefully.

5

Closed-End Fund Portfolios

The 99 funds in this book represent what the authors believe to be the best funds for any investor to consider when assembling an individual portfolio. We carefully scoured our database of 526 funds, interviewed portfolio managers, and read quarterly and annual reports during our selection process. The next step for you, the reader, is to determine what type of portfolio you wish to assemble and then select the appropriate issues from the list of 99. The following should assist you in your efforts.

BEFORE YOU INVEST

An investor should answer three basic questions before making an investment decision:

- What is the required real rate of return?
- What is the anticipated inflation factor?
- What is the risk premium?

Upon resolving these questions, you will be better prepared to decide whether an investment should be made in equity funds, bond funds, or both.

The real rate of return consists of what investors require for passing up immediate consumption and allowing others to use their savings for a given period. It is called a real rate because it is determined before the inclusion of any value for inflation or risk. Historically, the real rate of return in the U.S. economy has been approximately 3%. Therefore, let's use this figure for our computations.

To obtain a real rate of 3% we must add on the anticipated inflation factor. The current consensus would put that figure at about 4% through the rest of the decade: 3% + 4% = 7%.

We combine the two to arrive at an approximate 7% required rate of return. This is our required return on an investment before any explicit consideration of risk. For this reason, it is often called the risk free rate. This risk free rate is the minimum rate of return required of any investment (equities, bonds, real estate, etc.) to have a 3% real rate of return. If the risk free rate of return is less than the inflation rate, it would be better to spend the money now rather than invest it.

Finally, a third component must be considered, the risk premium. The risk premium is different for each type of investment. The higher the risk, the higher the risk premium. For example, U.S. Government Treasury bills or Federally insured certificates of deposit have risk premiums of nearly zero. All returns to the investor will be at the risk free rate of return. Corporate bonds fall between short-term Government obligations and common stock. Historically, the risk premium for these issues has run about 2% to 4%. For common stock, the investor's required return should be augmented with a 4% or 5% risk premium. Here are some required rates of return for three types of investments.

Short-Term Government Securities, CDs
Real Rate 3%
Anticipated Inflation .... +4%
Risk Free Rate 7%

Corporate Bonds
Real Rate 3%
Anticipated Inflation .... +4%
Risk Free Rate 7%
Risk Premium .... +2% to 4%
Required Rate of Return .... 9% to 11%

Common Stocks
Real Rate 3%
Anticipated Inflation .... + 4%
Risk Free Rate 7%
Risk Premium .... + 4% or 5%
Required Rate of Return .... 11% or 12%

BETA

Not all risk is compensated for by proportionally higher returns. Risk can also be tempered through diversification. For instance, the risk of investing in U.S. stock funds can be partially eliminated by investments in foreign or global funds. However, each investment carries risk that cannot be moderated through diversification. This is called systematic risk and can be determined by observing the correlation between the movement of a security and the market in general. This relationship is called the beta coefficient. If a fund moves in step with the market, it has a beta coefficient of 1. If a fund is 50% more volatile than the market, the beta coefficient is 1.5, meaning it will rise or fall about 15% when the market moves by 10%.

Conservative investors interested in preserving capital should focus on funds with low betas. Those willing to assume higher risk in an effort to earn greater rewards should look for funds with high betas.

The market is defined as the Standard & Poor's Index of 500 common stocks. The beta of the market is always 1. Money market funds have a beta coefficient of 0.

Betas are not meaningful with bond funds, funds with a preponderance of bonds, or precious metals funds. The market risk of a fixed-income security is determined primarily by maturity. The longer the maturity, the greater the risk of price change with interest rate fluctuations. These funds usually move independently of the S&P 500. For bond funds, the weighted average maturity of the portfolio holdings has been reported in this book. The Beta computations in this guide are based upon 36-month data whenever possible. Betas are helpful when used to estimate the market risk of an investment portfolio. This is figured by determining the weighted sum of the betas of the individual funds in the portfolio. If a portfolio is made up of four funds, with an equal market value for each, then the portfolio beta would be:

$$(0.25 \times \text{beta Fund 1}) + (0.25 \times \text{beta Fund 2}) + (0.25 \times \text{beta Fund 3}) + (0.25 \times \text{beta Fund 4}) = \text{Portfolio Beta}$$

A highly liquid, low-risk, short-term portfolio for an individual with a low tax exposure might be made up of:

	% of Portfolio	Average Beta
Growth Stock Funds	35	0.90
Growth & Income Funds	45	0.68
Money Market Fund	20	0.00
	100	

Portfolio Beta $[(0.35 \times 0.90) + (0.45 \times 0.68) + (0.20 \times 0.00)] = 0.62$

A higher risk, longer term, less liquid portfolio for an individual with high tax exposure might be:

	% of Portfolio	Average Beta
Aggressive Common Stock Funds	85	1.10
Money Market Fund	15	0.00
	100	

Portfolio Beta $[(0.85 \times 1.10) + (0.15 \times 0)] = 0.94$

Of course it's not necessary to wade through all these calculations to arrive at your own portfolio makeup.

However, it is important to determine your level of risk tolerance and the individual risk levels of each fund you consider.

AVERAGE MATURITIES

A maturity date is the date on which the principal amount of a note, bond, bill, or other debt instrument is due and payable. The bond fund data pages found in this book contain average maturity figures. This is an important analytical tool for determining interest rate exposure for the portfolio. The figures utilized in this book are the result of a weighted arithmetic mean for each portfolio examined.

Armed with this information, an investor can select those portfolios that correspond to his or her perception of what long- and short-term interest rates will do. For example, if it is determined that long-term rates will decline, then a portfolio with a higher average maturity would be desirable. The following is a generalized list of closed-end funds ranked according to the level of risk. As the level of risk increases, so does the potential for capital gains.

PORTFOLIO RISK LEVELS

Low Risk

Prime Rate Funds, U.S. Government Bond Funds, and Total Return Funds that invest in:

- Certificates of Deposit
- Commercial short-term paper
- Treasury securities

Maturities in this group range from 90 days up to several years.

Medium Risk

Corporate, Multi-Sector, Convertible, International, and Municipal Bond Funds that invest in:

- Bonds and debentures, with maturities ranging up to 25 years

Medium to High Risk

Domestic Equity Funds, Single Country Funds, Global and Multi Country Equity Funds that invest in:

- Common stocks

The danger associated with long-term, fixed-income securities is that inflation may outstrip the interest paid by the security, resulting in a loss of purchasing power when the capital is returned. Also, if the security is sold before maturity and interest rates rise higher than they were when the bond was purchased, this will result in a capital loss.

Convertible bonds, convertible debentures, and convertible preferreds all fall into the medium risk category. They offer investors a combination. Essentially, these are securities with a fixed interest or dividend rate. They differ from bonds in that they can be converted into the common shares of the issuing companies at the rate of a given number of shares per $100 of bonds. Convertible issues should offer a higher yield than common stocks and slightly lower yields than bonds, because the conversion privilege has a value as well. Preferred shares offer income but no fixed maturity date. Non-convertible preferreds must be sold on the open market in order to recover the investor's capital.

International bond funds can offer political, interest rate, and currency dangers. Common stocks provide only one guarantee, the right to participate in the growth or demise of a company. Dividends are not fixed but they can increase as profits rise. There is no promise of return of principal, but market values can rise handsomely. On the other hand, the company could go bankrupt, leaving the common shares worthless.

Single country and foreign equity funds also present inherent risks in investing overseas. These include currency fluctuations, political interference, and labor disputes.

After you have estimated your tax exposure, liquidity needs, appropriate holding period, and level of risk, you are ready to select the individual funds and assemble your portfolio.

MODEL PORTFOLIO FRAMEWORKS

There are three basic types of investment portfolios:

1. Bond/Income Portfolios for investors seeking income
2. Equity Portfolios for investors seeking growth
3. Balanced Portfolios for investors looking for both growth and income.

Each of these groups can be further divided into more specialized portfolios. For example, a bond/income portfolio can be tax-free, taxable, or international. In all likelihood, your actual portfolio will be determined by your position in life. However imprecise, Table 5.1 does indicate general investment settings.

Aggressive investors are generally early in their careers, have a high risk tolerance, a long investment horizon, and a low tax liability. They would prefer a low dividend paying growth equity portfolio. Conservative investors are primarily concerned with safeguarding principal and minimizing risk and would be more likely to assemble a bond/income portfolio. Investors should consider personal preferences, current market conditions, and individual investment requirements when structuring personal investment portfolios.

Table 5.1 Career Status and Investment Portfolios

Career Status	Risk Tolerance	Investment Horizon	Tax Liability
Early	High	Long	Low
Mid	High	Long	High
Late	Medium	Intermediate	Intermediate
Retired	Low	Intermediate	Low

The authors feel that todays' investor should select one of four investment portfolios: Income; Tax-Free Income; Balanced; or, Global Growth. The following sample model portfolios illustrate how the 99 closed-end funds presented in this book can be mixed and matched to structure your own investment portfolio. Of course, these should be viewed only as guidelines and do not reflect the only possible mix. They are fully invested portfolios.

INCOME PORTFOLIOS

Taxable Portfolio

- 50%   Government Funds
- 30%   Multi-Sector Funds
- 5%   Corporate and High-Yield Funds
- 10%   Flexible and International Funds
- 5%   Convertible Funds

Under current market conditions, this portfolio will produce an estimated annual return from distributions of around 9.5%. The yield could be maximized by putting a larger percentage in the higher yielding total return and international funds. If capital preservation or appreciation is required, a larger percentage could be put in total return funds.

Income Tax-Free Portfolio

- 100%   Municipal Funds

Since there is only one group to select from, assembling this portfolio might appear to be a simple task; it really is not. The funds in this group are quite diverse. There are insured, investment grade, high-yield or low-rated, leveraged, and Federal and State tax-free. With such a broad choice, careful selection is necessary to minimize risk.

With municipal bond funds there are two basic risk factors to consider: interest rate risk and credit risk. Generally, the longer the maturity of a bond, the higher the interest it pays. Therefore, unless the fund objective states otherwise, muni fund managers will always invest in longer maturity bonds in order to maximize yields. As interest rates rise and fall, the NAV of the fund will move inversely, to a greater degree, than shorter maturity portfolios.

Credit risk is always a factor to consider. The lower the rating, the higher the yield, and the greater the risk of default. You are relying on the expertise of the manager to correctly determine the actual risk involved with higher yielding muni bonds. Furthermore, non-rated bonds are not necessarily low quality bonds. Many municipalities do not bother with the expense of having their issues rated because they are known to be highly credit worthy communities.

With careful evaluation, it is possible to construct a portfolio with a tax-free return of between 6% and 7%. (Remember, Uncle Sam gets none of it.) If a consistent tax-free yield is of primary importance, then any interest rate induced fluctuation of NAV is of minimal significance.

EQUITY FUND PORTFOLIOS

Balanced Portfolio (Growth and Income) Average Beta

20%	Government or Municipal Bond Funds	na
5%	High-Yield Funds	na
20%	Total Return Bond Funds	na
30%	Domestic Equity Funds	0.30 x 0.63 = 0.19
10%	Specialized/Sector Equity Funds	0.10 x 0.51 = 0.05
5%	International Equity Funds	0.15 x 0.92 = 0.14
	Portfolio Beta	0.38

This type of portfolio dilutes risk by spreading it among several sectors. Several equity funds pay distributions equal to 10% of the NAV of the fund; these are particularly attractive for a balanced portfolio. Selecting from these fund groups with a mind toward high distributions, an investor can structure a portfolio with an annual return of 10% in cash, along with growth potential. This type of portfolio may not win a sprint race, but it should finish very well in a marathon. The conservative, long-term investor should find this portfolio particularly appealing.

Global Growth Average Beta

10%	Domestic Equity Funds	0.30 x 0.63 = 0.19
40%	Single Country Equity Funds	0.10 x 0.51 = 0.05
50%	Multi Country Equity Funds	0.15 x 0.92 = 0.14
	Portfolio Beta	0.38

This portfolio offers fund groups that invest not only in the U.S. securities markets but also in the foreign regional markets and in individual countries. Be sure to check the prospectuses to determine whether the selected funds concentrate on large or small capitalized companies. As with all mutual funds that are dedicated to equities, underlying economic cycles will affect the stock markets which in turn will be reflected in the performance of a portfolio's NAV. Also, keep abreast of currency moves and determine whether or not the fund utilizes hedging tactics.

A portfolio structured along the guidelines of these four groups should perform well under the anticipated market conditions. When selecting from domestic and international equity funds, locate the ones that have performed the best in uptrending markets. Because of the non-domestic sector, this type of portfolio requires careful monitoring. Foreign investments present added risks of currency fluctuations and potential political instability.

TRADING IN THE CLOSED-END FUND MARKET

Although closed-end funds are very attractive long-term investment vehicles, they also offer exceptional trading opportunities. It is still possible for a closed-end fund to trade at substantial discounts to their actual NAV. These discounts usually occur when overall stock market sentiment is bearish and investors and speculators are selling. The decreased demand causes the price of the funds to drop even further than the NAV of the underlying securities held in the fund.

For example, assume that during a bearish market the ABC Growth Fund is selling at $8 per share and that its NAV is $10 per share. The discount to the value of the underlying securities in the fund is 20%. When market sentiment begins to turn more positive, 500 shares are purchased at $8 per share or $4,000. The market rallies, increasing the NAV to $12 per share and the stock price rises accordingly to $12 per share, eliminating the bear market discount of 20%. The 500 shares purchased at $8 per share, or $4,000, will then be worth $6,000. This is a $2,000, or 50%, profit on the investment.

On the other hand, if $4,000 worth of open-end fund shares had been purchased at the same time, they would only be worth $5,000, a $1,000, or 25%, profit on the investment. This happened because the closed-end fund was purchased at a 20% discount, while the open-end fund was purchased at NAV. Under the right conditions, the profit potential in a bull market is twice as good for closed-end funds as it is for open-end funds.

But take warning, this can be a double-edged sword. For example, assume 500 shares had been purchased at $12, or $6,000, when the NAV was $12. If market sentiment turned bearish and caused the NAV to drop to $10 per share and a discount of 20% developed, making the shares sell at $8, a $2,000 loss would result. This is twice the loss than if the same amount of money had been invested in an open-end fund.

One might think that to become a wealthy and successful trader one only needs to buy shares when the discount is substantial, or approximately 20%, and sell when the discount shrinks or goes to parity. This is certainly possible for the astute or fortunate individual who knows what funds to buy (and when to buy them) and what funds to sell (and when to sell them). However, these senses of judgment and timing are precisely the problem.

Determining when and what to buy and/or sell is not easy and requires some sophistication and monitoring of the investment portfolio. This book should help increase an investor's knowledge and henceforth his or her ability to trade. The explosive growth in closed-end funds has made investing in them much more complex than it used to be.

Fortunately, there is much more information available now than in the past, and it may be necessary to subscribe to a newsletter or market timer to increase the chances for success. The financial press and several investment advisers have increased their coverage of closed-end funds. See the Appendix for examples.

TRADING OPPORTUNITIES

Trading opportunities exist when funds are trading at discounts historically deeper than average for the particular fund or on the short side at especially high premiums. The best trading opportunities exist in funds that may be takeover targets. This occurs when a fund is selling at a deep discount of 20% or more and an individual or group buys sufficient stock to have holdings beyond 5% of the outstanding shares. When this occurs, it becomes necessary for the group or individual to file a form 13D. A 13D filing is usually accompanied by a Statement of Purpose, which requires the individual or group to state whether holdings are for investment purposes only, or to seek control of the fund. These 13D filings are published weekly in *The Wall Street Journal* and *Barron's*. Sometimes these incursions are only made for a quick profit. An investor or group will accumulate a substantial position in order to create the impression of a takeover only to sell at a profit as the stock price moves up. Other times, it may be a serious, concerted effort to open-end the fund so that the full NAV is realized.

It is difficult to determine what an investor's motives are. There will often be a volume buildup prior to and shortly after an announcement in the press. It may be announced that an investor or group has taken a substantial position in the stock of the fund or has filed a form 13D. If the buildup in the stock has been substantial during this period and a good profit has been obtained, a trader usually considers selling into the strength. The ensuing pullback in price offers the trader a good reentry level. Because possible buyouts take a long time to be resolved, many holders lose patience and sell.

Criteria for trading in closed-end funds are changing in the new environment of narrow discounts. Currently the Country funds offer opportunities, as do Dual Purpose funds. For example, if the capital shares of a Dual Purpose fund are trading at a substantial discount, you make an automatic gain when it winds up and goes to NAV. While you are waiting, market risk can be hedged by selling options when the discounts widen. One strategy is to buy the fund and sell calls on the OEX Index. Stock index options can be a conservative way to increase income or insure your portfolio against losses, but it can also be a highly speculative way to buy or sell the dollar value of a basket of stocks.

MARKET TIMING

Short-term investment cycles, which reflect the state of the economy, have recently shortened, and investors and short-term traders can seek to enhance returns by moving in and out of the equity and bond markets in a timely manner. Closed-end funds, with their vast number of equity and bond funds, could prove to be an excellent vehicle for these short-term traders.

Switching services have used mostly no-load families of funds for short-term trading because switching transactions from fund to fund within the fund family required no transaction charges. Many fund families have found constant switching costly and detrimental to long-term investors and have begun to invoke transaction charges. These charges have made many open-end funds less attractive to the timing services and their short-term trading-oriented clients. As a result, some market timers have increased their use of closed-end funds.

As market timers increase their use of closed-end funds, volume will also increase. This added activity will help increase the liquidity but also adds to the volatility of the closed-end fund arena. Active traders or those who desire to trade may subscribe to a timing service that tells them when to be in the equity market and when to be in cash.

SOME POINTERS

Short-term trading is not for everyone. And no one can be told how to be a successful trader. But there are some things to keep in mind.

- *Avoid buying dividends.* When buying shares of a fund, buy a few days after the ex-dividend date. When selling, sell just before the ex-dividend date. Usually, the stock price will rise by the amount of the dividend during the week prior to the ex-dividend date. Then it typically falls by the amount of the dividend after the ex-dividend date. For example, if the XYZ Bond Fund is marked ex-dividend on April 10th, and the dividend is $0.10 per share during the week prior to April 10th, the stock will more than likely be selling at 9-7/8. On April 10th, and for a few days after, the stock will more than likely trade at 9-3/4. Waiting to purchase shares until April 10th or later will save $12.50, or $25 per 100 share purchase. A dividend of $10 per 100 shares would be missed, but $15 would be saved on the transaction.
- *Make sure the fund you buy has a history of substantial daily volume.* Illiquidity can increase the cost of trading. The spread between the bid and ask price is narrower when a stock normally trades at a substantial volume, usually 5,000 shares or more. In volume trades, a few thousand shares can move the stock significantly, even if the number of shares bid or offered is small.
- *Buy in multiple round lots.* Commissions are substantially lower per 100 shares when trading in higher multiples.
- *Ask for a discount.* Active traders are good clients and should be entitled to a break on commissions.
- *Use limit orders when buying or selling in size.* It is important to ask the broker how many shares are offered or bid for.
- *When buying in a somewhat soft market, try to buy on the bid side.* Conversely, if selling in a relatively strong market, limit the price to the offered side of the market.
- *Limit the downside of a losing trade to about 10%.* Remember, they who fight and run away live to fight another day.
- *Make sure your broker is working hard for you.* A good broker should help with executions and should save the client money in the long run.

Whether investing for the long term, actively trading, or using the services of a market timer, always be familiar with the investment product. Individual investors desiring to invest or trade in the closed-end fund market should seek the advice of their brokers.

KEEPING UP

The active investor or trader should keep up with worldwide economic and business news by reading the business section of local newspapers or *The Wall*

*Street Journa*l and *Barron's* on a regular basis. *Forbe*s and *Business Week* are also good sources of information. Hiring a professional money manager is an additional choice. Another alternative is to subscribe to an advisory newsletter, preferably one that specializes in closed-end funds. Many investors find *Frank Cappiello's Closed-End Fund Digest,* published monthly, to be a valuable resource. The Appendix also lists a number of other publications.

Remember, closed-end funds are pools of managed money. When you buy them, you are hiring the manager; when you sell, you are firing him or her.

6

Reading the Fund Summaries

SHAREHOLDER REPORT INFORMATION

The information contained in the fund summaries was obtained from company quarterly and annual reports. The following key is provided in way of explanation.

Fund Name. The fund name, address, and telephone number is included for ease in contacting the fund directly. A toll-free number is given whenever possible.

Exchange. The exchange tells in what organized market the fund shares are traded. There are two main stock and bond exchanges in the U.S.: the New York Stock Exchange (NYSE) and the American Stock Exchange (AMEX). At both exchanges brokers and dealers execute orders from institutional and individual investors to buy and sell securities. An additional market, the Over-The-Counter market (OTC), does not have a physical location. Rather, it is a market linked by telephone and computer networks allowing stock and bond dealers to buy and sell electronically, rather than on the floor of an exchange.

Symbol. The letters of the ticker symbol identify a security for trading purposes both on an exchange and over-the-counter.

Transfer Agent. The transfer agent is usually a commercial bank appointed by the fund to maintain a record of fund shareholders, to issue or cancel certificates, and to resolve problems arising from lost, destroyed, or stolen certificates.

Background. Here, the date, number of shares, stock price, and NAV for the fund's initial public offering is listed when available. This is important in order to see where the fund started and how it has performed since its inception.

Objective. The investment objectives and parameters of each fund are briefly enumerated in this paragraph. (The primary objective is briefly listed under the fund's address and phone number.)

Portfolio. This category should be taken with a grain of salt because the portfolios are actively managed and subject to rapid change. However, the date given in this book is the latest available from the fund's 1993 annual or 1994 quarterly reports and can give an indication of how management works by showing the quality, selection, and allocation of issues in the portfolio at that time. To obtain the latest portfolio allocations contact the fund and request the most current report. Negative figures under "cash & other" or "liabilities", result from accrued fund expenses and/or outstanding share purchases that had not been settled at reporting time.

Fund Manager and Fee. The investment adviser and the fee charged can be useful when comparing costs versus results.

Distributions. When the fund pays out distributions from both income and capital gains. This is particularly important information for investors seeking consistent income.

Reinvestment Plan. Most funds have reinvestment plans allowing shareholders to reinvest distributions at the lower of either share price or NAV. Many funds also offer IRA, Keogh, Pension, and Profit Sharing as well as automatic withdrawal programs. Check with the fund regarding these services.

Shareholder Reports. The frequency of shareholder reports is noted.

Capitalization. The number and class of shares outstanding plus the amount of debt, if any, are listed. This is important to determine the size of the fund, the amount of any leverage used, and the level of debt management must meet before paying out distributions to the shareholders.

STATISTICS

There are two data tables for each fund with operating histories of one year or more. To allow for performance comparisons over the same period, Table 1, at the top of the page, tabulates data for a 12-month period ending 4/29/94 (see Table 6.1 for an example). Table 2, at the bottom of the page, (see the example in Table 6.2) reports the fund's 5-year statistical history based on its Fiscal Year End (FYE).

Table 6.1: Results (Adams Express Company)

For 12-months Ending 4/29/94	Period End	Period Begin	Distributions	Yield Dist (%)	Total Return (%)
Share Price ($)	16.88	21.00	1.63	7.76	-11.86
NAV per Share ($)	19.05	20.38		8.00	1.47

Stock Price

Period. Beginning (April 29, 1993) and ending (April 29, 1994) period stock prices are shown for comparative purposes (in Table 1).

Distributions. Total of all distributions made during the 12-month period, as determined by the record date. This figure accounts for a change in the fund's NAV.

Yield from Distributions (%). Current yield from regular distributions (not counting extras) based upon stock price had fund shares been purchased on beginning date. The figure is calculated by dividing total distributions by period beginning stock price.

Table 6.2 Statistical History (Adams Express Company)

5 Year Performance

Fiscal Year Ending 12/31	1993	1992	1991	1990	1989
Net Assets ($mil)	840.60	696.90	661.90	529.50	550.10
Net Income Distribution ($)	0.45	0.46	0.54	0.66	0.70
Capital Gains Distribution ($)	1.18	1.16	1.09	1.06	1.36
Total Distribution ($)	1.63	1.62	1.63	1.72	2.06
Yield from Distribution (%)	8.15	8.53	11.05	11.00	13.97
Expense Ratio	0.36	0.49	0.58	0.50	0.51
Portfolio Turnover (%)	21.40	17.97	17.64	24.71	26.04
NAV per Share ($):	19.78	20.48	20.21	16.82	18.35
Market Price per Share ($)	17.88	20.00	19.00	14.75	15.63
Premium (Discount) (%)	-9.63	-2.34	-5.99	-12.31	-14.88
Total Return, Stock Price (%)	-2.45	13.79	39.86	5.37	19.93

Total Return (%). The percentage increase (or decrease) in stock price from beginning period to ending period with all distributions reinvested.

Average Maturity. Shown for all bond funds. Determined as a weighted arithmetic mean, it is an indication of interest rate risk.

Beta. Shown for all equity funds. It compares a fund's share price movement with that of the S&P 500 over the last 36 months. Funds without a 36 month history use at least a 12 month calculation.

NAV

Period. Beginning (April 29, 1993) and ending (April 24, 1994) period NAVs are shown for comparitive purposes (in Table 1).

Yield from Distributions (%). Current yield from regular distributions (not counting extras) calculated by dividing total distributions by period beginning NAV.

Total Return (%). The percentage increase (or decrease) in NAV from beginning period to ending period with all distributions reinvested.

Fiscal Year Ending. The fiscal year of the fund. Net Assets ($ mil.). The total aggregate value of the fund portfolio in millions of dollars.

Distributions: Net Income ($). The per share income distributions paid during the fiscal year.

Distributions: Capital Gains ($). Per share net distributions from realized capital gains paid during the fiscal year.

Total Distributions ($). The sum of Net Income and Capital Gains.

Yield From Distributions (%). Calculated by dividing total distributions by the beginning of year share price.

Expense Ratio (%). The ratio of the sum of all fund fees and expenses, divided by the average NAV, and stated as a percentage.

Portfolio Turnover Rate (%). A measure of fund trading activity. Expressed as a percentage, this is computed by dividing the lesser of fiscal year purchases or sales by the monthly average value of the securities owned by the fund. A figure of 100% implies complete portfolio turnover within one year.

NAV Per Share ($). The fiscal year end per share NAV.

Market Price Per Share ($). The fiscal year end per share market price.

Premium (Discount) (%). The percent difference between the fund NAV and the market price.

Total Return, Share Price ($). Calculated using the following formula:

$$\frac{(\text{Ending Value} - \text{Beginning Value}) + \text{Income} + \text{Capital Gains}}{\text{Beginning Value}}$$

Example: Adams Express Company
Ending Value: $17.88
Beginning Value: $20.00
Dividends, Net Income: $0.45
Distributions, Capital Gains: $1.18

$$\frac{(17.88 - 20.00) + 0.45 + 1.18}{20.00} = -0.025\% \text{ or } -2.45$$

7

Summaries of the 99 Best Closed-End Funds to Own Now

Domestic Equity Funds	57
Single Country Funds	77
Multi Country Funds	117
Single State—Tax Free Funds	131
Municipal Bond Funds—Leveraged	153
Municipal Bond Funds—Non-Leveraged	177
High Yield (Junk) Bond Funds	187
Convertible Bond Funds	197
Investment Grade Corporate Bond Funds	205
U.S. Government Bond Funds	219
Term Trust Bond Funds	229
International Bond Funds	241
Multi Sector Funds	257

Domestic Equity Funds

Adams Express Company

Seven St. Paul Street, Suite 1140
Baltimore, MD 21202
(800) 638-2479
(410) 752-5900

Growth & Income

NYSE: ADX

Transfer Agent:
The Bank of New York
101 Barclay St.
New York, NY 10007
(800) 524-4458

Results

For 12-months Ending 4/29/94	Period End	Period Begin	Distributions	Yield Dist (%)	Total Return (%)
Share Price ($)	16.88	21.00	1.63	7.76	-11.86
NAV per Share ($)	19.05	20.38		8.00	1.47

Background: Formed in 1858 as an express company. Shares have been publicly traded since 1873. Has a long-term interest in Petroleum and Resources Co., an affiliated investment company.

Objective: Seeks growth and income consistent with preservation of capital primarily through investments in large-cap, blue chip common stocks. Options may be utilized.

Portfolio: (12/31/93) Stocks & Convertibles 89.4%, Short-Term 10.7%. Sector Weightings: Basic Industries 8%, Consumer 27%, Energy 10%, Financial 17%, Producer Goods 9%, Transportation 2%, Utilities 16%.

Capitalization: (12/31/93) Common stock outstanding 42,497,665. No long-term debt.

Beta: 0.93
Fee: 0.00%
Income Distribution: Quarterly
Reinvestment Plan: Yes

Fund Manager: Adams Express Company
Capital Gains Distribution: Annually
Shareholder Reports: Quarterly

5 Year Performance

Fiscal Year Ending 12/31	1993	1992	1991	1990	1989
Net Assets ($mil)	840.60	696.90	661.90	529.50	550.10
Net Income Distribution ($)	0.45	0.46	0.54	0.66	0.70
Capital Gains Distribution ($)	1.18	1.16	1.09	1.06	1.36
Total Distribution ($)	1.63	1.62	1.63	1.72	2.06
Yield from Distribution (%)	8.15	8.53	11.05	11.00	13.97
Expense Ratio	0.36	0.49	0.58	0.50	0.51
Portfolio Turnover (%)	21.40	17.97	17.64	24.71	26.04
NAV per Share ($):	19.78	20.48	20.21	16.82	18.35
Market Price per Share ($)	17.88	20.00	19.00	14.75	15.63
Premium (Discount) (%)	-9.63	-2.34	-5.99	-12.31	-14.88
Total Return, Stock Price (%)	-2.45	13.79	39.86	5.37	19.93

Adams Express Company

Premium/Discount Spread

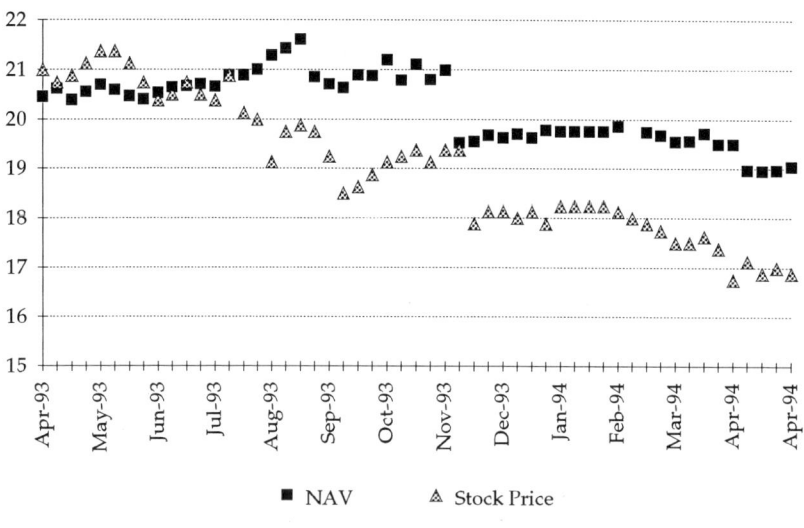

■ NAV   △ Stock Price

Fund Outlook (ADX): The fund is concerned that the equity market may have become overextended. There appears to be little room for disappointments in Wall Street estimates for the first half of 1994. Valuations of many stocks appear quite high by most traditional measures even on current earnings estimates. To some extent this can be attributed to the large amounts of new funds which were invested in equities in 1993, but there also appears to be a degree of unwarranted optimism about the near-term outlook. The fund believes there is more reason for optimism looking further out in the future as the rest of the developed world begins to recover. The fund expects to take advantage of market weakness to become more fully invested in companies which have superior long-term earnings prospects.

Authors' Comments (ADX): ADX is a conservatively managed fund, whose objectives are the preservation of capital. The portfolio contains a large percentage of energy and utility stocks which offer above average yield. The largest holding is Petroleum and Resources. There is a heavy commitment to cyclicals. The fund is staying away from consumer stocks because of the slow growth in personal disposable income. The portfolio is not limited to staid blue chips, but includes growth-oriented issues.

Baker, Fentress & Company

200 W. Madison Street, Suite 3510
Chicago, IL 60606
(312) 236-9190

NYSE: BKF

Transfer Agent
Harris Trust & Savings Bank
Corporate Trust Operations
111 W. Monroe St.
Chicago, IL 60603
(312) 461-2545

Growth

Results

For 12-months Ending 4/29/94	Period End	Period Begin	Distributions	Yield Dist (%)	Total Return (%)
Share Price	16.75	18.00	2.24	12.44	5.50
NAV per Share	20.29	21.19		10.57	6.32

Background: Formed in 1891 as an investment banker and broker-dealer in securities. Became a private investment company in 1960 and a registered investment company in 1970.

Objective: Seeks capital appreciation and income consistent with capital appreciation. Invests primarily in non-diversified, small-cap common stocks and other equity securities (preferred stocks, options to purchase equities, limited partnerships, business trusts, and convertible debt securities). The fund has an annual 8% payout policy.

Portfolio: (5/06/94) Equities 100%. Technology 21%, Basic Industry 16%, Capital Goods 13%, Energy 12%, Consumer Durables 11%. Top Holdings: Consolidated-Tacoma Land Company 14.1%, MCI Communications 9%, Wausau Paper 4%, American Barrick 3%, Nucor 3%, Mapco 3%.

Capitalization: (12/31/94) Common stock outstanding 25,318,433. No long-term debt.

Beta: 0.79
Fee: 0.00% *Fund Manager:* Internally Managed
Income Distribution: Semi-Annually *Capital Gains Distribution:* Annually
Reinvestment Plan: Yes *Shareholder Reports:* Quarterly

5 Year Performance

Fiscal Year Ending 12/31	1993	1992	1991	1990	1989
Net Assets ($mil)	516.90	419.80	417.40	350.20	456.20
Net Income Distribution ($)	0.48	0.39	0.58	0.70	0.72
Capital Gains Distribution ($)	1.76	1.42	1.15	1.25	2.72
Total Distribution ($)	2.24	1.81	1.73	1.95	3.44
Yield From Distribution (%)	13.18	10.27	11.93	9.07	17.30
Expense Ratio (%)	0.83	0.76	0.84	0.68	0.64
Portfolio Turnover (%)	31.45	28.36	50.70	26.19	35.47
NAV per Share ($)	20.42	20.82	21.49	18.66	25.18
Market Price per Share ($)	16.75	17.00	17.63	14.50	21.50
Premium (Discount)(%)	-17.97	-18.35	-18.01	-22.29	-14.61
Total Return, Stock Price (%)	11.71	6.69	33.52	-23.49	25.45

Baker, Fentress & Company

Premium/Discount Spread

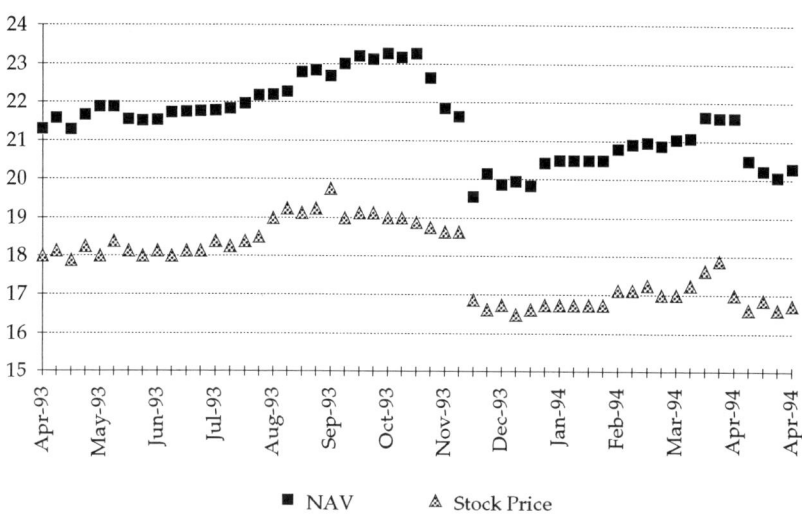

■ NAV △ Stock Price

Fund Outlook (BKF): BKF continues to be optimistic about the long-term renewal of the U.S. economy, led by more capital investment and dynamic smaller firms. The fund feels that risks to portfolio values from recession or adverse geopolitical developments seem to have receded. However, risks associated with the inadequate savings rate of the U.S. economy and its implications for rising interest rates remain. The fund feels that if household savings continue to decline, and no further progress is made in reducing government deficits, the probable result will be higher interest rates and slower growth. The long-term future remains bright for the U.S. economy. Global recovery, combined with a modest value for the dollar, bodes well for the revival of U.S. manufacturing and exports, particularly of capital equipment. Technology and services in many U.S. industries, including computers, communications, entertainment, financial services, and producers; and equipment, lead the world. Companies with competitive technology with costs in line with global competition, represent emerging investment opportunities.

Authors' Comments (BKF): The fund is a non-diversified, closed-end company whose objective is primarily capital appreciation. Consolidated-Tocoma Land Company, which represents a large portion of the portfolio, is engaged primarily in the operation of citrus groves and resort properties and, through subsidiaries, in property leasing, commercial real estate and real estate development. The company also leases properties for oil and mineral exploration.

Central Securities Corporation

AMEX: CET

375 Park Avenue
New York, NY 10152
(212) 688-3011

Transfer Agent:
First Chicago Trust Co. of New York
P.O. Box 2500
Jersey City, NJ 07303
(212) 791-6422

Growth & Income

Results

For 12-months Ending 4/29/94	Period End	Period Begin	Distributions	Yield Dist (%)	Total Return (%)
Share Price ($)	16.38	14.75	1.60	10.85	21.90
NAV per Share ($)	17.83	15.20		10.53	27.83

Background: Formed in 1929 as Central Illinois Securities Corp. Adopted current name in 1959.

Objective: Seeks long-term capital appreciation. Income is secondary. Invests primarily in relatively few situations. Balance invested in a broad general market portfolio. Will use borrowings when deemed advisable.

Portfolio: (12/31/93) Common Stock 91.3%, Notes & Debentures 3.4%, Short-Term Debt Investments 5.1%. Sector Weightings: Electronics 15.5%, Communications 13%, Business Services 11.8%, Insurance 8.9%, Energy 8.6%. Top Holdings: The Plymouth Rock Co., Reynolds and Reynolds Co., Analog Devices, Inc., Nextel Communications, Inc., M.A. Hanna Co.

Capitalization: (12/31/93) Common stock outstanding 11,667,795. Convertible preferred shares outstanding 398,436. No long-term debt.

Beta: 0.74

Fee: 0.40%

Income Distribution: Semi-Annually

Reinvestment Plan: No

Fund Manager: Internally Managed

Capital Gains Distribution: Annually

Shareholder Reports: Quarterly

5 Year Performance

Fiscal Year Ending 12/31	1993	1992	1991	1990	1989
Net Assets ($mil)	218.90	165.60	131.70	111.20	129.40
Net Income Distribution ($)	0.18	0.20	0.14	0.20	0.35
Capital Gains Distribution ($)	1.42	0.66	0.44	0.03	0.09
Total Distribution ($)	1.60	0.86	0.59	0.23	0.44
Yield From Distribution (%)	13.76	9.30	7.61	2.39	4.82
Expense Ratio (%)	0.77	0.88	0.96	0.98	0.92
Portfolio Turnover	15.14	18.56	16.69	7.25	14.33
NAV per Share ($)	17.90	14.33	11.87	10.00	12.24
Market Price per Share ($)	15.50	11.63	9.25	7.75	9.63
Premium (Discount) (%)	-13.41	-18.91	-22.07	-22.50	-21.41
Total Return, Stock Price (%)	47.03	35.03	26.97	-17.13	10.30

Central Securities Corporation

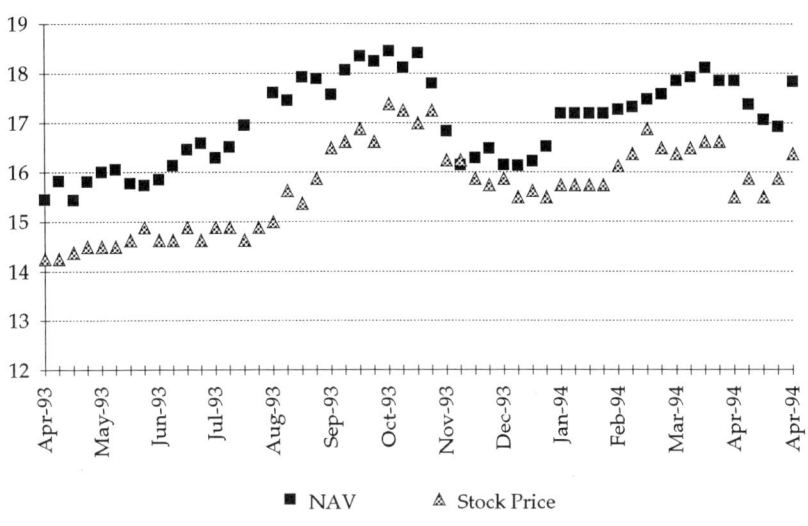

Fund Outlook (CET): The Corporation's practice has been to generally remain fully invested as opposed to buying and selling in anticipation of market moves. One qualification is that it is not always possible or desirable to immediately re-deploy funds from investment sales. The Corporation is always searching for excellent companies with good economic fundamentals, positive cash generation and shareholder oriented management which can be purchased at reasonable prices. Because such situations are difficult to find, CET prefers making significant long-term commitments and continues to believe that the best long-term results can be achieved by investing a substantial portion of the assets in a limited number of situations with the balance held in a broad general market portfolio. The Corporation believes that the risk associated with this approach can be reduced through active and intimate knowledge of the problems and opportunities of the companies in which it invests.

Authors' Comments (CET): The fund ranks first in total performance for the past trailing 12 months in its peer group of domestic equity funds. Management's investment philosophy can best be described as value investing, without any significant requirements as to sector weighting.

General American Investors

NYSE: GAM

450 Lexington Avenue
New York, NY 10017
(800) 436-8401
(212) 916-8400

Transfer Agent:
State Street Bank & Trust Co.
2 Heritage Drive
North Quincy, MA 02171
(800) 426-5523

Growth

Results

For 12 Months Ending 4/29/94	Period End	Period Begin	Distributions	Yield Dist (%)	Total Return (%)
Share Price	19.88	26.13	2.40	12.07	-14.73
NAV per Share ($)	23.27	25.46		10.31	0.82

Background: One of the nation's oldest publicly traded investment funds, it was established in 1927 by partners of Lazard Freres and Lehman Brothers.

Objective: Seeks long-term capital appreciation. Income is secondary. Normally remains fully invested in diversified equities.

Portfolio: (12/31/93) Stocks 96%, Short-Term 3%. Top Ten Holdings: The Home Depot 8%; Wal-Mart 6%; Buffets 4%, U.S. Healthcare 3%, Brinker International 3%, Luxottica Group 3%, Toys R Us 3%, Walt Disney 3%, American International 3%.

Capitalization: Common Stock Outstanding 22,378,764. No long-term debt.
Beta: 1.70
Fee: 0.50%   *Fund Manager:* Internally Managed
Income Distribution: Annually   *Capital Gains Distribution:* Annually
Reinvestment Plan: Yes   *Shareholder Reports:* Quarterly

5 Year Performance

Fiscal Year Ending 12/31	1993	1992	1991	1990	1989
Net Assets ($mil)	553.90	586.50	587.20	382.20	381.90
Net Income Distribution ($)	0.06	0.03	0.10	0.21	0.25
Capital Gains Distribution ($)	2.98	3.06	2.14	1.91	1.73
Total Distributions ($)	3.04	3.09	2.24	2.12	1.98
Yield from Distributions	10.13	10.66	13.18	11.70	14.80
Expense Ratio	1.16	1.16	1.02	1.07	1.04
Portfolio Turnover (%)	19.50	14.42	23.13	18.77	26.91
NAV per Share ($)	24.75	28.56	30.60	20.60	21.41
Market Price per Share ($)	22.25	30.00	29.00	17.00	18.13
Premium (Discount) (%)	-10.10	-18.91	-22.07	-22.50	-21.41
Total Return, Stock Price (%)	-15.70	14.10	83.76	5.46	48.60

General American Securities

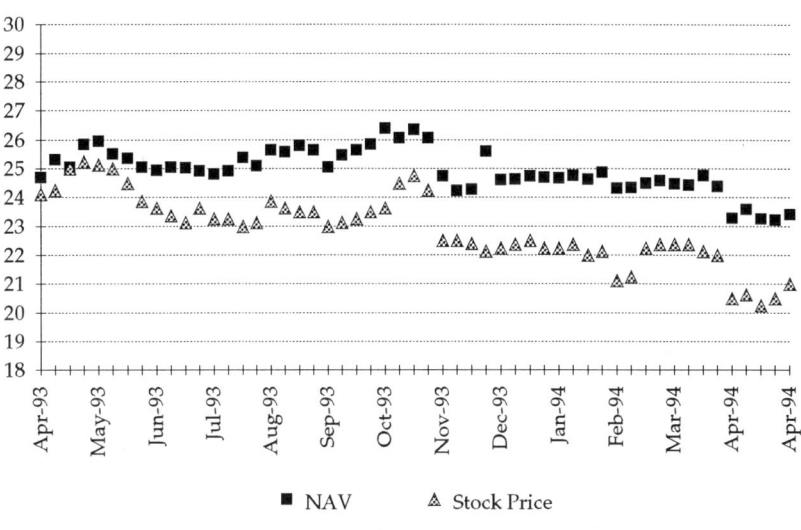

Premium/Discount Spread

■ NAV   △ Stock Price

Fund Outlook (GAM): The fund believes the economic recovery will continue in 1994 with slow to moderate real growth of 2.5-3.0% and modest inflation. This sustained recovery should favor General American's portfolio as the earnings per share of its investments on average should grow significantly more rapidly than the economy. With these securities selling at only a moderate price/earnings ratio premium to the S&P 500, the fund believes General American is well positioned for 1994 and beyond. Over longer periods of time, GAM's objective has proven successful as evidenced by long-term investment results.

Authors' Comments (GAM): Because of the fund's large stakes in the health care and specialty retailing sectors which have been relatively weak market performers, the fund has lagged the market and ranks 18th in total performance for the past trailing 12-months. The securities held in the portfolio may be characterized as quality blue chips with strong longer-term potential. GAM is recommended as a contrarian play on the assumption that the overvaluation in the health care and retailing stocks has been corrected.

H & Q Life Sciences Investors   NYSE: HQL

50 Rowes Wharf, 4th Floor
Boston, MA 02110
(800) 327-6679
(617) 574-0567

Transfer Agent:
State Street Bank & Trust Co.
225 Franklin St.
Boston, MA 02110
(800) 426-5523

Growth

Results

For 12-months Ending 4/29/94	Period End	Period Begin	Distributions	Yield Dist (%)	Total Return (%)
Share Price ($)	10.13	11.75	0.00	0.00	-13.79
NAV per Share ($)	10.96	11.86		0.00	-7.59

Background: Initial public offering May 8, 1992 of 3,850,000 shares at $15 per share. Initial NAV was $13.95 per share.

Objective: Seeks long-term capital appreciation. Invests in life-sciences companies. Normally, invests at least 65% in U.S./foreign health care companies, and agricultural/environmental management firms. May invest in preferreds, convertibles, junk bonds of health care issuers. In September 1993, trustees voted to allow fund to invest up to 40% in restricted securities. May invest up to 25% outside U.S. In December 1993, raised $31.5 million in a 73% subscribed rights offering.

Portfolio: (12/31/93) Stocks 75%, Convertibles 25%, Agri/Environmental 15%, Biotechnology 37%, Diagnostics 5%, Medical Supplies 15%, Medical Specialty 16%, Pharmaceuticals 10%. Top Holdings: Elan 5%, IDEXX Laboratories 5%, Chiron 5%, Ribi ImmunoChem Research 4%.

Capitalization: (12/31/93) Common stock outstanding 3,858,600. No long-term debt.

Beta: N/A
Fee: 1.00%   *Fund Manager:* Hambrecht & Quist Capital Mgt., Inc.
Income Distribution: Annually   *Capital Gains Distribution:* Annually
Reinvestment Plan: Yes   *Shareholder Reports:* Semi-Annually

5 Year Performance

Fiscal Year Ending 9/30	1993	1992	1991	1990	1989
Net Assets ($mil)	50.50	51.30	-	-	-
Net Income Distribution ($)	0.00	0.00	-	-	-
Capital Gains Distribution ($)	0.00	0.00	-	-	-
Total Distribution ($)	0.00	0.00	-	-	-
Yield From Distribution (%)	0.00	0.00	-	-	-
Expense Ratio (%)	2.17	1.97	-	-	-
Portfolio Turnover (%)	32.89	0.00	-	-	-
NAV per Share ($)	13.09	13.30	-	-	-
Market Price per Share ($)	12.88	12.75	-	-	-
Premium (Discount) (%)	-1.64	-4.11	-	-	-
Total Return, Stock Price (%)	1.02	-	-	-	-

H & Q Life Sciences Investors

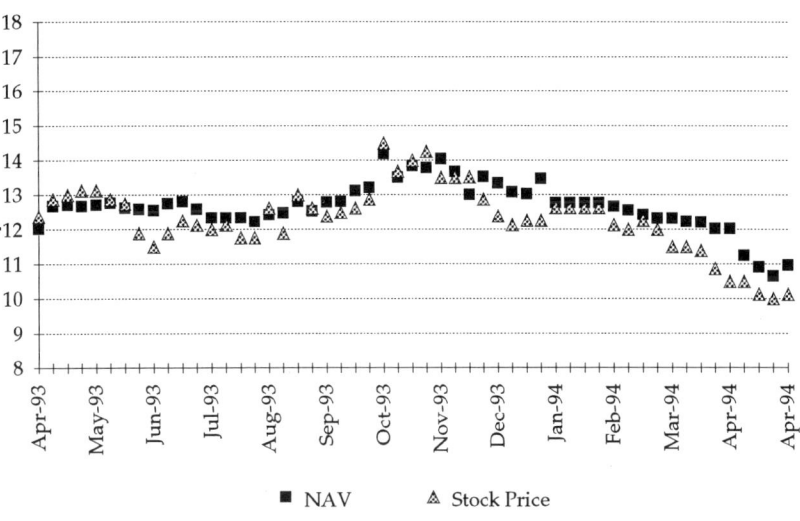

Fund Outlook (HQL): The fund believes that the pace of scientific discovery continues to accelerate and presents an ongoing flow of opportunities for private placement/venture investments. In the fourth quarter, two private companies were added to the portfolio. Bio-Transplant is developing products to enhance the success rate of organ transplantation and eliminating human organ shortages by transplanting pig organs into humans. Biofield is developing a system for the early detection of breast cancer. A follow-on investment was made in Transkaryotic Therapies which seeks to be a leader in the field of genetic therapy. Two private placements were made in public companies: Univax Biologics, a developer of therapeutic vaccines and antibodies; and Cortex Pharmaceuticals, whose lead product appears to materially enhance cognition. HQL continues to believe that long-term growth of many companies in the life sciences sectors will be above average and that investment returns from carefully selected common stocks will improve both relatively and absolutely.

Authors' Comments (HQL): Worries about the effects of any proposed Clinton health care plan have hit the health care industry hard. However, inflated P/E ratios have fallen back to more acceptable levels with the result that many bargains are now to be found. We are attracted to HQL because the new technologies, particularly biotechnology, medical supplies, and agricultural/environmental technologies.

Morgan Grenfell SMALLCap Fund, Inc.

885 Third Avenue, 32 Floor
New York, NY 10022
(212) 230-2600

Growth

NYSE: MGC
Transfer Agent:
The Bank of New York
101 Barclay St.
New York, NY 10286
(800) 524-4458

Results

For 12-months Ending 4/29/94	Period End	Period Begin	Distributions	Yield Dist (%)	Total Return (%)
Share Price ($)	9.88	10.25	1.14	11.12	7.51
NAV per Share ($)	11.67	11.46		9.95	11.78

Background: Diversified, team-managed fund. Initial public offering May 7, 1987 of 5,000,000 shares at $10 per share. Initial NAV was $9.27 per share. Fund manager is a subsidiary of London-based Morgan Grenfell Group PLC, a unit of Deutsche Bank AG.

Objective: Seeks long-term capital appreciation. Invests primarily in U.S. companies with capitalizations of $50 million to $500 million. Current income is secondary. Leverage may be employed up to 15% of assets.

Portfolio: (12/31/93) Common Stocks 94.4%, Commercial Paper 5.6%. Sector Weightings: Consumer 39.2%, Technology, 18.3%, Service Companies 11.6%, Energy 8%, Health Care 7.5%, Credit-Sensitive 4.9%, Transportation 2.5%, Process Industrial 2.4%.

Capitalization: (12/31/93) Common stock outstanding 5,682,063. No long-term debt.

Beta: 1.41
Fee: 1.00%   *Fund Manager:* Morgan Grenfell Capital Mgt.
Income Distribution: Quarterly   *Capital Gains Distribution:* Annually
Reinvestment Plan: Yes   *Shareholder Reports:* Quarterly

5 Year Performance

Fiscal Year Ending 12/31	1993	1992	1991	1990	1989
Net Assets ($mil)	67.30	68.00	64.50	45.60	54.10
Net Income Distribution ($)	0.00	0.00	0.00	0.00	0.00
Capital Gains Distribution ($)	1.14	0.82	0.97	0.65	0.25
Total Distribution ($)	1.14	0.82	0.97	0.65	0.25
Yield From Distribution (%)	9.31	6.37	11.09	6.75	3.39
Expense Ratio (%)	1.39	1.44	1.79	2.01	2.13
Portfolio Turnover (%)	89.00	89.00	70.00	75.00	80.00
NAV per Share ($)	11.85	11.97	12.30	8.70	10.80
Market Price per Share ($)	10.88	12.25	12.88	8.75	9.63
Premium (Discount) (%)	-8.23	2.34	4.63	0.57	-10.93
Total Return, Stock Price (%)	-1.88	1.48	58.29	-2.39	33.88

Morgan Grenfell SMALLCap Fund, Inc.

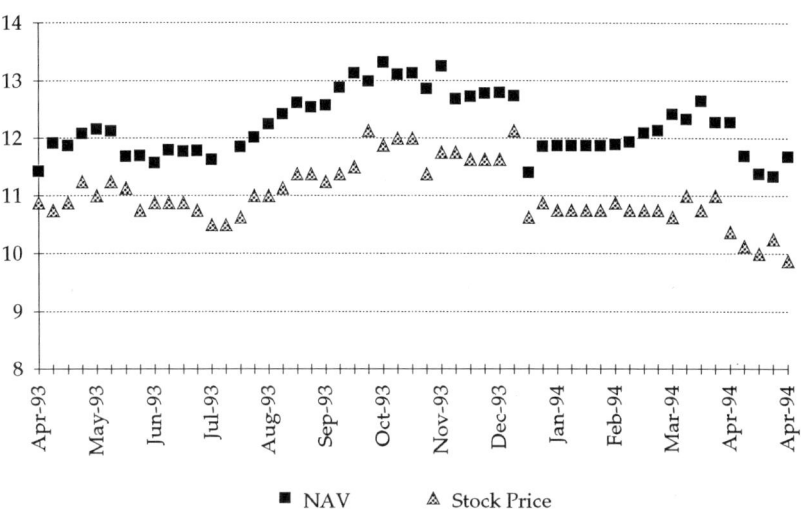

Premium/Discount Spread

■ NAV △ Stock Price

Fund Outlook (MGC): A fundamental approach to investment research represents the foundation of MGC's investment product. Original investment research encompasses not only the financial analysis of companies but also extensive team visititations companies to discuss business strategies with corporate management. The fund feels that the team approach along with investment expertise across all economic sectors provides the fund with the stability to structure a broadly diversified portfolio within the smaller company universe as well as the ability to shift investment emphasis among sectors. The fund's team is focused on selecting smaller companies which have the potential to be the highly successful medium-sized and larger companies of the future, and the fund's portfolio holdings reflect this approach to investment within the universe of smaller companies.

Authors' Comments (MGC): The fund concentrates on small cap companies with a market capitalization of between $100 million and $1 billion. These smaller cap companies are in a better position to restructure during a recession and, therefore are able to achieve significant earnings growth during an economic expansion. Prior to 1990 small cap stocks were out of favor, however. Since then, they have outperformed the big cap stocks. As the economy continues to improve, it is anticipated that this group will continue to outperform the big cap stocks. The fund ranks fifth in total performance on a 12-month trailing average among its peer group. MGC is an appropriate investment for growth-oriented investors.

Royce Value Trust, Inc.   NYSE: **RVT**

1414 Avenue of the Americas, 9th Floor
New York, NY 10019
(800) 221-4268

Transfer Agent:
State Street Bank & Trust Co.
P.O. Box 8200
Boston, MA 02266
(800) 426-5523

Growth

Results

For 12-months Ending 4/29/94	Period End	Period Begin	Distributions	Yield Dist (%)	Total Return (%)
Share Price ($)1	12.50	13.00	1.15	8.85	5.00
NAV per Share ($)	13.17	13.13		8.76	9.06

Background: Initial public offering November 19, 1986 of 10,000,000 shares at $10 per share. Initial NAV was $9.30 per share.

Objective: Seeks long-term capital appreciation. Invests in common stocks and other equity securities of small- and medium-sized companies (market capitalization of $15 million to $300 million), the selection of which emphasizes value investing.

Portfolio: (3/31/94) Common Stock 90%, Preferred Stocks & Corporate Bonds 1%, Cash & Other Assets Less Liabilities 9%. Largest Holdings: Avatar Holdings Inc.; Baldwin & Lyons, Inc. Class B; Ash Grove Cement Company; Alleghany Corporation; Wesco Financial Corporation.

Capitalization: (3/31/94) Common stock outstanding 19,453,875. No long-term debt.

Beta: 0.68

Fee: 1.00%   *Fund Manager:* Quest Advisory Corp.
Income Distribution: Annually   *Capital Gains Distribution:* Annually
Reinvestment Plan: Yes   *Shareholder Reports:* Quarterly

5 Year Performance

Fiscal Year Ending 12/31	1993	1992	1991	1990	1989
Net Assets ($mil)	246.60	202.50	166.50	118.30	130.50
Net Income Distribution ($)	0.09	0.15	0.17	0.17	0.17
Capital Gains Distribution ($)	1.06	0.75	0.44	0.15	0.35
Total Distribution ($)	1.15	0.90	0.61	0.32	0.52
Yield from Distribution (%)	9.39	8.67	7.50	3.37	6.40
Expense Ratio (%)	1.33	0.81	0.79	0.94	0.95
Portfolio Turnover (%)	33.00	40.40	34.01	28.16	36.06
NAV per Share ($)	13.47	12.5	11.23	8.58	10.35
Market Price per Share ($)	12.88	12.25	10.38	8.13	9.50
Premium (Discount) (%)	-4.42	-2.00	-7.66	-5.24	-8.21
Total Return, Stock Price (%)	14.53	26.69	35.18	-11.05	25.25

Royce Value Trust, Inc.

Premium/Discount Spread

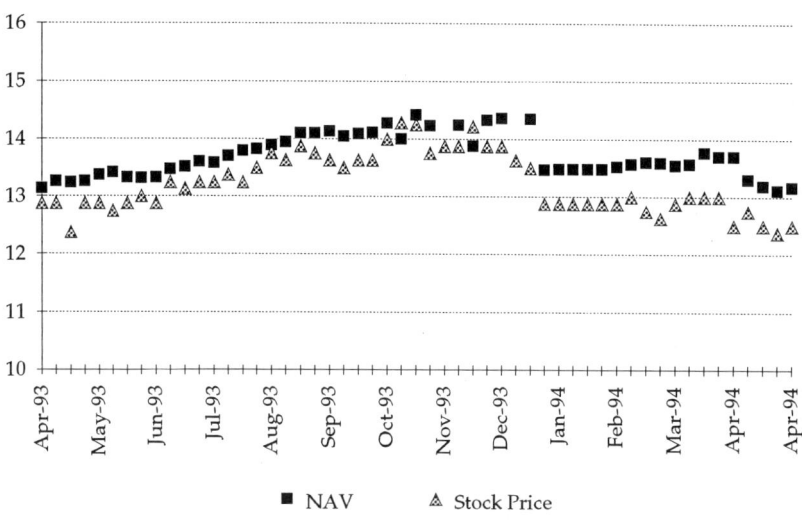

■ NAV △ Stock Price

Fund Outlook (RVT): The lessons of the first quarter bring back into focus the importance of capital preservation, an idea many investors forgot about because of the dazzling total returns provided by the high performance environment. To illustrate this point, consider that many of 1993's star performers, global hedge funds, posted 50% plus gains. Interestingly, several of these funds reportedly gave back 25% in the first quarter, for a cumulative return of 12.5% (9% annualized). RTV's less spectacular 17.9% gain in 1993 and modest loss of -1.2% in 1994's first quarter, produced a cumulative return of 16.5% (13% annualized). The contrast in returns conjures up images of a modern day "Tortoise And The Hare." The fund has always liked being the Tortoise. RTV will continue to use the market's volatility to their advantage—restocking the portfolio as prices become cheap and selling off securities as prices rise above their intrinsic business values. The fund feels that this approach, while at times out of sync with the market, has provided very respectable results over the long term.

Authors' Comments (RVT): This is a diversified closed-end fund that invests in small and medium-size companies. The investment philosophy uses a value (Graham & Dodd) rather than an earnings approach to investments. The value approach favors companies that have little or no debt, good cash flow and undervalued assets. There is an absence of technology and of stocks trading at high P/E ratios. RVT is good for growth-oriented accounts seeking an investment in small cap stocks.

Salomon Brothers Fund

7 World Trade Center
New York, NY 10048
(800) 725-6666
(212) 783-1301

Growth & Income

NYSE: **SBF**

Transfer Agent:
The Bank of New York
101 Barclay St.
New York, NY 10286
(800) 524-4458

Results

For 12-months Ending 4/29/94	Period End	Period Begin	Distributions	Yield Dist (%)	Total Return (%)
Share Price ($)	12.38	13.50	2.20	16.30	8.00
NAV per Share ($)	14.24	15.24		14.44	7.87

Background: Originally founded in 1929 by Lehman Brothers. The fund, formerly known as Lehman Corporation, was acquired by Salomon Brothers Asset Management on May 1, 1993. One of the largest traded public investment companies.

Objective: Seeks long-term capital growth through a portfolio of large capitalized blue chip stocks. Generally will be fully invested. No more than 25% of assets will be in a single industry.

Portfolio: (12/31/93) Common Stocks 90.6%, Corporate Bonds 4.9%, Repurchase Agreement 0.1%. Sector Weightings: Basic Industries 17%, Consumer Products & Services 10%, Defense 1.5%, Energy 9.8%, Financial Services 15%, Food & Beverages 1%, Health Care 8%, Machine & Equipment 1%, Merchandise 9%, Technologies 8%, Telecommunications 8%, Transportations 5%.

Capitalization: (12/31/93) Common stock outstanding 79,030,529. No long-term debt.

Beta: 1.00

Fee: 0.50% *Fund Manager:* Salomon Brothers Asset Mgt., Inc.
Income Distribution: Quarterly *Capital Gains Distribution:* Annually
Reinvestment Plan: Yes *Shareholder Reports:* Quarterly

5 Year Performance

Fiscal Year Ending 12/31	1993	1992	1991	1990	1989
Net Assets ($mil)	1176.00	1109.40	1115.20	906.00	1027.10
Net Income Distribution ($)	0.34	0.40	0.47	0.49	0.59
Capital Gains Distribution ($)	1.72	0.60	1.14	0.71	1.52
Total Distribution ($)	2.06	1.00	1.61	1.20	2.11
Yield from Distribution (%)	14.98	7.20	14.64	9.23	18.14
Expense Ratio (%)	0.41	0.43	0.43	0.46	0.44
Portfolio Turnover (%)	80.00	42.00	14.00	15.00	30.00
NAV per Share ($)	14.88	15.16	15.66	13.33	15.58
Market Price per Share ($)	12.75	13.75	13.88	11.00	13.00
Premium (Discount) (%)	-14.31	-9.30	-11.43	-18.45	-16.56
Total Return, Stock Price (%)	7.71	6.27	40.82	-6.15	29.92

Salomon Brothers Fund

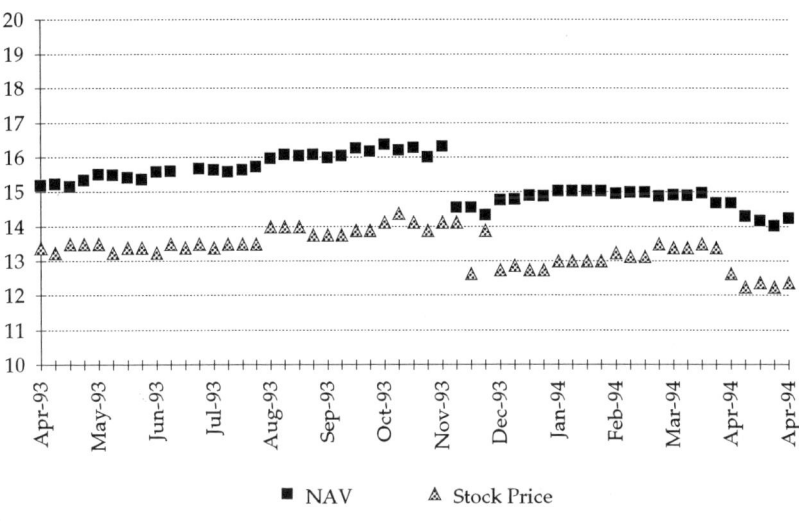

Premium/Discount Spread

■ NAV △ Stock Price

Fund Outlook (SBF): The fund's investment policy has been to concentrate a large portion of its investments in companies whose stocks generally have strong positions in industries with the potential to grow faster than the economy as a whole. Investments are monitored carefully and are changed from time to time into holdings the fund believes offer more favorable opportunities in light of changing economic, social and political conditions. The common thread of the fund has been to seek out and to hold stocks of well-managed, favorably situated companies it expects will produce above-average earnings and dividend growth over time. SBF also looks for opportunities in turn-around situations and in securities that appear to be priced substantially lower than their intrinsic value. With current income not primary, the fund is mindful of the income needs of shareholders. For the core of their holdings, the fund looks for companies able to increase earnings and dividends at an above-average rate and still retain enough cash to finance future growth.

Authors' Comments (SBF): In order to improve the overall performance of the fund, the responsibilities for management of the portfolio was recently divided between two managers. However, the overall investment philosophy remains unchanged, namely the selection of seasoned large and mid-cap growth stocks with substantial earnings visibility and good dividends. There is an absence of stocks with high P/E earnings multiples or stocks purchased on the basis of earnings momentum. This fund is good for investors seeking total return.

Tri-Continental Corporation

NYSE: TY

130 Liberty Street, 24th Floor
New York, NY 10006
(800) 221-2450
(212) 850-1864

Transfer Agent:
Union Data Service Center, Inc.
100 Park Avenue
New York, NY 10017
(212) 432-4100

Growth & Income

Results

For 12-months Ending 4/29/94	Period End	Period Begin	Distributions	Yield Dist (%)	Total Return (%)
Share Price ($)	22.38	25.00	2.41	9.64	-0.84
NAV per Share ($)	26.53	27.51		8.76	5.20

Background: Organized in 1929, it is now the nation's largest diversified, closed-end investment company with a capital structure consisting of three different types of securities: preferred stock, common stock, and warrants.

Objective: Seeks growth and income through a highly diversified portfolio of larger capitalized growth companies with emphasis on the medical and drug industries.

Portfolio: (12/31/93) Common Stock 77%, U.S. Government 8.3%, Convertibles 8.2%, Short-Term 4.0%, Corporate 2.7%. Sector Weightings: Automotive 5%, Basic Materials 5%, Communications 5%, Computers & Services 3%, Consumer Goods 9%, Diversified 2.9%, Drugs 4%, Utilities 4%, Other 38%.

Capitalization: (12/31/93) Common stock outstanding 78,812,785. Warrants outstanding 21,000. Preferred shares outstanding 752,740.

Beta: 0.95

Fee: 0.45%

Fund Manager: J. & W. Seligman & Co., Inc.

Income Distribution: Quarterly

Capital Gains Distribution: Annually

Reinvestment Plan: Yes

Shareholder Reports: Quarterly

5 Year Performance

Fiscal Year Ending 12/31	1993	1992	1991	1990	1989
Net Assets ($mil)	2203.90	2125.70	1871.30	1500.30	1632.10
Net Income Distribution ($)	0.80	0.78	0.78	0.86	0.84
Capital Gains Distribution ($)	1.80	0.70	1.80	1.60	2.55
Total Distribution ($)	2.60	1.48	2.58	2.46	3.39
Yield From Distribution (%)	10.20	5.33	12.07	10.70	17.61
Expense Ratio (%)	0.66	0.67	0.67	0.56	0.55
Portfolio Turnover (%)	69.24	44.35	49.02	41.23	59.87
NAV per Share ($)	27.49	28.03	28.57	24.60	27.44
Market Price per Share ($)	23.75	25.50	27.75	21.38	23.00
Premium (Discount) (%)	-13.60	-9.03	-2.87	-13.13	-16.18
Total Return, Stock Price (%)	3.33	-2.77	41.86	3.65	37.09

Tri-Continental Corporation

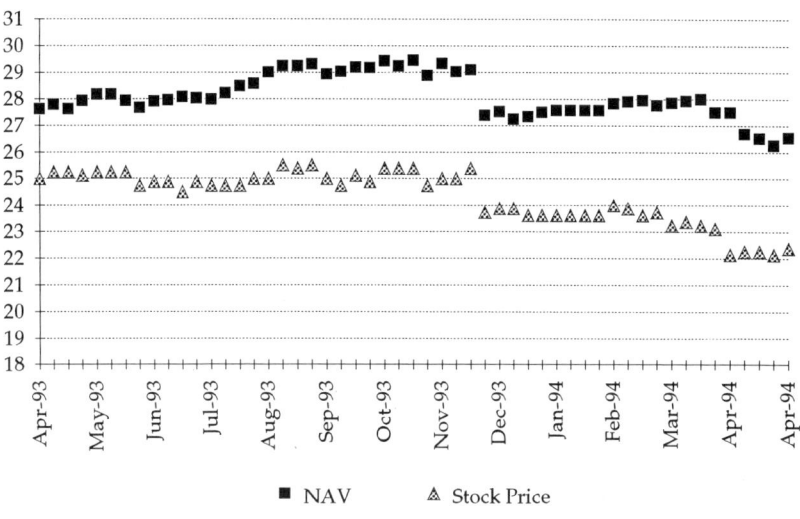

Premium/Discount Spread

■ NAV   △ Stock Price

Fund Outlook (TY): TY continues to seek investments that provide better-than-average growth of principal and income over time, while generating reasonable current income. Due to improving earnings potential in industrial companies, TY expects to further diversify its holdings to the economy's producer side. It believes the dynamics behind these restructured businesses, many active in the export markets, will surpass those of most consumer non-durable companies. TY will also look for signs of restructuring in the consumer and services industries where newly focused managements should begin to provide enhanced output cost-effectively. Finally, since market appreciation in foreign markets, particularly in Asia and Latin America, greatly exceeded expectations last year, TY hopes to take advantage of pullbacks to further increase exposure in these areas of rapid economic growth.

Authors' Comments (TY): TY is the largest and, founded in 1929, is one of the oldest closed-end funds. Unrealized appreciation is a factor that has affected performance. Profits taken on long-term positions, if paid out, result in a tax-liability for the shareholders. In 1993, financial stocks were increased, and international stocks were added to the portfolio. Currently, the portfolio is represented by foreign securities. Health-care holdings were reduced due to the cloud overhanging this sector. In anticipation of steady economic growth, improved corporate earnings, and subdued inflation, TY remains a good investment choice for those seeking better than average growth of principal and income over time along with the generation of current income.

Single Country Funds

Argentina Fund
345 Park Avenue
New York, NY 10154-0004
(800) 225-2470
(617) 330-5602

NYSE: **AF**
Transfer Agent:
State Street Bank & Trust Co.
P.O. Box 8300, Boston, MA 02266-8300
(617) 328-5000 ext. 6406

Growth **Results**

For 12-months Ending 4/29/94	Period End	Period Begin	Distributions	Yield Dist (%)	Total Return (%)
Share Price ($)	14.75	10.00	0.15	1.50	49.00
NAV per Share	13.99	10.03		1.50	40.98

Background: Initial public offering October, 1991 of 5,000,000 shares at $12 per share. Initial NAV was $10.98.

Objective: Seeks long-term capital appreciation. Invests at least 65% in equities of Argentine issuers including common and preferred stock, convertibles, warrants or rights, and partnership interests; up to 30% in Argentine Government and corporate debt securities of any maturity; up to 5% in securities rated C or below by S&P; up to 25% in unlisted securities. May also engage in hedging procedures utilizing futures and options.

Portfolio: (1/31/94) Equity Securities 82%, Argentine Debt Securities 7%, Repurchase Agreement 3%, U.S. Short-Term 9%. Sector Weightings: Telecommunications 19%, Beverage 15%, Food 13%, Petroleum 13%, Banking 11%, Conglomerates 11%, Construction 4%, Government 3%. Top Holdings: Quilmes Industrial, Nortel Inversora Preferred, YPF S.A. Bolinos Rio de la Plata.

Capitalization: (1/31/94) Common stock outstanding 5,795,644. No long-term debt.

Beta: N/A
Fee: 1.30% *Fund Manager:* Scudder, Stevens & Clark, Inc.
Income Distribution: Annually   *Capital Gains Distribution:* Annually
Reinvestment Plan: Yes   *Shareholder Reports:* Quarterly

5 Year Performance

Fiscal Year Ending 10/31	1993	1992	1991	1990	1989
Net Assets ($mil)	73.50	53.90	63.30	-	-
Net Income Distribution ($)	0.05	0.06	0.00	-	-
Capital Gains Distribution ($)	0.09	0.00	0.00	-	-
Total Distribution ($)	0.14	0.06	0.00	-	-
Yield from Distribution (%)	1.45	0.41	0.00	-	-
Expense Ratio (%)	2.37	2.24	2.55	-	-
Portfolio Turnover (%)	32.50	26.50	-	-	-
NAV per Share ($)	12.69	9.35	10.99	-	-
Market Price per Share ($)	14.00	9.63	14.63	-	-
Premium (Discount) (%)	10.32	2.99	33.12	-	-
Total Return, Stock Price (%)	46.83	-33.77	-	-	-

Argentina Fund

Premium/Discount Spread

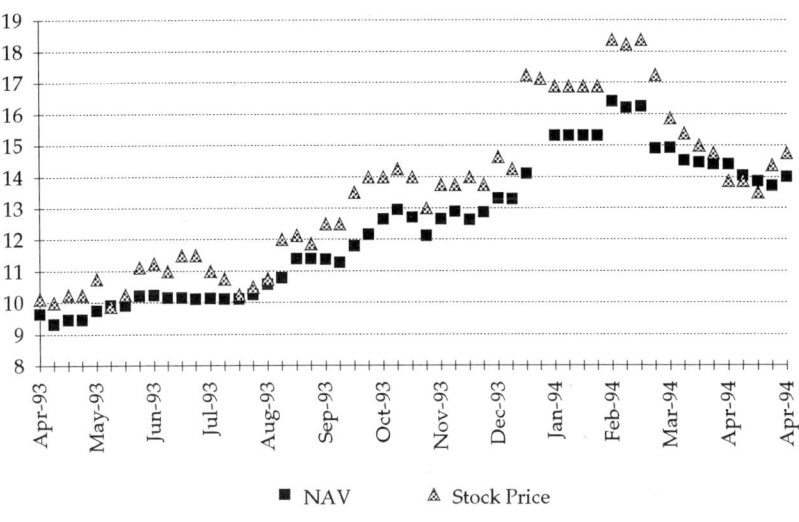

■ NAV   △ Stock Price

Fund Outlook (AF): The success in price stabilization is helping to strengthen the Argentine financial system, of which the rising capitalization and trading volume of the stock market is only one important aspect. The weak points are the reliance on net capital inflows from abroad to finance investment and the rising deficit on current account of the balance of payments. Although foreign inflows of capital continue to be strong (reserves rose to $3.6 billion in 1993), the economy is vulnerable to a slackening, leaving it exposed to a shortage of finance and a subsequent increase in domestic borrowing costs. This makes expansion more exposed to foreign or domestic shocks. At his point, no signs indicate Argentina will fail to attract the foreign funds needed to help finance a growth trend.

Authors' Comments (AF): In 1989, when Carlos Menem was elected President, he initiated a policy of privatization of state-owned companies, lifted trade barriers, curtailed government intervention in the economy and pegged the Argentine peso to the U.S. dollar. Resulting in reducing the monthly inflation rate of 200% to an annual rate of 6% by 1993. To compete in an open market, companies were forced to restructure. Economic reforms and restructuring have progressed enough to justify a more optimistic view of corporate profits and higher equity values. The financial markets are organized, automated and operate efficiently. No sectors are closed to foreign ownership nor a limit on the amount of equity ownership. Approximately 25% of the market float is owned by foreign investors. A good buy when the fund is sold at a discount.

Austria Fund (The)

1345 Avenue of the Americas
New York, NY 10105
(800) 247-4154
(212) 969-1000

NYSE: **OST**
Transfer Agent:
State Street Bank & Trust Co.
225 Franklin St.
Boston, MA 02110
(800) 426-5523

Growth

Results

For 12-months Ending 4/29/94	Period End	Period Begin	Distributions	Yield Dist (%)	Total Return (%)
Share Price ($)	9.75	8.00	0.10	1.25	23.13
NAV per Share	10.40	7.94		1.26	32.24

Background: Initial public offering September 28, 1989, of 5,750,000 shares at $12 per share. Initial NAV was $11.16 per share. A second offering was made February 1990, of 2,500,000 additional shares. Net proceeds were $16 per share.

Objective: Seeks long-term capital appreciation from a portfolio primarily of Austrian securities.

Portfolio: (3/31/94) Common Stocks 93%, Other 6%., Cash 1%. Sector Weightings: Financial Services 38%, Utility Companies 16%, Industrial Cyclicals 11%, Consumer Staples 8%. Top Holdings: EVN Energie Versorgung Niede, Creditnastalt-Bankverein, EA Generali, Oesterr Electrizitaets, OEMV.

Capitalization: (2/28/94) Common stock outstanding 8,260,963. No long-term debt.

Beta: 0.08

Fee: 1.00%   *Fund Manager:* Alliance Capital Management L.P.
Income Distribution: Annually   *Capital Gains Distribution:* Annually
Reinvestment Plan: Yes   *Shareholder Reports:* Quarterly

5 Year Performance

Fiscal Year Ending 8/31	1993	1992	1991	1990	1989
Net Assets ($mil)	79.50	73.40	89.90	120.10	-
Net Income Distribution ($)	0.01	0.00	0.06	0.06	-
Capital Gains Distribution ($)	0.01	0.14	0.36	0.01	-
Total Distribution ($)	0.02	0.14	0.42	0.07	-
Yield from Distribution (%)	0.26	1.47	3.73	-	-
Expense Ratio (%)	2.13	1.92	1.78	1.82	-
Portfolio Turnover (%)	42.00	56.00	34.00	24.00	-
NAV per Share ($)	9.62	8.89	10.89	14.54	-
Market Price per Share ($)	10.13	7.75	9.50	11.25	-
Premium (Discount) (%)	5.25	-12.82	-12.76	-22.63	-
Total Return, Stock Price (%)	30.97	-16.95	-11.82	-	-

Austria Fund (The)

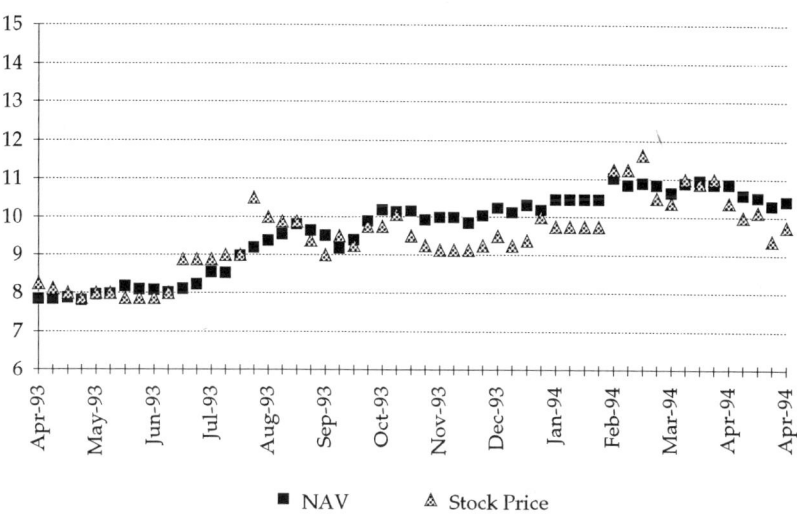

Premium/Discount Spread

Fund Outlook (OST): The Austrian stock market continued its strong recovery with the Credit Aktien Index gaining 11.1% over the first quarter 1994. An economic recovery and a continued decline in domestic interest rates has been encouraging. Within this framework the fund has increased the economic sensitivity of issues in its portfolio having benefited from a strategy that concentrated on earnings stability during 1993. The fund increased its weightings in the construction and engineering industries while reducing exposure to the defensive utility sector. The fund believes that the recent sell off in equities following the global decline in bond prices has given them an excellent opportunity to further pursue this strategy. The fund believes the outlook for equity values remains positive and is likely to be improved by European Union entry at the end of 1994.

Authors' Comments (OST): Austria's major trading partner is Germany, and so its monetary policy is closely tied to that of the Bundesbank. As it continues to ease interest rates to stimulate consumer demand and reduce the very high rate of unemployment, Austrian banks will be able to reduce their rates also. To take advantage of reduced interest rates OST's portfolio was heavily weighted with interest-rate sensitive issues (financials and utilities). However, Austrian stock capitalizations are usually small, and, thus tend to be relatively volatile, particularly medium cap. In 1994, the government raised the percentage of assets insurance companies can invest in equities and lowered individual tax rates on trading profits. OST is an attractive investment.

Chile Fund, Inc. (The)

153 E. 53rd Street, 58th Floor
New York, NY 10022
(212) 832-2626

NYSE: **CH**
Transfer Agent:
Provident Financial Processing Corp.
P.O. Box 8950
Wilmington, DE 19899
(800) 553-8080

Growth

Results

For 12-months Ending 4/29/94	Period End	Period Begin	Distributions	Yield Dist (%)	Total Return (%)
Share Price ($)	45.25	33.13	1.45	4.38	40.96
NAV per Share ($)	43.33	31.52		4.60	42.07

Background: Initial public offering October 3, 1989 of 5,300,000 shares at $15 per share. Initial NAV was $13.75 per share.

Objective: Seeks capital appreciation and dividend income through a portfolio of Chilean equities and bonds.

Portfolio: (12/31/93) Chilean Common Stock 92%, U.S. Government Securities 7%, Other 1%. Sector Weightings: Electrical Distribution 20%, Telecommunications 20%, Electrical Generators 13%, Beverages & Liquor & Tobacco 11%, Paper 4%.

Capitalization: (12/31/93) Common stock outstanding 6,979,533. No long-term debt.

Beta: 0.04
Fee: 1.20%
Income Distribution: Annually
Reinvestment Plan: Yes

Fund Manager: BEA Associates
Capital Gains Distribution: Annually
Shareholder Reports: Semi-Annually

5 Year Performance

Fiscal Year Ending 12/31	1993	1992	1991	1990	1989
Net Assets ($mil)	282.50	168.60	160.40	93.70	79.50
Net Income Distribution ($)	0.61	0.77	0.98	1.25	0.05
Capital Gains Distribution ($)	0.52	2.45	2.18	0.00	0.00
Total Distribution ($)	1.13	3.22	3.16	1.25	0.05
Yield from Distribution (%)	3.41	13.48	20.39	8.00	-
Expense Ratio (%)	1.72	1.71	1.75	2.04	1.98
Portfolio Turnover (%)	11.29	6.29	19.32	12.63	9.52
NAV per Share ($)	40.26	31.1	29.68	17.44	14.79
Market Price per Share ($) ($)	44.50	33.13	23.88	15.50	15.63
Premium (Discount) (%)	10.53	6.50	-19.58	-11.12	5.68
Total Return, Stock Price (%)	37.73	52.22	74.45	7.17	-

Chile Fund, Inc. (The)

Premium/Discount Spread

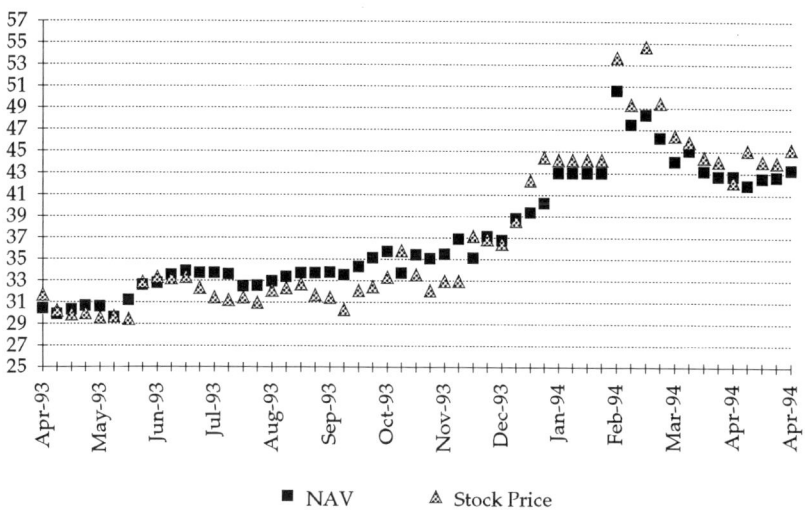

Fund Outlook (CH): The fund's long-term objective is to buy securities of well managed, profitable and cash-generating companies. The fund believes that they have made significant progress in meeting this objective while diversifying its holdings across sectors. In December 31, 1993, the Chilean market had an aggregate P/E ratio of 19.8 and a price-to-book of 1.95. The market as a whole had a weighted average yield of approximately 2.33%. The fund believes based on a number of relevant indicators, the Chilean market will continue to provide above-average returns for long-term investors.

Authors' Comments (CH): The stock market index is up 7.5% since December 31, 1993. GDP is expected to grow at a rate of 6%, unchanged from 1993, and down from 10.3% of 1992. The CPI is currently at the rate of 13.7%. The political climate has improved and the newly elected President, Eduardo Frei, is committed to pursuing policies emphasizing market economics. However, in March a Public Utility commission instituted new tariffs for Telefonos de Chile. It is expected that Chile will pursue entering into a NAFTA-type agreement. Should such a development take place, the equity market would take-off. Investors should be aware of the fact that there is a 10% repatriation tax upon any remittances. Because of a favorable long-term outlook for this economy, the shares of CH should be accumulated on any setback.

Emerging Germany Fund, Inc.

One Battery Park Plaza
New York, NY 10004
(800) 356-6122

NYSE: **FRG**
Transfer Agent:
State Street Bank & Trust Co.
P.O. Box 8200
Boston, MA 02266
(800) 426-5523

Growth

Results

For 12-months Ending 4/29/94	Period End	Period Begin	Distribution	Yield Dist (%)	Total Return (%)
Share Price ($)	8.63	7.38	0.00	0.00	16.94
NAV per Share	10.19	8.33		0.00	22.33

Background: Initial public offering April 5, 1990 of 14,000,000 shares at $12 per share. Initial NAV was $11.16 per share.

Objective: Seeks long-term capital appreciation. Invests in small- to medium-sized German companies. The fund may invest up to 20% of its assets in former East German companies and up to 10% in other Eastern European companies.

Portfolio: (3/31/94) Common Stocks 94%, Cash 6%. German Equity Securities 96%, Swiss Equity Securities 4%. Sector Weightings: Financial Services 36%, Industrial Cyclicals 26%, Consumer Durables 10%. Top Holdings: Deutsche Bank, Baterische Vereinsbank Commerzbank, Siemens, Berliner Hand und Frank.

Capitalization: (12/31/93) Common stock outstanding 14,008,334. No long-term debt.

Beta: 0.53
Fee: 0.70%
Income Distribution: Annually
Reinvestment Plan: Yes
Fund Manager: Dresdner Securities, Inc
Capital Gains Distribution: Annually
Shareholder Reports: Quarterly

5 Year Performance

Fiscal Year Ending 12/31	1993	1992	1991	1990	1989
Net Assets ($mil)	137.30	104.40	124.10	131.70	-
Net Income Distribution ($)	0.00	0.07	0.07	0.16	-
Capital Gains Distribution ($)	0.00	0.04	0.16	0.04	-
Total Distribution ($)	0.00	0.11	0.23	0.20	-
Yield from Distribution (%)	0.00	1.42	3.01	1.81	-
Expense Ratio (%)	1.46	1.49	1.70	1.51	-
Portfolio Turnover (%)	98.00	54.00	52.00	13.00	-
NAV per Share ($)	9.8	7.45	8.86	9.40	-
Market Price per Share ($)	9.38	6.38	7.75	7.63	-
Premium (Discount) (%)	-4.34	-14.36	-12.53	-18.94	-
Total Return, Stock Price (%)	47.02	-16.26	4.59	-29.20	-

Emerging Germany Fund, Inc.

Premium/Discount Spread

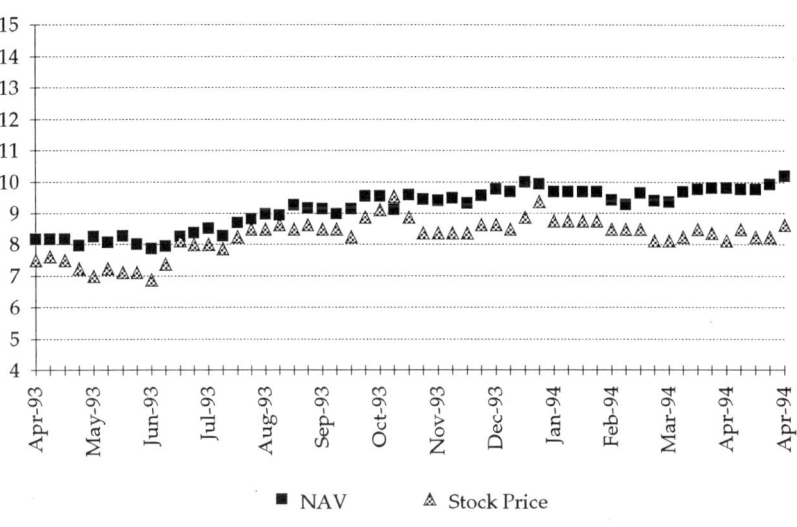

Fund Outlook (FRG): After 1993's outstanding performance, the German equity market consolidated early in 1994. FRG's general outlook remains positive as strong financial liquidity and expectation of cuts in short-term interest rates should support the market. FRG believes the currently inverted interest rate structure will return to normal. Driven by a rising dollar and a worldwide economic recovery, the German economy should show signs of slight upturn. With the effect of interest rate cuts waning, improvement in corporate earnings will gain in importance and the stock market will probably turn from sectors benefiting from lower interest rates and high liquidity towards those offering above-average earnings growth. The fund does expect this market transition to be accompanied by increasing volatility. FRG believes that after three years of declining corporate profits, 1994 will be a turnaround year and eventually produce strong double-digit earnings growth. FRG intends to further increase the cyclical and export-oriented sectors in the portfolio.

Authors' Comments (FRG): The German economy appears to be slowly picking up steam. The Bundesbank should continue to lower rates. CPI is projected to increase at the rate of 3.2% down the from 5.6% in 1993. The German stock exchange is up since December 31, 1993 to the interest rate declines. The portfolio is heavily weighted in banking and insurance which will benefit from further reductions in interest rates. There is a large representation of cyclicals which should benefit from the improved economic outlook and improved earnings. At a discount, FRG is very attractive.

Emerging Mexico Fund

1285 Avenue of the Americas
New York, NY 10019
(800) 852-4750

NYSE: **MEF**
Transfer Agent:
Provident Financial Processing Corp.
P.O. Box 8950
Wilmington, DE 19899
(800) 553-8080

Growth

Results

For 12-months Ending 4/29/94	Period End	Period Begin	Distributions	Yield Dist (%)	Total Return (%)
Share Price ($)	18.00	15.38	2.39	15.54	32.57
NAV per Share ($)	18.84	16.20		14.75	31.05

Background: Initial public offering October 2, 1990 of 5,000,000 shares at $12 per share. Initial NAV was $11.16 per share.

Objective: Seeks long-term capital appreciation through investing at least 65% in Mexican equities. Up to 25% of assets may be invested in unlisted securities, private placements, joint ventures, and partnerships.

Portfolio: (12/31/93) Common Stocks. 99.6%, Cash 0.4%. Sector Weightings: Industrial Cyclicals 30%, Utilities 18%, Retail 18%, Consumer Staples 15%. Top Holdings: Telefonos de Mexico, Cifra, Grupo Carso, Kimberly Clark de Mexico, Cemex.

Capitalization: (12/31/93) Common stock outstanding 6,678,666. No long-term debt.

Beta: 0.51
Fee: 0.90%   *Fund Manager:* Santander Management, Inc.
Income Distribution: Annually   *Capital Gains Distribution:* Annually
Reinvestment Plan: Yes   *Shareholder Reports:* Semi-Annually

5 Year Performance

Fiscal Year Ending 6/30	1993	1992	1991	1990	1989
Net Assets ($mil)	150.40	99.90	86.30	-	-
Net Income Distribution ($)	0.22	0.32	0.30	-	-
Capital Gains Distribution ($)	4.68	2.40	0.01	-	-
Total Distribution ($)	4.90	2.72	0.31	-	-
Yield from Distribution (%)	27.79	18.59	1.80	-	-
Expense Ratio (%)	1.82	1.72	2.22	-	-
Portfolio Turnover (%)	53.00	65.00	87.00	-	-
NAV per Share ($)	15.79	19.94	17.23	-	-
Market Price per Share ($)	14.13	17.63	14.63	-	-
Premium (Discount) (%)	-10.51	-11.58	-15.15	-	-
Total Return, Stock Price (%)	7.94	30.10	39.10	-	-

Emerging Mexico Fund

Premium/Discount Spread

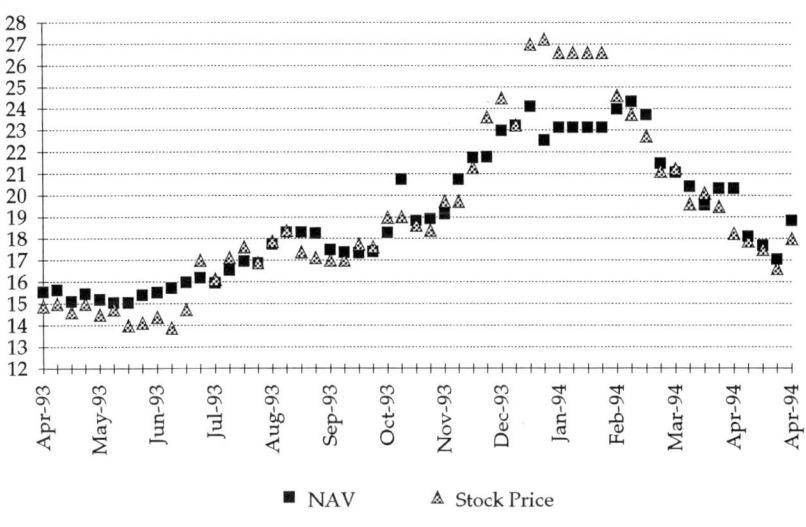

■ NAV △ Stock Price

Fund Outlook (MEF): In 1994, the Mexican Government intends to use its budget surplus to increase spending and stimulate the economy without pressuring the public sector's finances. Moreover, the ratification of NAFTA, coupled with the new foreign-investment law, will establish the conditions for a more stable economic environment. As a result, the fund anticipates a recovery in the second half of 1994 and expects the economy to grow approximately 3% by the end of the year.

Authors' Comments (MEF): NAFTA's adoption created the largest commercial bloc in the world with 371 million consumers. The fund has invested the portfolio to take advantage of the restructuring programs underway, as well as the need to modernize. In the fourth quarter of 1993 the fund issued rights to shareholders to raise additional funds to be available following the publishing of income reports after the first of the year. Because of some delays due to SEC requirements, funds did not become available until March of this year, at which time they were very favorably invested. The fund utilizes market timing, thus this fund may tend to be more volatile. MEF is a worthwhile investment and should be accumulated.

First Australia Fund

AMEX: **IAF**

One Seaport Plaza
New York, NY 10292
(212) 214-3334
(800) 451-6788

Transfer Agent:
State Street Bank & Trust Co.
One Heritage Drive
North Quincy, MA 02171
(800) 451-6788

Growth

Results

For 12-months Ending 4/29/94	Period End	Period Begin	Distributions	Yield Dist (%)	Total Return (%)
Share Price ($)	10.56	9.75	0.66	6.77	15.08
NAV per Share	12.29	10.21		6.46	26.84

Background: Initial public offering December 15, 1985 of 5,800,000 shares at $10 per share. Initial NAV was $9.25 per share.

Objective: Seeks long-term capital appreciation through equity investments in Australian securities and bonds. Current income is secondary. May engage in options strategies.

Portfolio: (3/31/94) Common Stocks 97%, Cash 3%. Sector Weightings: Industrial Cyclicals 53%, Services 20%, Financial Services 13%, Utility Companies 3%. Top Holdings: News Class A, Broken Hill Proprietary, National Australia Bank, Advance Bank of Australia, Nine Network Australia, St. George Bank.

Capitalization: (1/31/94) Common stock outstanding 9,781,200. No long-term debt.

Beta: 0.16

Fee: 1.10%   *Fund Manager:* EquitiLink Australia Ltd.
Income Distribution: Semi-Annually   *Capital Gains Distribution:* Annually
Reinvestment Plan: Yes   *Shareholder Reports:* Quarterly

5 Year Performance

Fiscal Year Ending 10/31	1993	1992	1991	1990	1989
Net Assets ($mil)	119.50	50.90	66.40	55.00	63.40
Net Income Distribution ($)	0.16	0.26	0.42	0.59	0.26
Capital Gains Distribution ($)	0.00	0.00	0.01	0.03	0.05
Total Distribution ($)	0.16	0.26	0.43	0.62	0.31
Yield from Distribution (%)	2.06	2.67	5.83	7.18	3.59
Expense Ratio (%)	1.87	1.90	2.25	2.14	2.18
Portfolio Turnover (%)	108.00	39.00	82.00	68.00	56.00
NAV per Share ($)	11.37	8.46	11.03	9.14	10.56
Market Price per Share ($)	10.38	7.75	9.75	7.38	8.63
Premium (Discount) (%)	-8.71	-8.39	-11.60	-19.37	-18.37
Total Return, Stock Price (%)	36.00	-17.85	37.94	-7.30	-0.67

First Australia Fund

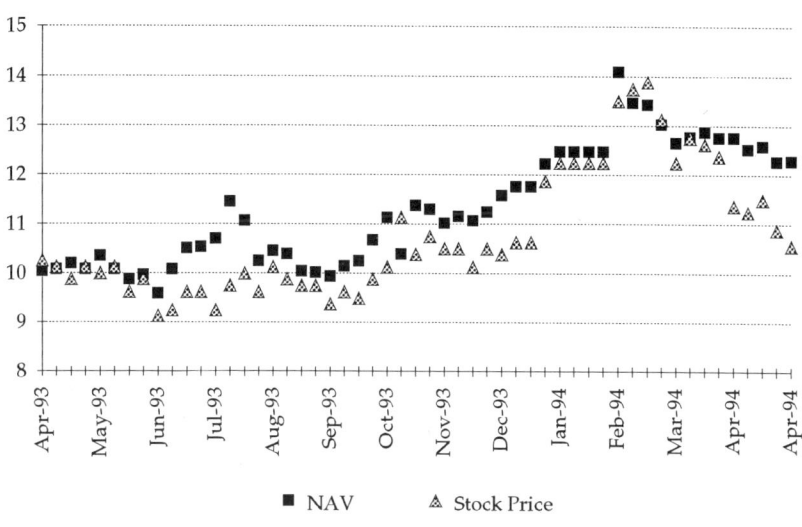

Premium/Discount Spread

■ NAV   △ Stock Price

Fund Outlook (IAF): Australia's economic growth and low inflation continue to provide a positive investment environment: the marked upturn in corporate earnings cycle, low inflation, low nominal interest rates, reduced corporate tax rate, improvements in corporate balance sheets, growing support from international investors. Foreign investors responded well to signs that base metal prices may have bottomed, taking positions in Australian resource stocks to gain exposure to anticipated recovery in metal prices. Corporate earnings cycle should strengthen further in 1994, pointing to considerable scope for the market to make further gains over the rest of 1994 into 1995. The Australian dollar strengthened against the U.S. dollar over three months to January 31, 1994 due to investment funds from Asia and the U.S. into the bond/equity markets. Better-than-expected current account figures released in January showed an improving balance of payments situation as did the successful completion of the GATT negotiations. After the end of January, the weakness of the U.S. bond market caused Australian bond yields to rise.

Authors' Comments (IAF): The Australian equity market has been strong reflecting positive domestic economic developments. Global economic recovery, as well as inflationary fears, should bolster demand for Australian commodities such as wool, coal, iron ore, and generate further economic gains. A recent rights offering valued at $33 million was placed in small cap stocks. Heretofore, IAF had confined all of their investments to larger cap stocks. The near- and long-term prospects for the Australian economy are positive.

First Iberian Fund, Inc.
345 Park Avenue
New York, NY 10154
(617) 330-5602

AMEX: IBF
Transfer Agent:
State Street Bank & Trust Co.
P.O. Box 8200
Boston, MA 02266-8200
(617) 328-5000

Growth

Results

For 12-months Ending 4/29/94	Period End	Period Begin	Distributions	Yield Dist (%)	Total Return (%)
Share Price ($)	8.13	6.88	0.06	0.87	19.04
NAV per Share ($)	9.01	7.91		0.76	14.66

Background: Initial public offering April 13, 1988 of 6,500,000 shares at $10 per share. Initial NAV was $9.16 per share.

Objective: Seeks capital appreciation through investments primarily in equity securities of Spanish and Portuguese companies.

Portfolio: (3/31/94) Common Stocks 100%. Country Exposure: Spain 79%, Portugal 21%. Sector Weightings: Financial Services 37%, Industrial Cyclicals 19%, Consumer Staples 8%. Top Holdings: Banco Popular Espanol, Zardoya Otis, Repsol, Empresa Nacional Electricid, Telefonica de Espana.

Capitalization: (12/31/93) Common stock outstanding 6,511,154. No long-term debt.

Beta: 0.89

Fee: 1.00% *Fund Manager:* Scudder, Stevens & Clark, Inc.
Income Distribution: Semi-Annually *Capital Gains Distribution:* Annually
Reinvestment Plan: Yes *Shareholder Reports:* Semi-Annually

5 Year Performance

Fiscal Year Ending 9/30	1993	1992	1991	1990	1989
Net Assets ($mil)	53.60	47.30	60.60	57.30	70.20
Net Income Distribution ($)	0.18	0.15	0.20	0.12	0.25
Capital Gains Distribution ($)	0.22	0.00	0.82	0.13	0.00
Total Distribution ($)	0.40	0.15	1.02	0.25	0.25
Yield from Distribution (%)	6.40	1.90	13.82	1.67	1.67
Expense Ratio (%)	2.31	2.45	2.30	2.18	2.08
Portfolio Turnover (%)	29.00	32.00	23.00	22.00	26.00
NAV per Share ($)	8.24	7.27	9.31	8.80	10.78
Market Price per Share ($)	7.75	6.25	7.88	7.38	15.00
Premium (Discount) (%)	-5.95	-14.03	-15.36	-16.25	39.15
Total Return, Stock Price (%)	30.40	-18.78	20.60	-49.13	81.98

First Iberian Fund, Inc.

Premium/Discount Spread

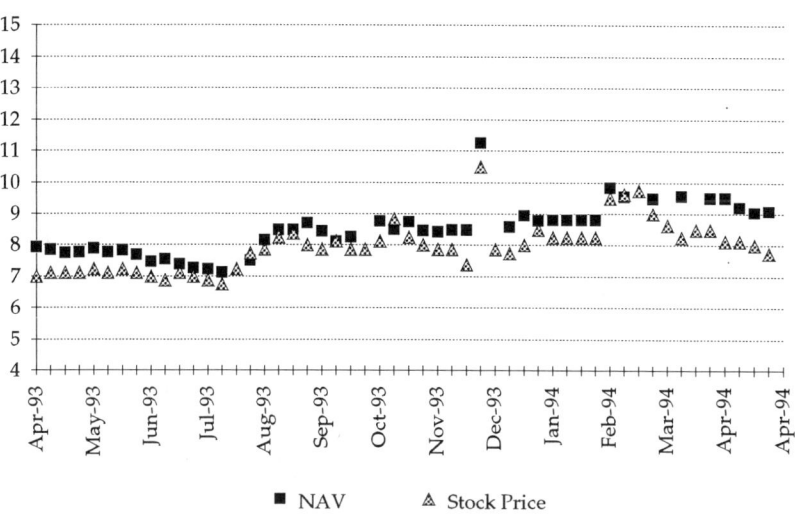

Fund Outlook (IBF): The fund has a positive outlook on the Spanish and Portuguese markets for 1994. Interest rates should fall further from their current levels, inflation will remain subdued and better earnings should start coming through as the year progresses. Domestic liquidity will also remain a key factor as local investors look for better returns in equity markets that do not look overly expensive relative to their European counterparts. In Portugal, since Europe absorbs 80% of its imports/exports, the government is projecting recovery in the 1994 economy based on economic recovery in Europe, increased EC funding for infrastructure and lower interest rates.

Authors' Comments (IBF): The fund invests in securities incorporated under the laws of Spain and Portugal. Prior to October 1, 1993 the fund was restricted to owning no more than 20% in Portuguese companies. With the exception of short-term interest rates and market performance, economic statistics for both are very similar. Both domestic economies still have negative growth and their CPI is increasing at a moderate rate. However, short-term interest rates in Portugal average 11.53%, contrasted to Spain's 7.68% down 6.95%. The Spanish stock market is up 3.9% since the first of the year, as contrasted with an increase of 21.1% for Portugal. To date the percentage of Portuguese equities that have been added to the account remains at 21%. In order to take advantage of the forthcoming economic recovery the fund has reduced the proportion of interest-related issues and switched into cyclicals. IBF is hedged into the U.S. dollar which explains, in part, recent poor performance.

First Philippine Fund, Inc.

152 W. 57th Street
New York, NY 10019
(800) 524-4458
(212) 765-0700

NYSE: **FPF**
Transfer Agent:
The Bank of New York
101 Barclay St.
New York, NY 10286
(800) 524-4458

Growth

Results

For 12-months Ending 4/29/94	Period End	Period Begin	Distributions	Yield Dist (%)	Total Return (%)
Share Price ($)	17.88	12.00	0.76	6.33	55.33
NAV per Share ($)	23.59	15.04		5.05	61.90

Background: Initial public offering November 15, 1989 of 7,800,000 shares at $12 per share. Initial NAV was $11.16 per share.

Objective: Seeks long-term capital appreciation. Invests at least 80% of assets in equity securities of Philippine companies.

Portfolio: (12/31/93) Common Stocks 88.9%, Philippine Treasury Bills 7.7%, U.S. securities 4.3%. Sector Weightings: Telecommunications 19.7%, Food & Beverage 13.7%, Conglomerates 7.7%, Electric Utilities 10.5%, Banking 7.3%. Top Holdings: Philippine Long Distance, San Miguel, Manila Electric, Ayala Land, Ayala Class A.

Capitalization: (12/31/93) Common stock outstanding 8,980,000. No long-term debt.

Beta: 0.22
Fee: 1.00% *Fund Manager:* Clemente Capital, Inc.
Income Distribution: Annually *Capital Gains Distribution:* Annually
Reinvestment Plan: Yes *Shareholder Reports:* Quarterly

5 Year Performance

Fiscal Year Ending 6/30	1993	1992	1991	1990	1989
Net Assets ($mil)	231.20	130.90	92.90	98.50	-
Net Income Distribution ($)	0.57	0.19	0.59	0.08	-
Capital Gains Distribution ($)	0.00	0.00	0.00	0.00	-
Total Distribution ($)	0.57	0.19	0.59	0.08	-
Yield from Distribution (%)	4.96	2.53	6.29	-	-
Expense Ratio (%)	1.72	1.79	1.90	2.00	-
Portfolio Turnover (%)	37.30	21.61	1.03	0.00	-
NAV per Share ($)	14.84	14.58	10.35	10.97	-
Market Price per Share ($)	13.00	11.50	7.50	9.38	-
Premium (Discount) (%)	-12.40	-21.12	-27.54	-14.59	-
Total Return, Stock Price (%)	18.00	55.87	-13.75	-	-

First Philippine Fund, Inc.

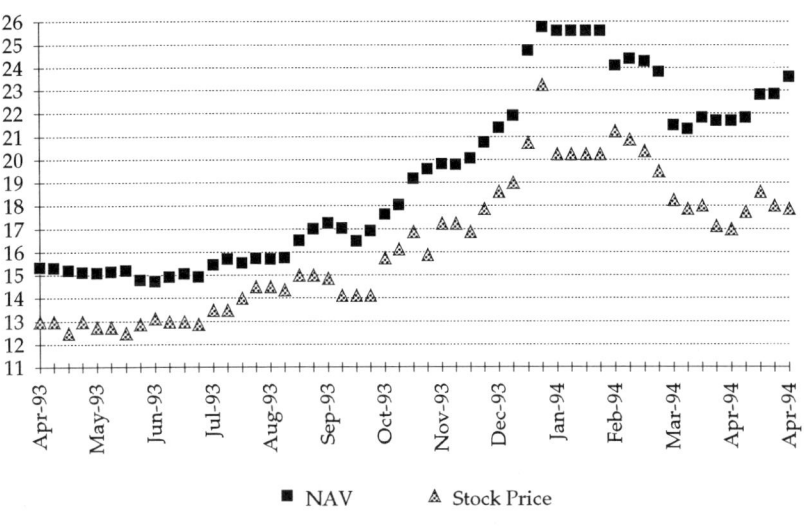

Fund Outlook (FPF): The fund believes that an economic recovery has evolved from being a mere vision into a very real possibility. Such belief is founded on a host of changes: The power shortage which befuddled the economy in 1993 has been resolved for the most part; deregulation of key industries is taking place; banking, telecommunications and power generation are among those being opened up to competition; real GDP and real GNP posted growth rates in the third quarter; domestic inflation remained stable; interest rates were about 400 basis points lower than the 1992 average. The fund believes these developments clearly set the stage for a take-off to faster and continued economic growth.

Authors' Comments (FPF): The Philippine economy could be another Tiger in fives years. In the past, power shortages were at times a hindrance to growth lasting up to 11 hours a day. Shares of the sell at a discount to B shares which are those held by foreigners. If FPF held the B shares of the same companies, the NAV would be greater and, consequently, the discount would be greater. Both the utilities and financial sectors of the portfolio will benefit as short-term interest rates are reduced. Francisco Rodrigo, portfolio manager since 1989, resigned, and interim manager, Leopoldo Clemente, has reduced the fund's positions in small cap stocks in favor of large cap blue chips.

France Growth Fund, Inc. (The)
1285 Avenue of the Americas
New York, NY 10019
(212) 713-2000

NYSE: **FRF**
Transfer Agent:
Provident National Bank
103 Bellevue Parkway
Wilmington, DE 19809
(800) 852-4750

Growth

Results

For 12-months Ending 4/29/94	Period End	Period Begin	Distributions	Yield Dist (%)	Total Return (%)
Share Price ($)	11.00	11.50	1.00	8.70	4.35
NAV per Share ($)	12.28	11.83		8.45	12.26

Background: Initial public offering May, 1990 of 10,000,000 shares at $12 per share. Initial NAV was $11.16 per share.

Objective: Seeks long-term capital appreciation through equity investments primarily in French companies. The fund may engage in hedging activities using futures and options.

Portfolio: (12/31/93) Common Stocks 95%, Short-Term & Other 5%. Sector Weightings: Capital Goods 10%, Distribution 8%, Energy 7%, Financial Services 18%, House Buildings 6%, Food & Beverages 8%, Other Services 13%. Top Holdings: Alcatel Alsthom General D'Electrique, TOTAL, Group BSN, Generale De Eaux, Carrefour.

Capitalization: (12/31/93) Common stock outstanding 11,509,000. No long-term debt.

Beta: 0.53
Fee: 0.90%   *Fund Manager:* Indosuez Intl. Invest. Ser.
Income Distribution: Annually   *Capital Gains Distribution:* Annually
Reinvestment Plan: Yes   *Shareholder Reports:* Semi-Annually

5 Year Performance

Fiscal Year Ending 12/31	1993	1992	1991	1990	1989
Net Assets ($mil)	148.90	121.20	123.80	118.80	-
Net Income Distribution ($)	0.00	0.02	0.14	0.35	-
Capital Gains Distribution ($)	0.00	0.02	0.10	0.17	-
Total Distribution ($)	0.00	0.04	0.24	0.52	-
Yield from Distribution (%)	0.00	0.45	2.78	-	-
Expense Ratio (%)	1.71	1.76	2.14	2.18	-
Portfolio Turnover (%)	57.00	40.00	75.00	16.00	-
NAV per Share ($)	12.94	10.53	10.75	10.33	-
Market Price per Share ($)	13.63	9.25	8.88	8.63	-
Premium (Discount) (%)	5.29	-12.16	-17.49	-16.46	-
Total Return, Stock Price (%)	47.35	4.62	5.68	-	-

France Growth Fund, Inc. (The)

Premium/Discount Spread

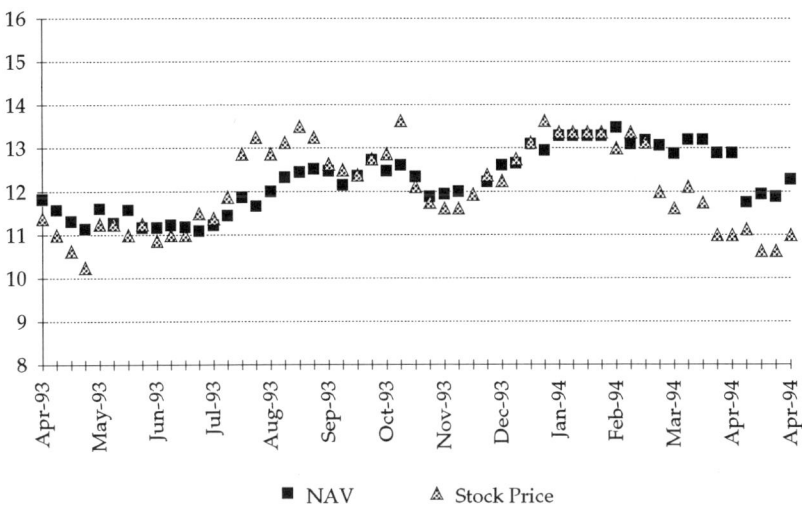

Fund Outlook (FRF): FRF believes in a moderate pick-up in growth led by exports and by a slight rebound in renewal and maintenance investments. Inventories were pared last year and will not be a drag on economic activity. Household saving will be less and, thus activity levels will remain flat. Corporate downsizing will further swell unemployment until around the turn of the year. A less restrictive budget policy and lower interest rates should stimulate the recovery. The structural throes in Germany and the lesser competitiveness of its manufacturing sector should further weaken the Deutsche mark against European currencies. This will ease convergence of European rates. The French franc stands to benefit from the trend as the interest-rate differential narrows and disappears. For the first time since 1989, equities have seemingly become credible alternatives to money market, bond and real estate investments. The switching from money market funds to equities will continue to bolster the French stock market.

Authors' Comments (FRF): GDP growth has been projected to grow at the rate of 1.2%. The CPI is projected to increase 2.2% in 1994. Unemployment is a record 12.2%. The French stock exchange index is down 3.8% since December 31, 1993. The portfolio's concentration in financial services will be well positioned to take advantage of the continued decline in interest rates. The concentration in the services sector, which was adversely affected by the recession, will be a prime beneficiary during the recovery. In March, the stock market experienced a step back due to student strikes which caused the government to back away from economic reforms. The government's plan for privatization is on schedule.

Growth Fund of Spain

120 S. LaSalle Street
Chicago, IL 60603
(800) 422-2848

Growth

NYSE: GSP
Transfer Agent:
Investors Fiduciary Trust Co.
127 W. 10th St.
Kansas City, MO 64105
(816) 474-8786

Results

For 12-months Ending 4/29/94	Period End	Period Begin	Distributions	Yield Dist (%)	Total Return (%)
Share Price ($)	10.13	8.38	0.00	0.00	20.88
NAV per Share ($)	12.57	9.94		0.00	26.46

Background: Initial public offering February 14, 1990 of 17,431,000 shares at $12 per share. Initial NAV was $11.16 per share.

Objective: Seeks long-term capital appreciation by investing primarily in Spanish equities.

Portfolio: (11/30/93) Common Stocks 83.4%, Government Bonds 2.1%, Cash Equivalent 9.5%. Sector Weightings: Electrical & Utilities 24.0%, Telecom & Motorways 15.1%, Banking 15.6%, Food & Tobacco 8.0%, Construction & Property Development 5.8%, Chemicals 5.9%, Metals & Engineering 8.3%, Investment & Diversification Companies 0.7%.

Capitalization: (11/30/93) Common stock outstanding 17,330,000. No long-term debt.

Beta: 0.80
Fee: 0.35%   *Fund Manager:* Kemper Financial Services, Inc.
Income Distribution: Annually   *Capital Gains Distribution:* Annually
Reinvestment Plan: Yes   *Shareholder Reports:* Semi-Annually

5 Year Performance

Fiscal Year Ending 11/30	1993	1992	1991	1990	1989
Net Assets ($mil)	184.90	156.20	192.90	186.60	-
Net Income Distribution ($)	0.00	0.15	0.36	0.00	-
Capital Gains Distribution ($)	0.00	0.00	0.00	0.00	-
Total Distribution ($)	0.00	0.15	0.36	0.00	-
Yield from Distribution (%)	0.00	1.52	4.30	0.00	-
Expense Ratio (%)	1.22	1.22	1.23	1.26	-
Portfolio Turnover (%)	50.00	72.00	104.00	19.00	-
NAV per Share ($)	10.67	8.99	11.08	10.71	-
Market Price per Share ($)	9.63	7.50	9.88	8.38	-
Premium (Discount) (%)	-9.79	-15.13	-10.92	-20.63	-
Total Return, Stock Price (%)	28.40	-22.57	22.20	-	-

Growth Fund of Spain

Premium/Discount Spread

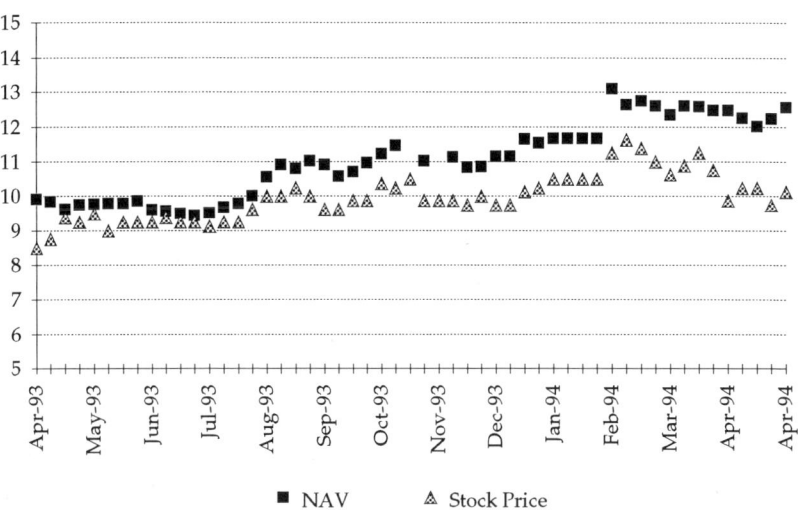

■ NAV △ Stock Price

Fund Outlook (GSP): The fund believes the positive case for Spanish equities continues to be based on lower interest rates. The depth of the current recession should put pressure on the Government to adopt a more growth oriented policy. This is likely to mean sharply lower interest rates in the coming year. Trading conditions for many companies have improved as the devaluation of the peseta greatly reduced competition from imports. The Bank of Spain lowered its benchmark rate from 13.75% to 9% over 1993. In 1994, companies should begin to benefit from lower financing expenses resulting from this significant decline in interest rates. Finally, the Spanish market, currently selling at approximately 12 times its estimated 1994 net earnings, is still reasonably priced compared to other European markets. The fund is invested in cyclicals, and according to the portfolio manager, more emphasis will be on cyclicals in the coming months, in anticipation of improving corporate earnings.

Authors' Comments (GSP): Current economic growth can be attributed to steps taken by the socialist government elected in June 1993. Labor reforms and pursued policies of deregulation have been instituted. Interest rates have declined steadily and, with the current CPI at 6.2% and the prime rate at 8.25%, there is ample room for further reductions. The portfolio is heavily weighted in interest-rate-sensitive companies that are expected to benefit as interest rates decline. GSP, currently at a discount, is extremely attractive.

India Growth Fund, Inc.
1285 Avenue of the Americas
New York, NY 10019
(212) 713-2000

NYSE: **IGF**
Transfer Agent:
Provident Financial Processing Corp.
P.O. Box 8950
Wilmington, DE 19899
(800) 852-4750

Growth

Results

For 12-months Ending 4/29/94	Period End	Period Begin	Distributions	Yield Dist (%)	Total Return (%)
Share Price ($)	20.00	13.75	0.25	1.82	47.27
NAV per Share ($)	20.48	11.67		2.14	77.63

Background: Initial public offering August 12, 1988 of 5,000,000 shares at $12 per share. Initial NAV was $11.16 per share.

Objective: Seeks long-term capital appreciation through investment in the Indian equity market.

Portfolio: (12/31/93): Common Stocks 106%, Other 4%, Liabilities 10%. Consumer Products 22%, Textiles 11%, Automobiles 8%, Tea & Plantation 6%, Chemicals & Dyes 6%. Top Holdings: ITC, Colgate Palmolive of India, Century Textiles, ITC Bhadrachalam Paper, Great Eastern Shipping, Tata Tea.

Capitalization: (12/31/93) Common stock outstanding 5,037,897. No long-term debt.

Beta: 0.18

Fee: 0.75%   **Fund Manager:** Unit Trust of India Advisory

Income Distribution: Annually   **Capital Gains Distribution:** Annually

Reinvestment Plan: Yes   **Shareholder Reports:** Quarterly

5 Year Performance

Fiscal Year Ending 6/30	1993	1992	1991	1990	1989
Net Assets ($mil)	94.90	80.20	83.30	69.70	74.10
Net Income Distribution ($)	0.00	0.00	0.00	0.37	0.15
Capital Gains Distribution ($)	1.56	0.93	0.16	0.73	0.15
Total Distribution ($)	1.56	0.93	0.16	1.10	0.30
Yield from Distribution (%)	9.75	7.91	1.00	9.36	2.55
Expense Ratio (%)	2.79	2.00	3.00	3.27	2.32
Portfolio Turnover (%)	19.00	27.00	14.00	19.00	39.00
NAV per Share ($)	12.49	18.57	14.12	12.86	14.23
Market Price per Share ($)	15.00	16.00	11.75	16.00	11.75
Premium (Discount) (%)	20.10	-13.84	-16.78	24.42	-17.43
Total Return, Stock Price (%)	3.50	44.09	-25.56	45.53	-

India Growth Fund, Inc.

Premium/Discount Spread

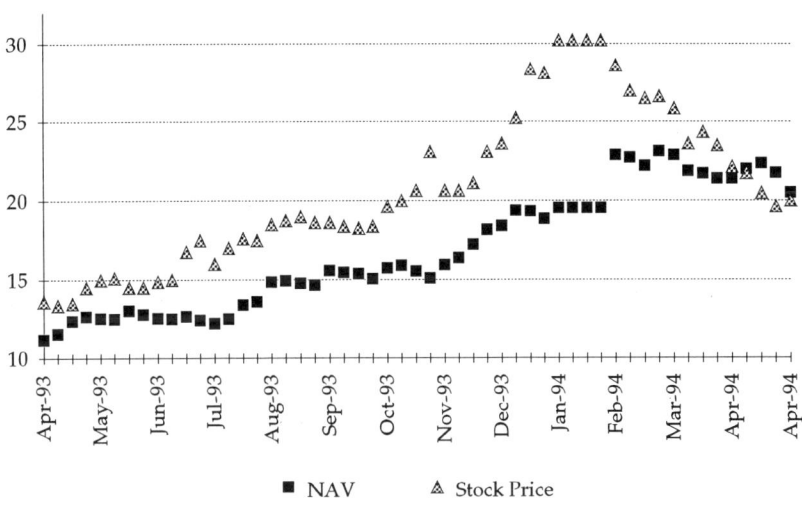

■ NAV △ Stock Price

Fund Outlook (IGF): The fund increasingly used its fundamental stock picking strategy to invest in new long-term growth stocks or to increase its investment in existing stocks through slow judicious stock selection. The strategy was more bottom up and focused on specific stock rather than sectors. The inability to increase stock concentrations was due to the low liquidity of the fund. The fund's strategy to move money into small- and medium-stocks began to translate into returns. For most of 1993, the fund's rupee portfolio performed on par with the BSE National Index and ahead of the BSESI.

Authors' Comments (IGF): India, the world's fifth largest economy, has abundant natural resources, low wages and a highly skilled labor force. Its population of 900 million is the second largest in the world. Inflation is at 9%. GDP is projected to grow. Exports are rising at an annual rate of 20%. IGF is overweighted in auto-related and textile manufacturing, two beneficiaries of increased exports. The portfolio also has a large position in the telecommunications industry which the government intends to deregulate. Foreign investors were not allowed into India's protected stock markets until September 1992. India has over 7,000 listed companies and a market capitalization of $110 billion on 22 exchanges. Net foreign investment was $1 billion in 1993, with most of that coming in November and December. Since December 31, 1993 the exchange has risen 11.5%. Investors excited about the potentials of China as an emerging market should be ecstatic about India's potential. IGF is one of the best ways to participate in the future development of India.

Irish Investment Fund

NYSE: IRL

Exchange Place—025-004B
Boston, MA 02109
(800) 468-6475

Transfer Agent:
American Stock Transfer & Trust Co.
40 Wall Street
New York, NY 10005
(212) 936-5100

Growth

Results

For 12 Months Ending 4/29/94	Period End	Period Begin	Distributions	Yield Dist (%)	Total Return (%)
Share Price ($)	9.13	8.13	0.07	0.86	13.17
NAV per Share ($)	10.52	9.06		0.77	16.89

Background: Initial public offering March 30, 1990 of 5,000,000 shares at $12 per share. Initial NAV was $11.16 per share.

Objective: Seeks long-term capital appreciation. At least 65% of assets will be invested in Irish equity securities. Up to 35% may be invested in fixed-income securities or equity securities outside of Ireland related to the Irish economy.

Portfolio: (4/30/94) Irish Common Stocks 95%, Irish Convertible Preferred Securities 3%, Irish Bonds 1%, Cash 1%. Top Holdings: Allied Irish Banks, Jefferson Smurfit Group, CRH of Ireland, Independent Newspapers, Kerry Group.

Capitalization: (6/30/94) Common stock outstanding 5,097,000. No long-term debt.

Beta: 0.73

Fee: 1.00% *Fund Manager:* Bank of Ireland Asset Mgt., Ltd.
Income Distribution: Annually *Capital Gains Distribution:* Annually
Reinvestment Plan: Yes *Shareholder Reports:* Quarterly

5 Year Performance

Fiscal Year Ending: 10/31	1993	1992	1991	1990 (9 mos.)	1989
Net Assets ($mil)	49.40	40.00	48.80	50.30	-
Net Income Distribution ($)	0.07	0.23	0.33	0.00	-
Capital Gains Distribution ($)	0.00	0.00	0.00	0.00	-
Total Distribution ($)	0.07	0.23	0.33	0.00	-
Yield from Distribution (%)	0.89	3.29	4.55	-	-
Expense Ratio	1.88	1.80	2.03	1.70	-
Portfolio Turnover (%)	15.00	7.00	28.00	6.00	-
NAV per Share ($)	9.59	7.99	9.75	10.04	-
Market Price per Share ($)	8.50	7.88	7.25	-	-
Premium (Discount) (%)	-11.37	-1.38	-28.21	-27.79	-
Total Return, Stock Price (%)	8.83	15.86	1.10	-	-

Irish Investment Fund

Premium/Discount Spread

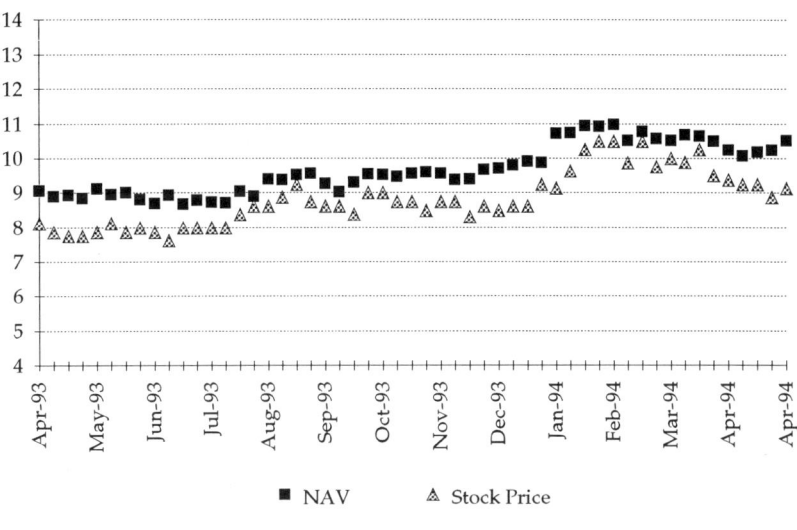

Fund Outlook (IRL): Economic releases in the second quarter confirmed that the Irish economy is in a very healthy position. Real GDP is currently growing at a 2.5% rate and is forecasted to increase to 4.5% in 1995, a remarkable performance given the recession seen in the U.K. and continental Europe. This growth has not been accompanied by inflationary pressures. The fundamental outlook for both the Irish economy and equity market is sound, and following its recent falls, the current valuation of the market is relatively attractive.

Authors' Comments (IRL): While a tight money stance at the Bundesbank is acting to prop up European rates, Ireland has been able to lower short-term rates twice this year. Their economy is expected to grow at a nearly 5% clip in 1995, without accompanying inflationary pressures. Due to the general reluctance of investors to enter the smaller markets at present, this fund offers a quiet, tidy way to invest in a growing European economy, at a double digit discount. IRL is a solid choice for the global investor.

Italy Fund, Inc. (The)

2 World Trade Center
New York, NY 10048
(212) 298-6263

NYSE: **ITA**
Transfer Agent:
Shareholders Services Group, Inc.
P.O. Box 1376
Boston, MA 02104
(800) 331-1710

Growth

Results

For 12-months Ending 4/29/94	Period End	Period Begin	Distributions	Yield Dist (%)	Total Return (%)
Share Price ($)	11.25	9.88	0.00	0.00	13.87
NAV per Share ($)	12.04	9.18		0.00	31.15

Background: Initial public offering February 28, 1986 of 6,333,961 shares at $12 per share. Initial NAV was $11.16 per share.

Objective: Seeks total return with at least 65% of assets invested in Italian equity and debt securities. May invest in non-Italian companies that have operations or sales in Italy. May invest up to 25% in unlisted securities.

Portfolio: (1/31/94) Stocks 66%, Fixed Income 3%, Convertible Bonds 1%, Commercial Paper 4%. Fixed-Income Investments 11.3%, Time Deposits 1.4%. Sector Weightings: Communications 23%, Insurance 22%, Banks 11%, Electromechanical Engineering & Autos 10%. Top Holdings: Government of Italy 12%, STRET, Eridania Beghin Say, Alleanza Assicurazioni, Parmalat Finanziaria.

Capitalization: (1/31/94) Common stock outstanding 6,334,901. No long-term debt.

Beta: 0.18
Fee: 0.75%   **Fund Manager:** Shearson Lehman Global Asset Mgt., Ltd.
Income Distribution: Annually   **Capital Gains Distribution:** Annually
Reinvestment Plan: Yes   **Shareholder Reports:** Quarterly

5 Year Performance

Fiscal Year Ending 1/31	1994	1993	1992	1991	1990
Net Assets ($mil)	60.90	49.50	69.60	72.80	81.30
Net Income Distribution ($)	0.07	0.00	0.25	0.34	0.15
Capital Gains Distribution ($)	0.00	0.00	0.24	0.58	0.00
Total Distribution ($)	0.07	0.00	0.49	0.92	0.15
Yield from Distribution (%)	0.79	0.00	4.90	5.26	0.86
Expense Ratio (%)	1.69	1.70	1.53	1.80	1.90
Portfolio Turnover (%)	46.00	33.00	24.00	15.00	15.00
NAV per Share ($)	9.84	8.43	11.08	11.37	13.24
Market Price per Share ($)	12.38	8.88	9.50	10.00	17.50
Premium (Discount) (%)	25.76	5.28	-14.26	-12.05	32.18
Total Return, Stock Price (%)	40.54	-6.58	1.00	-36.14	121.31

Italy Fund, Inc. (The)

Premium/Discount Spread

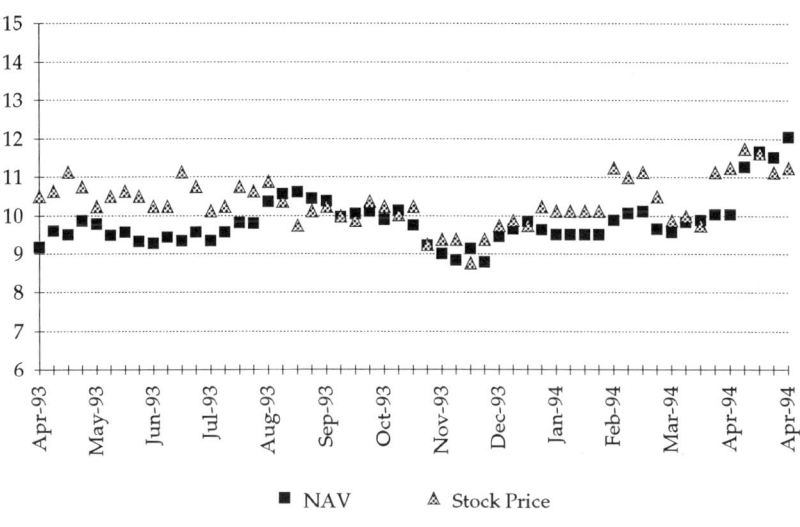

■ NAV   △ Stock Price

Fund Outlook (ITA): The fund's outlook for the Italian equity market depends on the continuation of the economic policies introduced by the Amato and Ciampi governments who are committed to policies of economic and financial stability. In the past it was less the endless rounds of elections and governments that undermined Italian assets than the failure of the old political establishment to control inflation and a budget deficit. Once the political uncertainty is removed, improved economic fundamentals will be there to focus on (primarily budget and trade surplus, low wages and inflation, lower interest rates). Indeed the Italian political and economic revolution has had greater positive impact on the economy of Italy than German unification has had on the economy of Germany.

Authors' Comments (ITA): The Italian economy is one of Europe's strongest due to a pick-up in exports as a result of currency devaluations. Political and economic reforms such as termination of indexing wages to the inflation rate and instead linking future wage increases to improvements in productivity have brought optimism to the equity markets. Several months of tight monetary policy has cut the rate of inflation. Italy is privatizing many large state-owned corporations. The CPI in 1993 was at the rate of a plus 4.2% down from a plus 5.3% in 1992 and is projected to approximate 3.8% in 1994, justifying further reduction in short-term rates. The equity market is expensive having risen 41% since the first of the year but at the current level of 817.2 (May 10) is well below its historic high of 906 reached in 1986. Despite the fact that the political turmoil does add some uncertainty, the fund represents sound value.

Malaysia Fund, Inc. (The)
126 High Street
Boston, MA 02110
(617) 557-8000

Growth

NYSE: MF
Transfer Agent:
The First National Bank of Boston
P.O. Box 644
Boston, MA 02102
(617) 575-2900

Results

For 12-months Ending 4/29/94	Period End	Period Begin	Distributions	Yield Dist (%)	Total Return (%)
Share Price ($)	23.38	16.75	0.00	0.00	39.58
NAV per Share ($)	21.52	17.45		0.00	23.32

Background: Initial public offering May 2, 1987 of 7,000,000 common shares at $12 per share. Initial NAV was $11.16 per share. This fund is the first vehicle available for investment primarily in the Malaysian economy.

Objective: Seeks long-term capital appreciation. Invests at least 80% in Malaysian equities with the balance in Malaysian debt securities. Distributions to foreign investors are exempt from Malaysian income tax.

Portfolio: (12/31/93) Malaysia Common Stocks 98%, Short-Term & Other Assets 4%, Liabilities (2%). Sector Weightings: Leisure & Tourism 19%, Building Materials & Components 25%, Construction & Housing 13%, Banking 10%, Telecommunications 10%. Top Holdings: Genting Bhd; Malayan Banking Bhd; Telekim Malaysia Bhd; United Engineers, Ltd.

Capitalization: (12/31/93) Common stock outstanding 9,712,922. No long-term debt.

Beta: 0.28
Fee: 0.90% *Fund Manager:* Morgan Stanley Asset Mgt. Inc.
Income Distribution: Annually *Capital Gains Distribution:* Annually
Reinvestment Plan: Yes *Shareholder Reports:* Quarterly

5 Year Performance

Fiscal Year Ending 12/31	1993	1992	1991	1990	1989
Net Assets ($mil)	265.40	118.20	98.30	90.10	99.90
Net Income Distribution ($)	0.13	0.00	0.07	0.21	0.11
Capital Gains Distribution ($)	0.96	0.00	0.00	0.00	0.00
Total Distribution ($)	1.09	0.00	0.07	0.21	0.11
Yield from Distribution (%)	6.71	0.00	0.62	1.12	1.47
Expense Ratio (%)	1.60	1.72	1.70	1.93	1.95
Portfolio Turnover (%)	43.00	37.90	14.90	17.80	30.20
NAV per Share ($)	27.32	16.28	13.55	12.41	13.77
Market Price per Share ($)	28.00	16.25	11.75	11.38	18.75
Premium (Discount) (%)	2.49	-0.18	-13.28	-8.30	36.17
Total Return, Stock Price (%)	79.02	38.30	3.87	-38.19	151.47

Malaysia Fund, Inc. (The)

Premium/Discount Spread

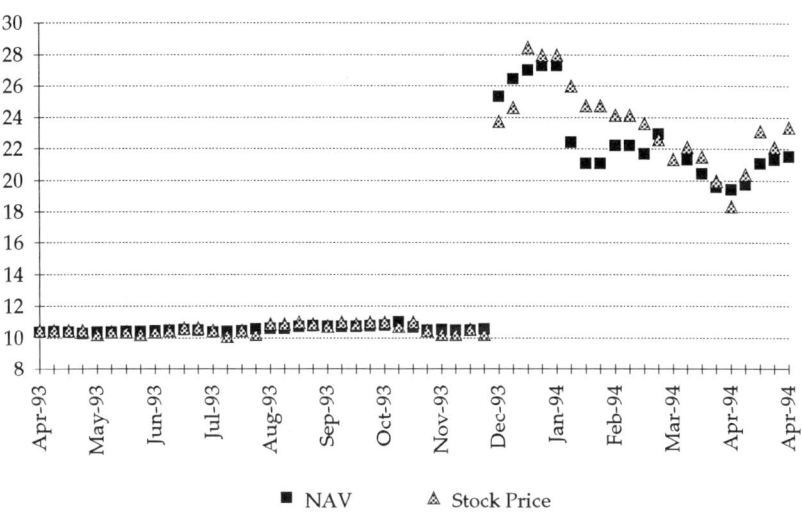

■ NAV   △ Stock Price

Fund Outlook (MF): The KLSE index experienced a sharp correction in January 1994 with the broad market off nearly 25% from its high. The fund's NAV also declined. The fund believes the decline was a result of some natural profit-taking and the government's concern that the market had gone too far, too fast. The central bank, Bank Negara, has tightened statutory reserve requirements to stem the tide of what they deem to be speculative flows. This has led to the Ringgit declining sharply against the world's major currencies. This volatility in the currency and fears of tighter liquidity touched off a wave of selling by retail investors and compounded by institutional investors selling as their shareholders redeemed. The fund believes the correction has brought prices to more reasonable levels. Although the Malaysia market is now trading at about 24 times prospective 1994 earnings, above the historic average, the market's valuation is underpinned by continued strong economic and corporate profits growth. Real GDP growth is estimated to be 8-8.5% in 1994; inflation 3.5%; and the CPI to 5%. The fund will constantly monitor its portfolio and reposition it in the best quality companies representing good value.

Authors' Comments (MF): The largest area of concentration is in consumer services; in companies that will benefit from higher disposable income. Other areas of concentration are in the construction and building-materials. There is ample liquidity in the financial markets, however the political situation could dampen the equity market. Long-term prospects for the Malaysian economy are excellent despite short-term risks.

Mexico Fund, Inc.
399 Park Avenue, 37th Floor
New York, NY 10022
(212) 750-4200

Growth

NYSE: MXF
Transfer Agent:
American Stock Transfer & Trust Co.
40 Wall St.
New York, NY 10004
(212) 936-5100

Results

For 12-months Ending 4/29/94	Period End	Period Begin	Distributions	Yield Dist (%)	Total Return (%)
Share Price ($)	29.38	23.63	0.70	2.96	27.30
NAV per Share ($)	31.30	25.82		2.71	23.93

Background: Initial public offering June 11, 1981. Beginning net assets equaled $104.7 million. Subsequent Rights Offerings in December 1983, March 1992, and September 1993 raised additional $28 million, $131.5 million, and $188 million respectively.

Objective: Seeks capital appreciation. Invests in securities and bonds traded on the Bolsa Mexicana de Valores, S.A. de C.V. the Mexican Stock Exchange.

Portfolio: (1/31/94) Common Stock 92%, Short-Term Securities 8%. Sector Weightings: Cement Industry 16%, Consumer Goods 13%, Financial Groups 12%, Holdings 15%, Retail Trade 17%. Top Holdings: Cifra, S.A. de C.V. Series B; Cemex, S.A. Series A; Grupo Financiero Banamex Accival, S.A. de C.V. Series C; Grupo Carso, S.A. de C.V. Series A1.

Capitalization: (1/31/94) Common stock outstanding 37,282,359. No long-term debt.

Beta: 0.29
Fee: 0.85%   **Fund Manager:** Impulsora del Fondo Mexico
Income Distribution: Annually   **Capital Gains Distribution:** Annually
Reinvestment Plan: Yes   **Shareholder Reports:** Quarterly

5 Year Performance

Fiscal Year Ending 10/31	1993	1992	1991	1990	1989
Net Assets ($mil)	1075.90	654.90	474.70	303.30	202.30
Net Income Distribution ($)	0.49	0.48	0.36	0.56	0.45
Capital Gains Distribution ($)	2.48	1.03	0.00	0.00	0.00
Total Distribution ($)	2.97	1.51	0.36	0.56	0.45
Yield from Distribution (%)	12.77	6.43	2.44	6.40	5.14
Expense Ratio (%)	1.08	1.08	1.37	1.80	1.77
Portfolio Turnover (%)	5.14	15.59	12.53	8.88	10.54
NAV per Share ($)	28.88	24.91	24.07	15.38	10.26
Market Price per Share ($)	27.00	23.25	23.50	14.75	8.75
Premium (Discount) (%)	-6.51	-6.66	-2.37	-4.10	-14.72
Total Return, Stock Price (%)	28.90	5.36	61.76	74.97	60.00

Mexico Fund, Inc.

Premium/Discount Spread

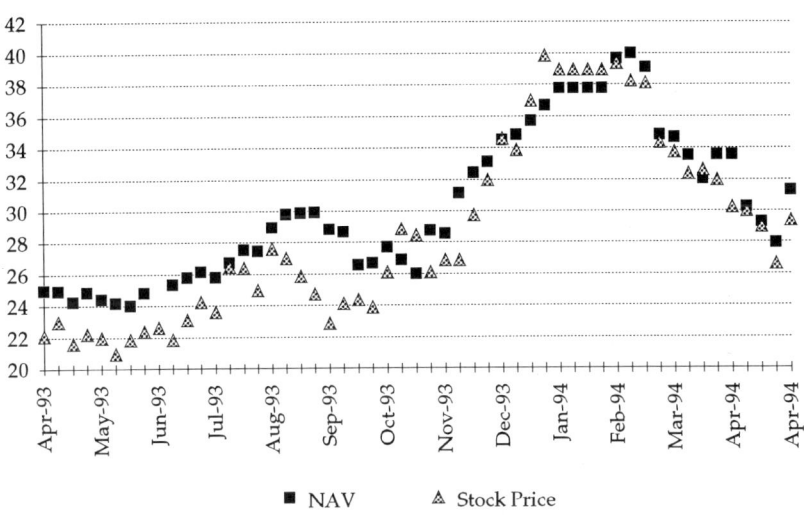

Fund Outlook (MXF): The new Mexican economic environment, created by the opening of the economy that started in 1988 and the approval of NAFTA in 1993, required the implementation of restrictive fiscal and monetary policies intended to reduce domestic inflation on a permanent basis. Mexico has achieved positive results in this respect. Measured by the CPI calculated by Banco de Mexico (central bank), domestic inflation decreased from less than 12% in 1992 to 8% in 1993, and to 7.5% for the 12-month period ended January 31, 1994. Banco de Mexico, recently designated as autonomous, is now charged with the protection of the domestic purchasing power. One of the undesirable secondary effects of the restrictive fiscal and monetary policies implemented has been the reduction of the economy's dynamism. The real growth of the Mexican GDP for all calendar 1993 was at 0.4% versus 2.6% in 1992. However, with inflation under control, Mexico may anticipate an increase in real economic growth in 1994.

Authors' Comments (MXF): The Mexican market had spectacular 1993 gains plus additional gains in January. But in February the markets began to tumble; interest rates rose more than 400-basis points; and additional market weakness developed when the leading presidential candidate, Luis Donaldo Colosio, was assassinated. If the ruling party is victorious in August, the economy is expected to gain momentum as the Chiapas uprising problems are addressed. The fund, with a large holding in cyclicals, will benefit as the new administration increases expenditures on infrastructure projects. MXF follows a buy and hold philosophy, and, therefore, has the lowest expense ratio of the three Mexico funds.

Portugal Fund, Inc.

One Citicorp Plaza
153 E. 53rd Street
New York, NY 10022
(212) 832-2626

NYSE: PGF

Transfer Agent
Provident National Bank
P.O. Box 8950
Wilmington, DE 19899
(800) 553-8080

Growth

Results

For 12 Months Ending 4/29/94	Period End	Period Begin	Distributions	Yield Dist (%)	Total Return (%)
Share Price	13.38	9.00	0.00	0.00	48.67
NAV per Share ($)	14.83	9.52		0.00	55.78

Background: Initial public offering November 1, 1989 of approximately 4,600,000 shares at $15 per share. Initial NAV was $13.95 per share.

Objective: Seeks total return including income and capital appreciation. The fund will invest at least 75% in Portuguese equity and debt securities. Up to 25% may be invested in non-Portuguese equity and debt securities. The fund may engage in hedging transactions.

Portfolio: (12/31/93) Common Stocks-Portugal 85.6%, U.S. Treasuries 14.4%, Sector Weightings: Auto 1.6%, Banks 9.4%, Construction & Public Works 10.8%, Consumer Products 7.4%, Film Distribution 6.7%, Food & Beverages 11%, Hotels 4.2%, Manufacturing 3.8%, Retail 24.7%, Telecommunications 2.4%, Transportation 1.8%.

Capitalization: (12/31/93) Common stock outstanding 5,298,570. No long-term debt.

Beta: 0.76

Fee: 1.20%   *Fund Manager:* BEA Associates
Income Distribution: Annually   *Capital Gains Distribution:* Annually
Reinvestment Plan: Yes   *Shareholder Reports:* Semi-Annually

5 Year Performance

Fiscal Year Ending 12/31	1993	1992	1991	1990	1989
Net Assets ($mill)	66.40	47.10	57.00	58.10	73.00
Net Income Distribution ($)	0.00	0.06	0.11	0.12	0.04
Capital Gains Distribution ($)	0.00	0.00	0.00	0.00	0.04
Total Distributions ($)	0.00	0.06	0.11	0.12	0.08
Yield from Distribution (%)	0.00	0.62	1.19	0.71	0.47
Expense Ratio	1.97	1.92	1.96	2.04	2.26
Portfolio Turnover (%)	24.47	39.07	13.31	10.09	0.00
NAV per Share ($)	12.52	8.90	10.77	10.96	13.79
Market Price per Share ($)	14.13	8.00	9.75	9.25	17.00
Premium Discount (%)	12.82	-10.11	-9.47	-15.60	23.28
Total Return, Stock Price (%)	76.63	-17.33	6.59	-44.88	-

Portugal Fund, Inc.

Premium/Discount Spread

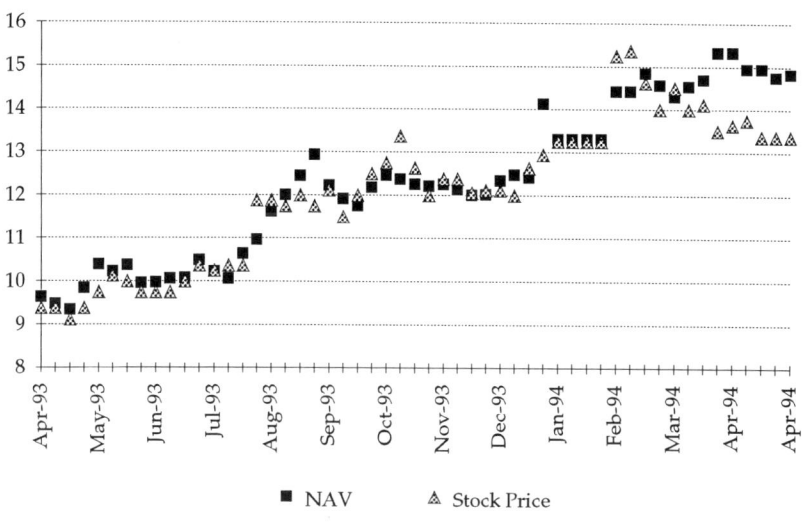

Fund Outlook (PGF): The Government's 1994 budget forecasts a recovery of growth for the calendar year. The pace of the recovery will largely be a function of how robustly Europe recovers. A stronger European recovery may allow Portugal to grow at 2% for 1994, which is in line with the OECD forecast. Healthy growth also depends on the extent to which investment will rise as a result of significant cuts in interest rates and an increase in European Community funding. The fund does not expect a recovery to be driven by meaningful growth in private consumption. Flat employment growth and wages will inhibit consumption. However, in light of the 1995 elections, the government is likely to feel the pressure to stimulate the economy.

Authors' Comments (PGF): The CPI is projected to increase 6.0% in 1994, down from 6.6% in 1993 and down from 8.4% in 1992. With the decline in the rate of inflation, interest rates have plummeted and the equity market has reacted accordingly. The stock market since December 31, 1993 has appreciated 14%, reflecting investor confidence in a number of reforms—access to a continuous trading system and an automated stock registration. Continued non-inflationary economic growth is forecasted, despite Prime Minister Cavaco Sila's introduction of an austerity program to reduce the budget deficit, which came in at 8.2% of GDP in 1993, well above the target of 4.8%. The fund manager has more than one-third of the portfolio weighted in the retail sector. Cyclicals are the second. The fund, on average, sold at a premium prior to the March sell off in the World Bond markets. PGF is an attractive purchase.

ROC Taiwan Fund, Inc.

100 E. Pratt Street
Baltimore, MD 21202
(800) 343-9567

NYSE: **ROC**
Transfer Agent:
State Street Bank & Trust Co.
225 Franklin St.
Boston, MA 02110
(800) 426-5523

Growth

Results

For 12-months Ending 4/29/94	Period End	Period Begin	Distributions	Yield Dist (%)	Total Return (%)
Share Price ($)	10.00	8.25	0.15	1.82	23.03
NAV per Share ($)	10.21	9.01		1.66	14.98

Background: Commenced operations on October 27, 1983 as an open-end fund. Converted to closed-end fund May 9, 1989. On date of reorganization, NAV was $13.50 per share.

Objective: Seeks long-term capital appreciation through investments in securities, primarily equities, traded on the Republic of China (ROC) Taiwan Exchange.

Portfolio: (12/31/93) Common & Preferred Stock 82%, Short-Term 20%, Liabilities (2%). Sector Weightings: Banking 26%, Electrical & Electronics 15%, Plastics 7%, Cement 6%, Textiles 5%. Top Holdings: First Commercial Bank 7%, Hua Nan Commercial Bank 6%, Chang Hwa Commercial Bank 5%, Teco Electric and Machinery Co. 4%.

Capitalization: (12/31/93) Common stock outstanding 27,870,676. No long-term debt.

Beta: 0.12
Fee: 1.45%   *Fund Manager:* International Investment Trust
Income Distribution: Annually   *Capital Gains Distribution:* Annually
Reinvestment Plan: Yes   *Shareholder Reports:* Quarterly

5 Year Performance

Fiscal Year Ending 12/31	1993	1992	1991	1990	1989
Net Assets ($mil)	295.90	237.20	244.10	235.70	370.70
Net Income Distribution ($)	0.15	0.02	0.75	0.22	0.43
Capital Gains Distribution ($)	0.00	0.00	0.00	0.00	0.00
Total Distribution ($)	0.15	0.02	0.75	0.22	0.43
Yield from Distribution (%)	1.71	0.20	9.68	1.68	-
Expense Ratio (%)	2.18	2.47	2.11	2.03	1.93
Portfolio Turnover (%)	151.00	45.00	35.00	27.00	30.00
NAV per Share ($)	10.62	8.51	9.53	9.15	14.38
Market Price per Share ($)	13.75	8.75	10.25	7.75	13.13
Premium (Discount) (%)	29.47	2.82	7.56	-15.30	-8.76
Total Return, Stock Price (%)	58.86	-14.44	41.94	-39.30	-

ROC Taiwan Fund, Inc.

Premium/Discount Spread

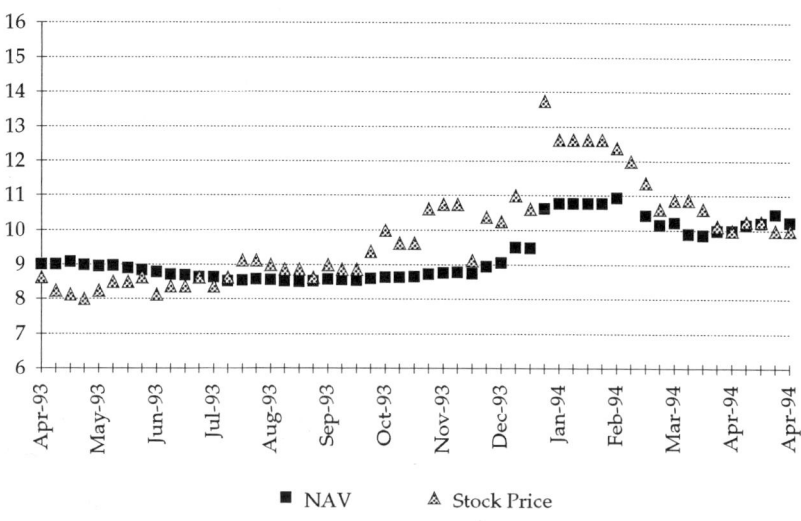

■ NAV   ▲ Stock Price

Fund Outlook (ROC): The market should be well supported by continued inflow of foreign capital and the relaxed monetary policy of the Taiwanese central bank. The fund will focus on stocks of companies benefiting from expansion into China and public infrastructure spending. The fund has above-average exposure in such blue-chip industrials. While the long-term outlook is positive, the fund is conscious of the rapid rise over the last quarter of the P/E multiple of the whole market above 35 times prospective earnings.

Authors' Comments (ROC): The Taiwan stock market was one of the better performing Asia markets in 1993, until the Taiwan government placed restrictions on investments by foreigners. As a result the market experienced a decline of 38% between February and March, at which time the Government eased restrictions. A rally followed. The Government has undertaken a six-year infrastructure program involving improvements in transportation and communications to enable Taiwan manufacturers to lower production costs. GDP growth is expected to grow at the rate of 6.1%, and the CPI is projected to increase at the rate of 3.1%. On April 1, 1994 the fund acquired a new manager, who, in addition to being a value investor, will maintain a fully invested position. Throughout 1993, the portfolio was 80% in cash and therefore underperformed. As the economies of Taiwan and China become more closely intertwined, Taipei stocks will be a way of participating in the China Market until the ban on direct investments is eliminated. Purchase of ROC should be made when the stock is available at a discount.

Swiss Helvetia Fund, Inc.
521 Fifth Avenue
New York, NY 10175
(212) 867-7660

NYSE: SWZ
Transfer Agent:
Provident National Bank
P.O. Box 8950
Wilmington, DE 19899
(800) 553-8080

Growth

Results

For 12-months Ending 4/29/94	Period End	Period Begin	Distributions	Yield Dist (%)	Total Return (%)
Share Price ($)	20.50	15.38	0.33	2.15	35.44
NAV per Share ($)	20.67	16.22		2.03	29.47

Background: Initial public offering August 27, 1987 of 8,000,000 shares at $15 per share. Net proceeds were approximately $111.6 million.

Objective: Seeks long-term capital appreciation through investment in equities and equity-linked Swiss securities. Does not intend to trade for short-term profits. May purchase private placements.

Portfolio: (12/31/93) Common Stocks & Warrants 98%, Short-Term 2%. Sector Weightings: Pharmaceuticals 22%, Banks 26%, Food & Beverages 12%, Insurance 14%, Machinery & Metals 9%. Top Holdings: Roche Holding AG, Union Bank of Switzerland, Nestle AG, Sandoz AG.

Capitalization: (12/31/93) Common stock outstanding 8,808,856. No long-term debt.

Beta: 0.50

Fee: 1.00%
Income Distribution: Annually
Reinvestment Plan: Yes

Fund Manager: Helvetia Capital Corporation
Capital Gains Distribution: Annually
Shareholder Reports: Quarterly

5 Year Performance

Fiscal Year Ending 12/31	1993	1992	1991	1990	1989
Net Assets ($mil)	184.70	128.80	110.50	105.40	104.40
Net Income Distribution ($)	0.08	0.03	0.03	0.05	0.00
Capital Gains Distribution ($)	0.25	0.00	0.00	0.00	0.00
Total Distribution ($)	0.33	0.03	0.03	0.05	0.00
Yield from Distribution (%)	2.38	0.23	0.25	0.33	0.00
Expense Ratio (%)	1.50	1.69	1.85	1.77	1.80
Portfolio Turnover (%)	19.64	13.09	41.08	43.83	30.46
NAV per Share ($)	20.96	14.62	13.80	13.17	13.04
Market Price per Share ($)	22.75	13.88	13.25	11.88	15.13
Premium (Discount) (%)	8.54	-5.06	-3.99	-9.87	15.95
Total Return, Stock Price (%)	66.28	4.98	11.78	-21.15	57.11

Swiss Helvetia Fund, Inc.

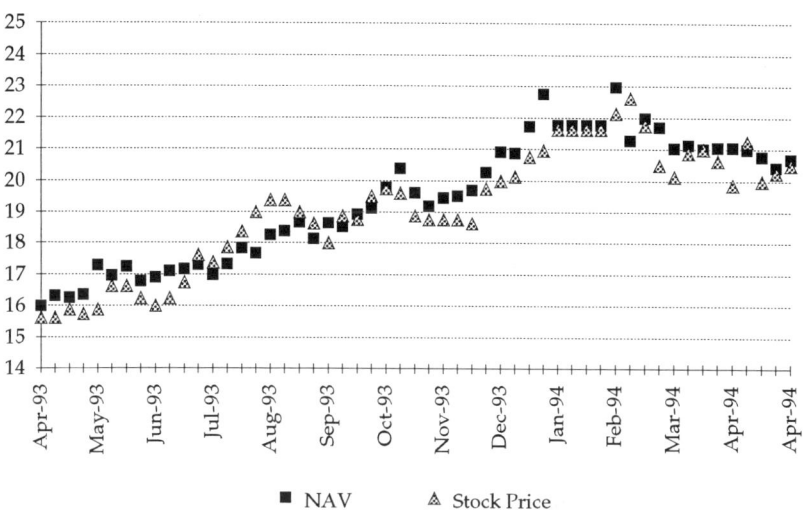

Premium/Discount Spread

■ NAV △ Stock Price

Fund Outlook (SWZ): The fund anticipates another good year in 1994, although it is unlikely to see anything like the market dynamics of 1993. However, with continuing low inflation and low interest rates combined with strong earnings growth and attractive valuations vis-à-vis other international markets, the fund believes it will continue to be a productive vehicle for investors who wish to achieve global exposure without having to assume multiple political and currency risks.

Authors' Comments (SWZ): Because many of the Swiss companies held in the fund's portfolio are multinational in scope, economic recovery in Europe, the U.S. and dollar-bloc countries is more significant than what happens domestically. The Swiss bank may reduce interest rates further from the current prime rate of 6.13% as the CPI currently projected at 2.1% continues to decline. Swiss Helvetia has a large position in financials which will benefit as rates decline and lending picks up. Because Swiss companies are heavily invested overseas, a strong dollar is of benefit to this fund. In 1993, investment in Swiss securities was made more attractive by the elimination of two classes of securities (one for locals and one for foreigners) and the standardized accounting procedures for financial reporting.

United Kingdom Fund, Inc.

245 Park Avenue
New York, NY 10167
(800) 524-4458
(212) 272-6404

NYSE: **UKM**
Transfer Agent:
The Bank of New York
101 Barclay St.
New York, NY 10286
(800) 524-4458/(212) 815 2315

Growth

Results

For 12-months Ending 4/29/94	Period End	Period Begin	Distributions	Yield Dist (%)	Total Return (%)
Share Price ($)	11.88	10.00	0.14	1.40	20.20
NAV per Share ($)	12.68	11.36		1.23	12.85

Background: Initial public offering August 6, 1987 of 4,000,000 shares at $12.50 per share. Initial NAV was $11.63 per share.

Objective: Seeks long-term capital appreciation. Under normal conditions at least 65% of the fund's assets will be invested in United Kingdom equity securities. The remainder will be in debt securities, private placements, or securities traded on the OTC market.

Portfolio: (12/31/93) Common Stocks 99%, Short-Term 1%. Sector Weightings: Banks 10.7%, Building Materials, 7.5%, Food Manufacturing & Retail 13.4%, Oil & Gas 10.5%, Stores 9.7%, Electricity 10.5%, Electronics 4.1%, Engineering 2.6%, Health & Household 3.1%, Pharmaceuticals 6.0%, Stores 9.7%.

Capitalization: (9/30/92) Common stock outstanding 4,010,135. No long-term debt.

Beta: 1.01
Fee: 0.75% *Fund Manager:* Warburg Invest. Mgt. Intl. Ltd.
Income Distribution: Annually *Capital Gains Distribution:* Annually
Reinvestment Plan: Yes *Shareholder Reports:* Quarterly

5 Year Performance

Fiscal Year Ending 3/31	1993	1992	1991	1990	1989
Net Assets ($mil)	43.50	39.80	46.80	41.60	48.70
Net Income Distribution ($)	0.14	0.45	0.00	0.35	0.22
Capital Gains Distribution ($)	0.41	0.38	0.73	0.25	0.43
Total Distribution ($)	0.55	0.83	0.73	0.60	0.65
Yield from Distribution (%)	6.02	8.10	8.34	6.00	7.32
Expense Ratio (%)	1.78	1.74	2.19	1.92	1.89
Portfolio Turnover (%)	45.54	47.30	36.37	22.07	40.91
NAV per Share ($)	10.84	9.93	11.67	10.38	12.15
Market Price per Share ($)	9.63	9.13	10.25	8.75	10.00
Premium (Discount) (%)	-11.16	-10.57	-12.17	-15.70	-17.70
Total Return, Stock Price (%)	11.50	-2.83	25.49	-6.50	19.93

United Kingdom Fund, Inc.

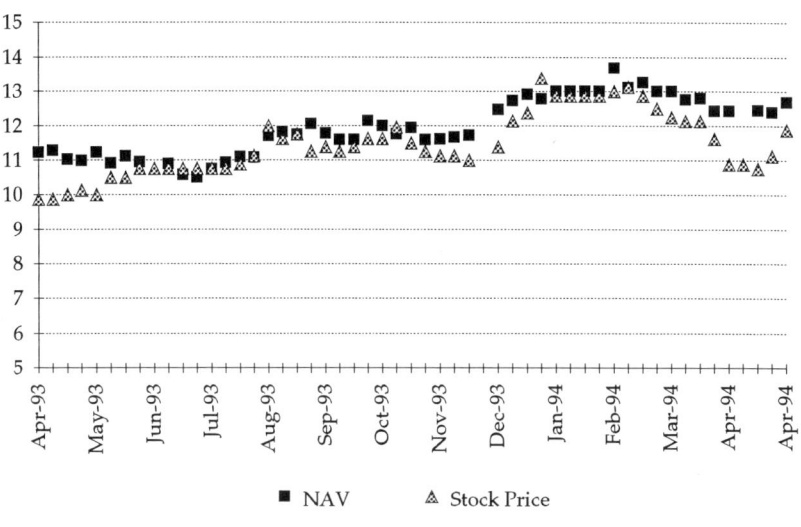

Premium/Discount Spread

■ NAV   △ Stock Price

Fund Outlook (UKM): The fund expects economic data to confirm that the U.K. economy continues to strengthen and expects GDP growth over 1994 of about 2.5%. Consumer expenditure at the beginning of the year has been buoyant. The delayed tax increases, effective from April, will pose a threat to rising consumer confidence although the Chancellor has the option of reducing base rates to soften the effect. The more positive influences are rising employment levels and very low inflation which should lead to growth in total real disposable income. Wage growth, is likely to remain subdued. The tone of company statements continues to be relatively cautious, particularly from those companies exporting to Continental European markets. The fund remains optimistic that aggregate corporate profits will grow by about 14% in 1994. Any increase in sales volumes will now lead to rapidly growing profits due to the much lower cost basis enjoyed by U.K. companies. Profits growth is now expected to be the main driver of share prices rather than further price earnings multiple expansion.

Authors' Comments (UKM): Further interest rate cuts may be anticipated as inflation continues to decline which should encourage investors to move money into equities. Higher corporate earnings should further fuel bullishness in the equity markets. The portfolio manager has shifted emphasis away from big-cap to smaller companies that are able to effectively restructure in order to reduce costs and increase competitiveness. Multinational companies that rely on exports have been reduced due to sluggish exports. UKM is well positioned to benefit from the improvement in the domestic and European economies.

Multi Country Funds

Alliance Global Environment Fund

1345 Avenue of the Americas
New York, NY 10105
(800) 247-4154
(212) 969-1000

NYSE: AEF
Transfer Agent:
State Street Bank & Trust Co.
225 Franklin St.
Boston, MA 02110
(800) 426-5523

Growth

Results

For 12-months Ending 4/29/94	Period End	Period Begin	Distributions	Yield Dist (%)	Total Return (%)
Share Price ($)	9.25	9.63	0.00	0.00	-3.95
NAV per Share ($)	11.36	11.13		0.00	2.07

Background: Initial public offering June 1, 1990 of 6,000,000 shares at $15 per share. Initial NAV was $13.95 per share.

Objective: Seeks long-term capital appreciation. Invests in companies expected to benefit from increased global awareness for a cleaner environment.

Portfolio: (10/31/93) Common & Preferred Stock 92.4%, Cash & Short-Term 7.1%, Convertible Bonds 0.5%. Country Exposure: U.S. 52.5%, U.K. 12.6%, France 11.1%, Japan 4.9%, Australia 1.4%, Canada 2.6%, Hong Kong 0.5%, Malaysia 1.7%, Philippines 2.7%, Spain 0.5%, Thailand 0.6%.

Capitalization: (10/31/93) Common stock outstanding 6,907,169. No long-term debt.

Beta: 0.74
Fee: 1.10%
Income Distribution: Annually
Reinvestment Plan: Yes
Fund Manager: Alliance Capital Mgt. L.P.
Capital Gains Distribution: Annually
Shareholder Reports: Semi-Annually

5 Year Performance

Fiscal Year Ending 10/31	1993	1992	1991	1990	1989
Net Assets ($mil)	75.80	74.40	90.60	86.00	-
Net Income Distribution ($)	0.00	0.10	0.25	0.00	-
Capital Gains Distribution ($)	0.00	0.08	0.09	0.00	-
Total Distribution ($)	0.00	0.18	0.34	0.00	-
Yield from Distribution (%)	0.00	1.58	3.36	-	-
Expense Ratio (%)	1.62	1.63	1.49	1.72	-
Portfolio Turnover (%)	25.00	41.00	32.00	4.00	-
NAV per Share ($)	10.97	10.78	13.12	12.46	-
Market Price per Share ($)	9.25	9.50	11.38	10.13	-
Premium (Discount) (%)	-15.68	-11.87	-13.26	-18.78	-
Total Return, Stock Price (%)	-2.63	-14.94	15.70	-	-

Alliance Global Environment Fund

Premium/Discount Spread

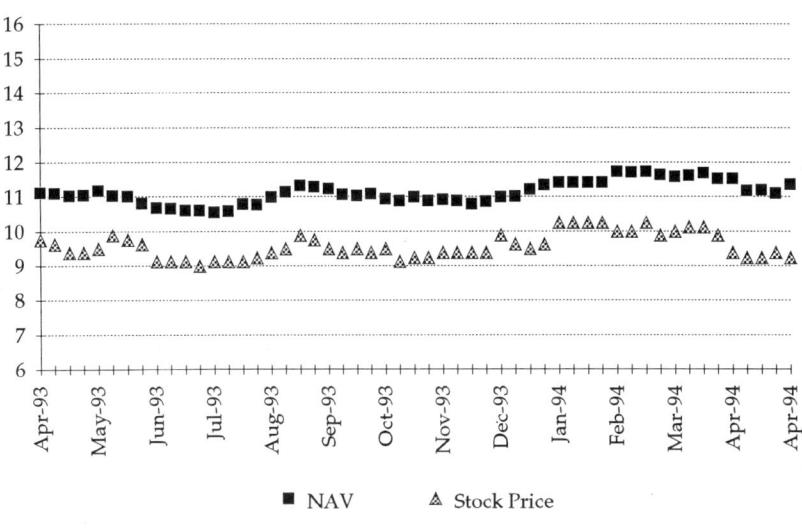

■ NAV   △ Stock Price

Fund Outlook (AEF): U.S. environmental stocks have begun to show better performance as economic activity continues to strengthen. The fund has focused on names that are involved with pollution prevention or minimization. The recent sharp decline in WMX Technologies (the industry leader which the fund did not own) demonstrates that the industry continues to show a spotty recovery. The fund believes that there are exciting opportunities for growth in water and air technologies. Internationally, the fund has benefited from its investments in traditional environmental companies in the U.K. and France, as well as in Mexico, Brazil and the Philippines. While the demand for environmental services in the latter countries is still relatively small, the growth rate is quite attractive.

Authors' Comments (AEF): The global environmental industry has been impacted by low levels of economic activity, as industry attempted to reduce costs and circumvent existing regulations. The absence of strong enforcement of existing regulations has also been a factor. A stronger sector performance can be anticipated due to economic recovery here and abroad as well as effective enforcement of current law dealing with acid rain, environmental standards required by NAFTA, stricter observance of regulations dealing with toxic waste and clean water. Corporate reports are reflecting improved trends and it is only a matter of time before the equity markets take note.

Clemente Global Growth Fund, Inc.   NYSE: **CLM**

152 W. 57th Street
New York, NY 10019
(212) 765-0700

Transfer Agent:
The Bank of New York
101 Barclay St.
New York, NY 10007
(800) 524-4458

Growth

Results

For 12-months Ending 4/29/94	Period End	Period Begin	Distributions	Yield Dist (%)	Total Return (%)
Share Price ($)	9.88	8.75	0.65	7.43	20.34
NAV per Share ($)	11.94	10.31		6.30	22.11

Background: Initial public offering on June 23, 1987 of 6,000,000 common shares at $10 per share. Initial NAV was $9.23 per share.

Objective: Seeks long-term capital appreciation. Invests in equity securities of small- and medium-sized companies throughout the world. Will invest between 50% and 75% in securities traded outside the U.S.

Portfolio: (12/31/93) Common Stock 90%, Short-Term 9%, Convertible Corporate Bonds 2%, Less Liabilities (5%). U.S. 19%, Latin America 18% (Mexico 7%, Colombia 3%, Chile 4%, Brazil 2%), Europe 14%, Japan 15%, Malaysia 9%, Indonesia 4%.

Capitalization: (12/31/93) Common stock outstanding 5,892,400. No long-term debt.

Beta: 0.55
Fee: 1.00%   *Fund Manager:* Clemente Capital, Inc.
Income Distribution: Annually   *Capital Gains Distribution:* Annually
Reinvestment Plan: Yes   *Shareholder Reports:* Quarterly

5 Year Performance

Fiscal Year Ending 12/31	1993	1992	1991	1990	1989
Net Assets ($mil)	72.80	55.50	63.80	57.70	69.00
Net Income Distribution ($)	0.00	0.02	0.00	0.00	0.00
Capital Gains Distribution ($)	0.65	1.03	0.35	0.16	0.16
Total Distribution ($)	0.65	1.05	0.35	0.16	0.16
Yield from Distribution (%)	8.39	11.50	4.12	1.58	2.17
Expense Ratio (%)	1.68	2.23	2.64	2.76	2.70
Portfolio Turnover (%)	125.31	82.49	66.11	28.69	67.35
NAV per Share ($)	12.36	9.43	10.82	9.79	11.71
Market Price per Share ($)	11.25	7.75	9.13	8.50	10.13
Premium (Discount) (%)	-8.98	-17.82	-15.71	-13.18	-13.58
Total Return, Stock Price (%)	53.55	-3.61	11.53	-14.51	39.43

Clemente Global Growth Fund, Inc.

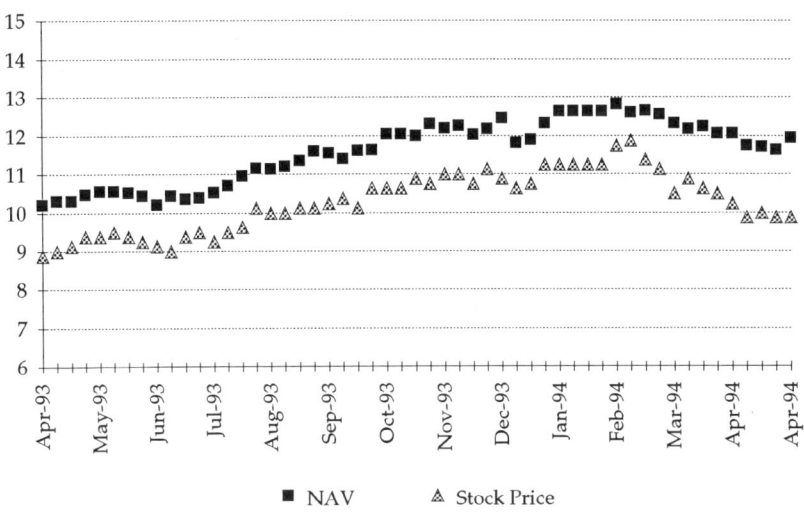

Premium/Discount Spread

■ NAV △ Stock Price

Fund Outlook (CLM): The fund trimmed its weighting in Japan from 26.1% to 14.6% (with some of that reduction coming from a weak Japanese market). Nearly two-thirds of the selling activity in Japan was completed before the middle of November 1993, allowing the fund to effectively sidestep the steep decline in the Japanese market that followed. Assets from the sales of the Japanese shares were directed to the emerging markets of Brazil, Chile, Indonesia, Malaysia, the Philippines, Thailand and Turkey. The coming year should bring many opportunities and challenges: a recovering Europe, the strong growth and emergence of the Pacific Rim and Latin American nations and a sustainable, albeit cautious, recovery in the U.S.

Authors' Comments (CLM): Because Clemente trades at a discount, it offers an inexpensive way for investors to diversify globally. The fund's largest country exposure is Japan at 15% of the portfolio. This should enhance performance over the rest of the year. Other allocations include the U.S. (6%), Latin America (15%) and Europe (21%). Diversification extends to the Pacific Rim countries of Indonesia, Malaysia, Thailand, and the Philippines. Over the last 5 years, the fund has averaged slightly better than 10% annualized. Although not a performance scorcher, this fund offers a steady pace for the conservative global investor.

Fidelity Advisor Emerging Asia

82 Devonshire Street
Boston, MA 02109
(800) 544-8888

Growth

NYSE: FAE
Transfer Agent:
State Street Bank & Trust Co.
225 Franklin Square
Boston, MA 02110
(800) 426-5523

Results

For 12 Months Ending 4/29/94	Period End	Period Begin	Distributions	Yield Dist (%)	Total Return (%)
Share Price ($)	13.63	-	-	-	-
NAV per Share ($)	14.50	-	-	-	-

Background: Initial public offering February 3, 1994 of 8,447,093 shares at $15 per share. Initial NAV was $14.10.

Objective: The fund seeks long-term capital appreciation through investments in equity and debt securities of Asian Emerging Market issuers. Securities are evaluated by Fidelity's own research staff, including on-site regional analysts. Regional economic growth, expected levels of inflation, and government policies that may affect investments are monitored continuously.

Portfolio: (4/30/94) Common Stock 83%, Convertibles 1%, Cash & Equivalents 16%. Top Country Holdings: Hong Kong 31%, Malaysia 15%, Taiwan 12%, Thailand 9%, Singapore 6%. Top Holdings: Hutchison Whampoa Ltd., Hong Kong Telecommunications, Sung Hung Kai Properties Ltd., Resorts World Bhd, Bank of East Asia.

Capitalization: (4/30/94) Common stock outstanding 7,757,093. No long-term debt.

Beta: None
Fee: 1.25%
Income Distribution: Annually
Reinvestment Plan: Yes

Fund Manager: Fidelity Intl. Adv. Ltd.
Capital Gains Distribution: Annually
Shareholder Reports: Quarterly

5 Year Performance

Fiscal Year Ending: 12/31	1994	1993	1992	1991	1990
Net Assets ($mil)	118.1	-	-	-	-
Net Distribution ($)	0.00	-	-	-	-
Capital Gains Distribution ($)	0.00	-	-	-	-
Total Distribution ($)	0.00	-	-	-	-
Yield from Distribution (%)	-	-	-	-	-
Expense Ratio (%)	-	-	-	-	-
Portfolio Turnover (%)	-	-	-	-	-
NAV per Share	-	-	-	-	-
Market Price per Share ($)	-	-	-	-	-
Premium (Discount) (%)	-	-	-	-	-
Total Return, Stock Price (%)	-	-	-	-	-

Fidelity Advisor Emerging

Premium/Discount Spread

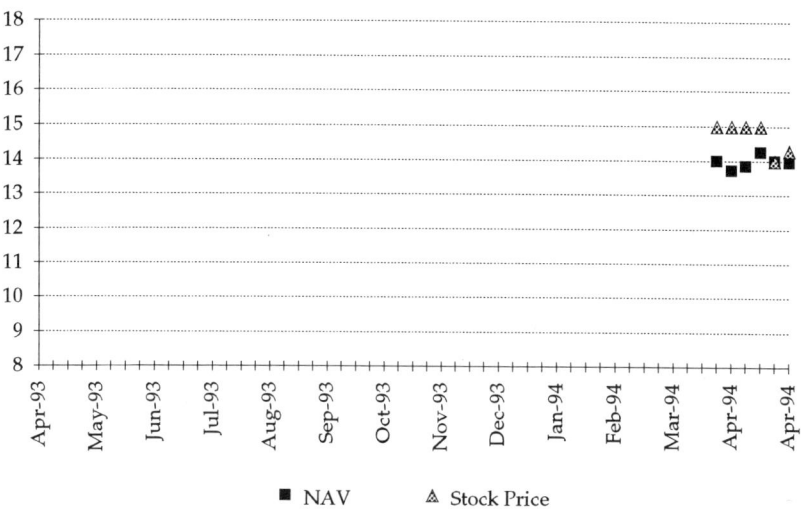

■ NAV   △ Stock Price

Fund Outlook (FAE): The Southeast Asian markets could rally at some point on good news, but the fund manager, in general, thinks it's going to be a much harder road to climb than last year. However, since stock valuations have returned to reasonable levels, FAE thinks Southeast Asian stocks will begin to look attractive to investors.

Authors' Comments (FAE): This fund is managed by an experienced on-sight manager, Peter Phillips. The authors agree with his recent assessment of the attractiveness of the Southeast Asian Markets. The feeble U.S. recovery, rising interest rates, and a weak U.S. dollar are, in the intermediate term, overshadowing the strong long-term fundamentals of the Southeast Asian region. The fund emphasizes companies with strong cash flow and sustainable growth rates with a mixture of large, mid- and small-cap stocks. With nearly all the other single country funds with a Southeast Asian focus trading at absurd premiums, this fund offers entry and diversification at a discount. A good selection for the bargain hunting global investor.

Global Health Sciences

NYSE: **GHS**

7800 E. Union Avenue, Suite 800
P.O. Box 2920
Denver, CO 80237
(800) 528-8765

Transfer Agent:
State Street Bank & Trust Co.
225 Franklin St.
Boston, MA 02110
(800) 426-5523

Growth

Results

For 12-months Ending 4/29/94	Period End	Period Begin	Distributions	Yield Dist (%)	Total Return (%)
Share Price ($)	10.00	10.25	0.20	1.95	-0.49
NAV per Share ($)	12.17	10.85		1.84	14.01

Background: Initial public offering January 20, 1992 at $15 per share. Initial NAV was $13.95.

Objective: Seeks capital appreciation by investing in health science companies around the world.

Portfolio: (10/31/93) Common Stock 85%, Convertibles 7%, Preferreds 4%. Sector Weightings: Pharmaceuticals 31%, Health Care Delivery 21%, Medical Devices & Supplies 14%, Biotechnology 19%, REITs 6%. Top Holdings: Medco Containment Services; HealthSource Inc., Creative BioMolecules, IVAX Corp., Roche Holdings Sponsored ADR.

Capitalization: (12/31/93) Common stock outstanding 20,507,200. No long-term debt.

Beta: N/A
Fee: 1.00%
Income Distribution: Annually
Reinvestment Plan: Yes
Fund Manager: Invesco Trust Co.
Capital Gains Distribution: Annually
Shareholder Reports: Semi-Annually

5 Year Performance

Fiscal Year Ending 10/31	1993	1992	1991	1990	1989
Net Assets ($mil)	248.60	259.30	-	-	-
Net Income Distribution ($)	0.08	0.00	-	-	-
Capital Gains Distribution ($)	0.00	0.03	-	-	-
Total Distribution ($)	0.08	0.03	-	-	-
Yield from Distribution (%)	0.70	0.29	-	-	-
Expense Ratio (%)	1.39	1.35	-	-	-
Portfolio Turnover (%)	226.00	215.00	-	-	-
NAV per Share ($)	12.12	12.64	-	-	-
Market Price per Share ($)	11.50	11.50	-	-	-
Premium (Discount) (%)	-5.12	-9.04	-	-	-
Total Return, Stock Price (%)	0.70	-	-	-	-

Global Health Sciences

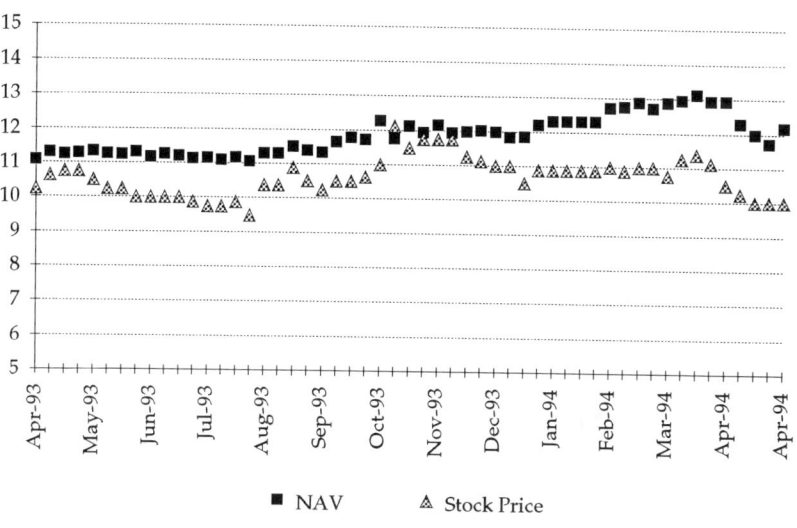

Fund Outlook (GHS): The health care industry has been in a state of rapid transition over the last few years. This transition was brought on by the demand for low-cost alternatives and the rapid pace of discovery in science and technology. The industry has reacted to these changes by creating new health care delivery systems and by introducing innovative new products. This change provides the investor with significant opportunities for long-term appreciation. Couple the transition in the industry with the aging worldwide population, increasing consumer demand for the best available health care and the growing demand for high-quality health care in the third world countries, and this sector is an attractive long-term area for investment.

Authors' Comments (GHS): The fund's investment strategy is to diversify the portfolio into five major sectors. Within these fields the managers are looking for discovery companies; those having new products or recently introduced new products in the market place that represent a substantial therapeutic advance. The fund is also focusing on companies dealing with cost containment; companies in the health care industry that are able to take a product or service out of a high-cost setting and move it into a low-cost procedure including prescription fulfillment. Because of the aging population, increasing consumer demand for better health care at lower costs, the prospects for this industry and this fund are bright.

Latin America Discovery Fund

NYSE: LDF

1221 Avenue of the Americas
New York, NY 10020
(212) 296-7100

Transfer Agent:
First National Bank of Boston
P.O. Box 644, Mail Stop 46-02-09
Boston MA 02102-0644
(617) 575-2900

Growth

Results

For 12 Months Ending 4/29/94	Period End	Period Begin	Distributions	Yield Dist (%)	Total Return (%)
Share Price ($)	22.13	15.00	0.00	0.00	47.50
NAV per Share ($)	21.58	16.18		0.00	33.37

Background: Initial public offering June 16, 1992 of 3,3000,000 shares at $15 per share. Initial NAV was $14.10 per share.

Objective: Seeks long-term capital appreciation. Normally invests at least 80% in equity securities of Latin American issuers and, from time to time, in debt securities issued or guaranteed by a Latin American Government or Government entity. At least 55% will be invested in listed securities of Argentine, Brazilian, Chilean and Mexican issuers. Will also actively invest in markets in other Latin American countries.

Portfolio: Common Stocks 97%, Convertible Debentures 3%. Country Holdings: Brazil 38%, Mexico 32%, Peru 5%, Chile 5%. Top Holdings: Telefonos de Mexico ADR, Grupo Sidek 'B', Electrobras Pfd., Petrobras Pfd.

Capitalization: (3/31/94) Common stock outstanding 7,885,082. No long-term debt.

Beta: 0.96

Fee: 1.25%

Fund Manager: Morgan Stanley Asset Mgt., Inc.

Income Distribution: Annually

Capital Gains Distribution: Annually

Reinvestment Plan: Yes

Shareholder Reports: Quarterly

5 Year Performance

Fiscal Year Ending 12/31	1993	1992	1991	1990	1989
Net Assets ($mil)	180.20	88.00	-	-	-
Net Income Distribution ($)	0.00	0.00	-	-	-
Capital Gains Distribution ($)	0.00	0.00	-	-	-
Total Distribution ($)	0.00	0.00	-	-	-
Yield from Distribution (%)	0.00	0.00	-	-	-
Expense Ratio (%)	2.23	2.74	-	-	-
Portfolio Turnover (%)	56.00	-	-	-	-
NAV per Share ($)	23.31	15.23	-	-	-
Market Price per Share ($)	27.13	13.25	-	-	-
Premium (Discount) (%)	16.37	-13.00	-	-	-
Total Return, Stock Price (%)	104.72	-11.67	-	-	-

Latin America Discovery Fund

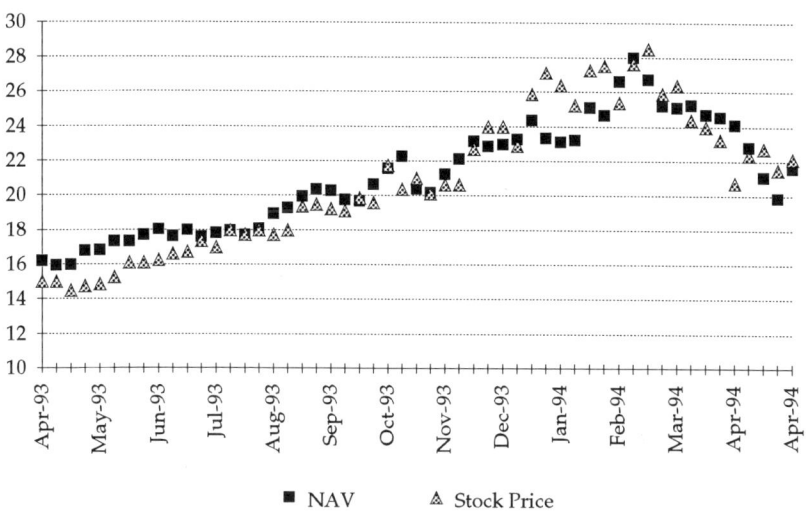

Premium/Discount Spread

■ NAV △ Stock Price

Fund Outlook (LDF): 1994 is the year of elections throughout the region. In Chile and Venezuela, new administration have come to power in the first quarter of 1994 expressing commitment to continuing economic reform. Mexico's presidential election will take place in August, Brazil's in October, Colombia's in May, and Argentina's in December. The fund expects the results to affirm Latin Americans' recognition that free markets and fiscal reform are the paths to sustainable growth. Thus, while LDF anticipates turbulence in each market, it remains positive on the outlook for Latin America's stock markets.

Authors' Comments (LDF): A resurgent market led by Brazil once again attracted capital south of the border. Brazil, the "sleeping giant," is expected to elect Cardosa, the Ralph Nader of Brazilian inflation fighters, as president this fall. Fund manager Robert Meyer sees both of the fund's major holdings, Mexico and Brazil, as grossly undervalued. The authors agree and see this fund as the best way to enter the arena and not pay a scalper's price.

Petroleum & Resources Corporation   NYSE: **PEO**

Seven St. Paul Street, Suite 1140
Baltimore, MD 21202
(800) 638-2479
(410) 752-5900

Transfer Agent:
The Bank of New York
101 Barclay St.
New York, NY 10007
(800) 524-4458

Growth

Results

For 12-months Ending 4/29/94	Period End	Period Begin	Distributions	Yield Dist (%)	Total Return (%)
Share Price ($)	28.75	28.50	2.12	7.44	8.32
NAV per Share ($)	29.60	30.79		6.89	3.02

Background: Founded in 1929 as the Petroleum Corporation of America. Name was changed to Petroleum & Resources Corporation in April 1977.

Objective: Seeks capital appreciation consistent with preservation of principal. Portfolio is made up primarily of energy and natural resources stocks that pay regular dividends.

Portfolio: (3/31/94) Stocks & Convertible Securities 95%, Short-Term 5%. Sector Weightings: Energy 73% (Internationals 25%, Domestics 13%, Producers 16%, Distributors 13%, Services 6%), Basic Industries 22% (Paper & Forest Products 10%, Environmental Control 2%, Other 10%).

Capitalization: (3/31/94) Common stock outstanding 12,006,671. 9.5% owned by Adams Express Company. No long-term debt.

Beta: 0.70
Fee: 0.20%   *Fund Manager:* Petroleum & Resources Corp.
Income Distribution: Quarterly   *Capital Gains Distribution:* Annually
Reinvestment Plan: Yes   *Shareholder Reports:* Quarterly

5 Year Performance

Fiscal Year Ending 12/31	1993	1992	1991	1990	1989
Net Assets ($mil)	355.80	350.10	343.90	308.60	352.80
Net Income Distribution ($)	0.82	0.77	0.92	1.10	1.20
Capital Gains Distribution ($)	1.30	1.23	1.23	1.25	1.20
Total Distribution ($)	2.12	2.00	2.15	2.35	2.40
Yield from Distribution (%)	8.40	7.69	8.56	8.70	11.43
Expense Ratio (%)	0.57	0.52	0.59	0.57	0.66
Portfolio Turnover (%)	10.16	15.06	11.41	18.41	18.68
NAV per Share ($)	29.64	27.66	28.07	28.59	31.09
Market Price per Share ($)	27.50	25.25	26.00	25.13	27.00
Premium (Discount) (%)	11.61	-8.71	-7.37	-12.10	-13.16
Total Return, Stock Price (%)	17.31	4.81	12.02	1.78	40.00

Petroleum & Resources Corporation

Premium/Discount Spread

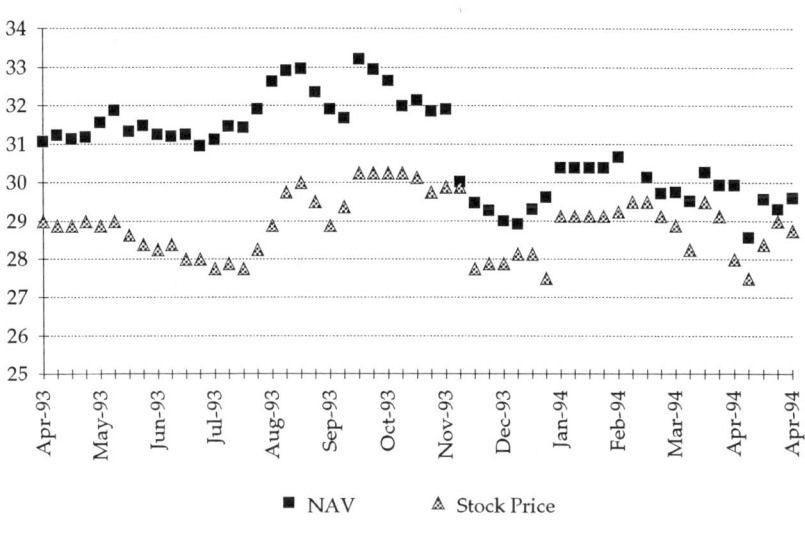

■ NAV   △ Stock Price

Fund Outlook (PEO): While oil markets will remain unsettled over the near term, oil prices are expected to recover slowly due to a plateau in non-OPEC supply, strengthening global economic activity and higher worldwide oil demand. However, political issues in both the Middle East oil exporting countries and the former Soviet Union will influence crude oil prices. The fund does not anticipate new Iraqi oil exports before year-end and should be accommodated with only limited disruptions through OPEC production cutbacks and higher worldwide consumption. The longer term prospects for the domestic natural gas industry remain quite favorable due to increased consumption, moderate levels of new drilling and gas reserve additions. In response to the current weakness in crude oil prices, both natural gas demand and gas prices are experiencing modest downward pressure. Once the oil price begins to rebound, a positive natural gas environment will reemerge.

Authors' Comments (PEO): Currently the oil industry is facing several problems, over supply and weaker than anticipated demand. However, the Energy Information Administration (EIA) has projected overall demand growth of 1% by the end of 1994, due to a surge in the North American economy and moderately higher demand in Europe, Asia and solid growth in China. The energy stocks have performed relatively well as investors have accumulated them in search of higher yields. Strong balance sheets made possible by intensive cost cutting early during the recession. PEO is recommended as an inflationary hedge and for income.

Single State—Tax Free Funds

Minnesota Municipal Term Trust   NYSE: **MNA**

Piper Jaffray Tower, 222 S. Ninth Street
Minneapolis, MN 55402
(800) 333-6000
(612) 342-6426

Transfer Agent:
Investors Fiduciary Trust Co.
127 W. 10th St.
Kansas City, MO 64105-1716
(816) 474-8786

Tax-Free Income

Results

For 12-months Ending 4/29/94	Period End	Period Begin	Distributions	Yield Dist (%)	Total Return (%)
Share Price ($)	10.50	10.88	0.51	4.69	1.19
NAV per Share ($)	10.51	10.76		4.74	2.42

Background: Initial public offering September 19, 1991 of 5,727,000 shares at $10 per share. Initial NAV was $9.45 per share.

Objective: Seeks high current income exempt from Federal and Minnesota State income taxes. The fund will terminate and distribute all of its assets to shareholders on or shortly before April 15, 2002. Termination may be extended to April 15, 2007. At least 65% of the fund's assets will be invested in municipal securities rated A or higher. The fund will not invest in any obligations rated below BB or non-rated.

Portfolio: (3/31/94) Minnesota Municipal Coupons 91%, Minnesota Municipal Zeros 9%. Portfolio Ratings: AAA 45%, AA 30%, A 24%, BBB 1%.

Capitalization: (12/31/93) Common stock outstanding 5,732,710. Leveraged with 576 shares preferred stock with $50,000 per share liquidation preference. No long-term debt.

Average Maturity (years): 18
Fee: 0.25%   *Fund Manager:* Piper Capital Management, Inc.
Income Distribution: Monthly   *Capital Gains Distribution:* Annually
Reinvestment Plan: Yes   *Shareholder Reports:* Semi-Annually

5 Year Performance

Fiscal Year Ending 12/31	1993	1992	1991	1990	1989
Net Assets ($mil)	93.70	87.00	84.30	-	-
Net Income Distribution ($)	0.61	0.61	0.10	-	-
Capital Gains Distribution ($)	0.00	0.01	0.00	-	-
Total Distribution ($)	0.61	0.62	0.10	-	-
Yield from Distribution (%)	5.88	5.83	-	-	-
Expense Ratio (%)	0.65	0.66	0.55	-	-
Portfolio Turnover (%)	1.00	17.00	23.00	-	-
NAV per Share ($)	11.32	10.15	9.68	-	-
Market Price per Share ($)	11.25	10.38	10.63	-	-
Premium (Discount) (%)	-0.62	2.27	9.71	-	-
Total Return, Stock Price (%)	14.26	3.48	-	-	-

Minnesota Municipal Term Trust

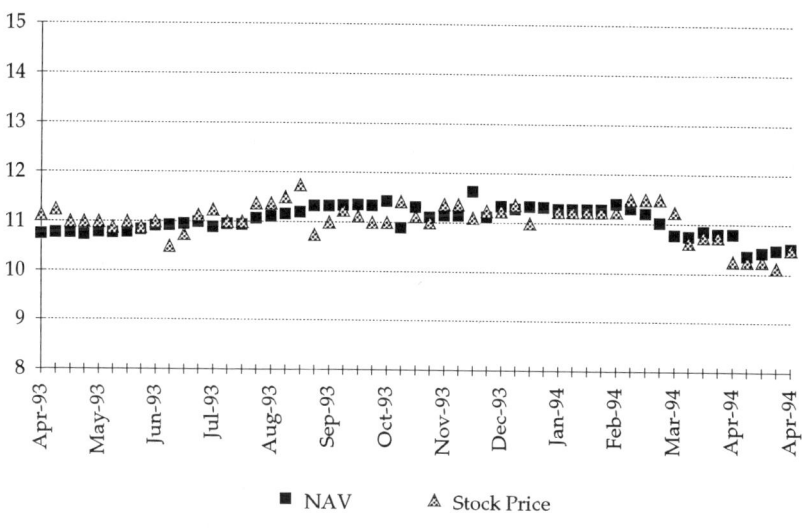

Premium/Discount Spread

■ NAV   △ Stock Price

Fund Outlook (MNA): To preserve a high level of tax-exempt income, trading activity in the fund has been minimal and will continue if interest rates maintain their relative stability or move lower over the life of the fund. The fund is constantly monitoring the credit quality of the portfolio and will restructure holdings as necessary. The fund continues to be invested in quality Minnesota bonds at yields substantially higher than yields on bonds available today with similar quality and maturities. Call protection extends to nearly the fund's termination date. The fund derives two major advantages from pre-refunded holdings. First, because these bonds are now backed by U.S. government obligations, credit risk is eliminated. Second, because these holdings now effectively mature on their first call date—approximately the fund's termination target—interest rate risk is eliminated on that date. In addition, the relatively low, short-term tax-exempt interest rate environment has allowed the fund to build a dividend reserve which should enable it to pay over 8.8% on its preferred stock for a full year before the common stock dividend would have to be lower than its current level.

Authors' Comments (MNA): The trust is to terminate on or about April 15, 2002, when a distribution of $10 share is the target payment. Despite being limited somewhat to shorter maturities to meet the termination objective, MNA does provide a satisfactory yield. The call protection extending near the fund's termination date is an attractive feature. The fund is leveraged. MNA's 12-month trailing return ranks first among the five Minnesota traded closed-end funds.

Nuveen California Investment Quality Municipal Fund

333 W. Wacker Drive
Chicago, IL 60606
(800) 252-4630
(312) 917-7700

Tax-Free Income

NYSE: NQC
Transfer Agent
U.S. Trust, Nuveen Exchange-Traded
Fund Investor Services
770 Broadway
New York, NY 10003
(800) 257-8787

Results

For 12 Months Ending 4/29/94	Period End	Period Begin	Distributions	Yield Dist (%)	Total Return (%)
Share Price ($)	15.13	16.88	1.15	6.81	-3.55
NAV per Share ($)	15.16	16.16		7.12	0.93

Background: Initial public offering November 20, 1990 of 11,500,000 shares at $15 per share. Initial NAV was $14.05 per share.

Objective: Seeks high current income exempt from Federal and California state income taxes and enhancement of portfolio value. At least 80% of the fund's assets will be invested in California municipal obligations rated in the top four categories by S&P or Moody's.

Portfolio: (2/28/94) Municipal Bonds 100%, Health Care Facilities 10%, Lease Rental Facilities 9%, Housing Facilities 7%, Water & Sewer Facilities 4%. Portfolio Ratings: AAA 41%, AA 29%, A 28%, BBB 12%.

Capitalization: (2/28/94) Common stock outstanding 12,955,280. Fund is leveraged with 3,600 shares preferred stock, stated value $50,000 per share.

Average Maturity (years): 23.9

Fee: 0.60%   *Fund Manager:* Nuveen Advisory Corporation
Income Distribution: Monthly   *Capital Gains Distribution:* Annually
Reinvestment Plan: Yes   *Shareholder Reports:* Annually

5 Year Performance

Fiscal Year Ending: 8/31	1993	1992	1991	1990	1989
Net Assets ($mil)	301.90	287.60	276.60	-	-
Net Income Distributions ($)	1.15	0.85	0.76	-	-
Capital Gains Distribution ($)	0.00	0.00	0.00	-	-
Total Distribution ($)	1.15	0.85	0.76	-	-
Yield from Distribution ($)	8.25	6.72	5.38	-	-
Expense Ratio (%)	0.78	0.76	0.78	-	-
Portfolio Turnover (%)	13.00	0.00	18.00	-	-
NAV per Share ($)	16.44	15.47	14.70	-	-
Market Price per Share ($)	17.00	16.00	15.63	-	-
Premium (Discount) ($)	3.41	3.43	6.33	-	-
Total Return, Stock Price (%)	14.50	9.09	-	-	-

Nuveen California Investment Quality Municipal Fund

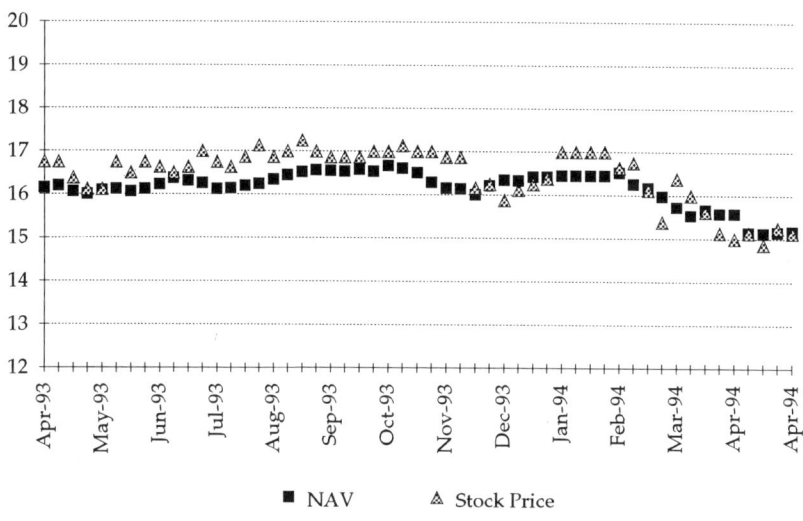

Premium/Discount Spread

■ NAV △ Stock Price

Fund Outlook (NQC): The fund is looking at revenue bonds, essential-purpose issues, such as water, sewer and public power bonds and tax allocated bonds with strong revenue streams. The fund is cautious about housing and health care revenue issues and some newer types of California bonds, such as certificates of participation. The fund is also watching a number of technical factors closely to identify value. For example, imbalances in supply and demand by sector or by individual issuer often can produce attractive investment opportunities. So can changes in the yield curve—the difference in yields on long- and short-term bonds. The fund will also find value by looking at the difference in yields on higher- and lower-quality bonds. Currently, the fund is finding opportunities in A-rated bonds, whose yields compare to BBB-rated bonds. The fund is also looking at bonds with maturities in the 20-year range.

Authors' Comments (NQC): The fund is leveraged with Auction Rate Preferred stock, with dividends reset every seven days by auction. The portfolio contains premium coupon bonds that are not as vulnerable to fluctuations in interest rates. The average weighted coupon is 7.34%. The portfolio contains a large percentage of Certificates of Participation (COP). Technically, the issuing authority has the right to refuse payment, however, failure to do so would have a huge impact on the ability of the municipality to access the municipal market as well as its financing costs. Apparently this is not a concern for the major rating services, in as much as California's COPs were upgraded.

Nuveen Florida Investment Quality Municipal Fund

NYSE: **NQF**

333 W. Wacker Drive
Chicago, IL 60606
(800) 252-4630
(312) 917-7700

Transfer Agent:
U.S. Trust, Nuveen Exchange-Traded Fund Investor Services
770 Broadway
New York, NY 10003
(800) 257-8787

Tax-Free Income

Results

For 12-months Ending 4/29/94	Period End	Period Begin	Distributions	Yield Dist (%)	Total Return (%)
Share Price ($)	15.00	16.75	0.99	5.91	-4.54
NAV per Share ($)	15.17	15.81		6.26	2.21

Background: Initial public offering February 21, 1991 of 15,680,000 shares at $15 per share. Initial net asset value $14.05 per share.

Objective: Seeks current income exempt from Federal income tax. The fund will invest primarily in investment-grade quality municipal bonds.

Portfolio: (12/31/93) Municipal Bonds 99%, Short-Term & Other 1%. Sector Weightings: Health Care Facilities 18%, Water & Sewer Facilities 13%, Housing Facilities 12%, Electric Utilities 9%. Portfolio Ratings: AAA 63%, AA 26%, A 3%, BBB 7 %.

Capitalization: (12/31/93) Common stock outstanding 15,962,568. Leveraged with 2,200 preferred shares, stated value $50,000 per share.

Average Maturity (years): 23.2

Fee: 0.60%
Income Distribution: Monthly
Reinvestment Plan: Yes

Fund Manager: Nuveen Advisory Corporation
Capital Gains Distribution: Annually
Shareholder Reports: Semi-Annually

5 Year Performance

Fiscal Year Ending 6/30	1993	1992	1991	1990	1989
Net Assets ($mil)	371.70	346.60	337.80	-	-
Net Income Distribution ($)	1.02	0.66	0.50	-	-
Capital Gains Distribution ($)	0.01	0.00	0.00	-	-
Total Distribution ($)	1.04	0.66	0.50	-	-
Yield from Distribution (%)	6.50	4.26	3.56	-	-
Expense Ratio (%)	0.80	0.77	0.76	-	-
Portfolio Turnover (%)	13.00	3.00	0.00	-	-
NAV per Share ($)	16.03	14.99	14.49	-	-
Market Price per Share ($)	16.63	16.00	15.50	-	-
Premium (Discount) (%)	3.71	6.74	6.14	-	-
Total Return, Stock Price (%)	10.44	7.71	-	-	-

Nuveen Florida Investment Quality Municipal Fund

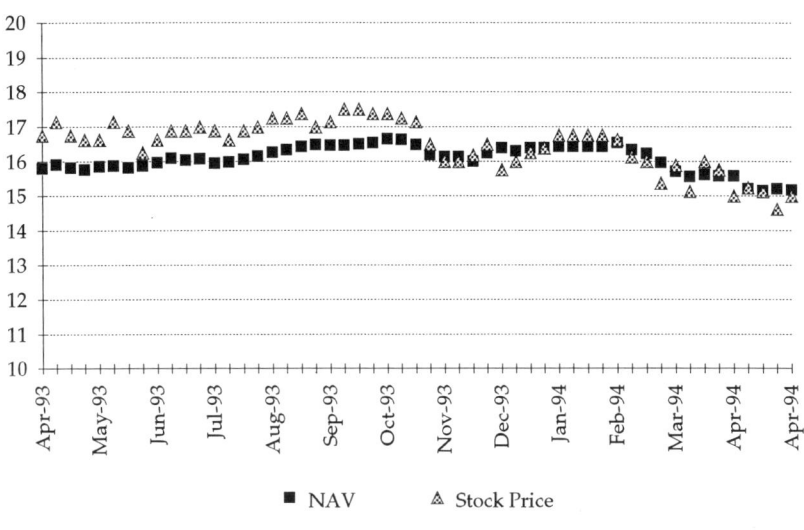

Fund Outlook (NQF): Florida is coming off a year of financial successes. In fiscal 1993, the state maintained a general fund balance of $294 million and had an operating surplus, ending a streak of two consecutive annual operating deficits. Can these results be sustained? On the positive side, the state continues to make significant strides in diversifying its economy away from dependence on tourism and agriculture. While tourism-related revenues were dealt a serious blow by highly publicized crimes against visitors, Florida's service industry—banking, finance and international trade—is surging. Employment growth has escalated, and the unemployment rate is now consistent with the national average. This growth may prove to be a mixed blessing. The state continues to face significant fiscal challenges in areas including health care financing, education funding, water management and transportation. The demands for infrastructure improvements coupled with the unwillingness of taxpayers to pay for services means the state's legislature will either have to reduce services or develop new sources of revenue.

Authors' Comments (NQF): Because the portfolio contains higher-coupon bonds (the average coupon is 7.27%) that are less sensitive to changes in interest rates, the market value decline in the NAV approximated 3%, as compared to the average decline of 4.3%. The fund also contains a number of pre-refunded bonds, which in essence shorten the maturities of the portfolio. The 12-month trailing return is 2.27% compared to its peer group of 0.39% The fund is leveraged and more volatile.

Nuveen Florida Quality Income Municipal Fund

NYSE: NUF

333 West Wacker Drive
Chicago, IL 60606
(800) 252-4630
(312) 917-7701

Transfer Agent:
U.S. Trust, Nuveen Exchange-Traded
Fund Investor Services
770 Broadway, New York, NY 10003
(800) 257-8787

Tax-Free Income

Results

For 12-months Ending 4/29/94	Period End	Period Begin	Distributions	Yield Dist (%)	Total Return (%)
Share Price ($)	14.13	16.13	0.97	6.01	-6.39
NAV per Share ($)	14.76	15.60		6.22	-0.83

Background: Initial public offering October 17, 1991 of 11,744,972 shares at $15 per share. Initial NAV $14.05 per share.

Objective: Seeks high current income exempt from Federal income tax and enhancement of portfolio value. The fund will invest substantially all of its assets in investment-grade Florida municipal obligations or in unrated securities that the fund adviser believes to be of investment-grade quality.

Portfolio: (12/31/93) Municipal Bonds 97%, Short-Term & Other 3%. Sector Weighting: Transportation 15%, Electric Utilities 15%, Health Care Facilities 12%, Pollution Control Facilities 12%. Portfolio Ratings: AAA 57%, AA 29%, A 7%, BBB 6%.

Capitalization: (12/31/93) Common stock outstanding 11,914,346. Leveraged with 1,700 shares preferred stock, stated value $50,000 per share.

Average Maturity (years): 24.4
Fee: 0.65%
Income Distribution: Monthly
Reinvestment Plan: Yes

Fund Manager: Nuveen Advisory Corporation
Capital Gains Distribution: Annually
Shareholder Reports: Semi-Annually

5 Year Performance

Fiscal Year Ending 6/30	1993	1992	1991	1990	1989
Net Assets ($mil)	276.70	256.70	-	-	-
Net Income Distribution ($)	0.97	0.46	-	-	-
Capital Gains Distribution ($)	0.03	0.00	-	-	-
Total Distribution ($)	1.00	0.46	-	-	-
Yield from Distribution (%)	6.84	-	-	-	-
Expense Ratio (%)	0.86	0.81	-	-	-
Portfolio Turnover (%)	14.00	0.00	-	-	-
NAV per Share ($)	15.87	14.57	-	-	-
Market Price per Share ($)	15.63	14.63	-	-	-
Premium (Discount) (%)	-1.54	0.41	-	-	-
Total Return, Stock Price (%)	13.67	-	-	-	-

Nuveen Florida Quality Income Municipal Fund

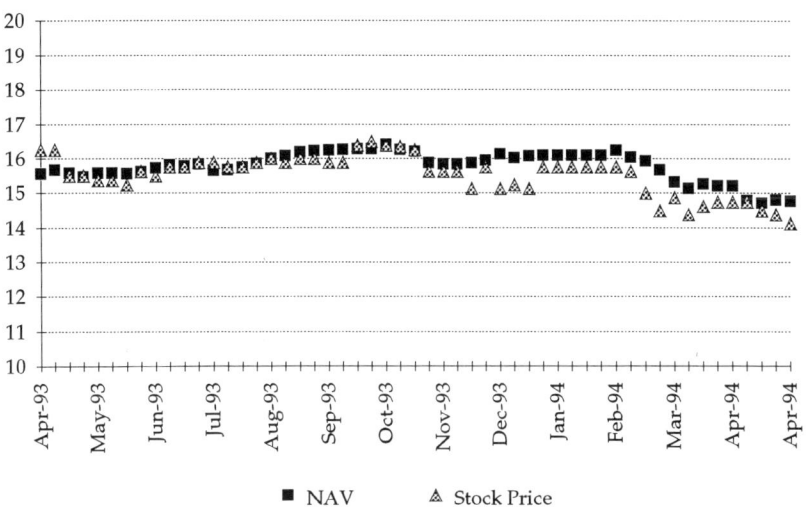

Fund Outlook (NUF): Florida is coming off a year of financial successes. In fiscal 1993, the state maintained a general fund balance of $294 million and had an operating surplus, ending a streak of two consecutive annual operating deficits. Can these results be sustained? On the positive side, the state continues to make significant strides in diversifying its economy away from dependence on tourism and agriculture. While tourism-related revenues were dealt a serious blow by highly publicized crimes against visitors, Florida's service industry—banking, finance and international trade—is surging. Employment growth has escalated, and the unemployment rate is now conistent with the national average. This growth, however, may prove to be a mixed blessing. The state continues to face significant fiscal challenges in areas including health care financing, education funding, water management and transportation. Demands for infrastructure improvements coupled with the unwillingness of Florida taxpayers to pay for services means the state's legislature will have to reduce services or develop new sources of revenue.

Authors' Comments (NUF): A relative newcomer (1991 IPO), this fund had relatively lower coupon bonds to select from. As a result, management had to reach out to longer maturities for yield. Currently, the average weighted coupon for the portfolio is 6.81%, while the average weighted maturity is 23.3 years. This has exposed the fund to interest rate sensitivity. A good choice for the aggressive Florida tax-free investor, this fund should outperform its peers if rates turn around and head southward.

Nuveen New Jersey Quality Income Municipal Fund

333 W. Wacker Drive
Chicago, IL 60606
(800) 252-4630
(312) 917-7702

Tax-Free Income

NYSE: NUJ
Transfer Agent:
U.S. Trust, Nuveen Exchange-Traded Fund Investor Services
770 Broadway
New York, NY 10003
(800) 257-8787

Results

For 12-months Ending 4/29/94	Period End	Period Begin	Distributions	Yield Dist (%)	Total Return (%)
Share Price ($)	14.63	15.63	1.02	6.53	0.13
NAV per Share ($)	14.54	15.22		6.70	2.23

Background: Initial public offering October 17, 1991 of 7,000,000 shares at $15 per share. Initial NAV was $14.05 per share.

Objective: Seeks current income exempt from Federal and New Jersey State income taxes. Capital appreciation is secondary. The fund will invest substantially all of its assets in New Jersey investment-grade municipal obligations.

Portfolio: (12/31/93) Municipal Bonds 99%, Short-Term & Other 1%. Sector Weightngs: Housing Facilities 16%, Transportation 12%, Health Care Facilities 10%, General Obligation 24%. Portfolio Ratings: AAA 34%, AA 26%, A 25%, BBB 6%.

Capitalization: (12/31/93) Common stock outstanding 7,193,880. Leveraged with 1,000 shares preferred stock, stated value $50,000 per share.

Average Maturity (years): 21.8
Fee: 0.65%
Income Distribution: Monthly
Reinvestment Plan: Yes
Fund Manager: Nuveen Advisory Corporation
Capital Gains Distribution: Annually
Shareholder Reports: Semi-Annually

5 Year Performance

Fiscal Year Ending 6/30	1993	1992	1991	1990	1989
Net Assets ($mil)	160.50	152.50	-	-	-
Net Income Distribution ($)	1.02	0.44	-	-	-
Capital Gains Distribution ($)	0.00	0.00	-	-	-
Total Distribution ($)	1.02	0.44	-	-	-
Yield from Distribution (%)	7.02	-	-	-	-
Expense Ratio (%)	0.90	0.87	-	-	-
Portfolio Turnover (%)	2.00	9.00	-	-	-
NAV per Share ($)	15.48	14.56	-	-	-
Market Price per Share ($)	16.13	14.50	-	-	-
Premium (Discount) (%)	4.17	-0.41	-	-	-
Total Return, Stock Price (%)	18.28	-	-	-	-

Nuveen New Jersey Quality Income Municipal Fund

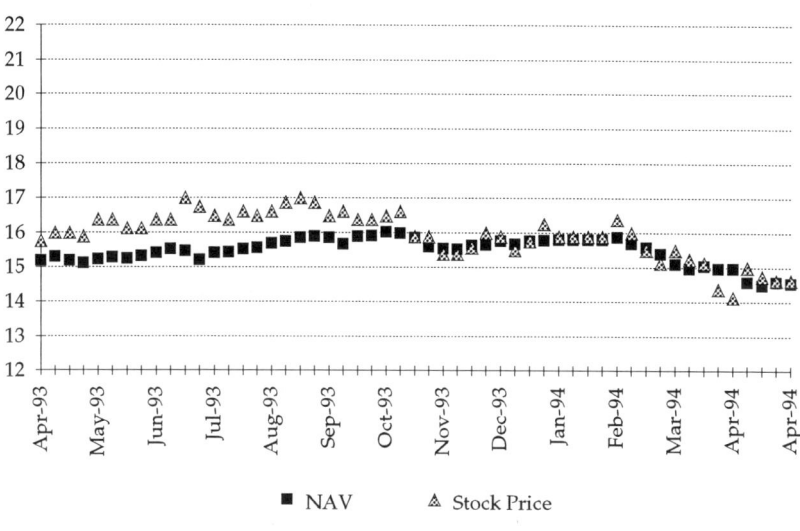

Fund Outlook (NUJ): Economic recovery was painfully slow in coming to New Jersey, but there are signs that it has at last arrived, and the outlook for the state is modestly positive. The state ended fiscal 1993 with a $792 million budget surplus, and the fiscal 1994 budget was adopted by the legislature without the acrimony or gimmickry that has surrounded the budget process in previous years. This new legislative focus has been matched by the state's voters, who in November elected a new governor. Together these developments signal that the political paralysis which as been one of New Jersey's chronic woes may be coming to an end. The state has significant strengths, notably a diverse economy, an educated workforce, a well-developed interstate transportation system, and its proximity to New York City.

Authors' Comments (NUJ): NUJ has been the top performer among the New Jersey tax frees. But we primarily like this fund for its inherent defensive nature. The secret to the fund's success is, surprisingly enough, its age. With a 1991 inception date, NUJ is one of the older New Jersey tax-free funds. It was therefore able to purchase higher-coupon issues when yields were higher. Plus, a significant percentage of its bonds have been pre-refunded which also tempers volatility. The fund is leveraged with auction rate preferreds which enhances yield, in both directions.

Nuveen New York Investment Quality Municipal Fund

333 W. Wacker Drive
Chicago, IL 60606
(800) 252-4630
(312) 917-7703

NYSE: **NQN**
Transfer Agent:
U.S. Trust, Nuveen Exchange-Traded Fund Investor Services
770 Broadway, New York, NY 10003
(800) 257-8787

Tax-Free Income

Results

For 12-months Ending 4/29/94	Period End	Period Begin	Distributions	Yield Dist (%)	Total Return (%)
Share Price ($)	15.50	17.25	1.01	5.86	-4.29
NAV per Share ($)	15.95	16.63		6.07	1.98

Background: Initial public offering November 20, 1990 of 15,000,000 shares at $15 per share. Initial NAV was $14.05 per share.

Objective: Seeks high current income exempt from Federal, New York State and City income taxes. Enhancement of portfolio value relative to the New York municipal bond market is secondary. The fund will invest substantially all of its assets in New York municipal bonds whose timely payment of principal and interest is guaranteed by AAA-rated insurers or backed by escrow accounts containing U. S. Government or U.S. Government Agencies securities.

Portfolio: (9/30/93) Municipal Bonds 98%, Short-Term & Other 2%. Sector Weightings: Transportation 13%, Housing Facilities 12%, Pollution Control Facilities 11%, Health Care Facilities 10%. Portfolio Ratings: AAA 87%, AA 11%, A 1%, BBB 1%.

Capitalization: (9/30/93) Common stock outstanding 16,941,389. Leveraged with 2,400 shares auction-rate preferred stock, stated value $50,000 per share.

Average Maturity (years): 25.8
Fee: 0.60%
Income Distribution: Monthly
Reinvestment Plan: Yes

Fund Manager: Nuveen Advisory Corporation
Capital Gains Distribution: Annually
Shareholder Reports: Semi-Annually

5 Year Performance

Fiscal Year Ending 9/30	1993	1992	1991	1990	1989
Net Assets ($mil)	412.90	385.10	368.30	-	-
Net Income Distribution ($)	1.10	0.97	0.77	-	-
Capital Gains Distribution ($)	0.00	0.02	0.00	-	-
Total Distribution ($)	1.10	0.99	0.77	-	-
Yield from Distribution (%)	6.57	6.29	-	-	-
Expense Ratio (%)	0.83	0.79	0.80	-	-
Portfolio Turnover (%)	1.00	5.00	9.00	-	-
NAV per Share ($)	17.29	15.83	14.98	-	-
Market Price per Share ($)	17.38	16.75	15.75	-	-
Premium (Discount) (%)	0.49	5.81	5.14	-	-
Total Return, Stock Price (%)	10.71	14.83	-	-	-

Premium/Discount Spread

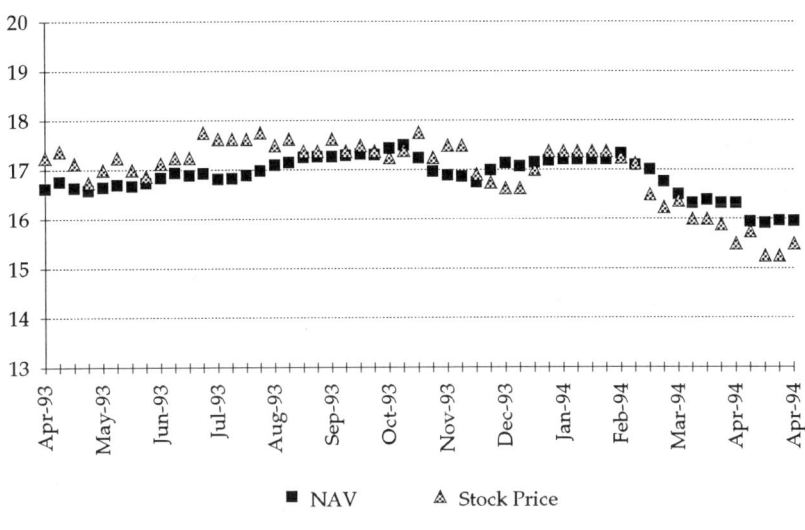

Fund Outlook (NQN): The New York State economy continues to show signs of strengthening after years of recession-related decline. Over the past 12 months, the state has achieved a revenue surplus, job losses to other states have slowed, and unemployment has declined steadily. Most important, the state legislature is becoming more focused on financial issues, notably the state's high business tax burden and inequities in school funding and the local costs of Medicare. While the legislature's budget debate was deadlocked over these issues in March and April, Governor Cuomo recently introduced a compromise plan which appears to balance revenues and spending, and should be acceptable statewide. This willingness to address financial issues before they become deficits has been welcomed by investors, a fact reflected most clearly in municipal bond insurers' willingness to insure larger state appropriation issues.

Authors' Comments (NQN): What with New York's infamous credit problems, it would make sense to select a fund with a preponderance of AAA issues. And that's exactly what NQN has going for it—85% AAA weighting. This, coupled with the age and low turnover allow for a cushy coupon buffer against interest rate sensitivity. However, the fund is leveraged. Should interest rates back down, this fund will soar.

Nuveen Pennsylvania Investment Quality Municipal Fund

NYSE: NQP

333 West Wacker Drive
Chicago, IL 60606
(800) 252-4630
(312) 917-7700

Transfer Agent:
U.S. Trust, Nuveen Exchange-Traded
Fund Investor Services
770 Broadway, New York, NY 10003
(800) 257-8787

Tax-Free Income

Results

For 12-months Ending 4/29/94	Period End	Period Begin	Distributions	Yield Dist (%)	Total Return (%)
Share Price ($)	15.38	17.63	1.15	7.47	-6.24
NAV per Share ($)	15.51	16.17		7.41	3.03

Background: Initial public offering February 21, 1991 of 8,200,000 shares at $15 per share. Initial NAV was $14.05 per share.
Objective: Seeks current income exempt from Federal and Pennsylvania State income taxes. Enhancement of portfolio value is secondary. The fund will invest at least 80% of its assets in Pennsylvania municipal obligations rated in the top four categories by S&P or Moody's. Up to 20% may be invested in non-rated Pennsylvania municipal obligations the adviser considers to be of investment-grade quality.
Portfolio: (12/31/93) Municipal Bonds 99%, Other 1%. Sector Weightings: Health Care 17%, Educational Facilities 15%, Housing 11%. Portfolio Rating: AAA 53%, AA 25%, A 7%, BBB 14%.
Capitalization: (12/31/93) Common stock outstanding 8,442,453. Leveraged with 1,200 shares preferred stock, stated value $50,000 per share.
Average Maturity (years): 21.4
Fee: 0.60%
Income Distribution: Monthly
Reinvestment Plan: Yes
Fund Manager: Nuveen Advisory Corporation
Capital Gains Distribution: Annually
Shareholder Reports: Semi-Annually

5 Year Performance

Fiscal Year Ending 6/30	1993	1992	1991	1990	1989
Net Assets ($mil)	197.90	185.60	187.80	-	-
Net Income Distribution ($)	1.12	0.66	0.50	-	-
Capital Gains Distribution ($)	0.00	0.00	0.00	-	-
Total Distribution ($)	1.12	0.66	0.50	-	-
Yield from Distribution (%)	7.14	4.26	3.56	-	-
Expense Ratio (%)	0.86	0.78	0.81	-	-
Portfolio Turnover (%)	2.00	0.00	0.00	-	-
NAV per Share ($)	16.42	15.14	14.60	-	-
Market Price per Share ($)	17.50	15.75	15.50	-	-
Premium (Discount) (%)	6.58	2.38	7.05	-	-
Total Return, Stock Price (%)	18.83	5.97	6.71	-	-

Nuveen Pennsylvania Investment Quality Municipal Fund

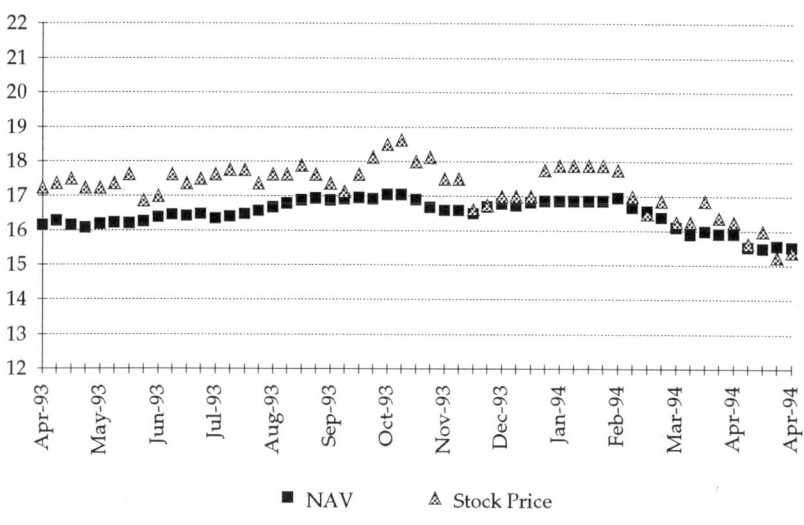

Premium/Discount Spread

■ NAV   △ Stock Price

Fund Outlook (NQP): Fiscal 1993 marked the second consecutive year in which Pennsylvania achieved a budget surplus, and budget for fiscal 1994 seems equally sound. The budget holds no tax increases, keeps expenses below revenues, and was passed five weeks before deadline. While the state's economy clearly faces major challenges, notably in the areas of income growth and job creation, the government has passed an economic development plan, touted as the nation's largest. While recent statistics are promising, a mood of pessimism continues to hang over much of the state's business community, which faces the highest corporate tax rate in the nation. It remains to be seen if the development plan will produce the desired results.

Authors' Comments (NQP): This fund is our top pick for a risk-averse Pennsylvanian seeking high tax-free yields. The fund has a generous portfolio of high yielding, older-issues purchased when yields were loftier. This has allowed handsome returns as rates fell, and because of the high yield, and large amount of pre-refunds, nearly 43%, the portfolio offers protection should rates continue to rise. The fund is not a perfect fortress as it is leveraged. However, the duration, coupon rate, and stability of the portfolio places it number one in its category.

Taurus MuniCalifornia Holdings, Inc.

P.O. Box 9011
Princeton, NJ 08543
(800) 543-6217
(609) 282-2800

Tax-Free Income

NYSE: MCF
Transfer Agent:
Bank of New York
110 Washington St.
New York, NY 10286
(800) 524-4458

Results

For 12-months Ending 4/29/94	Period End	Period Begin	Distributions	Yield Dist (%)	Total Return (%)
Share Price ($)	10.13	12.88	0.96	7.45	-13.90
NAV per Share ($)	10.88	12.11		7.93	-2.23

Background: Initial public offering January 25, 1990 of 5,000,000 shares at $12 per share. Initial NAV was $11.16 per share.
Objective: Seeks current income exempt from Federal and California State income taxes. Of the fund's assets, 80% will be invested in long-term California municipal obligations rated in the top four categories by S&P or Moody's. The fund may invest in certain tax-exempt securities classified as "private activity" bonds, which may be subject to the Alternative Minimum Tax (AMT).
Portfolio: (10/31/92) Municipal Bonds 97.7%, Other 2.3%. State Weightings: California 95.5%, Puerto Rico 2.2%. Portfolio Ratings: Investment Grade 100%.
Capitalization: (10/31/92) Common stock outstanding 5,121,232. Leveraged with 400 shares auction-rate preferred stock with $50,000 per share liquidation preference.
Average Maturity (years): 21.8
Fee: 0.50%
Income Distribution: Monthly
Reinvestment Plan: Yes
Fund Manager: Fund Asset Management, Inc.
Capital Gains Distribution: Annually
Shareholder Reports: Quarterly

5 Year Performance

Fiscal Year Ending 10/31	1993	1992	1991	1990	1989
Net Assets ($mil)	83.30	79.00	78.50	74.50	-
Net Income Distribution ($)	0.80	0.88	0.82	0.49	-
Capital Gains Distribution ($)	0.20	0.06	0.01	0.00	-
Total Distribution ($)	1.00	0.94	0.83	0.49	-
Yield from Distribution (%)	8.00	7.67	7.46	-	-
Expense Ratio (%)	0.94	0.88	0.91	0.97	-
Portfolio Turnover (%)	52.04	50.50	27.89	85.91	-
NAV per Share ($)	12.51	11.53	11.66	11.05	-
Market Price per Share ($)	13.00	12.50	12.25	11.13	-
Premium (Discount) (%)	3.92	8.41	5.06	0.72	-
Total Return, Stock Price (%)	12.00	9.71	17.52	-	-

Taurus MuniCalifornia Holdings, Inc.

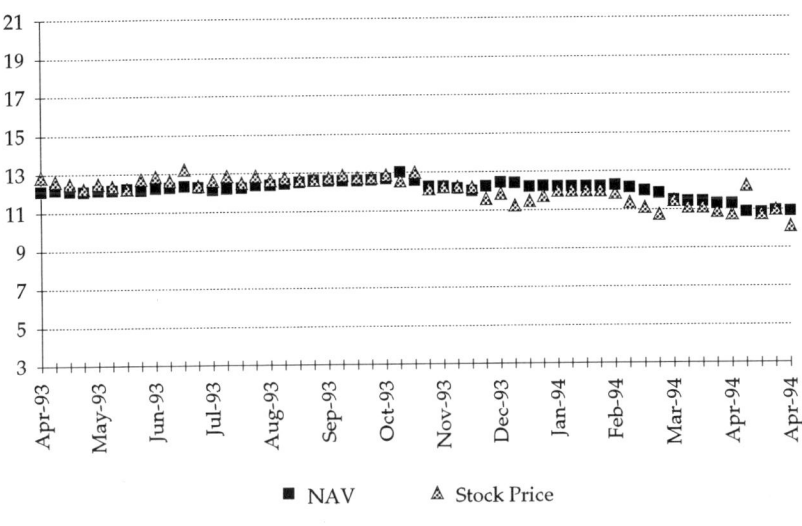

Premium/Discount Spread

■ NAV △ Stock Price

Fund Outlook (MCF): The fund currently enjoys a high current return of tax-exempt income generated through several of its high-coupon holdings that were purchased in a period of higher interest rates. During the October 1993 quarter, the fund sold a portion of these high-coupon holdings that were purchased in a period of higher interest rates because of their limited capacity for further price appreciation. A portion of the proceeds was committed to high-quality current coupon California bonds, and the balance was kept in short-term as equivalent reserves. The fund also made selective sales of serial maturity holdings with the proceeds remaining in similar short-term reserves. The fund anticipates using any future deterioration in bond prices to purchase lower-coupon, more performance oriented securities. This current cash reserve position will allow MCF the liquidity to put this plan into effect. This will be accomplished by using a heavy new issuance of high-grade California paper.

Authors' Comments (MCF): A relatively high premium coupon portfolio has helped to insulate MCF from rising interest rates. Fund management has been reallocating to current-coupon, more interest-rate sensitive issues in anticipation of sliding rates. The fund is leveraged to the tune of $20 million with auction rate preferreds. The investment across the investment-grade spectrum, and the 13% allocation in non-rated issues offers a diversified interest rate cushion of sorts. We like this fund for the more aggressive California tax-free investor.

Van Kampen Merritt New York Quality Municipal Trust

NYSE: VNM

One Parkview Plaza
Oakbrook Terrace, IL 60181
(800) 225-2222

Transfer Agent:
State Street Bank & Trust Co.
P.O. Box 366
Boston, MA 02266
(800) 426-5523

Tax-Free Income

Results

For 12-months Ending 4/29/94	Period End	Period Begin	Distributions	Yield Dist (%)	Total Return (%)
Share Price ($)	15.25	16.50	1.22	7.39	-0.18
NAV per Share ($)	16.50	17.37		7.02	-2.01

Background: Initial public offering September 20, 1991 of 3,033,763 shares at $15 per share. Net proceeds were $45,343,445.

Objective: Seeks a high level of current income exempt from Federal and New York State and City income taxes, consistent with preservation of capital.

Portfolio: (3/31/94) Municipal Bonds 98%, Other Assets 2%. Sector Weightings: General Purpose 20%, Education 8%, Housing 7%, Public Building 7%, Industrial Revenue 6%. Portfolio Ratings: AAA 25%, AA 22%, A 23%, BBB 23%, Non-Rated 6%.

Capitalization: (12/31/93) Common stock outstanding 5,643,496 shares. Leveraged with 900 shares preferred stock, stated value $50,000 per share.

Average Maturity (years): 20.35

Fee: 0.70% *Fund Manager:* Van Kampen Merritt Invest. Adv. Corp.
Income Distribution: Monthly *Capital Gains Distribution:* Annually
Reinvestment Plan: Yes *Shareholder Reports:* Semi-Annually

5 Year Performance

Fiscal Year Ending 8/31	1993	1992	1991	1990	1989
Net Assets ($mil)	147.10	136.70	130.80	-	-
Net Income Distribution ($)	1.20	0.74	-	-	-
Capital Gains Distribution ($)	0.00	0.00	-	-	-
Total Distribution ($)	1.20	0.74	-	-	-
Yield from Distribution (%)	7.68	-	-	-	-
Expense Ratio (%)	0.83	0.78	-	-	-
Portfolio Turnover (%)	25.00	65.00	-	-	-
NAV per Share ($)	17.96	16.30	-	-	-
Market Price per Share ($)	17.50	15.63	-	-	-
Premium (Discount) (%)	-2.56	-4.13	-	-	-
Total Return, Stock Price (%)	19.64	-	-	-	-

Van Kampen Merritt New York Quality Municipal Trust

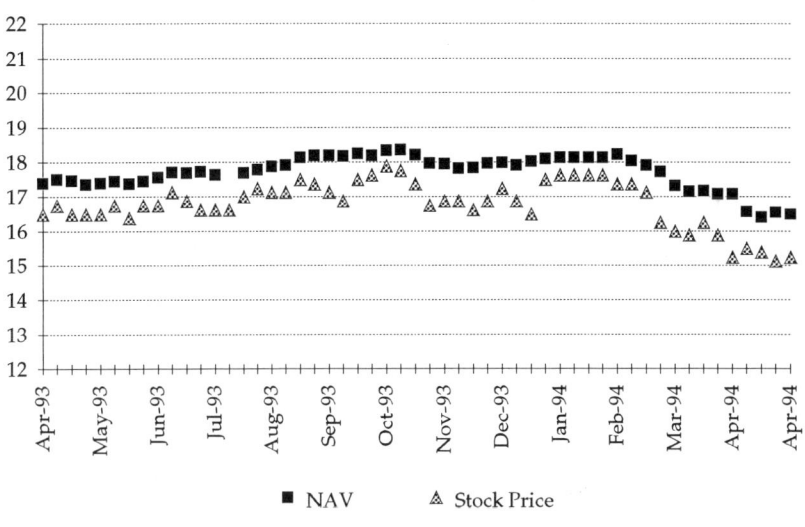

Premium/Discount Spread

■ NAV   △ Stock Price

Fund Outlook (VNM): The old investment adage about keeping a longer-term perspective was most likely phrased with difficult markets in mind. While the trust understands it is often easier to dispense such advice than to practice it, time has proven this axiom to be quite reliable. While the principal value of a tax-free investment will fluctuate over time, the trust offers a high and fairly stable stream of current income exempt from federal as well as New York State and New York city income taxes, consistent with preservation of capital. The non-diversified portfolio is composed of investment-grade tax-exempt New York municipal securities of which 80% are investment-grade at the time of investment.

Authors' Comments (VNM): This is a fund for aggressive New York tax-free investors. If you feel that rates could dip in the not-too-distant future this is the fund for you. The fund leveraged with $45 million of preferred shares and sports an interest rate sensitive portfolio with an average weighted coupon of 6.62% priced above par.

Van Kampen Merritt Pennsylvania Quality Municipal

NYSE: VPQ

One Parkview Plaza
Oakbrook Terrace, IL 60181
(800) 225-2222

Transfer Agent:
State Street Bank & Trust Co.
225 Franklin St.
Boston, MA 02266
(800) 426-5523

Tax-Free Income

Results

For 12-months Ending 4/29/94	Period End	Period Begin	Distributions	Yield Dist (%)	Total Return (%)
Share Price ($)	16.00	16.88	1.12	6.64	1.42
NAV per Share ($)	16.31	17.24		6.50	1.10

Background: Initial public offering September 20, 1991 of 5,798,057 shares at $15 per share. Initial NAV was $14.78 per share.

Objective: Seeks a high level of current income exempt from regular Federal and Pennsylvania State income taxes, consistent with the preservation of capital.

Portfolio: (3/31/94) Municipal Bonds 98%, Other Assets 2%. Sector Weightings: Health Care 36%, General Purpose 17%, Public Building 8%, Public Education 4%. Portfolio Ratings: AAA 41%, AA 4%, A 17%, BBB 35%, Non-Rated 4%.

Capitalization: (12/31/93) Common stock outstanding 8,060,902. Fund is leveraged with 1,300 shares preferred stock, stated value $50,000 per share.

Average Maturity (years): 20.4

Fee: 0.70%   *Fund Manager:* Van Kampen Merritt Invest. Adv. Corp.
Income Distribution: Monthly   *Capital Gains Distribution:* Annually
Reinvestment Plan: Yes   *Shareholder Reports:* Semi-Annually

5 Year Performance

Fiscal Year Ending 8/31	1993	1992	1991	1990	1989
Net Assets ($mil)	208.90	197.00	187.40	-	-
Net Income Distribution ($)	1.07	0.75	-	-	-
Capital Gains Distribution ($)	0.04	0.00	-	-	-
Total Distribution ($)	1.11	0.75	-	-	-
Yield from Distribution (%)	7.05	-	-	-	-
Expense Ratio (%)	1.64	1.11	-	-	-
Portfolio Turnover (%)	4.00	55.37	-	-	-
NAV per Share ($)	17.99	16.39	-	-	-
Market Price per Share ($)	17.50	15.75	-	-	-
Premium (Discount) (%)	-2.72	-3.89	-	-	-
Total Return, Stock Price (%)	18.16	-	-	-	-

Van Kampen Merritt Pennsylvania Quality Municipal

Premium/Discount Spread

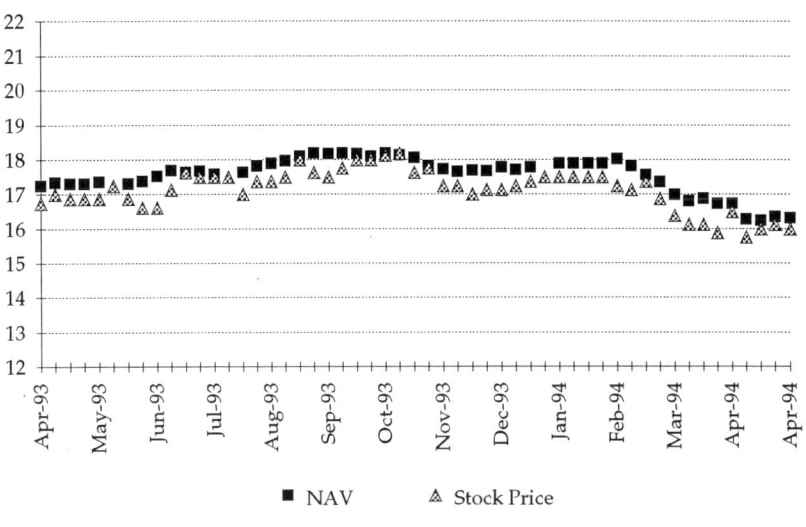

■ NAV △ Stock Price

Fund Outlook (VPQ): How high short rates will rise and where long rates will move in response remains to be seen. VPQ tends to believe, however, that long rates have to this point overreacted to the short rate pressure or at least have factored in further short-term rate increases at their current levels. In other words, the trust likes to believe that while long rates may move higher, most of the increase is behind us. VPQ continues to believe that municipals are undervalued and will likely outperform the Treasury market for the remainder of the year given the technical factors it suspects will eventually influence municipals this year.

Authors' Comments (VPQ): The averaged weighted coupon in the portfolio is 6.52%. The portfolio contains zero-coupon bonds, adding to the volatility in a sharply rising interest rate environment. During the February muni crash, the fund's NAV declined 4.2%, while the market value dropped 5.1%. The fund is leveraged, adding to volatility.

Municipal Bond Funds—Leveraged

American Municipal Term Trust, Inc.   NYSE: **AXT**

Piper Jaffray Tower, 222 S. Ninth Street
Minneapolis, MN 55402
(800) 866-7778
(612) 342-6223

Transfer Agent:
Investors Fiduciary Trust Co.
127 W. 10th St.
Kansas City, MO 64105-1716
(816) 474-8786

Tax-Free Income

Results

For 12-months *Ending 4/29/94*	Period End	Period Begin	Distributions	Yield Dist (%)	Total Return (%)
Share Price ($)	10.50	10.88	0.54	4.96	1.47
NAV per Share ($)	11.07	11.27		4.79	3.02

Background: Initial public offering March, 1991 of 7,500,000 shares at $10 per share. Initial NAV was $9.44 per share.

Objective: Seeks high current income exempt from regular Federal income tax and to return $10 per share to investors on termination of the trust on or shortly before April 15, 2001.

Portfolio: (3/31/94) Municipal Coupons 92%, Municipal Zeros 8%. 67% of bonds are insured. Sector Weightings: Electrical Revenue 20%, General Obligation 13%, Hospital Revenue 17%, Water & Sewer Utility Revenue 15%, Sales & Excise Tax Revenue 15%. Portfolio Ratings: AAA 79%, AA 8%, A 11%, BBB 2%.

Capitalization: (12/31/93) Common stock outstanding 8,455,000. Fund is leveraged with 850 shares of auction-rate preferred stock with stated liquidation value of $50,000.

Average Maturity (years): 17
Fee: 0.25%   *Fund Manager:* Piper Capital Management, Inc.
Income Distribution: Monthly   *Capital Gains Distribution:* Annually
Reinvestment Plan: Yes   *Shareholder Reports:* Quarterly

5 Year Performance

Fiscal Year Ending 12/31	1993	1992	1991	1990	1989
Net Assets ($mil)	142.90	131.80	127.00	-	-
Net Income Distribution ($)	0.65	0.65	0.49	-	-
Capital Gains Distribution ($)	0.00	0.00	0.00	-	-
Total Distribution ($)	0.65	0.65	0.49	-	-
Yield from Distribution (%)	6.19	6.42	-	-	-
Expense Ratio (%)	0.59	0.62	0.56	-	-
Portfolio Turnover (%)	2.00	4.00	24.00	-	-
NAV per Share ($)	11.89	10.57	9.99	-	-
Market Price per Share ($)	10.88	10.50	10.13	-	-
Premium (Discount) (%)	-8.54	-0.57	1.30	-	-
Total Return, Stock Price (%)	9.81	10.07	-	-	-

American Municipal Term Trust, Inc.

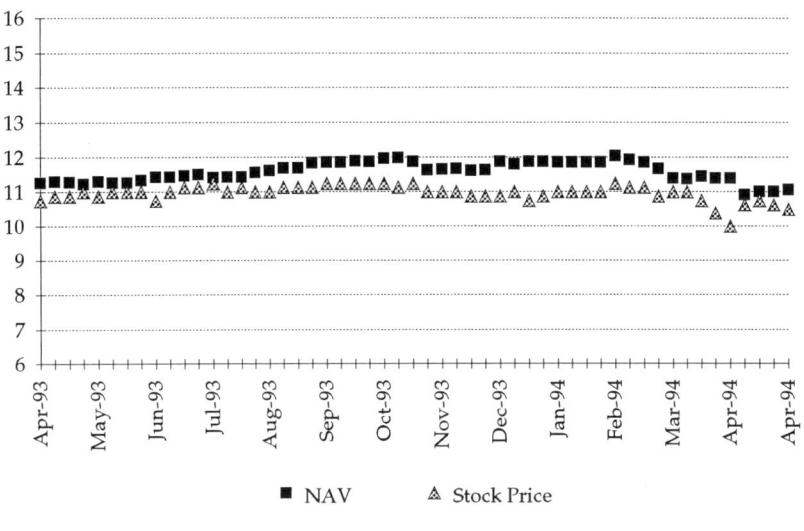

Fund Outlook (AXT): In order to preserve a relatively high level of tax-exempt income, trading activity in the fund has been minimal and is expected to be minimal if interest rates maintain their relative stability or continue to move lower over the life of the fund. The fund is, of course, constantly monitoring the credit quality of the portfolio. The fund will restructure holdings as necessary to assist in meeting the fund's objectives should credit or interest rate conditions dictate. The fund continues to be fully invested in high-quality municipal bonds at yields that are substantially higher than yields on bonds available today with similar quality and maturities. Call protection extends to nearly the fund's expected termination date.

Authors' Comments (AXT): The average weighted coupon is 6.57%. Despite the high-quality of the portfolio, the relatively high average coupon and relatively short maturities, the NAV has declined 8.9% since January 28, 1994. However, it should be pointed out that, as long as the NAV stays above the required liquidating value, $10, there is no concern. The trust is leveraged.

Kemper Municipal Income Trust

120 S. LaSalle Street
Chicago, IL 60603
(312) 781-1121
(800) 422-2848

Tax-Free Income

NYSE: KTF
Transfer Agent:
Investors Fiduciary Trust Co.
127 W. 10th St.
Kansas City, MO 64105
(816) 474-8786

Results

For 12-months Ending 4/29/94	Period End	Period Begin	Distributions	Yield Dist (%)	Total Return (%)
Share Price ($)	11.75	13.00	1.23	9.46	-0.15
NAV per Share ($)	12.02	12.92		9.52	2.55

Background: Initial public offering October 20, 1988 of 35,000,000 shares at $12 per share. Initial NAV was $11.11 per share.

Objective: Seeks a high level of current income exempt from regular Federal income tax by investing in a diversified portfolio of investment-grade, tax-exempt municipal securities. Average maturity of securities within the portfolio is expected to range from 10 to 30 years. The fund may not invest more than 20% of net assets in unrated securities.

Portfolio: (12/31/93) Municipal Bonds 98%, Cash & Other 2.0%. Portfolio Ratings: AAA 20.0%, AA 25%, A 27%, BBB 24%, Non-Rated 4%. Sector Weightings: Housing 26%, Health 11%, Utility 10%.

Capitalization: (12/31/93) Common stock outstanding 37,208,379. Leveraged with 43,000 preferred shares, stated value $5,000 per share.

Average Maturity (years): 22.9
Fee: 0.55%   *Fund Manager:* Kemper Financial Services, Inc.
Income Distribution: Monthly   *Capital Gains Distribution:* Annually
Reinvestment Plan: Yes   *Shareholder Reports:* Semi-Annually

5 Year Performance

Fiscal Year Ending 11/30	1993	1992	1991	1990	1989
Net Assets ($mil)	493.10	461.10	434.90	408.70	407.90
Net Income Distribution ($)	0.87	0.87	0.87	0.87	0.78
Capital Gains Distribution ($)	0.00	0.00	0.00	0.00	0.00
Total Distribution ($)	0.87	0.87	0.87	0.87	0.78
Yield from Distribution (%)	6.89	7.25	7.73	7.57	7.01
Expense Ratio (%)	0.69	0.71	0.72	0.66	0.62
Portfolio Turnover (%)	17.00	5.00	4.00	15.00	38.00
NAV per Share ($)	13.25	12.45	11.85	11.25	11.35
Market Price per Share ($)	12.75	12.63	12.00	11.25	11.50
Premium (Discount) (%)	-3.77	1.45	1.27	0.00	2.38
Total Return, Stock Price (%)	8.00	12.72	14.78	5.58	2.48

Kemper Municipal Income Trust

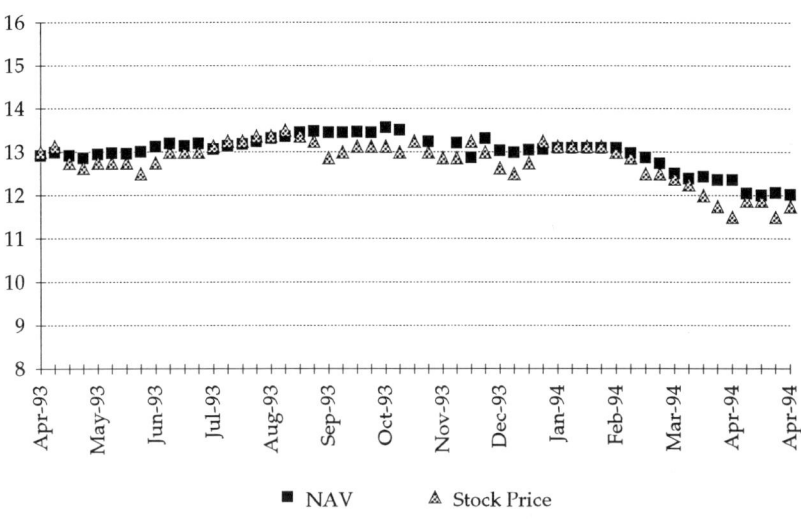

Premium/Discount Spread

Fund Outlook (KTF): The trust is very positive about the prospects for the municipal bond market for several reasons. First, with the passage of the Clinton plan in early August, increased taxes for higher-income Americans became a reality. Since these individuals are the primary buyers of municipal bonds, the fund expects demand for municipal securities to remain strong.

Authors' Comments (KTF): The trust's average weighted coupon is 7.36%. The trust's NAV fared well during the February muni crash, declining 3.4%, while the market value declined 8.3%. The portfolio contains over 50% AMT issues, which were acquired at the fund's inception primarily because of the higher yield. AMT bonds are not subject to pre-refunding. This accounts for the trust's ability to retain a larger percentage of high-coupon bonds and an attractive yield.

Municipal Premium Income Trust

NYSE: PIA

Two World Trade Center, 71st Floor
New York, NY 10048
(800) 869-3863
(212) 392-2550

Transfer Agent:
Dean Witter Trust Co.
Two Montgomery St.
Jersey City, NJ 07302
(800) 869-3863

Tax-Free Income

Results

For 12-months Ending 4/29/94	Period End	Period Begin	Distributions	Yield Dist (%)	Total Return (%)
Share Price ($)	9.75	11.00	0.73	6.36	-5.00
NAV per Share ($)	10.18	10.63		6.59	2.35

Background: Initial public offering February 1, 1989 of 6,900,000 shares at $10 per share. Initial NAV was $9.30 per share. Prior to 1993, the fund was managed by Allstate.
Objective: Seeks high current income exempt from regular Federal income tax. Invests in a leveraged portfolio of tax-free bonds.
Portfolio: (12/31/93) Municipal Bonds 94%, Short-Term & Other 5.4%. Portfolio Ratings: AAA 39%, AA 16%, A 18%, BBB 26.
Capitalization: (12/31/93) Common stock outstanding 26,243,024. Leveraged with 1,250 shares preferred stock, stated value $100,000 per share.
Average Maturity (years): 23.6
Fee: 0.50%   **Fund Manager:** Dean Witter Intercapital, Inc.
Income Distribution: Monthly   **Capital Gains Distribution:** Annually
Reinvestment Plan: Yes   **Shareholder Reports:** Quarterly

5 Year Performance

Fiscal Year Ending 5/31	1993	1992	1991	1990	1989
Net Assets ($mil)	291.10	388.00	373.20	368.10	249.60
Net Income Distribution ($)	0.78	0.72	0.70	0.69	0.15
Capital Gains Distribution ($)	0.00	0.05	0.07	0.11	0.00
Total Distribution ($)	0.78	0.77	0.77	0.80	0.15
Yield from Distribution (%)	7.51	8.00	8.56	8.42	-
Expense Ratio (%)	1.38	1.44	1.59	1.02	0.96
Portfolio Turnover (%)	7.00	16.00	56.00	150.00	106.00
NAV per Share ($)	10.67	10.02	9.61	9.35	9.59
Market Price per Share ($)	10.75	10.38	9.63	9.00	9.50
Premium (Discount) (%)	0.75	3.49	0.10	-3.74	-0.94
Total Return, Stock Price (%)	11.10	15.78	15.56	3.16	-

Municipal Premium Income Trust

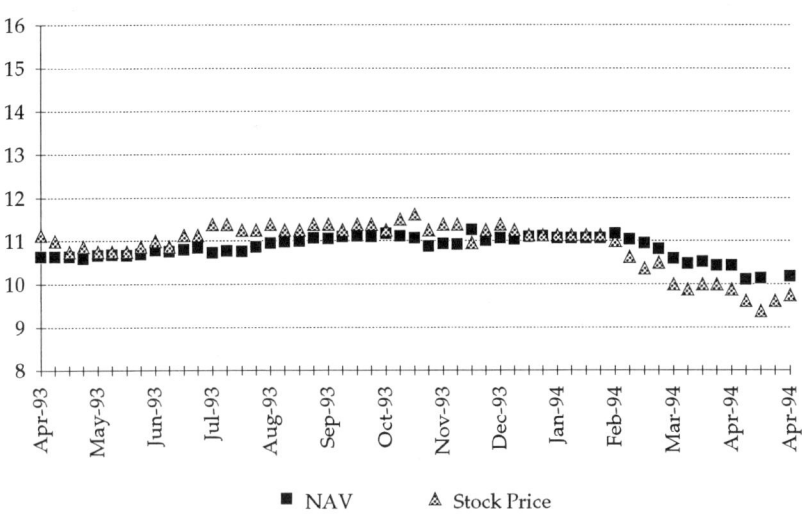

Premium/Discount Spread

■ NAV   △ Stock Price

Fund Outlook (PIA): Long-term municipal bond yields, as measured by The Bond Buyer Revenue Bond Index, were little changed in December 1993 and January 1994. However, in February and March 1994, the Index rose 89 basis points to 6.39% as yields reached levels not seen in over a year. Despite 15-20 basis point yield swings during April and May, the municipal market began to show signs of stability and the Index closed the period at 6.41%. The municipal market is influenced by unique supply and demand conditions. New-issue underwriting totaled a record $290 billion in 1993. The pace of new-issue activity in 1994 has slowed to an annual rate of $200 billion. By way of comparison, approximately $260 billion will leave the market as bonds mature or are called for redemption. Municipal issuance for the first five months of 1994 totaled $73 billion, 38% below the level for the comparable period of last year. This imbalance has helped municipal outperform U.S. government securities during mid-year 1994.

Authors' Comments (PIA): PIA has an average weighted coupon of 7.52% and is leveraged with adjustable-rate preferred shares. NAV did well during the February muni crash, declining 3% compared to an 8% decline in market value. In this period, the portfolio manager liquidated PIA's more defensive paper and took on more aggressive positions offering greater opportunities for appreciation. This was based on the assumption that long-term rates would not move much higher. However, in March 1994, rates did move up and PIA's NAV declined further for a total decline of 10% since January 28, 1994. Market value was down 16% for the same period. The current depressed market value affords a very attractive yield.

MuniEnhanced Fund, Inc.
P.O. Box 9011
Princeton, NJ 08543-9011
(609) 282-2800

AMEX: MEN
Transfer Agent:
State Street Bank & Trust Co.
225 Franklin Square
Boston, MA 02110
(800) 426-5523

Tax-Free Income

Results

For 12-months Ending 4/29/94	Period End	Period Begin	Distributions	Yield Dist (%)	Total Return (%)
Share Price ($)	10.75	12.88	1.26	11.72	-6.75
NAV per Share ($)	11.64	12.75		11.00	1.18

Background: Initial public offering February, 1989 of 25,000,000 shares at $12 per share. Initial NAV was $11.16 per share.
Objective: Seeks high current income from a portfolio of insured tax-exempt bonds of investment-grade quality.
Portfolio: (1/31/94) Sector Weightings: Water & Waste 15.5%, Health Care 15%, Transportation 10%, Utilities 8.2%, Government Obligations 9%. Portfolio Ratings: AAA & AA 99.3%, Other 0.7%.
Capitalization: (3/31/94) Common stock outstanding 29,007,770. Leveraged with auction-rate preferreds worth $150 million.
Average Maturity (years): 22.9
Fee: 0.50%
Income Distribution: Monthly
Reinvestment Plan: Yes
Fund Manager: Fund Asset Management, Inc.
Capital Gains Distribution: Annually
Shareholder Reports: Quarterly

5 Year Performance

Fiscal Year Ending 1/31	1993	1992	1991	1990	1989
Net Assets ($mil)	526.70	500.70	485.30	485.20	455.60
Net Income Distribution ($)	0.85	0.91	0.84	0.79	0.64
Capital Gains Distribution ($)	0.43	0.35	0.20	0.00	0.00
Total Distribution ($)	1.28	1.26	1.04	0.79	0.64
Yield from Distribution (%)	9.74	9.50	8.23	6.94	-
Expense Ratio (%)	68.00	69.00	70.00	71.00	66.00
Portfolio Turnover (%)	41.61	34.42	70.17	116.42	30.44
NAV per Share ($)	12.99	12.29	11.96	11.45	11.15
Market Price per Share ($)	13.13	13.25	12.63	11.38	10.75
Premium (Discount) (%)	1.04	7.81	5.52	-1.75	-3.59
Total Return, Stock Price (%)	8.75	14.88	20.12	13.20	-

MuniEnhanced Fund, Inc.

Premium/Discount Spread

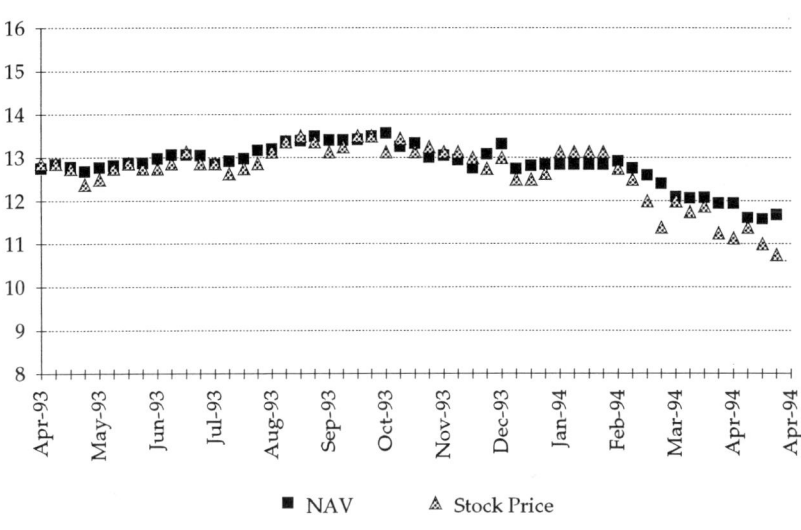

Fund Outlook (MEN): The fund's outlook for long-term municipal interest rates remains basically positive, and municipal securities are offering very attractive yields compared to alternative investments. The fund's cash reserves have been kept at a minimum to take advantage of the steep yield spread between short-term and long-term interest rates which continue to generate positive benefits to common stock shareholders as a result of the leveraging of the preferred stock. However, if the yield curve were to flatten, the benefits of leverage would decline and reduce the overall performance of the fund.

Authors' Comments (MEN): The fund has an average weighted coupon of 7.11%. The portfolio manager has been aggressively switching his premium bonds and pre-refunded bonds that are less sensitive to up-ticks in interest rates, to call-protected, current coupon issues. As a result, during the February-March muni crash, the NAV declined 11.5%, while the market value declined 24%. The fund is leveraged, which apparently adds to the concern of many investors. The current yield, however, is attractive.

MuniYield Fund

P.O. Box 9011
Princeton, NJ 08543-9011
(609) 282-2800

Tax-Free Income

NYSE: MYD
Transfer Agent:
The Bank of New York
110 Washington St.
New York, NY 10286
(800) 524-4458

Results

For 12-months Ending 4/29/94	Period End	Period Begin	Distributions	Yield Dist (%)	Total Return (%)
Share Price ($)	14.00	15.75	1.34	8.51	-2.60
NAV per Share ($)	14.99	15.93		8.41	2.51

Background: Initial public offering was November, 1991 at $15.00 per share. Initial NAV was $13.95 per share.

Objective: Seeks current income exempt from Federal income tax.

Portfolio: (10/31/93) Municipal Bonds 98%, Other Assets Less Liabilities 2%. State Weightings: Texas 15%, New York 14%, Washington 5%, Massachusetts 5%, Louisiana 4%. Portfolio Ratings: AAA 36%, AA 12%, A 36%, BBB 10%, Lower and Non-Rated 7%.

Capitalization: (10/31/93) Common stock outstanding 36,891,767. Fund is leveraged with 5,000 shares auction market preferred stock with a $50,000 per share liquidation preference.

Average Maturity (years): 25.2

Fee: 0.50%
Income Distribution: Monthly
Reinvestment Plan: Yes

Fund Manager: Fund Asset Management, Inc.
Capital Gains Distribution: Annually
Shareholder Reports: Quarterly

5 Year Performance

Fiscal Year Ending 10/31	1993	1992	1991	1990	1989
Net Assets ($mil)	619.80	526.30	-	-	-
Net Income Distribution ($)	1.11	0.89	-	-	-
Capital Gains Distribution ($)	0.16	0.00	-	-	-
Total Distribution ($)	1.27	0.89	-	-	-
Yield from Distribution (%)	8.39	5.88	-	-	-
Expense Ratio (%)	0.64	0.65	-	-	-
Portfolio Turnover (%)	25.58	66.45	-	-	-
NAV per Share ($)	16.80	14.69	-	-	-
Market Price per Share ($)	16.75	15.13	-	-	-
Premium (Discount) (%)	-0.30	3.00	-	-	-
Total Return, Stock Price (%)	19.90	-	-	-	-

MuniYield Fund

Premium/Discount Spread

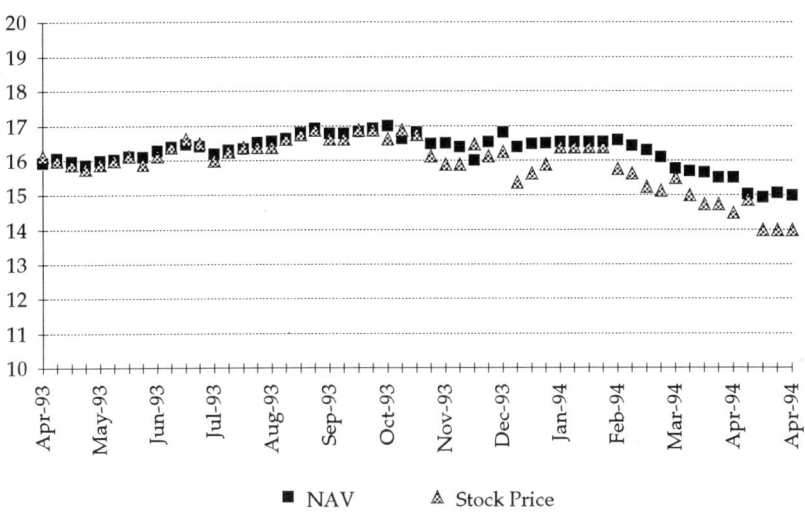

■ NAV   △ Stock Price

Fund Outlook (MYD): The tax-exempt marketplace continues to exhibit extraordinary value relative to its taxable counterpart. Tax-exempt issues are already at historically attractive levels. The prospect of higher taxes in conjunction with dwindling tax-exempt supply in the years ahead makes for an even more compelling investment argument. In light of these circumstances, it seems very likely that municipal bonds will outperform other fixed-income markets for some time to come.

Authors' Comments (MYD): The fund has an average weighted coupon of 7.01%. Approximately 20% of the portfolio is interest-rate sensitive, reflecting the fact that they bear current coupons. The lesser quality issues were less sensitive to the fluctuation in interest rates experienced in February-March. However, from January 28, 1994 to April 29, 1994 the NAV has declined 11%, and market value has dropped 17%. Management's strategy has been to hold a small percent of the portfolio in deep-discounted, lesser quality issues that in the past have outperformed the overall market, and the balance invested in good quality, investment-grade issues that can generate a higher than average yield. The current yield is attractive.

Nuveen Municipal Market Opportunity Fund   NYSE: **NMO**

333 W. Wacker Drive
Chicago, IL 60606
(800) 252-4630
(312) 917-7700

Transfer Agent:
U.S. Trust
770 Broadway
New York, NY 10003
(800) 257-8787

Tax-Free Income

Results

For 12-months Ending 4/29/94	Period End	Period Begin	Distributions	Yield Dist (%)	Total Return (%)
Share Price ($)	15.00	16.75	1.18	7.04	-3.40
NAV per Share ($)	15.30	16.22		7.27	1.60

Background: Initial public offering May 18, 1990 of 43,000,000 shares at $15 per share. Initial NAV was $14.05 per share.

Objective: Seeks current income exempt from Federal income tax from a leveraged portfolio of primarily long-term (20 to 30 year maturities) tax-free bonds rated BBB or better. Up to 20% may be invested in non-rated tax-free municipal obligations.

Portfolio: (10/31/93) Municipal Bonds 99%, Short-Term & Other 1%. Portfolio Ratings: AAA 28%, AA 35%, A 16%, BBB 21%. Sector Weightings: Housing Facilities 27%, Health Care Facilities 11%, Pollution Control Facilities 6%, Transportation 9%, Electric Utilities 8%.

Capitalization: (10/31/93) Common stock outstanding 44,489,216. Leveraged with 6,000 shares preferred stock, stated value $50,000 per share.

Average Maturity (years): 23.5
Fee: 0.60% *Fund Manager:* Nuveen Advisory Corporation
Income Distribution: Monthly   *Capital Gains Distribution:* Annually
Reinvestment Plan: Yes   *Shareholder Reports:* Semi-Annually

5 Year Performance

Fiscal Year Ending 10/31	1993	1992	1991	1990	1989
Net Assets ($mil)	1037.60	975.40	958.80	901.80	-
Net Income Distribution ($)	1.23	1.14	1.10	0.45	-
Capital Gains Distribution ($)	0.02	0.01	0.00	0.00	-
Total Distribution ($)	1.25	1.15	1.10	0.45	-
Yield from Distribution (%)	8.13	7.42	7.93	-	-
Expense Ratio (%)	0.76	0.74	0.75	0.73	-
Portfolio Turnover (%)	13.00	5.00	7.00	3.00	-
NAV per Share ($)	16.58	15.37	15.16	13.98	-
Market Price per Share ($)	17.25	15.38	15.50	13.88	-
Premium (Discount) (%)	4.04	0.07	2.24	-0.79	-
Total Return, Stock Price (%)	20.29	6.65	19.60	-	-

Nuveen Municipal Market Opportunity Fund

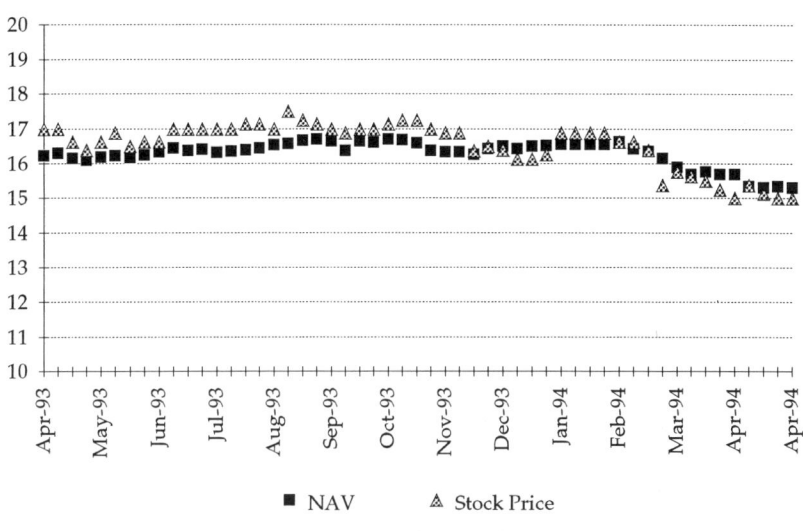

Fund Outlook (NMO): The outlook for the municipal market, at this writing, remains basically positive. While concern about inflation in a strengthening economy caused municipal yields to rise and bond prices to move lower from February to mid-May, four moves by the Federal Reserve Board to raise short-term interest have begun to calm inflationary fears about bond prices and continue to be well supported by market fundamentals. The muni market's positive supply and demand characteristics also remain essentially in place, and NMO believes that the prospects for the municipal market remain attractive.

Authors' Comments (NMO): The fund has an average weighted coupon of 8.2%. Management's investment strategy follows the theory of value investing which calls for seeking out bonds that are believed to be undervalued, under-researched and under-rated and also for holding higher coupon bonds selling at premiums and paying higher yields that are less sensitive to higher interest rates. In March 1994 the dividend rate was reduced from $0.096 per share to $0.093 bringing the monthly payment more in line with expected net investment income. The current yield is attractive.

Putnam Investment Grade Municipal Trust — NYSE: **PGM**

One Post Office Square
Boston, MA 02109
(617) 292-1000

Transfer Agent:
Putnam Investors Services, Inc.
P.O. Box 41203
Providence, RI 02940
(800) 634-1587

Tax-Free Income

Results

For 12-months Ending 4/29/94	Period End	Period Begin	Distributions	Yield Dist (%)	Total Return (%)
Share Price ($)	13.00	14.00	0.96	6.86	-0.29
NAV per Share ($)	12.19	13.02		7.37	1.00

Background: Initial public offering October, 1989 of 17,000,000 shares at $12 per share. Initial NAV was $11.11 per share.

Objective: Seeks high current income exempt from regular Federal income taxes through investment in long-term, investment-grade municipal bonds.

Portfolio: (12/31/93) Municipal Bonds 100%. Sector Weightings: Medical Facilities 11%, Investor Owned Utilities 10%, Transportation 10%, Pre-refunded 10%. Portfolio Ratings: AAA 46%, AA 10%, A 17%, BBB 24%.

Capitalization: (12/31/93) Common stock outstanding 19,782,075. Fund is leveraged with 1,400 remarketed preferred shares with $100,000 per share liquidation preference.

Average Maturity (years): 22.5
Fee: 0.70%
Fund Manager: Putnam Management Co., Inc.
Income Distribution: Monthly
Capital Gains Distribution: Annually
Reinvestment Plan: Yes
Shareholder Reports: Quarterly

5 Year Performance

Fiscal Year Ending 11/30	1993	1992	1991	1990	1989
Net Assets ($mil)	405.70	381.70	363.00	311.70	213.90
Net Income Distribution ($)	0.96	0.91	0.89	0.87	-
Capital Gains Distribution ($)	0.00	0.00	0.00	0.01	-
Total Distribution ($)	0.96	0.91	0.89	0.88	-
Yield from Distribution (%)	7.25	7.66	7.91	7.41	-
Expense Ratio (%)	1.40	1.45	1.46	1.21	0.12
Portfolio Turnover (%)	33.73	44.39	72.49	89.65	13.17
NAV per Share ($)	13.44	12.36	11.51	11.03	11.19
Market Price per Share ($)	14.00	13.25	11.88	11.25	11.88
Premium (Discount) (%)	4.17	7.20	3.13	1.99	6.08
Total Return, Stock Price (%)	12.91	19.19	13.51	2.10	-

Putnam Investment Grade Municipal Trust

Premium/Discount Spread

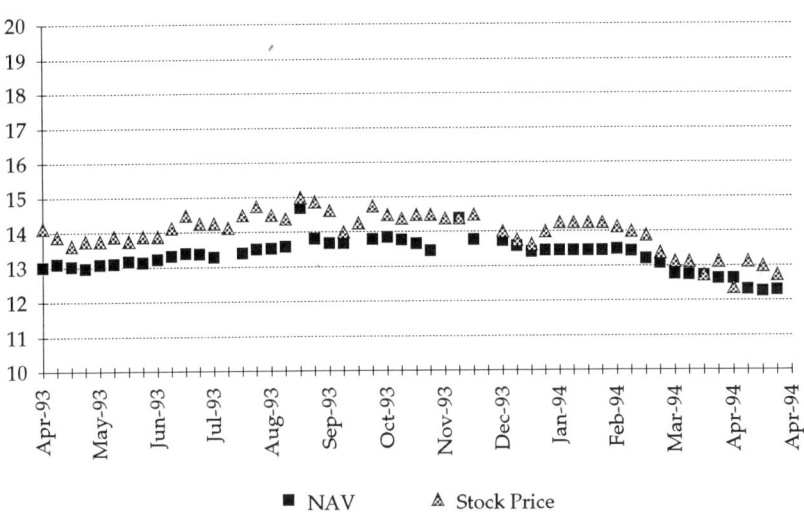

■ NAV △ Stock Price

Fund Outlook (PGM): The trust has continued to benefit from the effective use of leverage. Market conditions have made leverage a useful tool in the municipal bond market because of a steep yield curve, low inflation and low interest rates. The trust's use of both inverse floating obligations and the issuance of preferred shares have paid off in this environment. Of course, the trust is continually monitoring its use of leverage, and while it believes its usefulness is not yet outlived, will make adjustments to the trust's use of such tools as market conditions warrant. The trust continues to offer attractive tax-free income in an environment where municipal bonds are in demand.

Authors' Comments (PGM): The trust has an average weighted coupon of 7.72%. The 12-month trailing return is 6.18%, the best performance in its peer group. Management strategy involves the use of residual-interest bonds (RIBs); coupons that increase as short-term rates decline, hedged with variable rate issues whose coupons rise as short-term rates increase. PGM also ladders its portfolio by coupon to ensure that the portfolio holds a sufficient amount of higher coupon bonds in order to reduce the volatility of the portfolio and reduce the interest rate sensitivity.

Seligman Select Municipal Fund NYSE: SEL

100 Park Avenue
New York, NY 10017
(800) 874-1092
(800) 622-4597

Transfer Agent:
Union Data Service Center, Inc.
100 Park Avenue
New York, NY 10017
(800) 874-1092

Tax-Free Income

Results

For 12-months Ending 4/29/94	Period End	Period Begin	Distributions	Yield Dist (%)	Total Return (%)
Share Price ($)	11.75	13.25	0.99	7.47	-3.85
NAV per Share ($)	12.20	12.87		7.69	2.49

Background: Initial public offering February 15, 1990 of 12,750,000 shares at $12 per share. Initial NAV was $11.16 per share.

Objective: Seeks high current income exempt from regular Federal income tax. Capital appreciation is secondary. 80% of investments are rated AAA. The balance must be BBB or higher. All or a portion of the dividend may be subject to Federal Alternative Minimum Tax (AMT).

Portfolio: (3/31/94) Housing 24%, Utility 21%, Transportation 17%, Health Care 6%, General Obligation 6%, Private Placement 19%. Top Five States: Texas, Florida, New York, Massachusetts, and the District of Columbia. Portfolio Ratings: AAA 89%, AA 4%, A 5%, Low- and Non-Rated 2%.

Capitalization: (12/31/93) Common stock outstanding 12,985,671. Leveraged with 750 shares preferred stock, stated value $100,000 per share.

Average Maturity (years): 25.6
Fee: 0.55% *Fund Manager:* J. & W. Seligman & Co., Inc.
Income Distribution: Monthly *Capital Gains Distribution:* Annually
Reinvestment Plan: Yes *Shareholder Reports:* Quarterly

5 Year Performance

Fiscal Year Ending 12/31	1993	1992	1991	1990	1989
Net Assets ($mil)	245.60	235.80	228.50	217.40	-
Net Income Distribution ($)	0.84	0.84	0.84	0.63	-
Capital Gains Distribution ($)	0.22	0.02	0.00	0.00	-
Total Distribution ($)	1.06	0.86	0.84	0.63	-
Yield from Distribution (%)	8.31	7.02	7.47	-	-
Expense Ratio (%)	0.92	0.90	0.90	0.78	-
Portfolio Turnover (%)	15.83	3.90	7.36	10.75	-
NAV per Share ($)	13.14	12.45	11.95	11.15	-
Market Price per Share ($)	13.00	12.75	12.25	11.25	-
Premium (Discount) (%)	-1.07	2.41	2.51	0.90	-
Total Return, Stock Price (%)	10.27	11.10	16.36	-	-

Seligman Select Municipal Fund

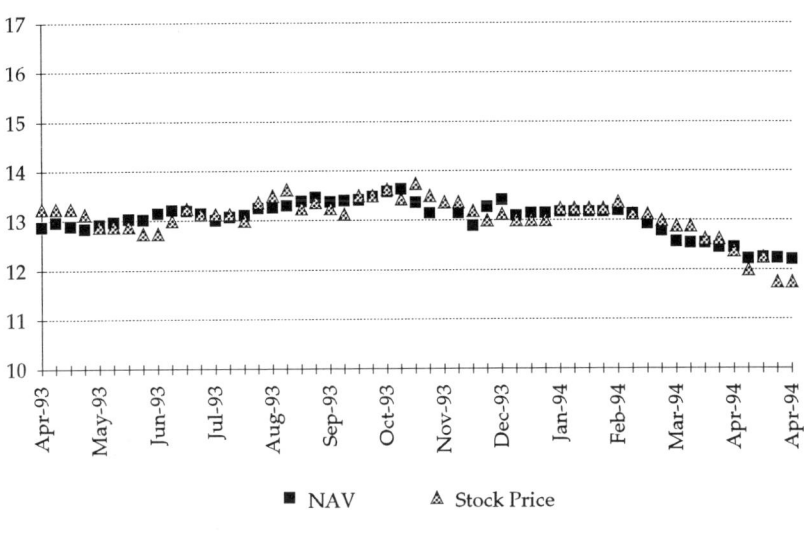

Premium/Discount Spread

■ NAV △ Stock Price

Fund Outlook (SEL): The fund remains positive regarding the performance of the municipal bond market. Because the fund anticipates little change in rates over the next 12-months, it will concentrate new purchases in current coupon bonds. Additionally, the fund will continue to hold many premium bonds because of their attractive current yields. Cash positions will be kept at minimum levels due to the steep yield curve. At present, the fund does not predict any one sector of the municipal market to outperform the others. For this reason, it plans to remain fairly diversified among many sectors. With the economy in a recovery, many municipal credits are beginning to stabilize or improve.

Authors' Comments (SEL): SEL is one of the more conservative muni funds around. From its inception, fund manager Thomas Moles gathered together a high-quality, high weighted average coupon rate portfolio and held on to it. The result was excellent performance as rates fell. At the end of 1993, some strategic changes were instituted as more current-coupon bonds were acquired, thus increasing yield while lowering current interest rate risk. This fund is still one of the best positioned muni funds in the market. It's good as a core for the tax-free investor.

Van Kampen Merritt Advantage Municipal Income Trust

NYSE: VKA

One Parkview Plaza
Oakbrook Terrace, IL 60181
(800) 225-2222

Transfer Agent:
State Street Bank & Trust Co.
225 Franklin St., P.O. Box 366
Boston, MA 02101
(800) 426-5523

Tax-Free Income

Results

For 12-months Ending 4/29/94	Period End	Period Begin	Distributions	Yield Dist (%)	Total Return (%)
Share Price ($)	14.00	15.00	1.07	7.13	0.47
NAV per Share ($)	14.99	16.33		6.55	-1.65

Background: Initial public offering September 25, 1992, of 19,100,085 shares at $15 per share. Initial NAV was $14.84.

Objective: Seeks high current income exempt from regular Federal income taxes. The fund's capital structure is leveraged.

Portfolio: (3/31/94) Tax Free Bonds 101%. Portfolio Ratings: AAA 22%, AA 17%, A 26%, BB 30%, BB 4%. Top States: New York 20%, Illinois 13%, Colorado 10%, California 5%, North Carolina 5%

Capitalization: (3/31/94) Common stock outstanding 19,106,785. Leveraged with 3,800 shares Auction Preferred in four series. Redeemable at $50,000.

Average Maturity (years): 22.4

Fee: 0.70%   *Fund Manager:* Van Kampen Merritt Invest. Adv. Corp.

Income Distribution: Monthly   *Capital Gains Distribution:* Annually

Reinvestment Plan: Yes   *Shareholder Reports:* Semi-Annually

5 Year Performance

Fiscal Year Ending 10/31	1993	1992	1991	1990	1989
Net Assets ($mil)	518.20	468.70	-	-	-
Net Income Distribution ($)	0.88	0.00	-	-	-
Capital Gains Distribution ($)	0.00	0.00	-	-	-
Total Distribution ($)	0.88	0.00	-	-	-
Yield from Distribution (%)	5.50	0.00	-	-	-
Expense Ratio (%)	1.66	1.12	-	-	-
Portfolio Turnover (%)	111.79	14.83	-	-	-
NAV per Share ($)	17.18	14.59	-	-	-
Market Price per Share ($)	16.00	13.88	-	-	-
Premium (Discount) (%)	-6.85	-4.88	-	-	-
Total Return, Stock Price (%)	21.60	-7.50	-	-	-

Van Kampen Merritt Advantage Municipal Income Trust

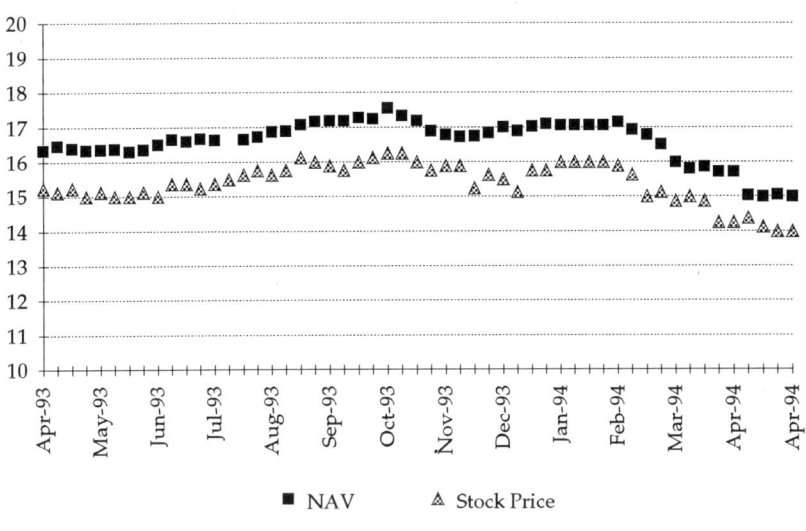

Fund Outlook (VKA): The trust's general economic forecast calls for low inflation and the continuation of relatively low interest rates. In the near term, it feels these conditions should generally lead to favorable performance for fixed-income securities. The trust's outlook for the national municipal market remains positive. It believes that as the realization of higher tax burdens becomes apparent, the demand for tax-exempt investment will increase. On the supply side, the market saw record levels of issuance in 1993 due mainly to refunding issues. If interest rates increase, the number of refunding issues could decrease drastically as it becomes less attractive for issuers to refinance. As with any fixed income investment, the immediate impact could be a partial loss of value in the trust share price. However, an environment of constrained supply and steady demand should support the municipal market and have a favorable impact upon the trust.

Authors' Comments (VKA): The trust has an average weighted coupon of 6.73%. The trust is leveraged with four classes of preferreds. Dividends for one class are reset every 28 days, the other three are reset every year. A portion of the portfolio is invested in embedded-caps which reflect increases in short-term rates. Because of the large spread between short- and long-term rates and the use of embedded-caps, VKA was able to increase dividends twice in 1993.

Van Kampen Merritt Municipal Opportunity Trust

One Parkview Plaza
Oakbrook Terrace, IL 60181
(800) 225-2222

Tax-Free Income

NYSE: VMO
Transfer Agent:
State Street Bank & Trust Co.
225 Franklin St., P.O. Box 366
Boston, MA 02101
(800) 426-5523

Results

For 12-months Ending 4/29/94	Period End	Period Begin	Distributions	Yield Dist (%)	Total Return (%)
Share Price ($)	14.00	15.63	1.02	6.53	-3.90
NAV per Share ($)	15.37	16.68		6.12	-1.74

Background: Initial public offering June 6, 1992 of 15,350,000 shares at $15 per share. Inial NAV was $15 per share.

Objective: Seeks a high level of current income exempt from Federal income tax, consistent with preservation of capital. The fund will invest primarily in a diversified portfolio of municipal securities which the fund's investment advisor believes do not involve undue risk to income or principal. Under normal market conditions, the fund will invest substantially all of its assets in municipal securities rated investment-grade at the time of investment.

Portfolio: (12/31/93) Municipal Bonds 106%, Other (6%). Portfolio Ratings: AAA 26%, AA 14%, A 40%, BBB 21%. Sector Weightings: Health Care 11%, Housing 12%, Utility 17%, Transportation 19%, Private Placements 18%.

Capitalization: (12/31/93) Common shares outstanding 27,352,891. Leveraged with 3,000 shares ARPs $50,000 stated value.

Average Maturity (years): 22.6

Fee: 0.70%   *Fund Manager:* Van Kampen Merritt Invest. Adv. Corp.
Income Distribution: Monthly   *Capital Gains Distribution:* Annually
Reinvestment Plan: Yes   *Shareholder Reports:* Semi-Annually

5 Year Performance

Fiscal Year Ending 10/31	1993	1992	1991	1990	1989
Net Assets ($mil)	415.60	380.10	-	-	-
Net Income Distribution ($)	1.02	0.34	-	-	-
Capital Gains Distribution ($)	0.06	0.00	-	-	-
Total Distribution ($)	1.08	0.34	-	-	-
Yield from Distribution (%)	7.45	-	-	-	-
Expense Ratio (%)	1.62	1.54	-	-	-
Portfolio Turnover (%)	52.40	53.37	-	-	-
NAV per Share ($)	17.30	14.99	-	-	-
Market Price per Share ($)	16.38	14.50	-	-	-
Premium (Discount) (%)	-5.33	-3.27	-	-	-
Total Return, Stock Price (%)	20.41	-	-	-	-

Van Kampen Merritt Municipal Opportunity Trust

Premium/Discount Spread

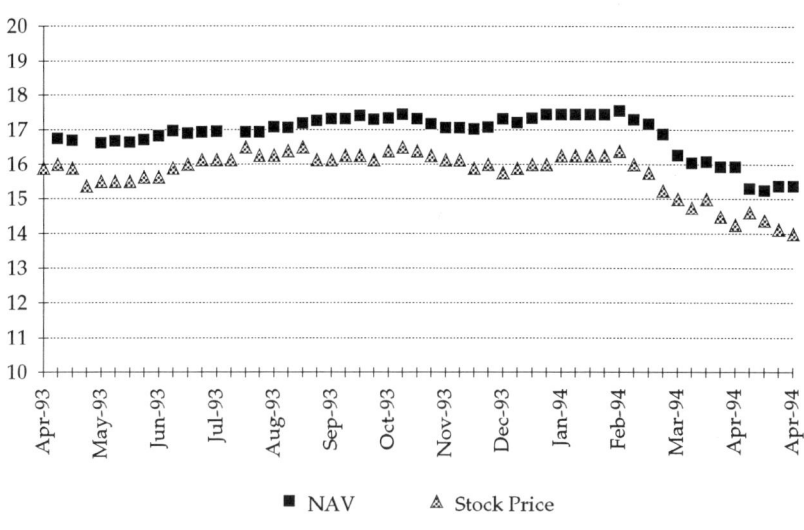

■ NAV △ Stock Price

Fund Outlook (VMO): The trust's general economic forecast calls for low inflation and the continuation of relatively low interest rates. In the near term, these conditions should generally lead to favorable performance for fixed-income securities. The trust's outlook for the national municipal market remains positive. As the realization of higher tax burdens becomes painfully apparent, the demand for tax-exempt investment should only increase. On the supply side of the equation, the market saw record levels of issuance in 1993 due mainly to refunding issues. If interest rates begin to increase, the number of refunding issues could decrease drastically as it becomes less attractive for issuers to refinance. As with any fixed income investment, the immediate impact could be a partial loss of value in the trust's share price. However, an environment of constrained supply and steady demand should support the municipal market and have a favorable impact.

Authors' Comments (VMO): The trust has an average weighted coupon of 6.5%. Because of the low average weighted coupon, the trust is interest sensitive. In the fourth quarter of 1993, its 7% position in zero coupons was reduced to 2.8% of the total portfolio.

Van Kampen Merritt Municipal Trust   NYSE: VKQ

One Parkview Plaza
Oakbrook Terrace, IL 60181
(800) 225-2222

Transfer Agent:
State Street Bank & Trust Co.
225 Franklin St., P.O. Box 366
Boston, MA 02101
(800) 426-5523

Tax-Free Income

Results

For 12-months Ending 4/29/94	Period End	Period Begin	Distributions	Yield Dist (%)	Total Return (%)
Share Price ($)	15.00	16.50	1.12	6.79	-2.30
NAV per Share ($)	15.46	16.63		6.73	-0.30

Background: Initial public offering October 17, 1991 of 30,577,325 shares at $15 per share. Initial net asset value was $15 per share.

Objective: Seeks a high level of current income exempt from Federal income tax, consistent with preservation of capital. The fund will invest at least 80% of its assets in investment-grade municipal securities.

Portfolio: (12/31/93) Municipal Bonds 98%. Sector Weightings: Housing 15%, Health 13%, Transportation 17%, Education 4%. Portfolio Ratings: AAA 16%, AA 10%, A 30%, BBB 29%, Non-Rated 15%.

Capitalization: (12/31/93) Common stock outstanding 36,270,469. Leveraged with 6,000 shares preferred stock, stated value $50,000 per share.

Average Maturity (years): 22.6

Fee: 0.70% *Fund Manager:* Van Kampen Merritt Invest. Adv. Corp.
Income Distribution: Monthly *Capital Gains Distribution:* Annually
Reinvestment Plan: Yes *Shareholder Reports:* Semi-Annually

5 Year Performance

Fiscal Year Ending 8/31	1993	1992	1991	1990	1989
Net Assets ($mil)	917.90	891.70	-	-	-
Net Income Distribution ($)	1.10	0.81	-	-	-
Capital Gains Distribution ($)	0.11	0.00	-	-	-
Total Distribution ($)	1.21	0.81	-	-	-
Yield from Distribution (%)	7.50	-	-	-	-
Expense Ratio (%)	1.06	1.03	-	-	-
Portfolio Turnover (%)	48.45	99.51	-	-	-
NAV per Share ($)	17.04	16.33	-	-	-
Market Price per Share ($)	16.75	16.13	-	-	-
Premium (Discount) (%)	-1.67	-7.40	-	-	-
Total Return, Stock Price (%)	11.35	-	-	-	-

Van Kampen Merritt Municipal Trust

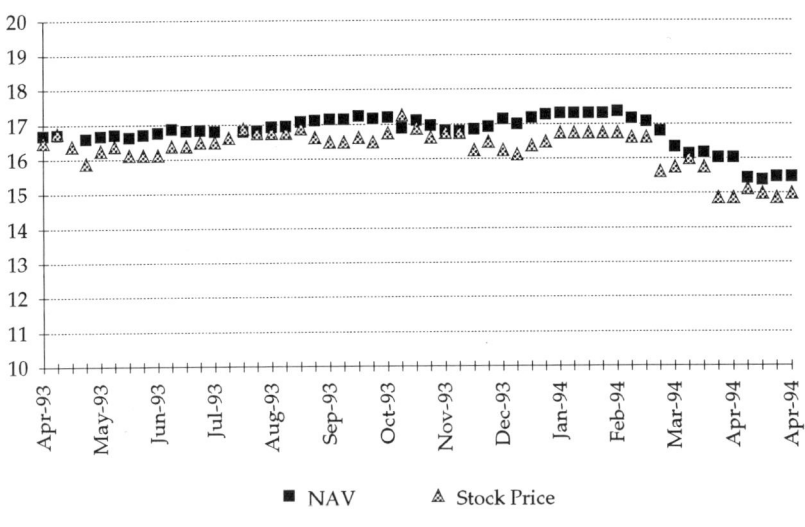

Fund Outlook (VKQ): Signs that the nation's economy is clearly doing better are irrefutable at this point. What remains unclear is the inflationary implications of a robust economy. While inflation at least to date has been low and unthreatening, the uncertainty looking forward continues to torment the financial markets. Rising, short-term exempt taxable rates will eventually filter through to the tax exempt market, but to a lesser degree. Short-term tax exempt rates should continue to benefit from higher tax rates, weak supply and, of course, an unstable market environment. But an increase in short municipal rates of any magnitude will likely impact the trust's preferred share financing costs, and while the trust is positioned to withstand a moderate increase in short-term interest rates, its dividend paying ability may diminish under the weight of a significant and protracted rate increase.

Authors' Comments (VKQ): The trust has an average weighted coupon of 6.7%. The trust is broadly diversified, as well as laddered by coupon. The trust is not sensitive to interest rate changes because of the large percentage of premium bonds held in the portfolio as well as the concentration of investments in lower grade and non-rated issues.

Municipal Bond Funds—Non-Leveraged

Municipal High Income Fund

Two World Trade Center
New York, NY 10048
(212) 2720-9218

Tax-Free Income

NYSE: **MHF**
Transfer Agent:
The Shareholder Services Group
Exchange Place
Boston, MA 02104
(617) 722-7000

Results

For 12-months *Ending 4/29/94*	Period End	Period Begin	Distributions	Yield Dist (%)	Total Return (%)
Share Price ($)	9.00	10.00	0.68	6.80	-3.25
NAV per Share ($)	9.21	9.65		7.05	2.49

Background: Initial public offering November 28, 1988 of 16,600,000 shares at $10 per share. Initial NAV was $9.35 per share.

Objective: Seeks high current tax-free income. Up to 100% of the portfolio may be invested in municipal obligations rated as low as BB. Up to 30% of the fund's assets may be invested in non-publicly traded municipal obligations, and up to 25% may be in municipal zeros.

Portfolio: (3/31/94) Municipal Bonds 98%, Short-Term & Other 2%. Sector Weightings: Hospitals & Nursing Homes & Health Care 21%, Industrial Development & Pollution Control & Resource Recovery 26%, Utility 10%. Portfolio Ratings: AAA 6%, AA 6%, A 10%, BBB 32%, BB 10%, Non-Rated 35%.

Capitalization: (3/31/94) Common stock outstanding 19,521,241. No long-term debt.

Average Maturity (years): 20.5

Fee: 0.40%

Income Distribution: Monthly

Reinvestment Plan: Yes

Fund Manager: Greenwich Street Advisors

Capital Gains Distribution: Annually

Shareholder Reports: Quarterly

5 Year Performance

Fiscal Year Ending 10/31	1993	1992	1991	1990	1989
Net Assets ($mil)	187.80	179.10	173.30	164.50	164.20
Net Income Distribution ($)	0.66	0.69	0.75	0.76	0.64
Capital Gains Distribution ($)	0.02	0.00	0.00	0.00	0.00
Total Distribution ($)	0.68	0.69	0.75	0.76	0.64
Yield from Distribution (%)	7.45	7.26	8.21	8.00	-
Expense Ratio (%)	0.87	0.87	0.90	0.87	0.86
Portfolio Turnover (%)	13.00	12.00	22.00	11.00	16.00
NAV per Share ($)	9.67	9.49	9.42	9.28	9.52
Market Price per Share ($)	9.63	9.13	9.50	9.13	9.50
Premium (Discount) (%)	-0.41	-3.79	0.85	-1.72	-0.21
Total Return, Stock Price (%)	12.92	3.37	12.27	4.11	-

Municipal High Income Fund

Premium/Discount Spread

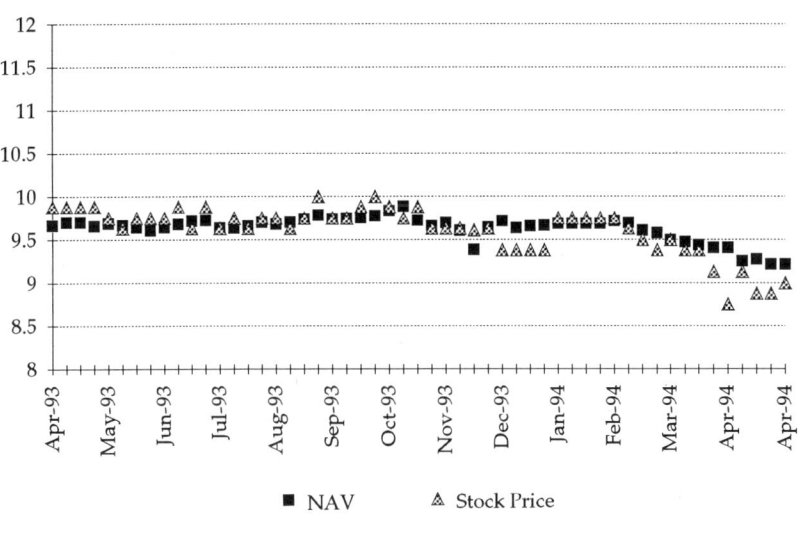

■ NAV △ Stock Price

Fund Outlook (MHF): Over the near term, the fund will tread cautiously as market forces continue to dwell on fears of increased inflation. Until this atmosphere improves, it will continue to be defensive in its asset allocation. The majority of the portfolio is in investment-grade securities rated BBB/BAA. The fund has invested the majority of its assets in industrial development bonds and hospital revenue bonds. The fund is invested in high coupon bonds that tend to cushion the NAV per share against market fluctuations.

Authors' Comments (MHF): The absence of leverage and the high incidence of premium coupon and non-rated bonds in the portfolio shield this fund somewhat from rising interest rates. While interest rates were falling, this hindered performance, but now that rates are on an upward bias, it has helped stabilize performance. The risks associated with such a portfolio include issuer default or calls. So far, management has avoided any defaults, and less than 10% of the portfolio is callable in 1994. Other risk factors include a high percentage of Texas bonds in the portfolio in anticipation of the implementation of a state income tax, as well as health care and utility issues. All these areas are vulnerable to unexpected twists. We feel the possible risks are outweighed by the rewards and should be attractive for tax-free investors.

MuniInsured Fund, Inc.

P.O. Box 9011
Princeton, NJ 08543-9011
(609) 282-2800

AMEX: MIF

Transfer Agent:
State Street Bank & Trust Co.
225 Franklin St.
Boston, MA 02101
(617) 328-5000

Tax-Free Income

Results

For 12-months Ending 4/29/94	Period End	Period Begin	Distributions	Yield Dist (%)	Total Return (%)
Share Price ($)	9.50	10.25	0.82	8.00	0.68
NAV per Share ($)	9.71	10.36		7.92	1.64

Background: Initial public offering October 19, 1987 of 7,475,000 shares at $10 per share. Initial NAV was $9.63 per share.

Objective: Seeks current income exempt from regular Federal income tax. Invests 80% in municipal obligations. Maturities are one year or more and are covered by insurance to guarantee the timely repayment of principal and interest. Will not invest more than 25% of total assets in municipal bonds whose issuers are located within the same state.

Portfolio: (12/31/93) Municipal Bonds 98.2%, Short-Term & Other 1.8%. Portfolio Ratings: AAA 82%, AA 8%, A 4%, BBB 3%.

Capitalization: (9/30/93) Common stock outstanding 7,916,616.

Average Maturity (years): 21.6

Fee: 0.50% **Fund Manager:** Fund Asset Management, Inc.
Income Distribution: Monthly **Capital Gains Distribution:** Annually
Reinvestment Plan: Yes **Shareholder Reports:** Quarterly

5 Year Performance

Fiscal Year Ending 9/30	1993	1992	1991	1990	1989
Net Assets ($mil)	85.50	80.70	77.80	74.30	76.60
Net Income Distribution ($)	0.60	0.62	0.64	0.65	0.66
Capital Gains Distribution ($)	0.22	0.40	0.08	0.22	0.15
Total Distribution ($)	0.82	1.02	0.72	0.87	0.81
Yield from Distribution (%)	7.54	10.20	8.00	8.70	8.80
Expense Ratio (%)	0.80	0.85	0.89	0.91	0.88
Portfolio Turnover (%)	27.89	84.01	92.07	132.60	76.62
NAV per Share ($)	10.72	10.26	10.21	9.68	10.00
Market Price per Share ($)	10.88	10.88	10.00	9.00	10.00
Premium (Discount) (%)	1.45	6.04	-2.06	3.31	-3.70
Total Return, Stock Price (%)	7.54	19.00	19.11	-1.30	5.10

MuniInsured Fund, Inc.

Premium/Discount Spread

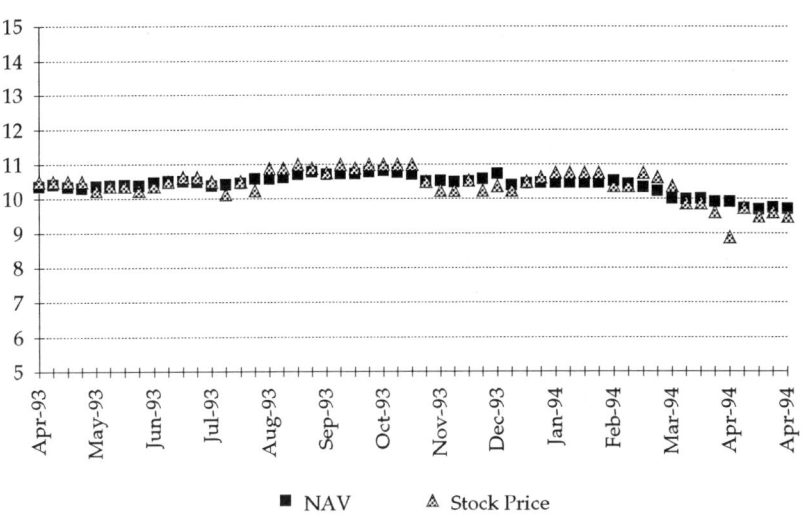

Fund Outlook (MIF): The authors regret to report that representatives from MuniInsured Fund did not wish to make a statement available to potential investors at this time.

Authors' Comments (MIF): The fund has an average weighted coupon of 7.19%. Initially offered in October of 1987 MIF is the oldest closed-end insured fund that is also not leveraged. More than one-third of the portfolio bears coupons of 7.5% or better. The portfolio is therefore not sensitive to interest rate changes, although the fund is currently making some switches into current coupon bonds in anticipation of a leveling out of interest rates.

Nuveen Municipal Value Fund, Inc.   NYSE: **NUV**

333 W. Wacker Drive   *Transfer Agent:*
Chicago, IL 60606   U.S. Trust, Nuveen Exchange-Traded
(800) 252-4630   Fund Investor Services
(312) 917-7700   770 Broadway, New York, NY 10003
       (800) 257-8787

Tax-Free Income

Results

For 12-months Ending 4/29/94	Period End	Period Begin	Distributions	Yield Dist (%)	Total Return (%)
Share Price ($)	10.25	11.50	0.68	5.91	-4.96
NAV per Share ($)	10.16	10.83		6.28	0.09

Background: Initial public offering June 17, 1987 of 150,000,000 shares at $10 per share. Initial NAV was $9.35 per share.

Objective: Seeks current income exempt from Federal income tax. Capital appreciation is secondary and obtained through selection of municipal securities undervalued in the opinion of the investment advisor. 100% of net assets are invested in tax-exempt municipal obligations of which 80% are rated BBB or higher. The fund intends to invest in longer-term maturities depending upon market conditions.

Portfolio: (10/31/93) Municipal Bonds 96%, Short-Term & Other 4%. Sector Weightings: Electric Utilities 16%, Health Care Facilities 12%, Escrowed Bonds 41%, Pollution Control Facilities 10%. Portfolio Ratings: AAA 36%, AA 18%, A 18%, BBB 21%, BB 2%, Lower and Non-Rated 4%.

Capitalization: (10/31/93) Common stock outstanding 166,370,908. No long-term debt.

Average Maturity (years): 22
Fee: 0.35%   *Fund Manager:* Nuveen Advisory Corporation
Income Distribution: Monthly   *Capital Gains Distribution:* Annually
Reinvestment Plan: Yes   *Shareholder Reports:* Semi-Annually

5 Year Performance

Fiscal Year Ending 10/31	1993	1992	1991	1990	1989
Net Assets ($mil)	1811.30	1726.30	1759.30	1595.20	1613.40
Net Income Distribution ($)	0.69	0.71	0.71	0.71	0.72
Capital Gains Distribution ($)	0.01	0.05	0.01	0.03	0.03
Total Distribution ($)	0.70	0.76	0.73	0.74	0.75
Yield from Distribution (%)	6.36	6.99	7.30	7.31	7.49
Expense Ratio (%)	0.74	0.77	0.83	0.86	0.89
Portfolio Turnover (%)	8.00	8.00	7.00	5.00	7.00
NAV per Share ($)	10.89	10.51	10.43	9.97	10.14
Market Price per Share ($)	11.50	11.00	10.88	10.00	10.13
Premium (Discount) (%)	5.60	4.66	4.41	0.30	-0.10
Total Return, Stock Price (%)	10.91	8.09	16.10	6.02	10.02

Nuveen Municipal Value Fund, Inc.

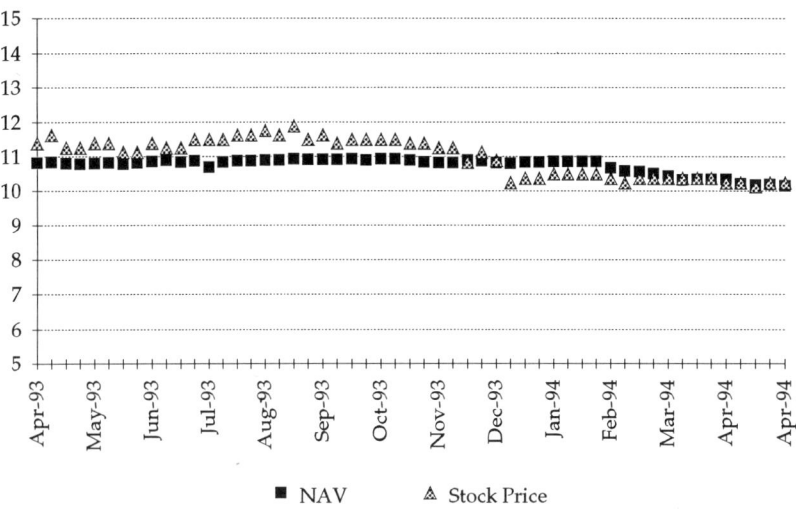

Fund Outlook (NUV): Given current conditions in the muni markets, it's easy to create headlines with sweeping predictions about directions in the economy or interest rates. The challenge comes in creating value, identifying bonds with the potential to perform well throughout economic and interest-rate cycles. NUV believes the best way to accomplish this goal is to hold to a tested value investing discipline. For instance, instead of trying to "call" temporary turns in interest rates or the economy, which it believes cannot be done consistently, NUV focuses on identifying specific bonds with the potential to perform well through the long-term.

Authors' Comments (NUV): NUV is one of the most defensive funds in its category, the primary reason we like it. It is not leveraged and has a large percentage of high coupon and pre-refunded bonds with shorter maturities. When interest rates fell, the fund lagged its peer group. But as rates have inched up, this portfolio mix has substantially helped the fund. The fund had a successful rights offering in January, raising nearly $256 million which management has been able to put to work buying undervalued current-coupon bonds. These purchases have effectively lowered the average coupon to around 7.8%. This is a good selection for defensive-oriented, tax-free investors. In this age of uncertainty, who needs fireworks?

Smith Barney Intermediate Municipal Fund

AMEX: SBI

1345 Avenue of the Americas
New York, NY 10105
800-221-9218
212-698-5349

Transfer Agent:
Provident National Bank
103 Bellevue Parkway
Wilmington, DE 19809
(800) 852-4750

Tax-Free Income

Results

For 12-months Ending 4/29/94	Period End	Period Begin	Distributions	Yield Dist (%)	Total Return (%)
Share Price ($)	10.38	10.63	0.60	5.64	3.29
NAV per Share ($)	10.27	10.64		5.64	2.16

Background: Initial public offering February 5, 1992 at $10 per share. Initial NAV was $10 per share. Offering expenses were reimbursed from management fees.

Objective: Seeks high current income exempt from regular Federal income taxes, consistent with prudent investment management.

Portfolio: (12/31/93) Municipal Bonds 100%. Sector Weightings: Health Care 18%, Housing 17%, Education 14%, General Obligation 13%, Private Placement 13%. Texas 14%, Illinois 9%, New Jersey 8%, New York 8%, Indiana 8%. Portfolio Ratings: AAA 36%, AA 12%, A 34%, BBB 17%, LNR 1%.

Capitalization: (12/31/93) Common shares outstanding 8,227,963. No long-term debt.

Average Maturity (years): 9.6

Fee: 0.60% **Fund Manager:** Mutual Management Corporation
Income Distribution: Monthly **Capital Gains Distribution:** Annually
Reinvestment Plan: Yes **Shareholder Reports:** Quarterly

5 Year Performance

Fiscal Year Ending 12/31	1993	1992	1991	1990	1989
Net Assets ($mil)	88.90	83.50	-	-	-
Net Income Distribution ($)	0.57	0.46	-	-	-
Capital Gains Distribution ($)	0.03	0.00	-	-	-
Total Distribution ($)	0.60	0.46	-	-	-
Yield from Distribution (%)	5.92	4.60	-	-	-
Expense Ratio (%)	0.73	0.59	-	-	-
Portfolio Turnover (%)	10.46	23.48	-	-	-
NAV per Share ($)	10.81	10.36	-	-	-
Market Price per Share ($)	11.13	10.13	-	-	-
Premium (Discount) (%)	2.91	4.66	-	-	-
Total Return, Stock Price (%)	15.79	-	-	-	-

Smith Barney Intermediate Municipal Fund

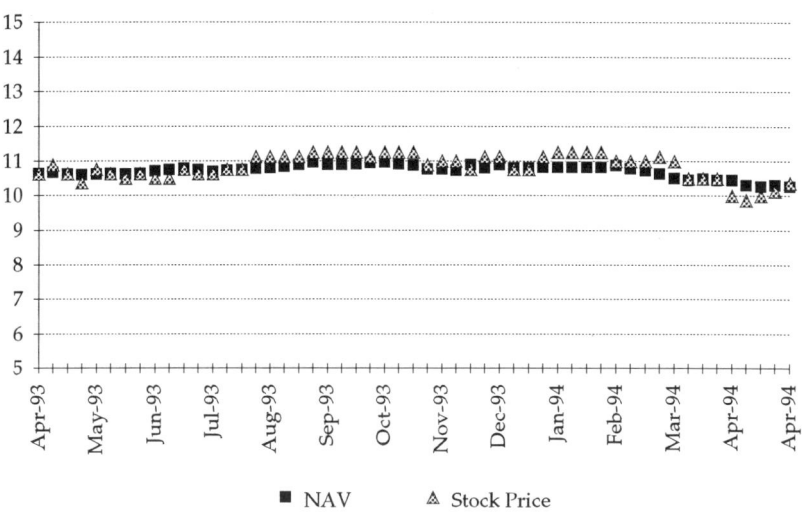

Fund Outlook (SBI): The fund is broadly diversified among sectors and continues to emphasize higher quality issues with a large percentage of assets allocated to bonds rated AA or better by at least one of the major rating agencies. On average, holdings are the long-end of the intermediate maturity range, which, in the fund's view, continues to provide strong municipal bond value. During 1993, trading levels in the portfolio were minimal in order to maintain the fund's dividend as long as possible and minimize the recognition of capital gains. The low portfolio turnover rate also contributed to a shortening of the average maturity. The fund believes it is well-positioned for the current market and, currently, does not anticipate any significant changes.

Authors' Comments (SBI): A defensive fund by definition, SBI's average weighted maturity must remain between 3 and 10 years. It's currently at about 7 years. When compared to its peers, where the average runs closer to 23 years, SBI wears a crew cut, glasses, is washed behind the ears and lives next door to the Cleavers. The fund has done well in both rising interest rates and in falling interest rates. Fund manager Peter Coffey has been able to shorten or lengthen maturities to capture as much total return as possible. Even though you can't buy it, put it in a drawer and forget about it, it's about as close as you can come in the muni bond fund sector.

High Yield (Junk) Bond Funds

Colonial Intermediate High Income Securities

NYSE: CIF

One Financial Center, 12th Floor
Boston, MA 02111
(800) 426-3750

Transfer Agent:
Shareholder Services Group
P.O. Box 1376
Boston, MA 02104
(800) 331-1710

Income Results

For 12-months Ending 4/29/94	Period End	Period Begin	Distributions	Yield Dist (%)	Total Return (%)
Share Price ($)	6.75	7.00	0.75	10.71	7.14
NAV per Share ($)	6.52	6.72		11.16	8.18

Background: Initial public offering July 21, 1988 of 11,000,000 shares at $10 per share. Net proceeds were approximately $102.3 million. Concurrently, the fund offered $33 million aggregate principal of Senior Extendible Notes for leveraging purposes.

Objective: Seeks high current income. Will invest at least 80% of total assets in high-yield fixed-income securities rated in the lower categories and unrated fixed-income securities regarded as comparable in quality.

Portfolio: (10/31/93) Corporate Bonds & Notes 94%, U.S. Government Bonds & Notes 4%, Other 2%. Sector Weightings: Consumer Non-Durables 31%, Manufacturing 48%, Transportation 4%, Energy 7%, Utilities 1%, Services 1%, Banking & Financial Services 2%.

Capitalization: (10/31/93) Common stock outstanding 13,760,000. $27,400,000 in Senior Extendable Notes.

Average Maturity (years): 8.4

Fee: 0.65% *Fund Manager:* Colonial Management Assn., Inc.
Income Distribution: Monthly *Capital Gains Distribution:* Annually
Reinvestment Plan: Yes *Shareholder Reports:* Semi-Annually

5 Year Performance

Fiscal Year Ending 10/31	1993	1992	1991	1990	1989
Net Assets ($mil)	95.10	87.10	83.60	64.90	107.80
Net Income Distribution ($)	0.72	0.78	0.78	1.11	1.20
Capital Gains Distribution ($)	0.00	0.00	0.00	0.00	0.00
Total Distribution ($)	0.72	0.78	0.78	1.11	1.20
Yield from Distribution (%)	11.52	13.00	17.81	15.04	12.63
Expense Ratio (%)	3.66	4.24	5.18	5.69	4.50
Portfolio Turnover (%)	135.00	78.00	30.00	12.00	23.00
NAV per share ($)	6.92	6.43	6.29	4.88	8.26
Market Price per Share ($)	6.63	6.25	6.00	4.38	7.38
Premium (Discount) (%)	-4.26	-2.80	-4.61	-10.45	-10.77
Total Return, Stock Price (%)	20.87	36.93	18.22	-28.55	-9.68

Colonial Intermediate High Income Securities

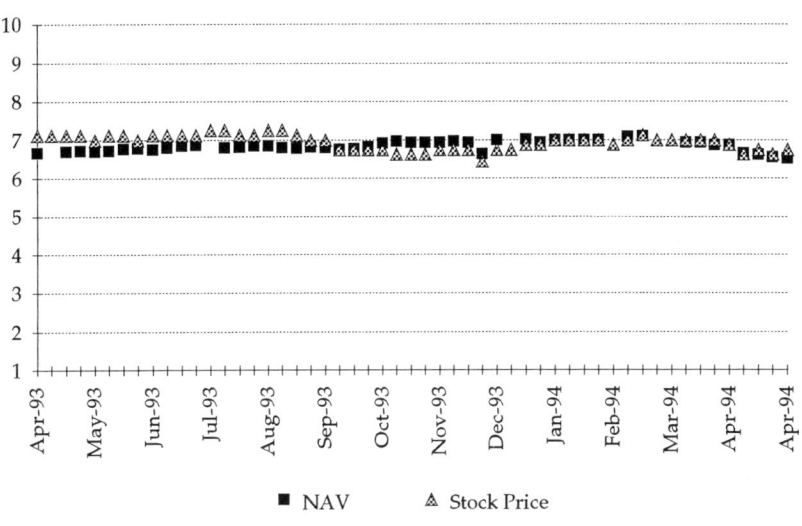

Fund Outlook (CIF): The fund is not averse to pursuing defensive strategies when warranted. For example, in early 1994, when the Fed hiked short-term rates, CIF purchased a 10% position in short-term treasuries. This created somewhat of a cushioning effect for NAV. The fund utilizes a top-down, bottom-up investment style. First, a particular sector is considered, then the best issues within that sector based upon fundamental analysis and management. Management currently likes the cyclical companies including TV and radio, paper and forest-products.

Authors' Comments (CIF): The fund has a NAV trailing 12-month return of 9.08% which exceeds the peer group performance of 6.09%. The majority of the portfolio is rated B or better. The portfolio includes high-yielding cyclical issues, where the issuer will benefit during the early stages of an economic recovery such as in the automotive, home-building and steel industries. The fund is leveraged in notes that will mature in 1998. The high fiscal yield justifies purchase when available at a discount.

High Income Advantage Trust

Two World Trade Center
New York, NY 10048
(800) 869-3863
(212) 392-2550

NYSE: **YLD**
Transfer Agent:
Dean Witter Trust Co.
2 Montgomery St.
Jersey City, NJ 07302
(800) 526-3143

Income

Results

For 12-months Ending 4/29/94	Period End	Period Begin	Distributions	Yield Dist (%)	Total Return (%)
Share Price ($)	5.88	6.13	0.61	9.95	5.87
NAV per Share ($)	6.03	5.72		10.66	16.08

Background: Initial public offering October 23, 1987 of 25,000,000 shares at $10 per share. Initial NAV was $9.25 per share.

Objective: Seeks high current income; capital appreciation is secondary. Invests primarily in lower-rated or unrated bonds of domestic corporations. May invest up to 10% in private placements. May also invest in common stocks and securities of foreign issuers and enter into repurchase agreements.

Portfolio: (9/30/93) Corporate Bonds 90%, Common Stock 8%, Other 2%. Sector Weightings: Forest & Paper Products 11%, Manufacturing 10%, Retail Food Chains 9%, Aerospace 5%. Top Holdings: Georgia Gulf Corp, Cablevision Systems Corp., Alco Health Services Corp., Presidio Oil, Container of America.

Capitalization: (9/30/93) Shares of beneficial interest outstanding 30,017,252. No long-term debt.

Average Maturity (years): 8.1

Fee: 0.75% *Fund Manager:* Dean Witter Reynolds InterCap. Div.
Income Distribution: Monthly *Capital Gains Distribution:* Annually
Reinvestment Plan: Yes *Shareholder Reports:* Quarterly

5 Year Performance

Fiscal Year Ending 9/30	1993	1992	1991	1990	1989
Net Assets ($mil)	179.80	174.70	162.00	158.50	247.90
Net Income Distribution ($)	0.82	0.59	0.69	1.13	1.20
Capital Gains Distribution ($)	0.00	0.00	0.00	0.00	0.05
Total Distribution ($)	0.82	0.59	0.69	1.13	1.25
Yield from Distribution (%)	14.26	12.74	15.33	14.34	12.65
Expense Ratio (%)	0.97	1.00	1.07	1.01	0.90
Portfolio Turnover (%)	140.00	108.00	149.00	20.00	44.00
NAV per share ($)	5.99	5.81	5.23	4.96	7.68
Market Price per Share ($)	6.13	5.75	4.63	4.50	7.88
Premium (Discount) (%)	2.25	-1.03	-11.66	-9.27	2.47
Total Return, Stock Price (%)	20.87	36.93	18.22	-28.55	-7.59

High Income Advantage Trust

Premium/Discount Spread

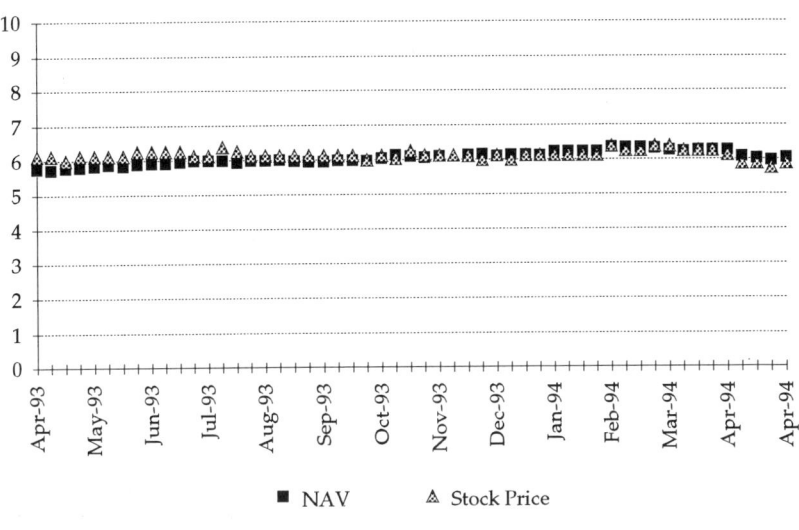

Fund Outlook (YLD): The trust focuses on financially sound issuers with improving credit quality. The trust is optimistic about the prospects for the high-yield bond market, based on expectations for a slowly improving economy and further corporate de-leveraging and debt-refinancing. If the economy continues to recover, the trust anticipates that the attractive yields available today will provide investors not only with a healthy yield advantage over alternative fixed-income products, but also with an excellent opportunity for further capital appreciation in the event yields decline.

Authors' Comments (YLD): The trust's NAV 12-month trailing performance is 15.51% compared to 9.38% for the group. Cyclical issues included in the portfolio have experienced credit quality enhancement and therefore considerable capital appreciation. Outstanding fiscal total return performance and high current yield make the trust attractive.

High Income Advantage Trust II

Two World Trade Center
New York, NY 10048
(800) 869-3863
(212) 938-4500

Income

NYSE: YLT

Transfer Agent:
Dean Witter Trust Co.
2 Montgomery St.
Jersey City, NJ 07302
(800) 526-3143

Results

For 12-months Ending 4/29/94	Period End	Period Begin	Distributions	Yield Dist (%)	Total Return (%)
Share Price ($)	6.38	6.50	0.64	9.85	5.87
NAV per Share ($)	6.76	6.32		10.66	16.08

Background: Initial public offering October 4, 1988 of 40,000,000 shares at $10 per share. Initial NAV was $9.30 per share.

Objective: Seeks high current income; capital appreciation is secondary. Invests primarily in lower-rated or unrated bonds of domestic corporations. May invest up to 10% in private placements. May also invest in common stocks and securities of foreign issuers and enter into repurchase agreements.

Portfolio: (1/31/94) Corporate Bonds 80%, Common Stocks 7%, Short-Term 8%, Other 5%. Sector Weightings: Entertainment, Gaming & Lodging 11%, Forest & Paper Products 7%, Manufacturing 7%, Food Chains 6%, Health Care Products 5%. Top Holdings: Georgia Gulf, Alco Health Services, Unisys, American Standard, Presidio Oil.

Capitalization: (1/31/94) Shares of beneficial interest outstanding 35,611,307. No long-term debt.

Average Maturity (years): 7.9

Fee: 0.75% *Fund Manager:* Dean Witter Reynolds InterCap. Div.
Income Distribution: Monthly *Capital Gains Distribution:* Annually
Reinvestment Plan: Yes *Shareholder Reports:* Quarterly

5 Year Performance

Fiscal Year Ending 7/31	1993	1992	1991	1990	1989
Net Assets ($mil)	235.00	229.30	210.60	251.80	343.60
Net Income Distribution ($)	0.91	0.66	0.77	1.19	0.92
Capital Gains Distribution ($)	0.00	0.00	0.00	0.00	0.00
Total Distribution ($)	0.91	0.66	0.77	1.19	0.93
Yield from Distribution (%)	14.00	12.87	12.83	14.42	-
Expense Ratio (%)	0.95	0.98	1.07	0.93	0.85
Portfolio Turnover (%)	138.00	99.00	129.00	31.00	101.00
NAV per share ($)	6.60	6.43	5.68	6.44	8.76
Market Price per Share ($)	6.88	6.50	5.13	6.00	8.25
Premium (Discount) (%)	4.17	1.09	-9.68	-8.70	-7.19
Total Return, Stock Price (%)	19.85	39.57	-1.67	-12.85	-

High Income Advantage Trust II

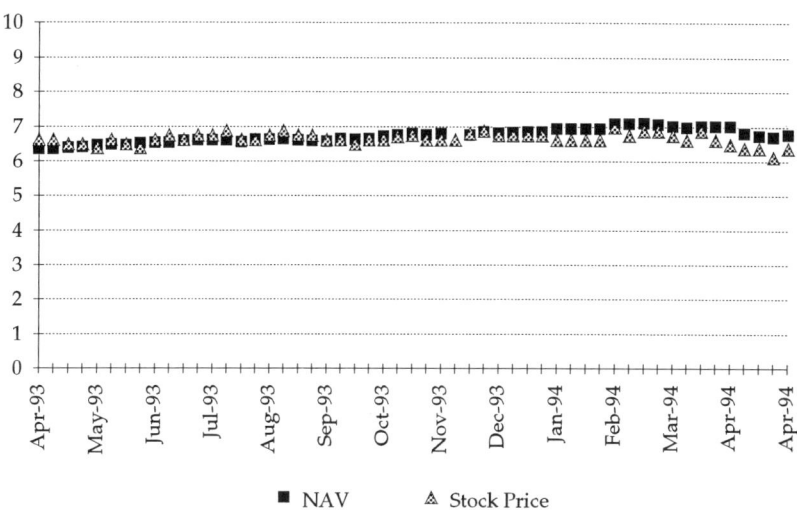

Premium/Discount Spread

■ NAV △ Stock Price

Fund Outlook (YLT): 1993 marked the third successive year of excellent returns for the high-yield market. Looking further into 1994, the trust remains optimistic about the prospects for the high-yield bond market, based on their expectations for continued growth in the economy and further improvements in corporate credit quality. The trust would anticipate that the attractive yields available today will provide investors not only with a healthy yield advantage over alternative fixed-income products, but also with an excellent opportunity for further capital appreciation in the event yields decline.

Authors' Comments (YLT): The trust's portfolio concentration consists of a large percentage of cyclical issues that will benefit from corporate deleveraging and debt refinancing. Fund Manager Peter Avelar has already shown his abilities in this arena. In the first quarter of 1994, he correctly determined that the high income bond market was trading in dangerous territory as rates tracked up. He moved out of issues he felt were trading too rich, parked assets in shorter term maturities, and then bought back the very same issues later in the year, picking them up at lower prices than he sold them for. That's good management and causes us to rate this fund as the best choice for high income investors.

High Income Advantage Trust III

Two World Trade Center
New York, NY 10048
(800) 869-3863
(212) 938-9500

Income

NYSE: YLH

Transfer Agent:
Dean Witter Trust Co.
2 Montgomery St.
Jersey City, NJ 07302
(800) 869-3863

Results

For 12-months Ending 4/29/94	Period End	Period Begin	Distributions	Yield Dist (%)	Total Return (%)
Share Price ($)	7.13	7.00	0.72	10.29	12.14
NAV per Share ($)	7.21	6.87		10.48	15.43

Background: Initial public offering February 8, 1989 of 10,760 shares at $10 per share. Initial NAV was $9.30 per share.

Objective: Seeks high current income from a portfolio of lower-rated or unrated bonds. The fund also invests in common stocks and securities of foreign issuers. The fund may also enter into repurchase agreements.

Portfolio: (1/31/94) Corporate Bonds 83%, Common Stocks 6%, Warrants 1%, Short-Term 7%. U.S. Government Obligations 6.4%. Sector Weightings: Health Care Products 6%, Entertainment, Gaming & Lodging 12%, Food Chains 7%. Top Holdings: Health Services, Georgia Gulf, Unisys, American Standard, Aztar Mortgage Funding.

Capitalization: (1/31/94) Shares of beneficial interest outstanding 12,876,779. No long-term debt.

Average Maturity (years): 8

Fee: 0.75%   *Fund Manager:* Dean Witter Reynolds InterCap. Div.
Income Distribution: Monthly   *Capital Gains Distribution:* Annually
Reinvestment Plan: Yes   *Shareholder Reports:* Semi-Annually

5 Year Performance

Fiscal Year Ending 1/31	1993	1992	1991	1990	1989
Net Assets ($mil)	86.30	89.10	68.50	101.10	-
Net Income Distribution ($)	0.91	0.77	1.15	0.95	-
Capital Gains Distribution ($)	0.00	0.00	0.00	0.00	-
Total Distribution ($)	0.91	0.77	1.15	0.95	-
Yield from Distribution (%)	14.00	17.11	15.58	-	-
Expense Ratio (%)	1.06	1.17	1.05	0.93	-
Portfolio Turnover (%)	118.00	137.00	44.00	59.00	-
NAV per share ($)	6.70	6.83	5.18	7.59	-
Market Price per Share ($)	6.88	6.50	4.50	7.38	-
Premium (Discount) (%)	2.61	-4.83	-13.13	-2.90	-
Total Return, Stock Price (%)	19.85	61.56	-23.44	-	-

High Income Advantage Trust III

Premium/Discount Spread

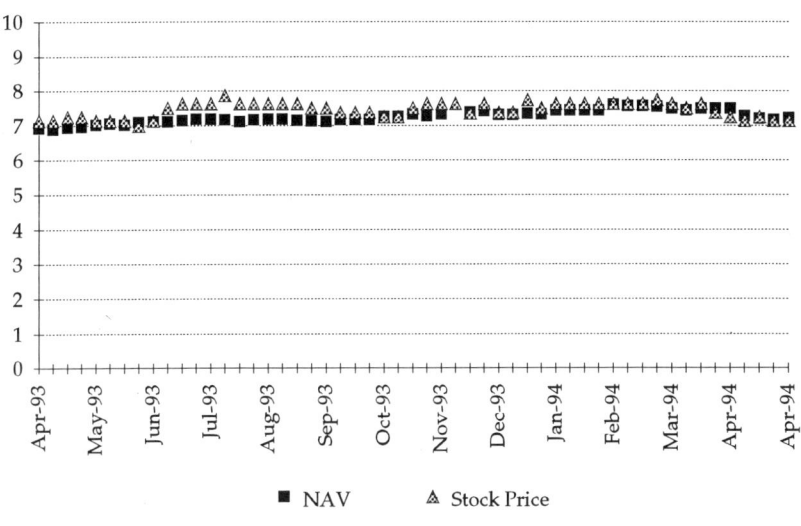

■ NAV △ Stock Price

Fund Outlook (YLH): Looking further into 1994, the trust remains optimistic about the prospects for the high-yield bond market, based on their expectations for continued growth in the economy and further improvements in corporate credit quality. If the economy continues to recover and high-yield issuers work toward strengthening their balance sheets, the trust would anticipate that the attractive yields available today will provide investors not only with a healthy yield advantage over alternative fixed-income products, but also with an excellent opportunity for further capital appreciation in the event yields decline.

Authors' Comments (YLH): The trust has a NAV relative performance for the past 12 months of 14.70% versus 9.38% for the peer group. In July 1992 41% of the portfolio was invested in zeros. By July 1993 this position was reduced to 1.4% and investments shifted to cyclicals that will benefit from the upturn in the economy. The fund is well-positioned for income investors seeking above average total return potential with high current yield.

Convertible Bond Funds

Lincoln National Convertible Securities Fund, Inc.

1300 S. Clinton Street
Fort Wayne, IN 46801
(219) 455-2210

NYSE: **LNV**
Transfer Agent:
First National Bank of Boston
P.O. Box 644
Boston, MA 02102
(800) 442-2001

Income

Results

For 12-months Ending 4/29/94	Period End	Period Begin	Distributions	Yield Dist (%)	Total Return (%)
Share Price ($)	17.25	18.13	1.53	8.44	3.59
NAV per Share ($)	17.80	18.87		8.11	2.44

Background: Initial public offering June 19, 1986 of 6,900,000 shares at $15 per share. Initial NAV was $13.96 per share.

Objective: Seeks a high level of total return through capital appreciation and current income. Invests at least 65% of assets in convertible securities, including direct placements.

Portfolio: (12/31/93) Public Debt Securities 4%, Convertible Securities 102%, Other (6%). Top Holdings: Agco Convertible Preferreds, California Energy Convertible, Owens-Corning Fiberglass Convertible, Riverwood International Convertibles, EMC Convertibles.

Capitalization: (12/31/93) Common stock outstanding 6,292,442. No long-term debt.

Average Maturity (years): 10.4

Fee: 0.60% *Fund Manager:* Lincoln National Invest. Mgt. Co.
Income Distribution: Quarterly *Capital Gains Distribution:* Annually
Reinvestment Plan: Yes *Shareholder Reports:* Quarterly

5 Year Performance

Fiscal Year Ending 12/31	1993	1992	1991	1990	1989
Net Assets ($mil)	118.60	110.70	113.40	85.40	95.70
Net Income Distribution ($)	1.05	0.97	1.02	1.02	1.07
Capital Gains Distribution ($)	1.87	1.17	0.00	0.00	0.50
Total Distribution ($)	2.92	2.14	1.02	1.02	1.57
Yield from Distribution (%)	17.70	13.81	8.87	7.62	11.63
Expense Ratio (%)	102.00	0.83	0.89	0.97	0.94
Portfolio Turnover (%)	222.00	166.26	132.99	134.64	147.31
NAV per Share ($)	18.84	17.62	18.04	13.59	15.21
Market Price per Share ($)	19.25	16.50	15.50	11.50	13.38
Premium (Discount) (%)	2.18	-6.36	-14.08	-15.38	-12.10
Total Return, Stock Price (%)	34.36	20.26	43.65	-6.43	10.74

Lincoln National Convertible Securities

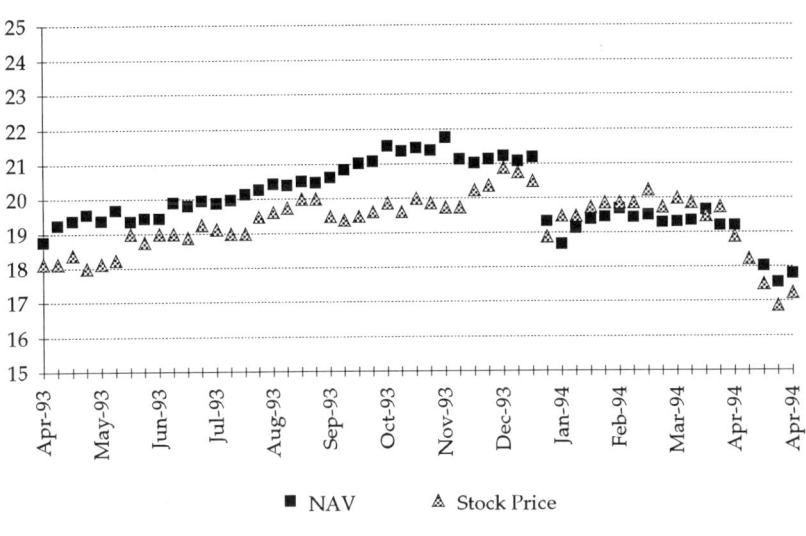

Premium/Discount Spread

■ NAV △ Stock Price

Fund Outlook (LNV): For 1993 and the cumulative five-year period ending December 31, 1993. LNV was the top performing convertible fund according to Lipper Analytical Services, Inc. The fund provides an easy method of investing in a diversified portfolio of convertible bonds. It would be very difficult for investors to do this on their own as many convertibles are not actively quoted on listed exchanges. The fund provides a means of participating in the potential return of a rising stock market while receiving an above-average market yield.

Authors' Comments (LNV): Convertible funds offer a little of both worlds, income and growth. While many criticize the group as really only benefitting the issuing company, as an asset class, they have their days in the sun. LNV is a fund that has shown what a successfully managed convertible strategy can do. With a highly aggressive style, it seeks out smaller capitalized companies and special situations. The turnover ratio is very high, reflective of its lively investment policies. Rapid turnover and sector reallocations make predictions of portfolio composition difficult. However, in the case of this fund we like the dynamic management philosophy. It has proven to be extremely successful over the years. Fund manager Robert Schwartz has proven admirably adept at the helm. The fund is an excellent choice for the more aggressive convertible investor—if there is such a thing.

Putnam High Income Convertible & Bond Fund

One Post Office Square
Boston, MA 02109
(617) 292-1000

Growth & Income

NYSE: PCF
Transfer Agent:
Putnam Investor Services
P.O. Box 2701
Boston, MA 02208
(800) 634-1587

Results

For 12-months Ending 4/29/94	Period End	Period Begin	Distributions	Yield Dist (%)	Total Return (%)
Share Price ($)	9.75	9.75	0.87	8.92	8.92
NAV per Share ($)	9.38	9.05		9.61	13.26

Background: Initial public offering July 9, 1987 of 125,000,000 shares at $10 per share. Initial NAV was $9.30 per share.

Objective: Seeks high current income. Capital appreciation is secondary. The fund will invest in high-yielding convertible securities which at the time of purchase are trading principally on their current yield rather than on the value of the underlying equity. Will also invest in lower-rated, higher-yielding securities to augment income.

Portfolio: (12/31/93) Corporate Bonds & Notes 35%, High-Yield Bonds 46%, Convertible Preferred 8%, Preferred Stocks 1%, Other 6%. Portfolio Ratings: AAA 10%, A 3%, BBB 3%, BB 8%, B 66%, Lower or Non-Rated 11%.

Capitalization: (8/31/93) Common stock outstanding 12,945,798. No long-term debt.

Average Maturity (years): 10.3
Fee: 0.75%
Income Distribution: Monthly
Reinvestment Plan: Yes
Fund Manager: Putnam Mgt. Co., Inc.
Capital Gains Distribution: Annually
Shareholder Reports: Quarterly

5 Year Performance

Fiscal Year Ending 8/31	1993	1992	1991	1990	1989
Net Assets ($mil)	123.30	108.90	95.80	87.90	105.80
Net Income Distribution ($)	0.84	0.94	0.85	0.92	0.85
Capital Gains Distribution ($)	0.00	0.00	0.01	0.02	0.00
Total Distribution ($)	0.84	0.94	0.86	0.94	0.85
Yield from Distribution (%)	9.46	12.32	14.63	11.93	10.63
Expense Ratio (%)	1.03	1.13	1.31	1.26	1.15
Portfolio Turnover (%)	71.63	45.84	68.36	53.30	69.68
NAV per Share ($)	9.52	8.49	7.56	6.94	8.37
Market Price per Share ($)	10.00	8.88	7.63	5.88	7.88
Premium (Discount) (%)	5.04	4.48	0.93	-15.42	-5.97
Total Return, Stock Price (%)	22.07	28.70	44.39	-13.45	9.12

Premium/Discount Spread

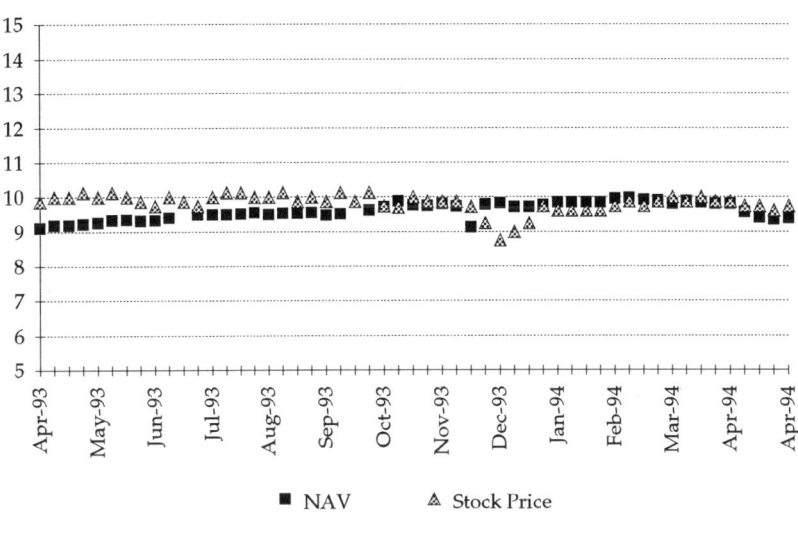

■ NAV △ Stock Price

Fund Outlook (PCF): High-yield bonds continued to rally despite higher rates on Treasury securities. News of continued economic growth is one reason for the high demand for these securities. Additionally, a shortage of attractive yields elsewhere in the taxable market brought many new investors into the high-yield market. The fund continues to maintain approximately a 50/50 split between high-yielding convertible and straight bonds. The fund also continues to emphasize cyclically oriented securities with broad diversification across industry groups. On the convertible side, the fund has selectively taken profits on some energy, technology and early cyclical issues. On the straight bond side, they have also favored cable company investments, which have demonstrated improved performance as a result of acquisition activity in the industry.

Authors' Comments (PCF): Outstanding total performance. The NAV trailing 12-month performance is the highest in the peer group. This fund has always sold at a slight premium because of its consistently strong performance. The above average yield results from the large concentration in high yielding bonds and adds to total performance making this issue extremely attractive. The large exposure to environmental and health care sectors offers great appreciation potential as both areas have been depressed of late.

TCW Convertible Securities Fund, Inc.   NYSE: CVT

865 S. Figueroa Street
Los Angeles, CA 90017
(213) 244-0662

Growth & Income

Transfer Agent:
The Bank of New York
Church Street Station, P.O. Box 11002
New York, NY 10277-0770
(800) 524-4458

Results

For 12-months Ending 4/29/94	Period End	Period Begin	Distributions	Yield Dist (%)	Total Return (%)
Share Price ($)	9.13	9.50	1.06	11.16	7.26
NAV per Share ($)	8.17	8.69		12.20	6.21

Background: Initial public offering February 26, 1987 of 20,000,000 shares at $10 per share. Initial NAV was $9.27 per share.

Objective: Seeks a high rate of total return (both income and capital appreciation). Under normal market conditions, 65% of total assets will be in convertible securities. Securities may be BB or lower as rated by S&P. The balance of the portfolio may be in non-convertible equity and investment-grade debt securities issued or guaranteed by the U.S. Government.

Portfolio: (12/31/93) Convertible Securities: 99%. Sector Weightings: Banks & Financial Services & Building 17%, Leisure & Entertainment & Photo & Media 12%, Health Care 10%, Information Processing 8%, Energy & Oil Services 7%. Top Holdings: Roche Holdings 3%, Delta Air Lines 3%, Chiron Corp. 2.4%, Omnicom Group Inc. 2.3%, Storage Tech. Corp. 2.2%.

Capitalization: (12/31/93) Common stock outstanding 31,047,913. No long-term debt.

Average Maturity (years): 10.4
Fee: 0.75%   *Fund Manager:* TCW Funds Management, Inc.
Income Distribution: Quarterly   *Capital Gains Distribution:* Annually
Reinvestment Plan: Yes   *Shareholder Reports:* Semi-Annually

5 Year Performance

Fiscal Year Ending 12/31	1993	1992	1991	1990	1989
Net Assets ($mil)	273.20	215.20	172.30	144.60	175.70
Net Income Distribution ($)	0.84	0.84	0.84	0.84	0.84
Capital Gains Distribution ($)	0.37	0.00	0.00	0.00	0.00
Total Distribution ($)	1.21	0.84	0.84	0.84	0.84
Yield from Distribution (%)	13.25	9.60	12.21	10.50	11.38
Expense Ratio (%)	0.80	0.88	0.94	0.94	0.95
Portfolio Turnover (%)	173.79	139.39	114.13	99.53	84.17
NAV per Share ($)	8.79	8.36	8.09	6.85	8.36
Market Price per Share ($)	9.25	9.13	8.75	6.88	8.00
Premium (Discount) (%)	5.23	9.21	8.16	0.44	-4.31
Total Return, Stock Price (%)	14.75	13.94	39.39	-3.50	19.78

TCW Convertible Securities Fund, Inc.

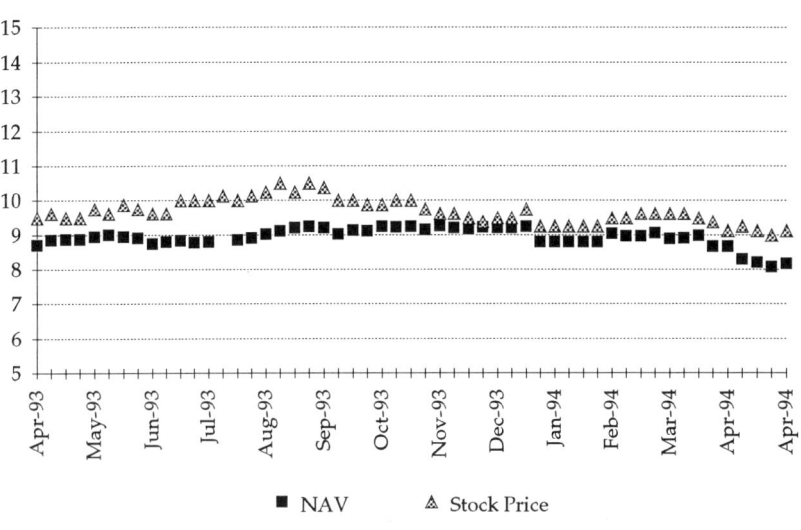

Premium/Discount Spread

■ NAV　△ Stock Price

Fund Outlook (CVT): The convertible new issue calendar continued its remarkable rise in 1993—over $23 billion. From this the fund makes two observations: first, new security issuance greatly facilitates the portfolio management process as new issues must be priced to sell in order to convince investors to buy. Thus, market power is shifted from sellers to buyers. Second, new issues with attractive terms and prices and are convertible into desirable stocks are identifiable in the market. Overall, CVT considers the vitality of the new issue calendar to be a major plus for management of convertible securities. Also important was the continued decline in intermediate- and long-term interest rates which enabled many companies to refinance existing debt at attractive rates. This had a positive effect on both the credit quality and the stock prices. CVT believes the combination of modest but rising economic growth, low inflation and slightly higher interest rates will create an environment in which stocks could again provide returns of approximately 10%. However, should CVT's forecast prove faulty and stocks experience a significant correction, convertibles will provide a good measure of protection from any downturn.

Authors' Comments (CVT): This fund has been selected on the basis of its top performance, second only to Putnam High Income Convertible & Bond Fund. The NAV trailing performance for the past 12-months ranked second in the convertible bond group. The four largest sectors should benefit from an improving economy. This is an excellent fund, but be selective. The current premium will have to diminish somewhat.

Investment Grade Corporate Bond Funds

Current Income Shares, Inc.

NYSE: CUR

P.O. Box 30151, Terminal Annex
Los Angeles, CA 90030
(213) 236-4056

Transfer Agent:
Harris Trust Co.of California
601 South Figueroa St., 49th Floor
Los Angeles, CA 90017
(213) 239-0670

Income

Results

For 12-months Ending 4/29/94	Period End	Period Begin	Distributions	Yield Dist (%)	Total Return (%)
Share Price ($)	12.00	13.63	0.96	7.04	-4.92
NAV per Share ($)	13.25	14.05		6.83	1.14

Background: Organized under sponsorship of Unionamerica, Inc., a financial services company. Initial public offering March 27, 1973 at $15 per share. Initial NAV was $13.80 per share.

Objective: Seeks high current income by investing 75% of total assets in high-quality straight-debt securities, with the balance invested in other debt securities, preferred stocks, and high-quality income-producing common stocks. Up to 10% of assets may be invested in private placements. The fund may also hold up to 25% of assets in issues rated below investment-grade. To supplement interest income, may lend its securities; it may also engage in short-term trading. The fund may leverage up to one third of its assets.

Portfolio: (12/31/93) Bonds 98%. Sector Weightings: Utilities 36%, Industrial 29.2%, Canadian 18%, U.S. Government 5%, Transportation 4%. Portfolio Ratings: AAA 13%, AA 91%, A 30%, BBB 38%, Lower or Non-Rated 9%.

Capitalization: (12/31/93) Common stock outstanding 3,673,334. No long-term debt.

Average Maturity (years): 19.6

Fee: 0.50%

Income Distribution: Quarterly

Reinvestment Plan: Yes

Fund Manager: Union Bank

Capital Gains Distribution: Annually

Shareholder Reports: Semi-Annually

5 Year Performance

Fiscal Year Ending 12/31	1993	1992	1991	1990	1989
Net Assets ($mil)	52.10	48.90	48.40	43.40	45.20
Net Income Distribution ($)	0.97	1.03	1.09	1.10	1.12
Capital Gains Distribution ($)	0.00	0.00	0.00	0.00	0.00
Total Distribution ($)	0.97	1.03	1.09	1.10	1.12
Yield from Distribution (%)	7.68	7.77	9.08	8.98	10.18
Expense Ratio (%)	0.80	0.90	0.90	0.90	0.90
Portfolio Turnover (%)	24.15	87.06	82.38	106.20	84.50
NAV per Share ($)	14.19	13.33	13.16	11.80	12.30
Market Price per Share ($)	13.00	12.63	13.25	12.00	12.25
Premium (Discount) (%)	-8.39	-5.25	0.68	1.69	-0.41
Total Return, Stock Price (%)	10.61	3.09	19.50	6.94	21.55

Current Income Shares, Inc.

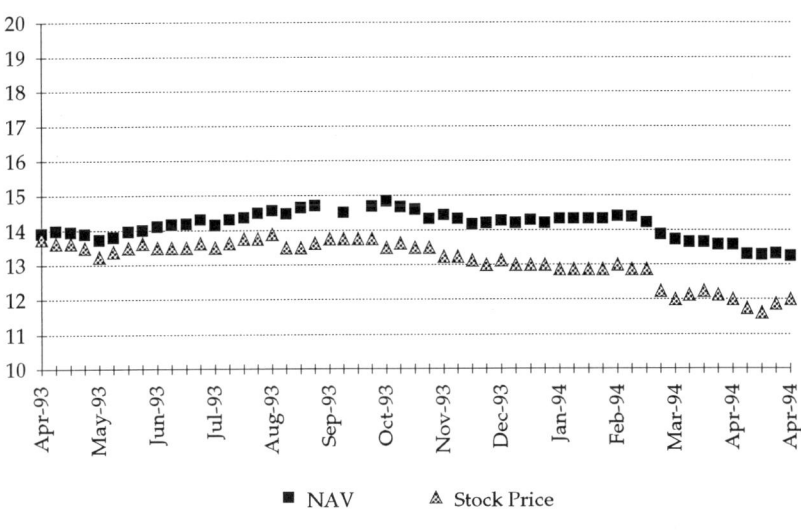

Fund Outlook (CUR): Fund management is optimistic that the negative returns experienced from bond investments over the first five months of 1994 will be reversed during the second half of the year. The sharp rise in interest rates is about over and the second half of the year should see lower interest rates as the economy slows and inflation remains dormant. In 1995 the fund is looking for significantly lower rates. Call protected corporate bonds will in all likelihood produce higher total returns than Government bonds as interest rates drop. Therefore, shareholders can benefit from a high level of current income while the portfolio's NAV gains from the rising bond prices.

Authors' Comments (CUR): Dividend stability can be attributed to portfolio manager James V. Atkinson's preference for call-protected bonds. However, with everything in life there are trade-offs. Longer call protection often goes hand in hand with longer maturities which increases interest rate risk. Exposure to electric utilities attracts us to this fund. Plus, the current discount offers a pleasing way to buy a very savvy portfolio manager with an excellent five-year total return record.

John Hancock Income Securities Trust

NYSE: JHS

101 Huntington Avenue
Boston, MA 02199-7603
(800) 843-0090

Transfer Agent:
Bank of Boston
P.O. Box 644
Boston, MA 02102
(617) 575-2900

Income

Results

For 12-months Ending 4/29/94	Period End	Period Begin	Distributions	Yield Dist (%)	Total Return (%)
Share Price ($)	15.00	17.50	1.37	7.83	-6.46
NAV per Share ($)	15.93	17.03		8.04	1.59

Background: Initial public offering February 14, 1973. Net proceeds were $176.7 million.

Objective: Seeks high current income consistent with prudent risk. Invests at least 75% of total assets in debt securities rated within the four highest categories by S&P or Moody's. Up to 20% of fund's assets may consist of income-producing preferred and common stocks.

Portfolio: (12/31/93) Banks & Finance 18%, Utilities 12%, U.S. Government Agency Issues 29%, Cyclicals 19%, Broadcasting 5%, Foreign Government Issues 5%, Other 12%. Largest Holdings: U.S. Treasuries, U.S. Agencies, Barclay's, American Airlines.

Capitalization: (12/31/93) Common stock outstanding 10,076,240. No long-term debt.

Average Maturity (years): 17.1

Fee: 0.50%

Fund Manager: John Hancock Advisors, Inc.

Income Distribution: Quarterly

Capital Gains Distribution: Annually

Reinvestment Plan: Yes

Shareholder Reports: Quarterly

5 Year Performance

Fiscal Year Ending 12/31	1993	1992	1991	1990	1989
Net Assets ($mil)	170.90	162.50	160.00	147.70	149.70
Net Income Distribution ($)	1.32	1.38	1.46	1.47	1.47
Capital Gains Distribution ($)	0.13	0.00	0.00	0.00	0.00
Total Distribution ($)	1.45	1.38	1.46	1.47	1.47
Yield from Distribution (%)	8.79	8.12	9.73	9.48	10.14
Expense Ratio (%)	0.84	0.81	0.74	0.70	0.71
Portfolio Turnover (%)	95.00	110.78	91.97	84.67	61.79
NAV per Share ($)	16.97	16.31	16.25	15.19	15.61
Market Price per Share ($)	16.50	16.75	17.00	15.00	15.50
Premium (Discount) (%)	-2.71	2.70	4.62	-1.25	-0.70
Total Return, Stock Price (%)	7.16	6.65	23.07	6.26	17.03

John Hancock Income Securities Trust

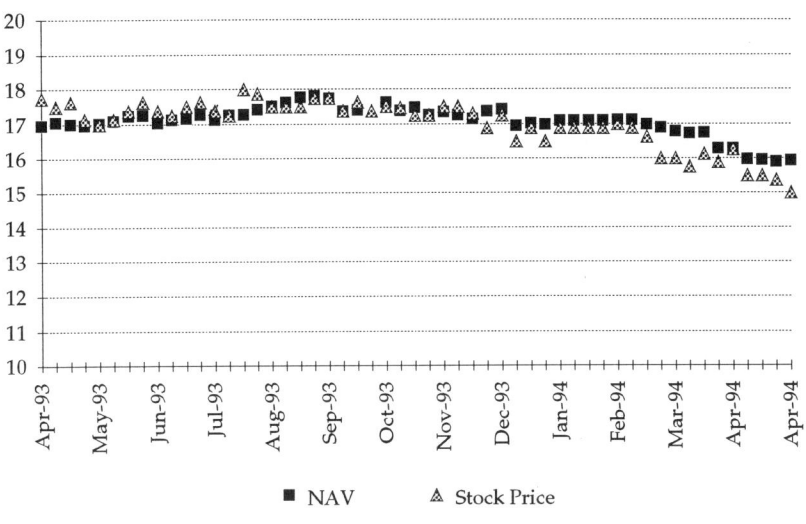

Fund Outlook (JHS): The trust believes that double-digit returns are going to be harder to come by in 1994, but that opportunities exist. With growth expected to remain moderate and inflation under control, bonds should generate decent single-digit returns. The trust offers a word of caution: The ride could be somewhat bumpy, as investors worry about the Federal Reserve raising short-term rates. In anticipation of some volatility, the trust scaled back their maturity barbell slightly at the end of last year. That should reduce the trust's interest-rate sensitivity and provide some protection against any rise in rates. Overall, the trust is still sticking with a barbell structure because it expects the yield curve to flatten further as long-term rates remain stable or fall slightly and short-term rates edge up. Even though prices aren't likely to rise sharply, JHS is still optimistic about high-yield bonds. Because its yields are four to five percentage points higher than U.S. Treasuries, they should continue to provide decent returns just by earning their coupons, and it will benefit as the economy gains strength. For the first time in three years, the trust started building up its stage in mortgage-backed securities. In 1993, a wave of mortgage refinancing battered mortgage-backed bonds. However, their future is looking brighter.

Authors' Comments (JHS): The quality of the portfolio is 76% rated BBB or better while 24% is below investment grade. This fund will outperform in the current interest rate environment precisely because they are currently invested in mortgage-backed securities.

Montgomery Street Income Securities
101 California Street, Suite 4100
San Francisco, CA 94111
(415) 981-8191
Income

NYSE: MTS
Transfer Agent:
First National Bank of Boston
P.O. Box 644, Boston, MA 02102
(617) 575-2900

Results

For 12-months Ending 4/29/94	Period End	Period Begin	Distributions	Yield Dist (%)	Total Return (%)
Share Price ($)	17.75	21.63	1.47	6.80	-11.14
NAV per Share ($)	18.86	20.08		7.32	1.25

Background: Initial public offering February 14, 1973 of 8,000,000 shares at $25 per share. Initial NAV was $23.11 per share.

Objective: Seeks high income consistent with prudent risk. Capital appreciation is secondary. Invests 70% in straight debt securities rated in the top four categories by S&P or Moody's; obligations of, or debt guaranteed by, the U.S. or Canadian Governments not to exceed 25% of assets, provincial or municipal securities, commercial paper, and cash. May invest up to 30% in lower-equity bonds, debt issues with equity features, preferred stock, and dividend-paying utility common stocks.

Portfolio: (12/31/93) Long-Term Bonds 86%, Intermediate-Term Bonds 11%, Short-Term Investments 1%. Sector Weightings: U.S. Treasury & Agency 33%, Energy 11%, Financial 11%, Utilities 9%, Media 7%.

Capitalization: (12/31/93) Common stock outstanding 9,958,150. No long-term debt.

Average Maturity (years): 12.5
Fee: 0.50%   *Fund Manager:* Scudder, Stevens & Clark, Inc.
Income Distribution: Quarterly   *Capital Gains Distribution:* Annually
Reinvestment Plan: Yes   *Shareholder Reports:* Semi-Annually

5 Year Performance

Fiscal Year Ending 12/31	1993	1992	1991	1990	1989
Net Assets ($mil)	200.50	191.00	157.10	139.80	144.80
Net Income Distribution ($)	1.54	1.67	1.76	1.78	1.85
Capital Gains Distribution ($)	0.00	0.00	0.00	0.00	0.00
Total Distribution ($)	1.54	1.67	1.76	1.78	1.85
Yield from Distribution (%)	7.38	8.51	10.06	9.49	10.35
Expense Ratio (%)	0.73	0.75	0.69	0.57	0.52
Portfolio Turnover (%)	122.80	137.60	72.00	69.10	97.10
NAV per Share ($)	20.13	19.3	19.17	17.21	17.97
Market Price per Share ($)	19.75	20.88	19.63	17.50	18.75
Premium (Discount) (%)	-1.89	8.19	2.35	1.69	4.34
Total Return, Stock Price (%)	1.96	14.88	22.23	2.83	15.21

Premium/Discount Spread

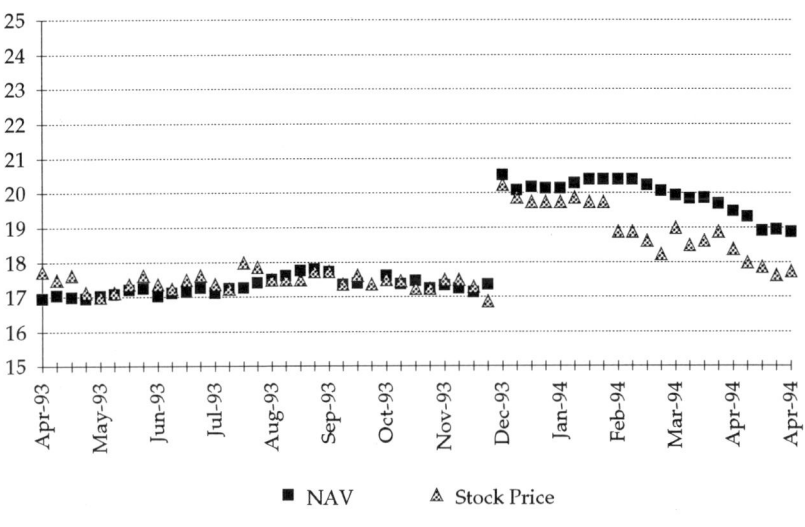

■ NAV   △ Stock Price

Fund Outlook (MTS): Looking ahead, economic activity is expected to improve but not at the rate experienced in the fourth quarter 1993. The combined effects of the tax increase and poor weather should hold the recovery down to a rate which will not strain production capacity or burden the capital markets, at least until the summer. Similarly, the best inflation news may be over, but the picture is not likely to deteriorate very much. Employment costs are under control, and weak economies in Europe and Japan add weight to the conclusion that price restraint and slow growth will continue to be the order of the day.

Authors' Comments (MTS): The current discount exceeds the average for its group. The yield is attractive. NAV trailing 12-month performance has exceeded the group average. The majority of the portfolio is rated BB or better. The fund experienced above average returns in 1991, 1992 and 1993 because 15% of the portfolio was in inverse-floaters. This position, because of pre-payments, has been reduced to 6%, and funds were shifted to foreign and junk bond positions. This is a quality issue available at a discount.

Pilgrim Prime Rate Trust

10100 Santa Monica Blvd.
Los Angeles, CA 90067
(800) 331-1080

NYSE: PPR

Transfer Agent:
Investors Fiduciary Trust Company
P.O. Box 419368
Kansas City, MO 64141

Income

Results

For 12-months Ending 4/29/94	Period End	Period Begin	Distributions	Yield Dist (%)	Total Return (%)
Share Price ($)	9.75	9.25	0.55	5.95	11.35
NAV per Share ($)	9.99	10.03		5.48	5.08

Background: Commenced operations May 12, 1988. Prior to PPR's listing on the NYSE on March 9, 1992 its shares were continuously offered through broker-dealers at net asset value plus a sales charge of up to 3% of the offering price.

Objective: Seeks high current income consistent with preservation of capital. The trust seeks to achieve its objective by investing in Senior Collateralized Corporate Loans, the interest rates on which reset periodically at various spreads above established short-term lending rates.

Portfolio: (3/31/94) Senior Collateralized Bonds 91%, Cash 8%, Stocks 1%. Top Holdings: Northwest Airlines Loan Participation of '97, USG Loan Participation of '00, Playtex Family Products Loan Participation of '96, Saks Loan Participation of '00, Aviall Loan Participation of' '00.

Capitalization: (2/28/94) Common stock outstanding 71,835,000. No long-term debt.

Average Maturity (years): 4.7

Fee: 0.85%   **Fund Manager:** Pilgrim Management Corporation

Income Distribution: Monthly   **Capital Gains Distribution:** Annually

Reinvestment Plan: Yes   **Shareholder Reports:** Quarterly

5 Year Performance

Fiscal Year Ending 2/28	1993	1992	1991	1990	1989
Net Assets ($mil)	719.90	738.80	874.10	1158.20	1036.50
Net Income Distribution ($)	0.60	0.57	0.75	0.96	1.06
Capital Gains Distribution ($)	0.00	0.00	0.00	0.00	0.00
Total Distribution ($)	0.60	0.57	0.75	0.96	1.06
Yield from Distribution (%)	6.57	-	-	-	10.60
Expense Ratio (%)	1.31	1.42	1.38	1.46	1.46
Portfolio Turnover (%)	87.00	81.00	53.00	55.00	100.00
NAV per Share ($)	10.02	10.05	9.96	9.97	10.00
Market Price per Share ($)	9.25	9.13	-	-	-
Premium (Discount) (%)	-7.68	-9.15	-	-	-
Total Return, Stock Price (%)	7.89	-	-	-	-

Pilgrim Prime Rate

Premium/Discount Spread

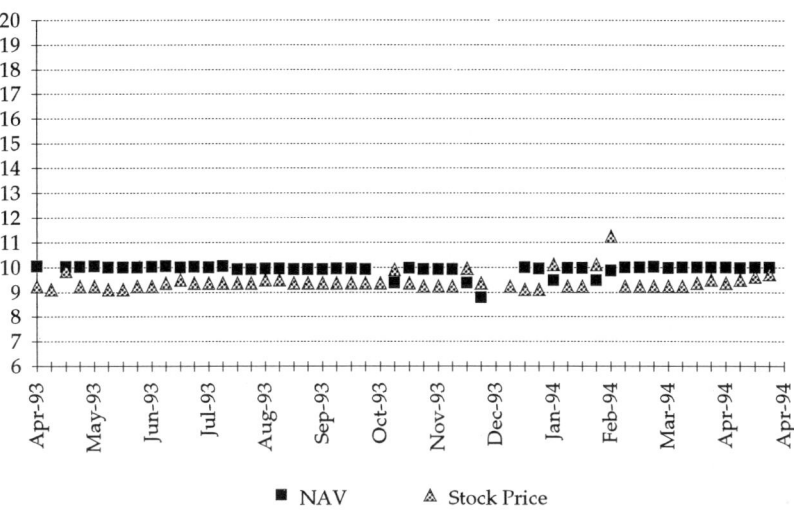

■ NAV △ Stock Price

Fund Outlook (PPR): Looking forward, the trust believes that in the coming months securities markets will exhibit a continuation of interest rate induced volatility. In such an environment, the trust expects to continue to be able to pay a dividend that would in time adjust to the new level of interest rates with little impact on net asset value. The trust also believes that the months ahead represent an unusual opportunity for a portfolio of senior, secured floating-rate loans to well-managed companies. And, in spite of widespread uncertainty in most financial markets, the trust believes it will continue to win the long-term race in investment performance against more volatile investments through its strategy of slow but steady delivery of results consistent with its objective of high current income and relative stability of net asset value.

Authors' Comments (PPR): Steady as a rock, this fund is an excellent hedge against rising short-term interest rates. By its very nature, this fund rises and falls with the yield tide. The fund is specifically structured to maintain a stable NAV while providing a variable current yield close to the prime rate by investing in participation of senior collateralized corporate loans. The loans to corporations restructured to have stable prices since changes in the interest rate environment are reflected by similar changes in the interest rates corporations pay. The quality of the loan paper should improve as corporate balance sheets improve with a stronger economy. A good core in the taxable portfolio.

State Mutual Securities Trust

440 Lincoln Street
Worchester, MA 01653
(508) 855-1000

Income

NYSE: SMS

Transfer Agent:
The Bank of New York
P.O. Box 11002
Church Street Station, NY 10249
(800) 524-4458

Results

For 12-months Ending 4/29/94	Period End	Period Begin	Distributions	Yield Dist (%)	Total Return (%)
Share Price ($)	10.38	11.63	0.90	7.74	-3.01
NAV per Share ($)	11.14	11.79		7.63	2.12

Background: Initial public offering February 20, 1973 of 7,700,000 shares at $15 per share. Initial NAV was $13.80 per share.

Objective: Seeks high current income. Capital appreciation is secondary. Invests primarily in fixed-income securities. Invests at least 40% of total assets in securities rated in the top four categories by S&P or Moody's, obligations issued or guaranteed by the U.S. or Canadian Governments, high-grade commercial paper, and cash equivalents. May invest up to 50% of net assets in private placements. May borrow short-term up to 25%.

Portfolio: (12/31/93) Corporate Bonds 78.33%, U.S. Government & Agencies 13.37%, Foreign 4.64%. Sector Weightings: Electric, Gas & Sanitary 19.87%, Communication 9.72%, Petroleum Refining 7.45%, Air Transportation 7.04%, Banking 5.22%.

Capitalization: (12/31/93) Common stock outstanding 8,592,305. No long-term debt.

Average Maturity (years): 11.6

Fee: 0.30% **Fund Manager:** State Mut. Life Assur. Co. of America
Income Distribution: Quarterly **Capital Gains Distribution:** Annually
Reinvestment Plan: Yes **Shareholder Reports:** Semi-Annually

5 Year Performance

Fiscal Year Ending 12/31	1993	1992	1991	1990	1989
Net Assets ($mil)	101.20	95.40	93.60	85.40	89.60
Net Income Distribution ($)	0.91	0.97	0.97	1.04	1.09
Capital Gains Distribution ($)	0.00	0.00	0.00	0.00	0.00
Total Distribution ($)	0.91	0.97	0.97	1.04	1.09
Yield from Distribution (%)	7.74	9.13	10.07	9.56	10.02
Expense Ratio (%)	0.74	0.76	0.77	0.82	0.84
Portfolio Turnover (%)	55.00	55.00	43.00	39.00	31.00
NAV per Share ($)	11.77	11.3	11.08	10.11	10.68
Market Price per Share ($)	11.63	11.75	10.63	9.63	10.88
Premium (Discount) (%)	-1.19	3.96	-4.10	-4.85	1.87
Total Return, Stock Price (%)	6.72	19.66	20.46	-1.93	10.02

State Mutual Securities Trust

Premium/Discount Spread

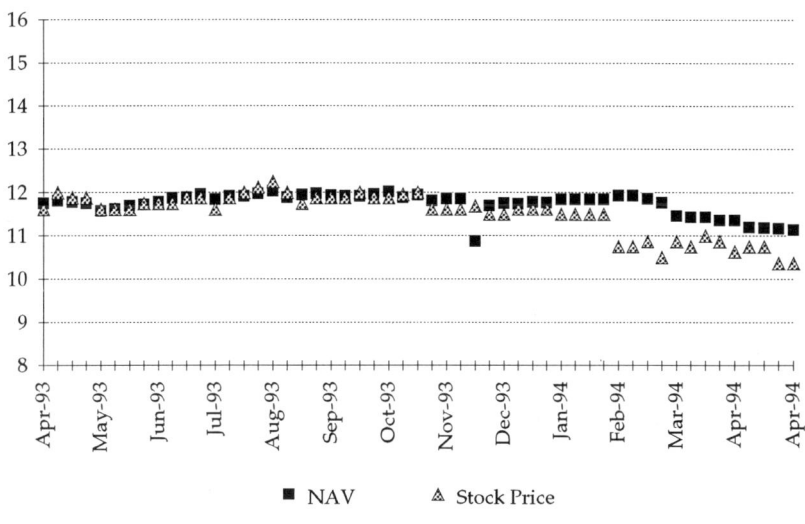

Fund Outlook (SMS): Although long-term rates are unlikely to fall as much in 1994 as they did in 1993, long-term rates remain high relative to short-term rates. With most economic indicators pointing toward slow growth and low inflation, there is room for a further decline in long-term rates. For these reasons, the trust expects to maintain investments in longer-term issues with an emphasis on corporate securities. As interest rates stabilize further, the trust will likely add to the mortgage-backed securities in its portfolio and continue to look for bonds in undervalued industries seeking to provide a high level of current income.

Authors' Comments (SMS): The NAV trailing 12-month return exceeds the average for its peer group. The majority of the portfolio is rated B or better. Investment in lesser rated issues has permitted the trust to maintain current high yield. The trust's philosophy is to invest in industries that are depressed and where earnings growth is in doubt, and where attractive valuations are available, such as the airline industry, public utility and various cyclical issues. Recently the trust increased its position in mortgaged-back securities at very attractive values and at a time when this type of security was out of favor. The trust is well managed and the current yield and discount make this a very attractive purchase.

USLife Income Fund, Inc.
125 Maiden Ln.
New York, NY 10038
(212) 709-6000

Income

NYSE: UIF
Transfer Agent:
Chemical Bank
450 W. 33rd St.
New York, NY 10001
(212) 270-6000

Results

For 12-months Ending 4/29/94	Period End	Period Begin	Distributions	Yield Dist (%)	Total Return (%)
Share Price ($)	9.63	10.88	0.68	6.25	7.06
NAV per Share ($)	9.95	10.25		6.63	6.83

Background: Initial public offering December 7, 1972 of 4,400,000 shares at $15 per share. Initial NAV was $13.80 per share.

Objective: Seeks high current income. Invests 50% in straight debt securities of the four highest grades determined by S&P, obligations guaranteed by the U.S. or Canadian Governments, and investment-grade commercial paper. May invest the balance in lower-rated fixed income debt securities, convertible bonds and preferred shares. May hold 10% in common shares, with a limit of 30% in private placements. The fund may borrow up to 25% of total assets.

Portfolio: (3/31/94) Corporate Obligations 97%, Cash 3%. Portfolio Ratings: AA 7%, BBB 57%, BB 25%, B 4%. Top Holdings: Canadian Pacific Forest, Delta Air Lines, Gulf Canada Resources, Toro, Long Island Lighting.

Capitalization: (3/31/94) Common stock outstanding 5,611,350. No long-term debt.

Average Maturity (years): 18.6
Fee: 0.04%
Income Distribution: Quarterly
Reinvestment Plan: Yes
Fund Manager: USLife Advisors, Inc.
Capital Gains Distribution: Annually
Shareholder Reports: Semi-Annually

5 Year Performance

Fiscal Year Ending 12/31	1993	1992	1991	1990	1989
Net Assets ($mil)	57.00	52.40	47.00	46.70	52.30
Net Income Distribution ($)	0.90	0.92	0.93	0.93	0.92
Capital Gains Distribution ($)	0.00	0.00	0.00	0.00	0.00
Total Distribution ($)	0.90	0.92	0.93	0.93	0.92
Yield from Distribution (%)	8.37	10.82	11.80	10.05	10.51
Expense Ratio (%)	1.23	1.29	1.38	1.37	1.32
Portfolio Turnover (%)	45.01	36.55	59.73	36.53	41.97
NAV per Share ($)	10.28	9.75	8.50	7.88	9.00
Market Price per Share ($)	10.75	9.75	8.50	7.88	9.00
Premium (Discount) (%)	0.05	6.00	4.82	-14.09	-5.23
Total Return, Stock Price (%)	19.48	25.53	19.67	-2.11	16.23

USLife Income Fund, Inc.

Premium/Discount Spread

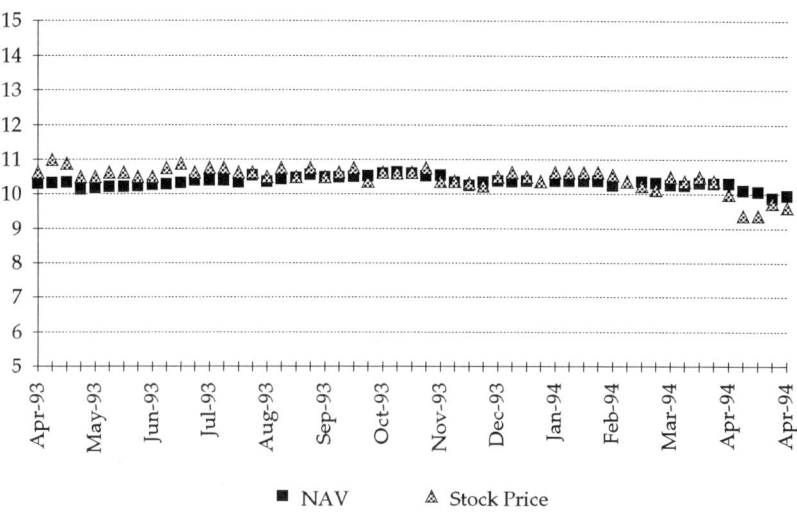

■ NAV   △ Stock Price

Fund Outlook (UIF): Maximum investment income and preservation of capital value are the two primary goals that influence the investment strategy of the fund. The emphasis on dynamic asset management can be illustrated by the period from June 30 to September 30, 1993. During that period, the portfolio was reallocated from a nearly 50% weighting in lower than BBB-rated bonds in June, to only 38% by September with the remainder invested in investment grade bonds. The resulting portfolio mix enabled the fund to weather the two interest rate moves in November and February with relative ease.

Authors' Comments (UIF): The NAV trailing 12-month return is the highest of its peer group. The majority of the portfolio is rated B or better. Electric utility issues were increased in the portfolio, which may create a problem with regard to the NAV, should S&P down-grade the quality of the utility bonds because of de-regulation and increased competition in this industry. Because a large percentage of portfolio was in junk bonds, NAV was relatively stable during the bond market correction in February. However, it was hit by the tidal wave of selling that took place in March, despite the fact that this type of bond is supposed to be more sensitive to the credit worthiness of the issuer than to vacillations in the bond market. Very attractive yield.

U.S. Government Bond Funds

Dean Witter Government Income Trust   NYSE: **GVT**

Two World Trade Center
New York, NY 10048
(800) 869-3863
(212) 392-2550

Transfer Agent:
Dean Witter Trust Co.
Harborside Financial Center, Plaza Two
Jersey City, NJ 07311
(800) 526-3143

Income

Results

For 12-months Ending 4/29/94	Period End	Period Begin	Distributions	Yield Dist (%)	Total Return (%)
Share Price ($)	7.88	9.00	0.72	8.00	-4.44
NAV per Share ($)	8.85	9.64		7.47	-0.73

Background: Initial public offering February 29, 1988 of 70,173,901 shares of beneficial interest at $10 per share. Initial NAV was $9.50 per share.

Objective: Seeks high current income consistent with preservation of capital. Invests 65% in U.S. Government securities; up to 35% in other debt securities, non-governmental issuers in the U.S., and Foreign Governments. The fund may be leveraged up to 25%.

Portfolio: (9/30/93) U.S. Government Agencies 64.8%, U.S. Treasuries 40.1%, Short-Term Investment 0.3%.

Capitalization: (9/30/93) Shares of beneficial interest outstanding 57,818,800. No long-term debt.

Average Maturity (years): 7.9
Fee: 0.60%
Income Distribution: Monthly
Reinvestment Plan: Yes
Fund Manager: Dean Witter InterCapital Inc.
Capital Gains Distribution: Annually
Shareholder Reports: Quarterly

5 Year Performance

Fiscal Year Ending 9/30	1993	1992	1991	1990	1989
Net Assets ($mil)	551.70	561.70	561.30	538.90	538.80
Net Income Distribution ($)	0.70	0.76	0.84	0.87	0.98
Capital Gains Distribution ($)	0.00	0.00	0.00	0.00	0.00
Total Distribution ($)	0.70	0.76	0.84	0.87	0.98
Yield from Distribution (%)	7.57	8.10	9.60	9.80	10.59
Expense Ratio (%)	0.70	0.72	0.72	0.76	0.74
Portfolio Turnover (%)	132.00	70.00	10.00	20.00	64.00
NAV per Share ($)	9.54	9.72	9.70	9.32	9.31
Market Price per Share ($)	9.13	9.25	9.38	8.75	8.88
Premium (Discount) (%)	-4.30	-3.50	-3.40	-6.12	-4.62
Total Return, Stock Price (%)	6.27	6.72	16.80	8.33	6.59

Dean Witter Government Income Trust

Premium/Discount Spread

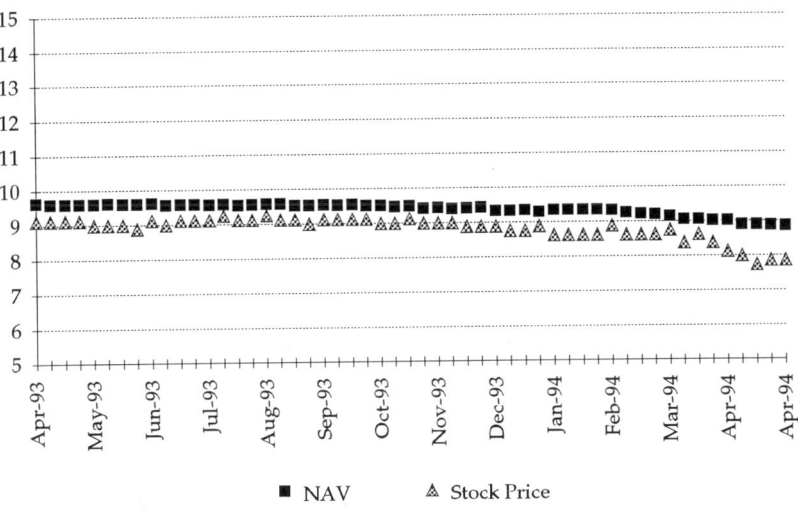

■ NAV △ Stock Price

Fund Outlook (GVT): As a result of falling interest rates, principal pre-payments on mortgage-backed securities (MBSs) increased from already high historical levels. During the trust's previous fiscal year, certain structural changes were made in anticipation of this extended period of declining interest rates and increased mortgage pre-payments. These included a reduction in the portfolio's high coupon mortgages, as well as the purchase of short-term, high coupon U.S. Treasury notes. This strategy enabled the trust to increase its monthly dividend. Also, the trust purchased more lower-costing, current-coupon MBSs and Treasuries. The trust feels these instruments will provide greater potential for price appreciation in the ongoing low interest rate environment.

Authors' Comments (GVT): The trailing 12-month performance is (0.62%) as contrasted with a (8.04%) for the group. The fund may leverage up to 25% of its assets, however, it is presently unleveraged. A large portion of the portfolio is represented by mortgaged-back securities. In a stable to rising interest rate environment, the trust's portfolio of mortgage-backed securities will do well. High credit quality and current discount makes it attractive.

Kemper Intermediate Government Trust   NYSE: **KGT**

120 S. LaSalle Street
Chicago, IL 60603
(800) 422-2848
(312) 781-1121

Transfer Agent:
Investors Fiduciary Trust Co.
127 W. 10th St.
Kansas City, MO 64105
(816) 474-8786

Income

Results

For 12-months Ending 4/29/94	Period End	Period Begin	Distributions	Yield Dist (%)	Total Return (%)
Share Price ($)	7.63	8.88	0.72	8.11	-5.97
NAV per Share ($)	8.18	8.91		8.08	-0.11

Background: Initial public offering July 2, 1988 of 28,000,000 shares at $10 per share. Initial NAV was $9.30 per share.

Objective: Seeks high current income consistent with preservation of capital. Invests at least 65% of assets in obligations issued or guaranteed by the U.S. Government and its Agencies. Average maturity of between three and ten years is maintained. May use hedging strategies.

Portfolio: (11/30/93) U.S. Government Obligations 121%, Municipal Bonds 0.5%, Repurchase Agreements 5%, Total Investments 127%, Liabilities, less Cash & Other (26.8%).

Capitalization: (11/30/93) Common stock outstanding 33,996,000. No long-term debt.

Average Maturity (years): 3.8
Fee: 0.80%
Income Distribution: Monthly
Reinvestment Plan: Yes

Fund Manager: Kemper Financial Services, Inc.
Capital Gains Distribution: Annually
Shareholder Reports: Quarterly

5 Year Performance

Fiscal Year Ending 11/30	1993	1992	1991	1990	1989
Net Assets ($mil)	295.50	298.90	301.20	288.40	302.10
Net Income Distribution ($)	0.71	0.75	0.88	0.91	0.99
Capital Gains Distribution ($)	0.00	0.00	0.00	0.00	0.01
Total Distribution ($)	0.71	0.75	0.88	0.91	1.00
Yield from Distribution (%)	8.00	8.33	10.06	9.33	10.95
Expense Ratio (%)	0.92	0.93	0.93	0.95	0.95
Portfolio Turnover (%)	326.00	494.00	368.00	253.00	115.00
NAV per Share ($)	8.69	8.81	8.97	8.70	9.16
Market Price per Share ($)	8.50	8.88	9.00	8.75	9.75
Premium (Discount) (%)	-2.19	2.16	0.33	0.57	3.92
Total Return, Stock Price (%)	3.72	7.00	12.91	-0.92	17.74

Kemper Intermediate Government Trust

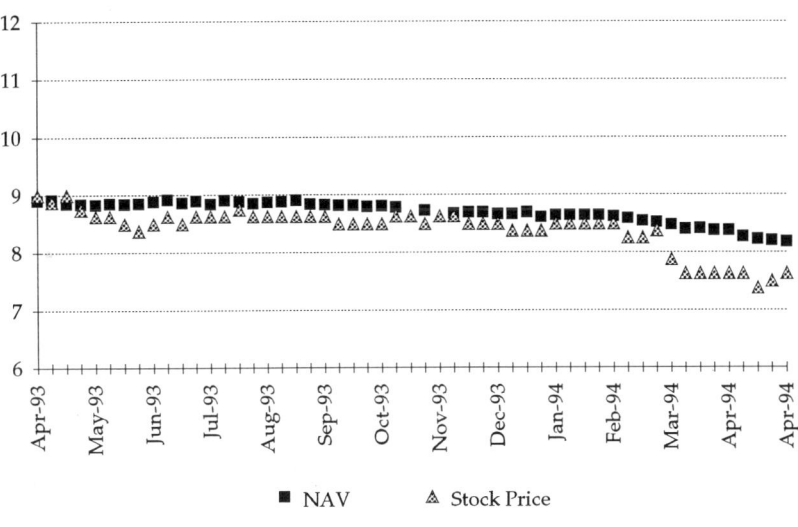

Premium/Discount Spread

■ NAV △ Stock Price

Fund Outlook (KGT): Historically interest rates have risen as expansion ages. Because the current economic expansion began in 1991, it seems likely that the next significant move in interest rates will be upward. As bond prices generally move inversely to interest rates, the result would be a decline in bond prices. In order to reduce this effect, the trust currently intends to maintain an average portfolio life on the lower end of the 3-to-10 year range. In addition, the fund intends to continue to invest a small percentage in foreign securities due to the possibility of declining rates abroad.

Authors' Comments (KGT): We tend to prefer the paranoid bond fund manager. During halcyon days, their results are acceptable, while during turbulent times their defenses protect. KGT is just such a fund. Original management strategy was to purchase high coupon Treasuries set to mature in only a few years. The high percentage of these issues shielded the portfolio as interest rates began to tick up earlier in February. At that time, the manager sold half of these Treasuries and moved into two year notes. Those remaining bonds mature in August of 1994 when they will be replaced with mortgage-backed securities to better track any further interest rate increases. As new issues are purchased, the dividend will most likely be cut. However, this is an excellent, defensive fund for the taxable income investor.

Mentor Income Fund
Riverfront Plaza, 901 East Byrd Street
Richmond, VA 23219
(800) 825-5353
(804) 782-3747

Income

NYSE: MRF
Transfer Agent:
State Street Bank & Trust Co.
P.O. Box 366
Boston, MA 02101
(800) 426-5523

Results

For 12-months Ending 4/29/94	Period End	Period Begin	Distributions	Yield Dist (%)	Total Return (%)
Share Price ($)	9.88	12.00	0.99	8.25	-9.42
NAV per Share ($)	10.20	11.26		8.79	-0.62

Background: Initial public offering December 23, 1988 with 10,000,000 common shares at $12 each. Initial per share net asset value $11.16.
Objective: Seeks high current monthly income while preserving capital.
Portfolio: (10/31/93) U.S. Government Agencies 71%, Private Issues 56.9%, Residual Interests 23.9%.
Capitalization: (10/31/93) Common stock outstanding 11,786,222. The fund is approximately 31% leveraged with reverse repurchase agreements.
Average Maturity (years): 24.3
Fee: 0.65%   **Fund Manager:** Commonwealth Invest. Counsel
Income Distribution: Monthly   **Capital Gains Distribution:** Annually
Reinvestment Plan: Yes   **Shareholder Reports:** Quarterly

5 Year Performance

Fiscal Year Ending 10/31	1993	1992	1991	1990	1989
Net Assets ($mil)	133.10	126.90	120.10	112.40	112.10
Net Income Distribution ($)	1.05	1.26	1.26	1.27	0.85
Capital Gains Distribution ($)	0.00	0.02	0.00	0.00	0.05
Total Distribution ($)	1.05	1.28	1.26	1.27	0.90
Yield from Distribution (%)	8.48	10.67	11.72	12.10	10.95
Expense Ratio (%)	1.09	1.13	1.17	1.28	1.37
Portfolio Turnover (%)	269.16	219.43	132.44	155.40	241.81
NAV per Share ($)	11.29	11.06	11.57	11.12	11.09
Market Price per Share ($)	10.50	12.38	12.00	10.75	10.50
Premium (Discount) (%)	-7.00	11.93	3.72	-3.33	-5.32
Total Return, Stock Price (%)	-6.70	13.83	23.35	14.48	-6.65

Mentor Income Fund

Premium/Discount Spread

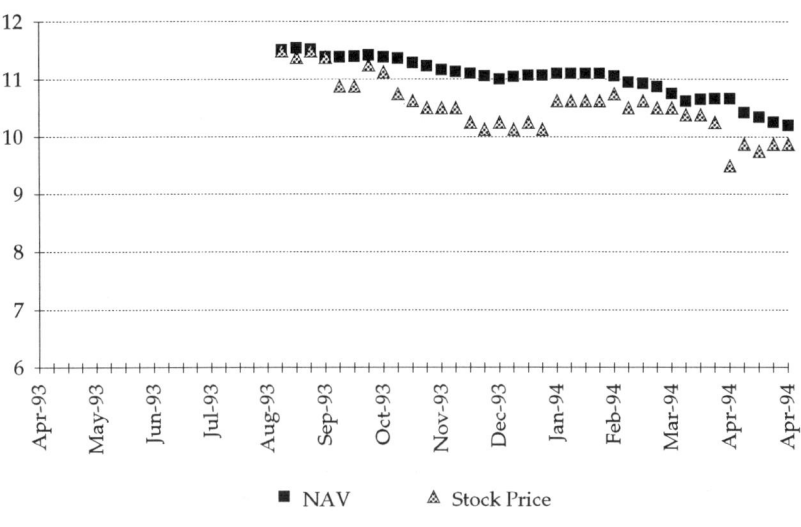

Fund Outlook (MRF): The fund's investment strategy remains focused on generating high monthly income while preserving capital. To achieve this objective, the fund's portfolio is currently concentrated in high-quality, short-duration mortgage-backed securities. The portfolios interest-rate risk is being managed with the objective of holding volatility in net asset value at or below levels generated by intermediate Treasury securities.

Authors' Comments (MRF): The portfolio is invested in 3-5 year maturity, derivative mortgage-backed securities which did well as interest rates were declining and is one of the reasons the fund performed as well as it did in 1993. The portfolio also includes a large position of adjustable-rate mortgages, which are less volatile because coupons are reset based on short-term rates. With the continued slowdown in pre-payment activities, mortgage-backed securities are attractive for value conscious fixed income investors.

Putnam Intermediate Government Income Trust

One Post Office Square
Boston, MA 02109
(617) 292-1000

NYSE: PGT
Transfer Agent:
Putnam Investor Services, Inc.
P.O. Box 41203
Providence, RI 02940
(800) 634-1587

Income

Results

For 12-months Ending 4/29/94	Period End	Period Begin	Distributions	Yield Dist (%)	Total Return (%)
Share Price ($)	7.63	8.50	0.60	7.06	-3.18
NAV per Share ($)	8.48	9.23		6.50	-1.63

Background: Initial public offering June 17, 1988 of 60,000,000 shares at $10 per share. Initial NAV was $9.30 per share.

Objective: Seeks current income and stable NAV primarily by investing in U.S. or Foreign Government and Government Agency bonds with average maturities between three and ten years. At least 65% of assets are invested in U.S. Government and Agency securities, options, futures and repurchase agreements. Up to 35% may be invested in Foreign Government securities.

Portfolio: (12/31/93) U.S. Government & Agencies 73%, International 27%.

Capitalization: (12/31/93) Shares of beneficial interest outstanding 65,098,252. No long-term debt.

Average Maturity (years): 13.5

Fee: 0.75%

Income Distribution: Monthly

Reinvestment Plan: Yes

Fund Manager: Putnam Mgt. Co., Inc.

Capital Gains Distribution: Annually

Shareholder Reports: Quarterly

5 Year Performance

Fiscal Year Ending 11/30	1993	1992	1991	1990	1989
Net Assets ($mil)	589.20	601.60	585.60	567.10	562.10
Net Income Distribution ($)	0.55	0.60	0.68	0.73	0.79
Capital Gains Distribution ($)	0.44	0.17	0.05	0.08	0.22
Total Distribution ($)	0.99	0.77	0.73	0.81	1.01
Yield from Distribution (%)	10.84	8.43	8.11	9.00	11.54
Expense Ratio (%)	0.89	0.92	1.01	1.02	1.00
Portfolio Turnover (%)	303.68	216.24	255.49	268.42	174.57
NAV per Share ($)	9.05	9.32	9.21	9.08	9.11
Market Price per Share ($)	8.13	9.13	9.13	9.00	9.00
Premium (Discount) (%)	-10.22	-2.04	-0.87	-0.88	-1.21
Total Return, Stock Price (%)	-0.11	8.43	9.56	9.00	14.40

Putnam Intermediate Government Income Trust

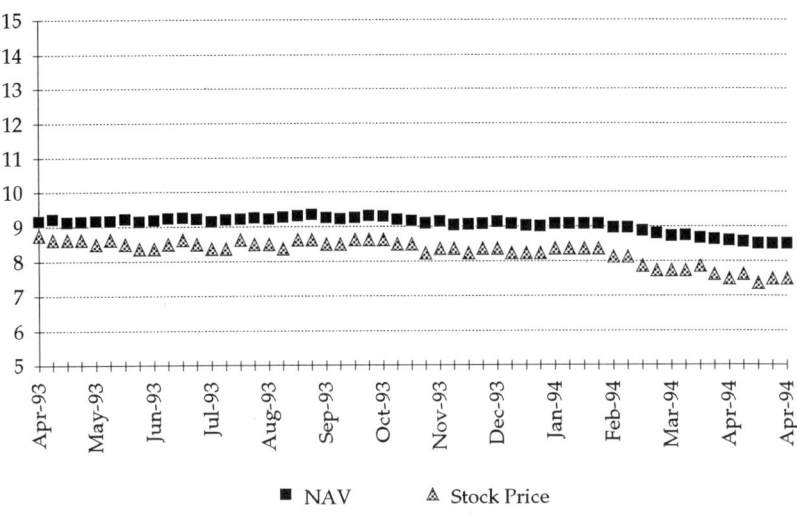

Premium/Discount Spread

■ NAV   △ Stock Price

Fund Outlook (PGT): The trust expects to move its concentration of maturities from a barbelled position toward a higher-yielding bulleted position in coming months. The trust believes this strategy will help to increase the portfolio's yield. Also, the trust intends to add selectively to its mortgage-backed holdings. However, the trust will continue to be conscious of the prepayment risk that has kept many investors away from these securities in recent months. The trust has continued to maintain about half of the trust's foreign securities in European countries. The trust believes these countries, led by Germany, will be forced to face the inevitable in 1994 and lower interest rates more substantially than they did in 1993.

Authors' Comments (PGT): The NAV trailing 12-month return is 1.07% which ranks second highest in this category, as contrasted with the average performance for the peer group of (8.04%). PGT is currently selling at the largest discount to NAV and is a good purchase at this level.

Term Trust Bond Funds

BlackRock Advantage Term Trust, Inc.   NYSE: **BAT**

One Seaport Plaza *Transfer Agent:*
New York, NY 10292 State Street Bank & Trust Co.
(800) 227-7236 One Heritage Drive
(212) 214-3334 North Quincy, MA 02171
 (800) 451-6788

Income

Results

For 12-months Ending 4/29/94	Period End	Period Begin	Distributions	Yield Dist (%)	Total Return (%)
Share Price ($)	8.88	10.38	0.74	7.13	-7.32
NAV per Share ($)	9.71	10.68		6.93	-2.15

Background: Initial public offering April 17, 1990 of 9,375,000 shares at $10 per share. Initial NAV was $9.30 per share.

Objective: Seeks high monthly income and return of $10 per share on or shortly before December 31, 2005. At least 80% of the fund's assets are in mortgage-backed securities and zero-coupon securities rated AAA or guaranteed by the U.S. Government.

Portfolio: (4/29/94) Mortgage-Backed Securities 47%, U.S. Government & Agencies 5%, Taxable Zero-Coupon Bonds 31%, Municipal Zero-Coupon Bonds 9%, Asset-Backed Securities 8%.

Capitalization: (12/31/93) Common stock outstanding 9,510,667. No long-term debt.

Average Maturity (years): 12
Fee: 0.60% **Fund Manager:** BlackRock Financial Mgt. L.P.
Income Distribution: Monthly **Capital Gains Distribution:** Annually
Reinvestment Plan: Yes **Shareholder Reports:** Quarterly

5 Year Performance

Fiscal Year Ending 12/31	1993	1992	1991	1990	1989
Net Assets ($mil)	153.20	147.00	104.20	94.00	-
Net Income Distribution ($)	0.83	0.90	1.06	0.51	-
Capital Gains Distribution ($)	0.00	0.00	0.00	0.06	-
Total Distribution ($)	0.83	0.90	1.06	0.57	-
Yield from Distribution (%)	7.81	8.00	10.60	-	-
Expense Ratio (%)	1.14	1.37	1.30	1.17	-
Portfolio Turnover (%)	-	3.00	254.00	180.00	-
NAV per Share ($)	10.72	10.43	10.96	9.89	-
Market Price per Share ($)	8.88	10.63	11.25	10.00	-
Premium (Discount) (%)	-17.21	1.92	2.65	1.11	-
Total Return, Stock Price (%)	-8.65	2.49	23.10	-	-

BlackRock Advantage Term Trust, Inc.

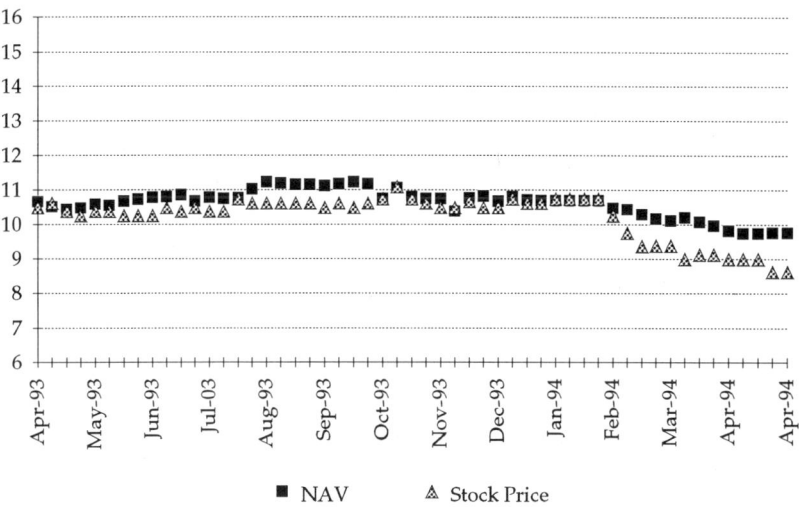

Premium/Discount Spread

■ NAV   ▲ Stock Price

Fund Outlook (BAT): In April, the Federal Reserve once again took preemptive measures to combat potential inflationary pressures and increased the Federal funds rate for the third time in three months to 3.75%. Bond prices across all points of the yield curve continued to decline as the yield of the 10-year Treasury eclipsed the 7% mark since July 1992. The recent volatility of fixed income markets should prevail in the short term as the possibility of additional Federal funds increases keeps investors wary. However, the trust expects a decline in longer term interest rates toward the latter half of 1994 with the yield of the 30-year Treasury expected to end 1994 closer to the 6.5% level. To combat the threat of extension risk associated with continued rising interest rates, the trust has emphasized 15-year mortgages which offer more protection from duration extension than traditional 30-year mortgages.

Authors' Comments (BAT): Approximately 40% of the fund's assets are held in zeros scheduled to mature at the time the fund is terminated, providing funds are available. Because of the extreme volatility of the zeros, the NAV is subject to wide swings, rising during periods when interest rates are declining and dropping when interest rates are rising. The trust dividend was recently reduced from $0.06875 to $0.06042 due to the level of pre-payment of mortgaged-back securities held in the portfolio and the reinvestment in a low-interest rate environment. The trust should be attractive for risk-tolerant investors.

BlackRock Target Term Trust, Inc.   NYSE: BTT

One Seaport Plaza
New York, NY 10292
(800) 227-7236
(212) 214-3334

Transfer Agent:
State Street Bank & Trust Co.
One Heritage Drive
North Quincy, MA 02172
(800) 451-6788

Income

Results

For 12-months Ending 4/29/94	Period End	Period Begin	Distributions	Yield Dist (%)	Total Return (%)
Share Price ($)	9.13	10.13	0.78	7.70	-2.17
NAV per Share ($)	9.52	10.68		7.30	-3.56

Background: Initial public offering November 8, 1988 of 83,000,000 shares at $10 per share. Initial NAV was $9.39 per share.

Objective: Seeks high monthly income and to return $10 per share to common shareholders on or about December 31, 2001.

Portfolio: (12/31/93) Mortgage-Backed Securities 45%, Taxable Zero-Coupon Bonds 45%, Municipal Zero-Coupon Bonds 3%, Asset Backed Securities 2%, U.S. Government and High-Quality Market Securities 5%.

Capitalization: (12/31/93) Common stock outstanding 95,460,639. No long-term debt.

Average Maturity (years): 7
Fee: 0.60%   *Fund Manager:* BlackRock Financial Mgt. L.P.
Income Distribution: Monthly   *Capital Gains Distribution:* Annually
Reinvestment Plan: Yes   *Shareholder Reports:* Semi-Annually

5 Year Performance

Fiscal Year Ending 12/31	1993	1992	1991	1990	1989
Net Assets ($mil)	992.00	981.30	967.70	882.40	902.10
Net Income Distribution ($)	0.73	0.87	0.95	0.96	0.83
Capital Gains Distribution ($)	0.00	0.00	0.00	0.00	0.00
Total Distribution ($)	0.73	0.87	0.95	0.96	0.83
Yield from Distribution (%)	7.30	8.09	9.50	9.85	-
Expense Ratio (%)	0.73	0.89	0.92	0.92	0.92
Portfolio Turnover (%)	0.00	30.00	279.00	114.00	177.00
NAV per Share ($)	10.41	10.28	10.14	9.24	9.45
Market Price per Share ($)	10.00	10.00	10.75	10.00	9.75
Premium (Discount) (%)	-3.94	-2.72	6.02	8.23	3.17
Total Return, Stock Price (%)	7.30	1.12	17.00	12.41	-

BlackRock Target Term Trust, Inc.

Premium/Discount Spread

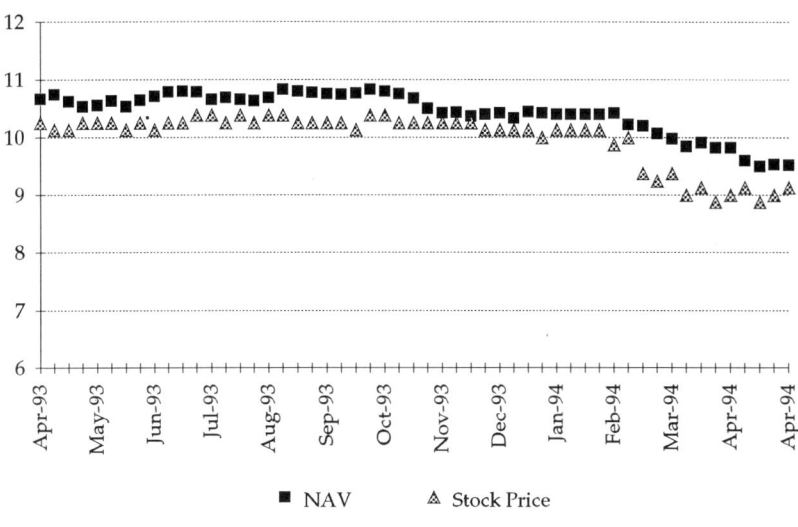

Fund Outlook (BTT): In April, the Federal Reserve once again took preemptive measures to combat potential inflationary pressures and increased the Federal funds rate for the third time in three months to 3.75%. Bond prices across all points of the yield curve continued to decline as the yield of the 10-year Treasury eclipsed the 7% mark since July 1992. The recent volatility of the fixed income markets should prevail in the short term as the possibility of additional Federal funds increases keeps investors wary. However, the trust expects a decline in longer term interest rates toward the latter half of 1994 with the yield of the 30-year Treasury expected to end 1994 closer to the 6.5% level. To combat the threat of extension risk associated with continued rising interest rates, the trust has emphasized 15-year mortgages, as these securities offer more protection from duration extension than traditional 30-year mortgages.

Authors' Comments (BTT): Approximately one-third of the portfolio is invested in zero-coupon bonds that will mature at termination, and if held to maturity, funds will be available to make distributions. On the other hand, because of pre-payments of mortgaged-back securities held in the portfolio and the reinvestment during a period of declining interest rates, the monthly dividend was recently reduced from $0.0667 to $0.05833. The yield is attractive despite the volatility due to the zero component in the portfolio.

Hyperion 1999 Term Trust, Inc.   NYSE: **HTT**

520 Madison Avenue
New York, NY 10022
(800) HYPERION
(212) 214-3334

Transfer Agent:
Boston Financial Data Services, Inc
2 Heritage Drive
North Quincy, MA 02171
(800) 426-5523

Income

Results

For 12-months Ending 4/29/94	Period End	Period Begin	Distributions	Yield Dist (%)	Total Return (%)
Share Price ($)	7.38	9.00	0.62	6.89	-11.11
NAV per Share ($)	7.53	8.15		7.61	0.00

Background: Initial public offering June 18, 1992 of 6,000,000 shares at $10 per share. Initial NAV was $9.40 per share.

Objective: Seeks to provide a high level of current income consistent with investing in securities of the highest credit quality and to return at least $10 per share (the trust's initial public offering price per share) to investors on or shortly before November 30, 1999. All trust securities are either rated AAA by S&P, or are issued or guaranteed by the U.S. Government or one of its Agencies or Instrumentalities.

Portfolio: (4/7/94) Mortgage-Backed Securities 5%, CMOs 45%, Multi-Family CMOs 2%, Municipal Securities 14%, Interest-Only Securities (IOs) 35%.

Capitalization: (10/30/93) Shares outstanding 63,260,639. No long-term debt.

Average Maturity (years): 7

Fee: 0.50%   *Fund Manager:* Hyperion Capital Mgt., Inc.
Income Distribution: Monthly   *Capital Gains Distribution:* Monthly
Reinvestment Plan: Yes   *Shareholder Reports:* Semi-Annually

5 Year Performance

Fiscal Year Ending 11/30	1993	1992	1991	1990	1989
Net Assets ($mil)	444.00	554.90	-	-	-
Net Income Distribution ($)	0.74	0.27	-	-	-
Capital Gains Distribution ($)	0.00	0.00	-	-	-
Total Distribution ($)	0.74	0.27	-	-	-
Yield from Distribution (%)	7.40	2.70	-	-	-
Expense Ratio (%)	0.76	0.80	-	-	-
Portfolio Turnover (%)	1175.00	111.00	-	-	-
NAV per Share ($)	7.02	8.77	-	-	-
Market Price per Share ($)	6.75	10.00	-	-	-
Premium (Discount) (%)	-3.85	14.03	-	-	-
Total Return, Stock Price (%)	-25.10	-	-	-	-

Hyperion 1999 Term Trust, Inc.

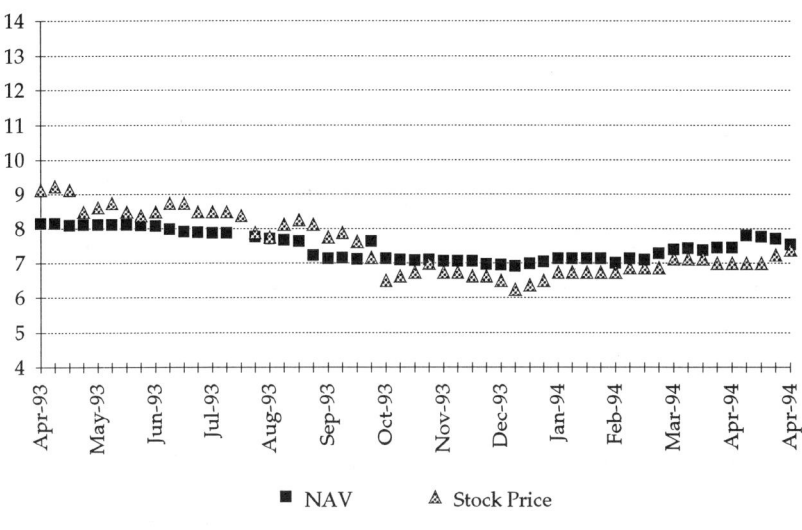

Premium/Discount Spread

■ NAV   ▲ Stock Price

Fund Outlook (HTT): The trust is actively managed to take advantage of relative value opportunities in various sectors of the mortgage market. The trust is currently managed with an average duration of negative 5 years; currently the average life is approximately 7 years.

Authors' Comments (HTT): Declining interest rates resulted in a decline in the value of the funds interest-only securities (IOs) which represent the interest payments from the cash flows of a pool of mortgages. As the principal in the mortgage pool declines due to pre-payments, less cash in the form of interest is received and as a result the value of the IOs declines. The trust experienced an approximate 25% decline in its IOs in 1993. The fund was able to hedge the portfolio with the purchase of principal-only strips securities (POs) and U.S. Treasury futures and thus avoided any serious decline in NAV. The trust's NAV 12-month trailing performance is 0.41% as contrasted with the group average of (1.61%). The fund is actively managed.

Income Opportunities Fund 1999

Box 9011
Princeton, NJ 08543-9011
(800) 543-6217
(609) 282-2800

Income

NYSE: IOF
Transfer Agent:
The Bank of New York
110 Washington St.
New York, NY 10286
(800) 524-4458

Results

For 12-months Ending 4/29/94	Period End	Period Begin	Distributions	Yield Dist (%)	Total Return (%)
Share Price ($)	8.13	9.50	0.62	7.62	-7.89
NAV per Share ($)	8.67	9.47		6.55	-1.90

Background: Initial public offering September 21, 1992 at $10 per share. Initial NAV was $9.50 per share.

Objective: Seeks high current income and to return $10 per share to common shareholders on or about December 31, 1999.

Portfolio: (12/31/93) Mortgage Backed Obligations 130%, Municipal Bonds 18%, U.S. Government Agency Obligations 3%, Treasury Notes 2%, Short-Term Securities 0.1%.

Capitalization: (12/31/93) Common shares outstanding 55, 510,527. Leveraged with 31% repurchase agreements with daily weighted average interest rate of 3.73%.

Average Maturity (years): 16.2

Fee: 0.75%
Income Distribution: Monthly
Reinvestment Plan: Yes

Fund Manager: Fund Asset Mgt.
Capital Gains Distribution: Annually
Shareholder Reports: Semi-Annually

5 Year Performance

Fiscal Year Ending 12/31	1993	1992	1991	1990	1989
Net Assets ($mil)	517.30	520.30	-	-	-
Net Income Distribution ($)	0.59	0.18	-	-	-
Capital Gains Distribution ($)	0.08	0.00	-	-	-
Total Distribution ($)	0.67	0.18	-	-	-
Yield from Distribution (%)	7.24	1.95	-	-	-
Expense Ratio (%)	2.30	1.63	-	-	-
Portfolio Turnover (%)	185.20	48.17	-	-	-
NAV per Share ($)	9.32	9.37	-	-	-
Market Price per Share ($)	8.75	9.25	-	-	-
Premium (Discount) (%)	-6.12	-1.28	-	-	-
Total Return, Stock Price (%)	1.84	-	-	-	-

Income Opportunities Fund 1999

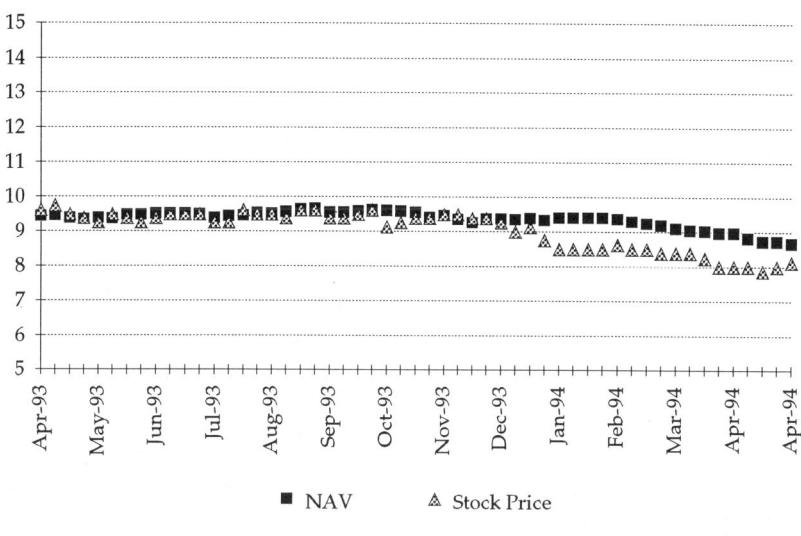

Fund Outlook (IOF): Looking ahead, the fund's strategy will continue to focus on reaching a net asset value of $10 per share on the termination date. Therefore, the fund will invest in securities with maturities that are either shorter than or only marginally beyond the termination date. Although an increase in interest rates would impact the fund's net asset value, the effect will lessen as portfolio securities approach maturity. In addition, municipal income will be retained in the fund's net asset value.

Authors Comments (IOF): The NAV's trailing 12-month performance is 1.14% versus 0.12% for the peer group. The portfolio includes IOs that have recently been reduced in favor of 10-year Treasuries and adjustable-rate-mortgage securities (ARMs). ARMs are also subject to mortgage prepayments in declining interest rate markets, but their value is enhanced when interest rates rise. That's because their rates are adjusted upward.

Liberty Term Trust 1999

Federated Investors Tower
Pittsburgh, PA 15222-3779
(412) 288-1900

Income

NYSE: LTT

Transfer Agent:
State Street Bank & Trust Co.
1776 Heritage Drive
North Quincy, MA 02171
(800) 426-5523

Results

For 12-months Ending 4/29/94	Period End	Period Begin	Distributions	Yield Dist (%)	Total Return (%)
Share Price ($)	7.88	9.25	0.66	7.14	-7.68
NAV per Share ($)	8.47	9.31		7.09	-1.93

Background: Initial public offering April 2, 1992 at $10 per share. Initial NAV was $9.50 per share.

Objective: Seeks high monthly income and a return of $10 per share to shareholders on or about December 31, 1999. The fund seeks to preserve capital by investing in high-quality debt securities and in municipal securities including municipal zeros. It will attempt to achieve high monthly income by investing primarily in mortgage-backed securities, asset-backed securities, and non-U.S. issued debt. The fund will invest at least 65% of assets in mortgage-backed securities. The fund is able to leverage through borrowings up to one-third of the value of its assets.

Portfolio: (12/31/93) Long-Term Municipal Securities 12%, U.S. Government Obligations 88%, Repurchase Agreements 35%.

Capitalization: (12/31/93) Common shares outstanding 5,625,018. No long-term debt.

Average Maturity (years): 5.8
Fee: 0.5%
Income Distribution: Monthly
Reinvestment Plan: Yes
Fund Manager: Federated Advisers
Capital Gains Distribution: Annually
Shareholder Reports: Semi-Annually

5 Year Performance

Fiscal Year Ending 12/31	1993	1992	1991	1990	1989
Net Assets ($mil)	51.20	51.10	-	-	-
Net Income Distribution ($)	0.75	0.59	-	-	-
Capital Gains Distribution ($)	0.00	0.00	-	-	-
Total Distribution ($)	0.75	0.59	-	-	-
Yield from Distribution (%)	7.32	5.76	-	-	-
Expense Ratio (%)	0.90	0.90	-	-	-
Portfolio Turnover (%)	402.00	164.00	-	-	-
NAV per Share ($)	9.1	9.09	-	-	-
Market Price Share ($)	8.63	10.25	-	-	-
Premium (Discount) (%)	-5.22	12.76	-	-	-
Total Return, Stock Price (%)	-8.49	-	-	-	-

Liberty Term Trust 1999

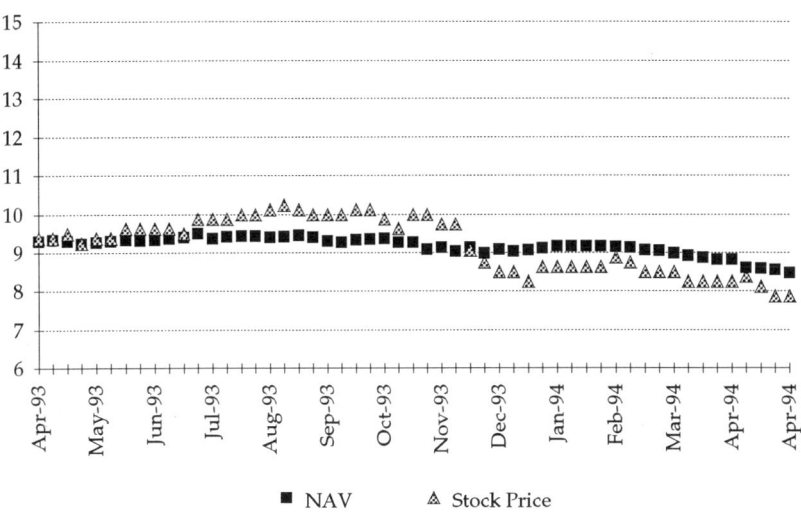

Premium/Discount Spread
■ NAV △ Stock Price

Fund Outlook (LTT): Continues on the conservative end of the closed-end term trust matrix. Remains committed to $10 per share term price. In 1993 gave up income to reach that goal and saw declining interest rates and higher mortgage pre-payments than predicted. So, mortgage-backed securities underperformed U.S. Treasuries. LLT's performance lagged due to its mortgage security allocations. LLT responded by reducing mortgage derivative securities by 5.3% with the remaining position limited to an interest-only inverse floater backed by 6.5% 15-year collateral resulting in a more defensive portfolio at reduced distribution levels. Current dividend supports a yield in excess of the trust's goal of 50 basis points over the comparable U.S. Treasuries, as related to the time to maturity.

Authors' Comments (LTT): Term trusts have one glaring weakness. To offer the possibility the money will be there, they stash what is considered to be an appropriate portion of assets in zero-coupon municipals and Treasuries that will mature in the year the trust terminates. These issues are highly sensitive to rising interest rates. Add the use of leverage and a mix of mortgage-backed derivatives and you have a ticking time bomb if interest rates suddenly rise. However, LTT's management, while placing about a third of assets into zeros moved out of derivatives in early 1994. That didn't stop investors from getting a queasy feeling as they watched the NAV and share price sink below the surface. But, opportunity knocks. The zeroes eventually return to par. Derivatives are at a minimum, and management is savvy. Set to return $10 per share in 1999, LTT should get pretty close. This is a good bet at current discounts for the taxable investor.

International Bond Funds

ACM Managed Multi-Market Trust

NYSE: MMF

1345 Avenue of the Americas
New York, NY 10105
(800) 247-4154
(212) 969-1000

Transfer Agent:
State Street Bank & Trust Co.
225 Franklin St.
Boston, MA 02110
(800) 426-5523

Income Results

For 12-months Ending 4/29/94	Period End	Period Begin	Distributions	Yield Dist (%)	Total Return (%)
Share Price ($)	8.38	9.00	0.66	7.33	0.44
NAV per Share ($)	9.22	9.60		6.88	2.92

Background: Initial public offering January 21, 1990. Initial NAV was $11.16 per share.

Objective: Seeks high current income. Invests in high-quality debt securities with maturities under five years. The fund expects to maintain at least 70% of its assets in debt securities denominated in foreign currencies, but not more than 25% of the fund's total assets may be invested in debt securities denominated in a single currency other than the U.S. dollar. The fund will invest at least 25% of its total assets in debt instruments issued by domestic or foreign banks and bank holding companies.

Portfolio: (2/28/94) Short- and Medium-Term Notes 94%, Cash 6%. Country Exposure: U.S. 69%, Mexico 11%, New Zealand 5%, Malaysia 4%, Australia 3%, Indonesia 2%.

Capitalization: (12/31/93) Common stock outstanding 9,973,931. Bank borrowing $28,750,000.

Average Maturity (years): 2.7
Fee: 0.65%
Income Distribution: Monthly
Reinvestment Plan: Yes
Fund Manager: Alliance Capital Mgt., Inc.
Capital Gains Distribution: Annually
Shareholder Reports: Semi-Annually

5 Year Performance

Fiscal Year Ending 11/30	1993	1992	1991	1990	1989
Net Assets ($mil)	97.90	95.80	111.10	113.30	-
Net Income Distribution ($)	0.74	1.09	1.34	1.18	-
Capital Gains Distribution ($)	0.00	0.00	0.17	0.00	-
Total Distribution ($)	0.74	1.09	1.51	1.18	-
Yield from Distribution (%)	8.00	8.90	13.13	-	-
Expense Ratio (%)	1.42	3.06	3.37	2.90	-
Portfolio Turnover (%)	319.00	176.00	95.00	101.00	-
NAV per Share ($)	9.75	9.61	11.22	11.53	-
Market Price per Share ($)	9.00	9.25	12.25	11.50	-
Premium (Discount) (%)	-7.69	-3.75	9.18	-0.26	-
Total Return, Stock Price (%)	5.30	-15.59	19.65	-	-

ACM Managed Multi-Market Trust

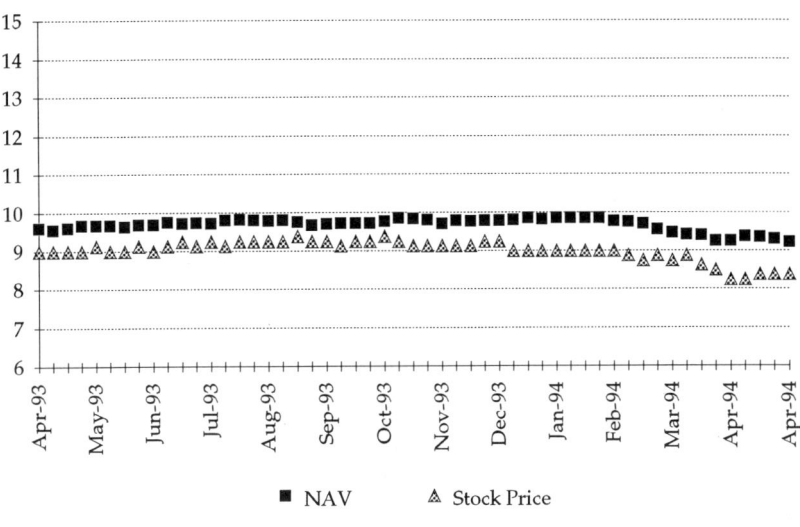

Premium/Discount Spread

■ NAV △ Stock Price

Fund Outlook (MMF): The trust's portfolio was well positioned for the rise in U.S. interest rates, with very little exposure to duration in U.S. block markets. The increase in U.S. rates combined with disappointment over the slow rate of the Bundesbank-easing led to weakness in European bond prices. The trust increased the portfolio's European holdings. The portfolio's four- and five-year government bonds appear greatly undervalued and the trust believes that recent disappointing performance should lay the foundation for future price appreciation. The portfolio has increased cross-currency hedged investments in European exchange rates recently. These economies are expected to grow faster than Germany's. This growth should underpin currency values at today's low and undervalued levels and should generate currency appreciation. The Mexican Peso weakened slightly in February. In part this weakness reflects very poor economic performance in 1993. With NAFTA signed and the restructuring of the Mexican economy continuing, the trust believes that the necessary elements for growth in 1994 are in place.

Authors' Comments (MMF): The largest portfolio concentrations are in the U.S., followed by Europe where the currency is hedged, rate of inflation is low, and the central banks are reducing interest rates in order to stimulate their economies. The fund is also invested in U.S. dollar bloc countries in Asia and Latin America. Here the fund is benefitting from the high yields available. The fund is leveraged, which adds a degree of risk. However, the large discount and high yield warrant consideration for the balanced portfolios and the taxable.

First Commonwealth

800 Scudders Mill Road
Plainsboro, NJ 08536
(609) 282-4600
(800) 543-6217

NYSE: FCO
Transfer Agent:
State Street Bank & Trust Co.
P.O. Box 8200
Boston, MA 02266
(800) 426-5523

Income Results

For 12-months Ending 4/29/94	Period End	Period Begin	Distributions	Yield Dist (%)	Total Return (%)
Share Price ($)	11.38	13.25	1.18	8.91	-5.21
NAV per Share ($)	12.45	13.84		8.53	-1.52

Background: Initial public offering February 20, 1992 with 9,009,200 shares at $15 per share. Initial NAV per share was $13.89.

Objective: Seeks high current income by investing in high-grade fixed income securities denominated in the currencies of Australia, Canada, New Zealand and the U.K. (Commonwealth Currencies). Capital appreciation is secondary. Normally, the fund will invest in debt securities denominated in at least three of these currencies and will not hold more than 50% of its assets in any one Commonwealth Currency. At least 75% of investments will be in securities rated not less than AA by S&P.

Portfolio: (1/31/94) Medium- to longer-term maturities in: Australia 44%, Canada 27%, U.K. 21%, New Zealand 8%, U.S. 0.3%. Portfolio Ratings: AAA 52%, AA 33%, A 16%.

Capitalization: (12/31/93) Common shares outstanding 9,249,430. Leveraged with 600 shares $50,000 per share liquidation value Auction Market Preferred Stock.

Average Maturity (years): 7.7
Fee: 0.65%
Income Distribution: Monthly
Reinvestment Plan: Yes

Fund Manager: EquitiLink Intl. Mgt. Ltd.
Capital Gains Distribution: Annually
Shareholder Reports: Quarterly

5 Year Performance

Fiscal Year Ending 10/31	1993	1992	1991	1990	1989
Net Assets ($mil)	124.10	119.30	-	-	-
Net Income Distribution ($)	0.96	0.80	-	-	-
Capital Gains Distribution ($)	0.26	0.00	-	-	-
Total Distribution ($)	1.22	0.80	-	-	-
Yield from Distribution (%)	9.04	5.76	-	-	-
Expense Ratio (%)	1.73	1.59	-	-	-
Portfolio Turnover (%)	41.00	18.00	-	-	-
NAV per Share ($)	13.42	13.00	-	-	-
Market Price per Share ($)	12.63	13.50	-	-	-
Premium (Discount) (%)	-5.92	3.85	-	-	-
Total Return, Stock Price (%)	2.59	-	-	-	-

First Commonwealth

Premium/Discount Spread

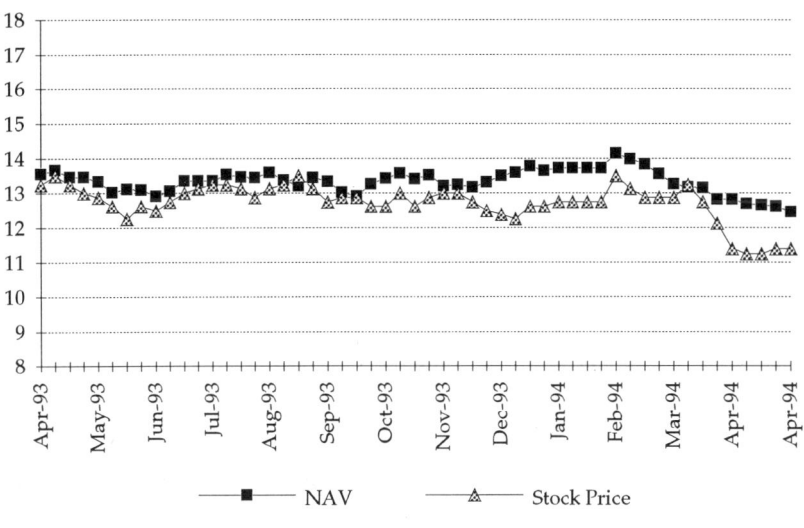

Fund Outlook (FCO): The nervousness in U.S. fixed-income markets following the Federal Reserve Bank's decision to raise interest rates in mid-February resulted in considerable increases in bond yields in the fund's countries' bond markets. This followed overall strong performance for the three months to the end of January. The change in market sentiment has provided the fund with opportunities to buy some longer-dated bonds at significantly higher yields and to position the portfolio to benefit from any renewed market firmness in the months ahead.

Authors' Comments (FCO): In January the dividend was reduced from $0.0925 to $0.0875. The dividend currently exceeds the net investment income and is supplemented with the payment of capital gains in order to maintain a stable dividend disbursement. The 12-month trailing return is 2.16% as compared with the group's 0.52%. The currency is hedged. Because of reduced rates of inflation in the U.K., the fund's three bond markets have provided sound returns.

Global Governments Plus Fund, Inc. NYSE: **GOV**

One Seaport Plaza
New York, NY 10292
(212) 214-3334

Transfer Agent:
State Street Bank & Trust Co.
One Heritage Dr., North Quincy, MA 02171
(800) 426-5523

Income

Results

For 12-months Ending 4/29/94	Period End	Period Begin	Distributions	Yield Dist (%)	Total Return (%)
Share Price ($)	6.25	7.38	0.32	4.34	-10.98
NAV per Share ($)	7.29	7.91		4.05	-3.79

Background: Initial public offering July 24, 1987 of 52,011,000 shares at $10 per share. Initial NAV was $9.30 per share.

Objective: Seeks high income through interest and capital appreciation. Invests in longer-term U.S. and Foreign Government securities. At least 65% of assets invested in debt securities issued or guaranteed by governmental entities in the U.S. and 20 other major countries. Will normally expose no more than 30% of assets to any one foreign currency, with the exception of Germany, Great Britain, or Japan. For defensive purposes, U.S. securities may comprise a majority of assets. May try to protect or enhance dividend return through the use of options, futures, and foreign-currency transactions.

Portfolio: (2/28/94) Long-Term Bonds 92%, Short-Term & Other 8%. Country Exposure: U.S. 22%, Italy 12%, Spain 9%, Japan 8%, Denmark 7%, New Zealand 7%. Credit Breakdown: AAA 76%, AA 20%, Cash & Options 5%.

Capitalization: (12/31/93) Common stock outstanding 45,642,508. No long-term debt.

Average Maturity (years): 8.6
Fee: 0.75%   *Fund Manager:* Prudential Mutual Fund Mgt., Inc.
Income Distribution: Quarterly   *Capital Gains Distribution:* Annually
Reinvestment Plan: Yes   *Shareholder Reports:* Semi-Annually

5 Year Performance

Fiscal Year Ending 12/31	1993	1992	1991	1990	1989
Net Assets ($mil)	357.80	336.80	377.90	376.70	434.20
Net Income Distribution ($)	0.23	0.67	0.66	0.59	0.59
Capital Gains Distribution ($)	0.54	0.20	0.00	0.00	0.00
Total Distribution ($)	0.77	0.87	0.66	0.59	0.59
Yield from Distribution (%)	11.00	11.23	9.10	7.87	6.46
Expense Ratio (%)	1.07	1.15	1.29	1.47	1.59
Portfolio Turnover (%)	441.00	346.00	267.00	503.00	477.00
NAV per Share ($)	7.84	7.38	8.28	8.25	8.25
Market Price per Share ($)	7.00	7.00	7.75	7.25	7.50
Premium (Discount) (%)	-10.71	-5.15	-6.40	-12.12	-9.09
Total Return, Stock Price (%)	11.00	1.55	16.00	4.53	-11.39

Global Governments Plus Fund, Inc.

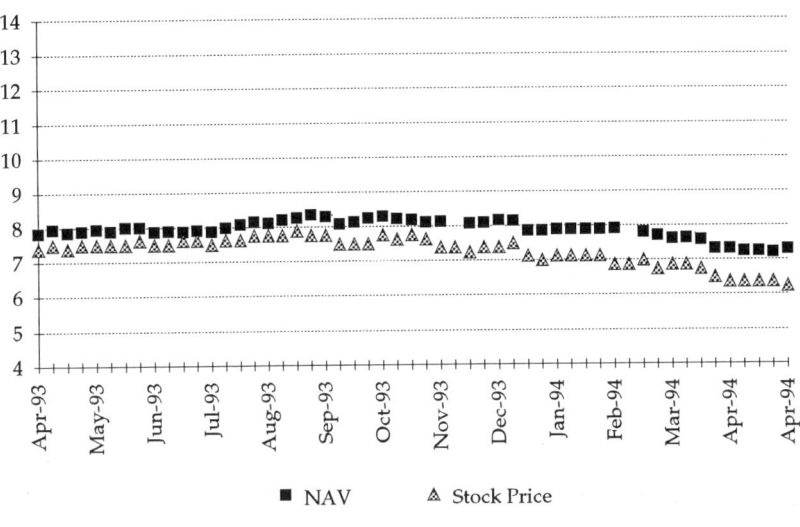

Premium/Discount Spread

■ NAV   △ Stock Price

Fund Outlook (GOV): The move to raise the Federal funds rate by 25 basis points effectively signaled the end of the cycle of lower domestic interest rates. Though this was intended to reassure the bond market, further anticipated action by the Fed and surging credit demand have only helped to push rates higher. Since the Bundesbank lowered official rates further, European-U.S. interest rate differentials narrowed. As Europe continues to struggle with double-digit unemployment and weak industrial demand, the resulting low inflation has fundamentally supported bonds. Nevertheless, the sell-off in the U.S. bond market adversely affected many European markets. The U.S.-Japan trade dilemma and political and economic reform discussions have caused nervousness in Japanese bond markets. In addition, the Japanese yen appreciated against all major currencies as the threat of trade sanctions emerged. This recent appreciation hindered exports. Despite large moves in the global bond markets, the U.S. dollar and German deutschemark currencies were steady during February. While fundamentals support a higher U.S. dollar, upside momentum has failed to materialize. The dollar bloc currencies should outperform going forward given their relative economic strength.

Authors' Comments (GOV): A substantial portion of the currency exposure is hedged. Rising interest in the U.S. caused prices of debt markets worldwide to drop in March. However, recent moves by the central banks in Europe indicate that the decoupling of the credit markets may be developing.

Global Yield Fund, Inc. (The)   NYSE: **PGY**

One Seaport Plaza
New York, NY 10292
(212) 214-3332
(800) 451-6788

Transfer Agent:
State Street Bank & Trust Co.
One Heritage Dr., North Quincy, MA 02171
(800) 426-5523

Income Results

For 12-months Ending 4/29/94	Period End	Period Begin	Distributions	Yield Dist (%)	Total Return (%)
Share Price ($)	7.00	8.13	0.36	4.43	-9.47
NAV per Share ($)	8.09	8.45		4.26	0.00

Background: Initial public offering June 30, 1986 of 65,550,000 shares at $10 per share. Initial NAV was $9.29 per share.

Objective: Seeks high current income through investment in U.S. dollar debt securities. Capital appreciation is secondary. The fund invests in debt securities denominated in a variety of currencies. Will not hold more than 40% of assets in any one currency, except for U.S. dollars for temporary defensive purposes. Will invest at least 65% of assets in governments or agencies, the remainder in corporate debt. Average weighted maturity is not to exceed 10 years. The dividend policy of the fund is to pay out essentially all of the net investment income on a quarterly basis without regard to capital or currency losses.

Portfolio: (2/28/94) Long-Term Bonds 99%, Short-Term 1%. Country Exposure: U.S. 14%, Japan 13%, Spain 11%, Italy 10%, U.K. 7%. Credit Breakdown: AAA 63%, AA 34%, A 1%.

Capitalization: (12/31/93) Common stock outstanding 66,207,299. No long-term debt.

Average Maturity (years): 6.6
Fee: 0.75%   *Fund Manager:* Prudential Mutual Fund Mgt., Inc.
Income Distribution: Quarterly   *Capital Gains Distribution:* Annually
Reinvestment Plan: Yes   *Shareholder Reports:* Semi-Annually

5 Year Performance

Fiscal Year Ending 12/31	1993	1992	1991	1990	1989
Net Assets ($mil)	579.90	535.60	593.40	591.30	595.80
Net Income Distribution ($)	0.30	0.75	0.62	0.88	0.94
Capital Gains Distribution ($)	0.23	0.05	0.00	0.00	0.00
Total Distribution ($)	0.72	0.80	0.62	0.88	0.94
Yield from Distribution (%)	9.60	9.84	7.75	11.17	10.02
Expense Ratio (%)	1.02	1.01	0.99	1.03	1.07
Portfolio Turnover (%)	370.00	192.00	141.00	221.00	734.00
NAV per Share ($)	8.76	8.10	8.99	8.96	8.57
Market Price per Share ($)	8.00	7.50	8.13	8.00	7.88
Premium (Discount) (%)	-8.68	-7.41	-9.68	-10.71	-8.05
Total Return, Stock Price (%)	11.00	1.55	16.00	4.53	-5.97

Global Yield Fund, Inc. (The)

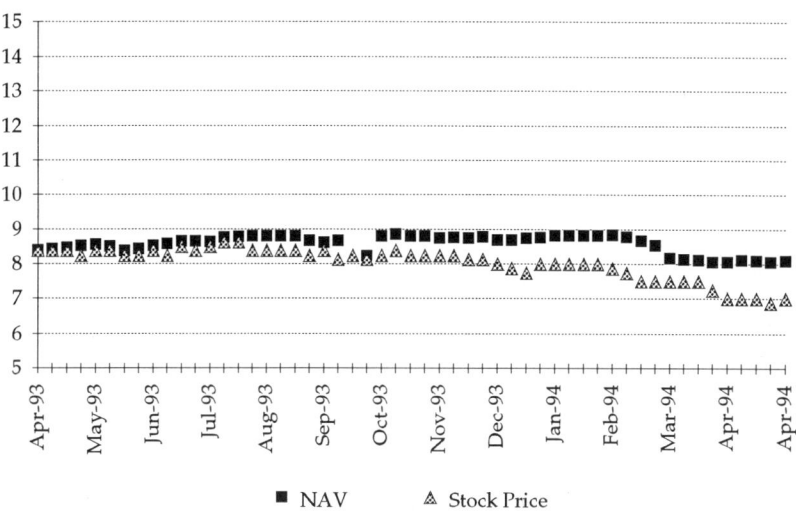

Premium/Discount Spread

■ NAV   ▵ Stock Price

Fund Outlook (PGY): The fund believes that the prospects for the global bond market are positive. Given the low level of U.S. interest rates, economic weakness abroad and generally stable worldwide inflation, global bonds should remain attractive in 1994. The fund will attempt to maintain diversified holdings in various world bond markets in order to capture both high current yields and potential capital gains resulting from falling interest rates. In coming months, the fund will continue to focus on investments outside the U.S. In addition, if the U.S. dollar appreciates further the fund will apply currency hedges as necessary to help protect the portfolio.

Authors' Comments (PGY): Large exposure to European credit markets should prove rewarding. The discount is currently larger than the average for the group and merits consideration for purchase for appreciation.

Kleinwort Benson Australian Income Fund, Inc.

NYSE: KBA

200 Park Avenue
New York, NY 10166
(800) 237-4218
(212) 687-2515
Income

Transfer Agent:
U.S. Trust Co. of New York
c/o Mutual Funds Service Co., 126 High St.
Boston, MA 02110
(800) 292-4224/(617) 482-9300

Results

For 12-months Ending 4/29/94	Period End	Period Begin	Distributions	Yield Dist (%)	Total Return (%)
Share Price ($)	9.13	10.13	0.66	6.52	-3.36
NAV per Share ($)	10.31	10.89		6.06	0.73

Background: Initial public offering November 20, 1986 of 5,500,000 shares at $10 per share. Initial NAV was $9.35 per share.

Objective: Seeks high current income by investing primarily in high quality Australian dollar denominated debt securities of Australian issuers. Long-term capital appreciation is secondary. The fund may invest up to 25% of assets in New Zealand government debt.

Portfolio: (1/31/94) Australian Government Bonds 22.6%, Other Semi-Government Bonds 23%, New South Wales Treasury Bonds 23.6%, Eurobonds 19%, Australian Corporate Bonds 4.4%, New Zealand Government Bonds 5%.

Capitalization: (12/31/93) Common stock outstanding 7,172,740. No long-term debt.

Average Maturity (years): 5.6

Fee: 0.70% *Fund Manager:* Kleinwort Benson Intl. Invest. Ltd.
Income Distribution: Monthly *Capital Gains Distribution:* Annually
Reinvestment Plan: Yes *Shareholder Reports:* Quarterly

5 Year Performance

Fiscal Year Ending 10/31	1993	1992	1991	1990	1989
Net Assets ($mil)	75.00	69.60	74.70	65.30	62.70
Net Income Distribution ($)	0.74	1.02	1.01	1.06	0.97
Capital Gains Distribution ($)	0.00	0.57	0.00	0.00	0.58
Total Distribution ($)	0.74	1.59	1.01	1.06	1.55
Yield from Distribution (%)	7.68	14.45	11.88	11.01	13.78
Expense Ratio (%)	1.47	1.48	1.62	1.61	1.75
Portfolio Turnover (%)	9.69	53.66	11.39	23.78	11.87
NAV per Share ($)	10.45	9.97	11.77	10.29	9.88
Market Price per Share ($)	9.75	9.63	11.00	8.50	9.63
Premium (Discount) (%)	-6.70	-3.51	-6.54	-17.40	-2.63
Total Return, Stock Price (%)	8.93	2.00	41.29	-0.73	-0.62

Kleinwort Benson Australian Income Fund, Inc.

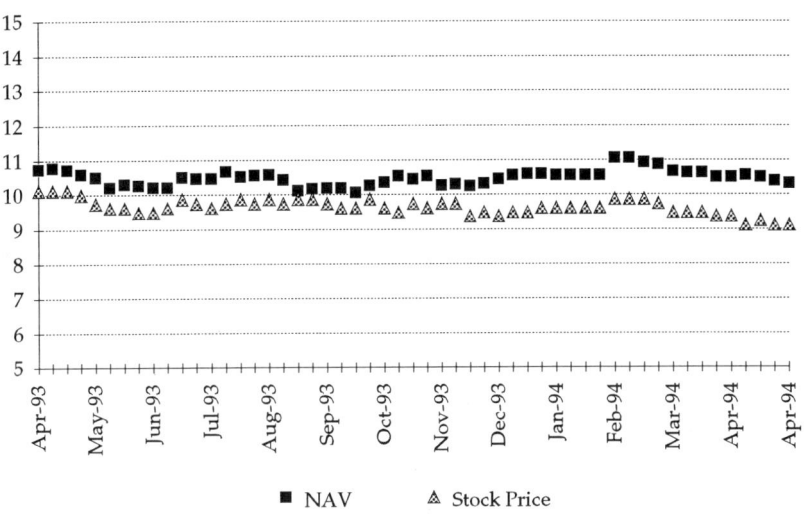

Fund Outlook (KBA): To continue to benefit from the prolonged bond rally in Australia, the fund will maintain the investment policy of emphasizing medium- and long-dated securities. This approach enables the attainment of higher yields and offers the greatest scope for further capital gain. The fund will retain its holding of Eurobonds and increase the exposure to such securities, if appropriate, to maintain the income yield enhancement due to withholding tax exemption. In addition, diversification into the New Zealand market also provides gross coupon income and enables the fund to take advantage of often dissimilar economic and political developments between the Australian countries. With this overall approach to investment, the fund should continue to provide an attractive income return, especially by comparison with U.S. dollar cash and bond equivalents, while also seeking to ensure long-term capital appreciation.

Authors' Comments (KBA): The discount is currently considerably greater than the average for the peer group. The 12-month trailing return is 2.14% versus the group average of 3.03%. Most of the portfolio is invested in Australian government and semi-government bonds, with the balance representing investments in New Zealand government bonds. The portfolio is largely concentrated in short- to medium-term issues where the yields are higher. The fund is not leveraged and does not engage in currency hedging. The Australian inflation rate is at historically low levels and, with a declining CPI, interest rates should drop more. The Australian economy is commodity driven and therefore should benefit from worldwide improvement in economic activity.

Strategic Global Income

1285 Avenue of the Americas
New York, NY 10019
(212) 713-2000

Income

NYSE: SGL

Transfer Agent:
Provident National Bank
P.O. Box 8950
Wilmington, DE 19899
(800) 553-8080

Results

For 12-months Ending 4/29/94	Period End	Period Begin	Distributions	Yield Dist (%)	Total Return (%)
Share Price ($)	12.63	13.75	1.26	9.97	1.02
NAV per Share ($)	13.38	14.35		9.42	2.02

Background: Initial public offering January 24, 1992 of 19,000,000 shares at $15 per share. Initial NAV was $14.03 per share.

Objective: Seeks high current income. Capital appreciation is secondary. Normally, the fund will invest at least 65% of assets in U.S. Government debt securities, Foreign Government debt securities, corporate obligations or preferred stock rated no lower than BBB.

Portfolio: (3/31/94) Government and other public issuers, Long-Term 73%, Short-Term/Cash 27%. Country Exposure: U.S. 40%, Mexico 10%, U.K. 7%, Canada 7%, Germany 7%.

Capitalization: (1/30/93) Common stock outstanding 21,407,128. No long-term debt.

Average Maturity (years): 13.2

Fee: 1.00% **Fund Manager:** Mitchell Hutchins Asset Mgt., Inc.
Income Distribution: Quarterly **Capital Gains Distribution:** Annually
Reinvestment Plan: Yes **Shareholder Reports:** Semi-Annually

5 Year Performance

Fiscal Year Ending 11/30	1993	1992	1991	1990	1989
Net Assets ($mil)	319.50	288.30	-	-	-
Net Income Distribution ($)	1.12	0.70	-	-	-
Capital Gains Distribution ($)	0.06	0.03	-	-	-
Total Distribution ($)	1.18	0.73	-	-	-
Yield from Distribution (%)	9.17	5.67	-	-	-
Expense Ratio (%)	1.58	1.34	-	-	-
Portfolio Turnover (%)	111.29	94.08	-	-	-
NAV per Share ($)	14.92	13.47	-	-	-
Market Price per Share ($)	14.25	12.88	-	-	-
Premium (Discount) (%)	-4.49	-4.42	-	-	-
Total Return, Stock Price (%)	19.80	-	-	-	-

Strategic Global Income

Premium/Discount Spread

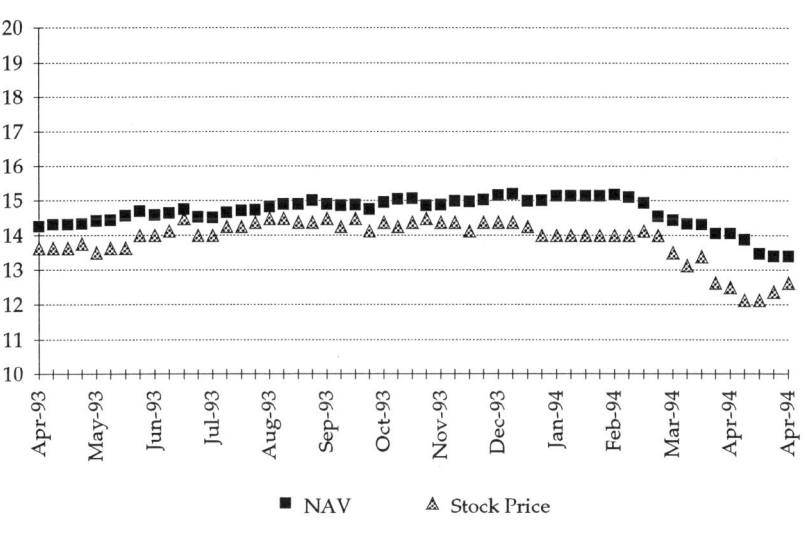

■ NAV   △ Stock Price

Fund Outlook (SGL): The fund believes the U.S. is ahead of the world in a recovery phase of the economic cycle. Significantly more space capacity exists in Europe and Japan than in the U.S. Therefore, inflation is likely to be lower, and credit conditions are likely to be easier overseas than in the U.S. A low inflation, low interest rate environment in Europe continues to make investing in European bonds compelling. The Bundesbank is expected to reduce interest rates further, which will allow other European governments to ease their interest rates. Economic reform in countries like Mexico, Argentina and Chile is another important factor in the global picture. These countries have opened and deregulated their markets in the last several years and have developed more efficient, competitive economies in the process. They have privatized and reduced their outstanding debt levels substantially, significantly enhancing their creditworthiness.

Authors' Comments (SGL): The 12-month trailing return is 2.89% versus a 3.30% for the peer group. The European credit market sell-off that occurred in February-March did not substantially depress SGL's NAV because of defensive positions established with maturities in the two- to five-year range. The portfolio is rated BBB or better.

Templeton Global Income Fund, Inc.   NYSE: **GIM**

700 Central Avenue
St. Petersburg, FL 33701
(800) 237-0738
(813) 823-8712

Transfer Agent:
Mellon Financial Services
85 Challenger Road, Overpark Center
Ridgefield Park, NJ 07660
(800) 526-0801

Income

Results

For 12-months Ending 4/29/94	Period End	Period Begin	Distributions	Yield Dist (%)	Total Return (%)
Share Price ($)	7.00	8.13	0.55	6.77	-7.13
NAV per Share ($)	7.94	8.57		6.42	-0.93

Background: Initial public offering March 17, 1988 of 110,000,000 shares at $10 per share. Initial NAV was $9.35 per share.

Objective: Seeks high current income. Capital appreciation is secondary. Invests 85% of its assets in a portfolio of fixed-income securities rated AA or AAA, including debt securities and preferred stock of U.S. and Foreign issuers. May borrow against its portfolio and invest 35% in dividend-paying common stocks of U.S. and foreign corporations.

Portfolio: (8/31/93) Government Bonds 70.7%, Corporate Bonds 13.6%, Indexed Securities 10.6%, Short-Term Obligations 2.9%. Country Exposure: North America 59%, Europe 21.7%, Australia & New Zealand 12%, Japan 7.3%.

Capitalization: (8/31/93) Common stock outstanding 120,453,400. No long-term debt.

Average Maturity (years): 8.9
Fee: 0.55%   *Fund Manager:* Templeton, Galbraith, & Hansberger Ltd.
Income Distribution: Monthly   *Capital Gains Distribution:* Annually
Reinvestment Plan: Yes   *Shareholder Reports:* Quarterly

5 Year Performance

Fiscal Year Ending 8/31	1993	1992	1991	1990	1989
Net Assets ($mil)	1032.80	1055.50	991.00	992.60	994.90
Net Income Distribution ($)	0.66	0.84	0.86	0.96	0.98
Capital Gains Distribution ($)	0.06	0.00	0.09	0.00	0.00
Total Distribution ($)	0.72	0.84	0.95	0.96	0.98
Yield from Distribution (%)	7.78	10.02	12.87	10.51	9.92
Expense Ratio (%)	0.79	0.81	0.82	0.81	0.81
Portfolio Turnover (%)	264.61	189.94	257.11	130.40	78.73
NAV per Share ($)	8.57	8.86	8.48	8.51	8.62
Market Price per Share ($)	8.00	9.25	8.38	7.38	9.13
Premium (Discount) (%)	-6.65	4.40	-1.30	-13.40	5.80
Total Return, Stock Price (%)	-5.73	20.41	26.42	-8.65	2.33

Templeton Global Income Fund, Inc.

Premium/Discount Spread

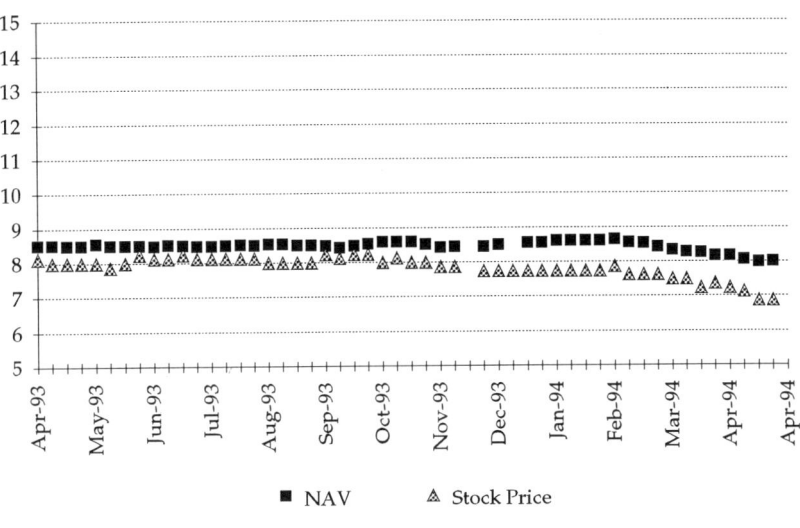

■ NAV   △ Stock Price

Fund Outlook (GIM): The fund believes that the North American Free Trade Agreement (NAFTA) will help to foster free trade in North America and should contribute to the region's long-term economic growth. The fund also believes that the successful completion (after seven years) of the Uruguay Round of talks under the General Agreement on Tariffs and Trade (GATT) may have a favorable influence on global markets. With 117 member nations, GATT promises less-restricted trade around the world through a gradual reduction of trade barriers, such as tariffs and government subsidies, during the next 50 years. Both NAFTA and GATT may have long-term, positive implications for global investors by lowering the costs of trade and investment.

Authors' Comments (GIM): The current discount is the widest discount in more than three years. The 12-month trailing return in 3.09% compared to the group 3.30%. During the recent world bond market correction, GIM was relatively unaffected inasmuch as the fund held a fairly substantial amount of cash. Additional funds were added in January, positioning the fund to take advantage of any future weakness in world markets.

Multi Sector Bond Funds

American Capital Income Trust

NYSE: ACD

2800 Post Oak Blvd., P.O. Box 1411
Houston, TX 77251-1411
(800) 421-5666
(713) 993-0500

Transfer Agent:
Boston Financial Services, Inc.
P.O. Box 366
Boston, MA 02101
(800) 421-9696

Income

Results

For 12-months Ending 4/29/94	Period End	Period Begin	Distributions	Yield Dist (%)	Total Return (%)
Share Price ($)	6.88	7.88	0.68	8.63	-4.06
NAV per Share ($)	7.79	8.02		8.48	5.61

Background: Initial public offering April 22, 1988 of 13,000,000 shares of beneficial interest at $10 per share. Initial NAV was $9.30 per share.

Objective: Seeks high current income consistent with preservation of capital. Balances investments between U.S. Government and corporate fixed-income securities, including high-yielding lower-rated or non-rated issues. Typically, allocations are nearly equal though the fund may invest in one security class to the exclusion of the other. May hedge with options and futures strategies.

Portfolio: (12/31/93) Corporate Bonds & Notes 41%, U.S. Government & Agency Obligations 49%, Preferred Stocks 6%, Stocks 1%, Cash 3%. Portfolio Ratings: BB 17%, B 24%, Low- & Non-Rated 10%. Top Holdings: GNMA, SuperMarkets General Preferred, Federal Farm Credit Bank, Unisys.

Capitalization: (3/31/94) Shares of beneficial interest outstanding 15,290,019. No long-term debt.

Average Maturity (years): 15.1

Fee: 0.65% *Fund Manager:* American Capital Asset Mgt., Inc.
Income Distribution: Monthly *Capital Gains Distribution:* Annually
Reinvestment Plan: Yes *Shareholder Reports:* Semi-Annually

5 Year Performance

Fiscal Year Ending 12/31	1993	1992	1991	1990	1989
Net Assets ($mil)	124.70	119.60	116.30	100.60	119.40
Net Income Distribution ($)	0.77	0.86	0.89	0.97	1.08
Capital Gains Distribution ($)	0.00	0.00	0.00	0.00	0.03
Total Distribution ($)	0.77	0.86	0.89	0.97	1.11
Yield from Distribution (%)	10.09	11.65	15.81	12.93	12.05
Expense Ratio (%)	1.01	0.99	1.03	1.00	0.97
Portfolio Turnover (%)	42.00	54.00	50.00	29.00	20.00
NAV per Share ($)	8.16	7.85	7.70	6.66	7.90
Market Price per Share ($)	7.75	7.63	7.38	5.63	7.50
Premium (Discount) (%)	-5.02	-2.80	-4.29	-15.47	-5.06
Total Return, Stock Price (%)	11.64	15.04	46.89	-12.00	-5.81

American Capital Income Trust

Premium/Discount Spread

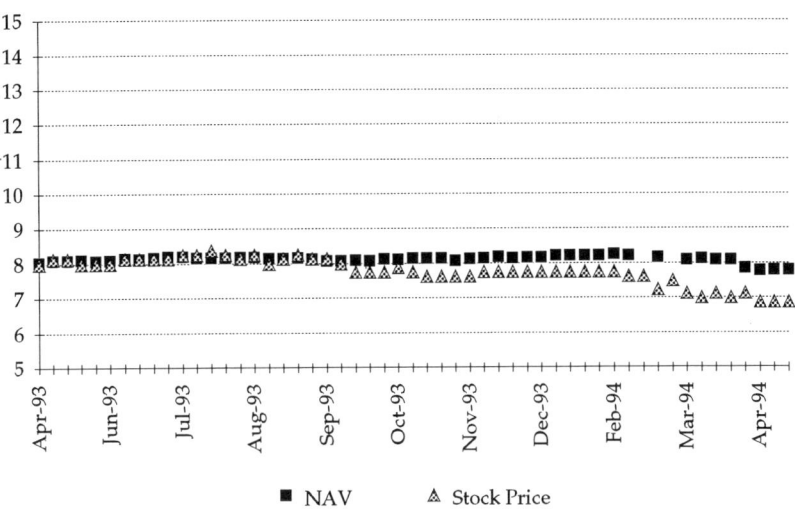

■ NAV   △ Stock Price

Fund Outlook (ACD): The trust expects to see moderate economic growth during 1994, as improving corporate earnings and rising consumer confidence are counterbalanced by a heavier tax burden, ongoing concerns about the effects of health care reform and higher short-term interest rates. Inflation should remain low and long-term interest rates should stay close to current levels. In the current environment, it will be difficult for high yield bonds to generate the record levels of returns ACD experienced through the third quarter of 1993, but they will continue to offer opportunities which compare favorably with other available investments. ACD believes that any eventual increases in long-term interest rates will be gradual and moderate. Thus "real" returns from bonds and bond funds remain attractive, and these investments continue to be appropriate for income-oriented investors.

Authors' Comments (ACD): The 12-month trailing return is 8.43% as contrasted with 5.08% for the peer group. This superior performance may be attributed to the very fine performance of the high-yield portion of the portfolio.

Colonial Intermarket Income Trust I

One Financial Center, 12th Floor
Boston, MA 02111
(800) 426-3750

Income

NYSE: CMK
Transfer Agent:
State Street Bank & Trust Co.
P.O. Box 8200
Boston, MA 02266
(800) 426-5523

Results

For 12-months Ending 4/29/94	Period End	Period Begin	Distributions	Yield Dist (%)	Total Return (%)
Share Price ($)	10.75	11.75	1.37	11.66	3.15
NAV per Share ($)	11.01	11.84		11.57	4.56

Background: Initial public offering September 22, 1989 of 10,000,000 shares at $12 per share. Initial NAV was $11.16 per share.

Objective: Seeks high current income. Invests in securities issued or guaranteed by the U.S. Government, its Agencies or Instrumentalities; debt secured by Foreign Governments; high-yield securities, some of which may be convertible. The percentage of assets in any one sector is limited to 50%. The fund may engage in hedging transactions.

Portfolio: (11/30/93) Corporate 44.2%, Banking & Financial Services 4.6%, Consumer Non-Durables 17.1%, Energy 4%, Manufacturing 16.1%, Transportation 1.8%, Utilities 0.6%, Foreign Government Obligations 23.3%, U.S. Government & Agency Obligations 21.5%, Convertible Bonds 0.1%.

Capitalization: (11/30/93) Common stock outstanding 11,009,000. No long-term debt.

Average Maturity (years): 11.9
Fee: 0.75%
Income Distribution: Monthly
Reinvestment Plan: Yes

Fund Manager: Colonial Mgt. Associates, Inc.
Capital Gains Distribution: Annually
Shareholder Reports: Semi-Annually

5 Year Performance

Fiscal Year Ending 11/30	1993	1992	1991	1990	1989
Net Assets ($mil)	132.30	123.60	124.80	117.10	123.90
Net Income Distribution ($)	1.08	1.13	1.23	1.35	0.12
Capital Gains Distribution ($)	0.00	0.00	0.01	0.00	0.00
Total Distribution ($)	1.08	1.13	1.24	1.35	0.12
Yield from Distribution (%)	9.70	10.27	12.88	11.61	-
Expense Ratio (%)	1.02	1.04	1.07	1.11	0.90
Portfolio Turnover (%)	179.00	129.00	109.00	153.00	0.00
NAV per Share ($)	12.01	11.22	11.33	10.64	11.26
Market Price per Share ($)	11.88	11.13	11.00	9.63	11.63
Premium (Discount) (%)	-1.12	-0.89	-2.91	-9.59	3.20
Total Return, Stock Price (%)	16.44	11.45	27.10	-5.59	-

Colonial Intermarket Income Trust I

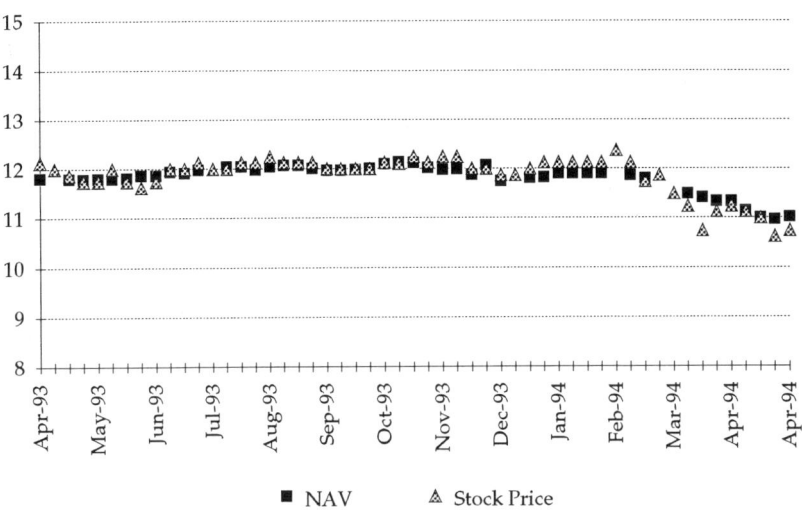

Premium/Discount Spread

■ NAV △ Stock Price

Fund Outlook (CMK): Seeks to provide high current income by investing in three fixed-income markets. All three markets—U.S. and foreign government, and high yield, high risk U.S. corporate—contributed to the strong performance during the fiscal year ended November 30, 1993. Members of the management team have positioned the portfolio in sectors they believed were likely to perform well in the early stages of an economic recovery. These included automotive-related industries, steel, and home building. The management also maintained the trust's position in food and beverages.

Authors' Comments (CMK): The current monthly distribution of $0.085 was reduced from $0.090 in February. Recent NAV weakness during the February-March sell-off in the world debt markets can be attributed to the fund's position in the emerging-market debt, as well as the bond positions held in the U.K., Australia and Spain. The 12-month trailing return is 8.75% as contrasted to 5.08% for the group.

Dreyfus Strategic Governments Income, Inc.   NYSE: **DSI**

144 Glenn Curtiss Blvd.
Uniondale, NY 11556
(800) 334-6899

Transfer Agent:
Mellon Bank, N. A.
One Mellon Bank Center
Pittsburgh, PA 15258
(412) 236-8000

Income

Results

For 12-months Ending 4/29/94	Period End	Period Begin	Distributions	Yield Dist (%)	Total Return (%)
Share Price ($)	9.88	11.88	0.85	7.15	-9.68
NAV per Share ($)	10.36	11.16		7.62	-0.45

Background: Initial public offering June 23, 1988 of 13,000,000 shares at $12 per share. Initial NAV was $11.15 per share.

Objective: Seeks current income consistent with capital preservation. Invests at least 65% in securities issued by the U.S. Government and its agencies and Foreign Governments. May invest up to 35% in non-government securities. May use options.

Portfolio: (11/30/93) Corporate Bonds 2.4%, Foreign Government Bonds & Notes 32.9%, Foreign & Supranational Bonds & Notes 5.2%, U.S. Government & Agencies 47.1%, Short-Term 6.4%.

Capitalization: (11/30/93) Common stock outstanding 14,960,617. No long-term debt.

Average Maturity (years): 8.1

Fee: 0.70% *Fund Manager:* The Dreyfus Corporation
Income Distribution: Monthly *Capital Gains Distribution:* Annually
Reinvestment Plan: Yes *Shareholder Reports:* Semi-Annually

5 Year Performance

Fiscal Year Ending 5/31	1993	1992	1991	1990	1989
Net Assets ($mil)	162.70	163.20	159.80	156.20	157.00
Net Income Distribution ($)	0.94	1.08	1.08	1.03	0.91
Capital Gains Distribution ($)	0.00	0.03	0.00	0.00	0.03
Total Distribution ($)	0.94	1.11	1.08	1.03	0.94
Yield from Distribution (%)	8.17	9.97	10.93	9.47	-
Expense Ratio (%)	0.88	0.88	0.87	0.89	0.89
Portfolio Turnover (%)	43.00	56.29	26.38	16.34	83.78
NAV per Share ($)	11.03	11.06	10.92	10.70	10.76
Market Price per Share ($)	11.50	11.50	11.13	9.88	10.88
Premium (Discount) (%)	4.26	3.98	1.83	-7.66	1.02
Total Return, Stock Price (%)	8.17	13.30	23.58	0.28	-

Dreyfus Strategic Governments Income, Inc.

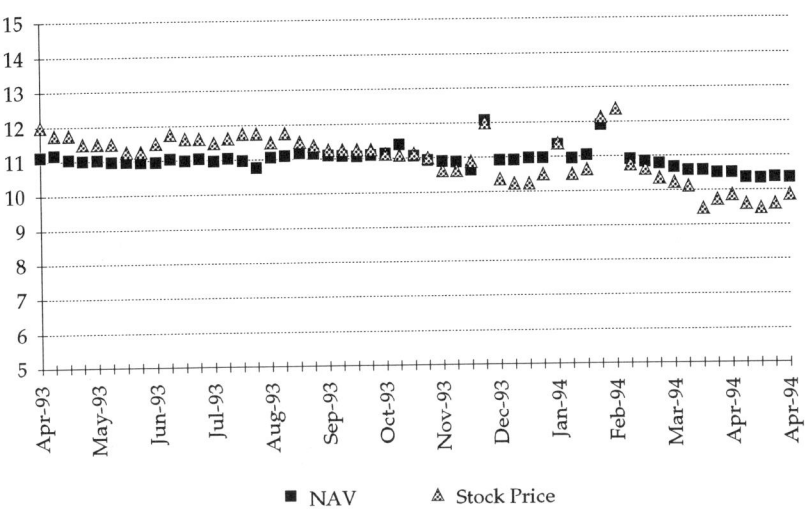

Fund Outlook (DSI): Recent concerns regarding the acceleration of U.S. economic activity and a potential jump in the U.S. inflation rate has led to an increase in U.S. interest rates with the greatest pressure on the longer-maturity issues in the market. Since the dollar-weighted average maturity of the holdings in the fund cannot exceed 10 years, the portfolio's net asset value per share was somewhat protected during the February sell-off. It is the fund's judgment that 1994 will see greater day-to-day price volatility and therefore the fund may increase the turnover rate in the portfolio, especially in U.S. Treasury holdings.

Authors' Comments (DSI): The fund is restricted to investing in investment-grade securities and, therefore, was not able to participate in the bull market in high-yield securities. The fund is also restricted from investing in a number of emerging-market debt instruments because of the low credit quality. In addition, DSI must maintain a weighted maturity of less than 10 years and cannot leverage. Despite these restrictions the fund has been able to maintain an above average yield by investing in high premium Treasuries. The 12-month trailing return is 0.94%. However, market risk is below average and appropriate for those seeking less volatility.

Kemper Multi-Market Income Trust

120 S. LaSalle Street
Chicago, IL 60603
(800) 537-6006

NYSE: **KMM**
Transfer Agent:
Investors Fiduciary Trust Co.
127 W. 10th St.
Kansas City, MO 64105
(800) 422-2848

Income

Results

For 12-months Ending 4/29/94	Period End	Period Begin	Distributions	Yield Dist (%)	Total Return (%)
Share Price ($)	9.88	11.38	1.05	9.23	-3.95
NAV per Share ($)	10.59	11.16		9.41	4.30

Background: Initial public offering January 23, 1989 of 10,000,000 shares at $12 per share. Initial NAV was $11.16.

Objective: Seeks high income consistent with a prudent total return. Invests in a diversified portfolio of income-producing securities. The fund may invest in: U.S. Government & Agency paper, Foreign Government obligations, and foreign corporate securities. No limitation on portfolio allocation percentages. The fund may leverage with preferreds.

Portfolio: (11/30/93) U.S. Government Obligations 3.9%, Foreign Government Obligations 25.2%, Corporate Obligations 42.3%, Common Stocks & Other 3.7%.

Capitalization: (11/30/92) Common shares outstanding 19,993,000. No long-term debt.

Average Maturity (years): 8.1

Fee: 0.85%
Income Distribution: Monthly
Reinvestment Plan: Yes
Fund Manager: Kemper Financial Services, Inc.
Capital Gains Distribution: Annually
Shareholder Reports: Quarterly

5 Year Performance

Fiscal Year Ending 11/30	1993	1992	1991	1990	1989
Net Assets ($mil)	225.10	215.40	204.50	155.40	203.20
Net Income Distribution ($)	1.08	1.09	1.16	1.40	1.05
Capital Gains Distribution ($)	0.00	0.00	0.00	0.00	0.00
Total Distribution ($)	1.08	1.09	1.16	1.40	1.05
Yield from Distribution (%)	10.40	11.03	15.72	-	-
Expense Ratio (%)	0.97	0.99	1.00	1.00	0.94
Portfolio Turnover (%)	240.00	101.00	24.00	32.00	38.00
NAV per Share ($)	11.29	10.88	10.36	7.88	10.33
Market Price per Share ($)	11.00	10.38	9.88	7.38	-
Premium (Discount) (%)	-2.57	-4.60	-4.73	-6.47	-100.00
Total Return, Stock Price (%)	16.38	16.09	49.59	-15.41	-

Kemper Multi-Market Income Trust

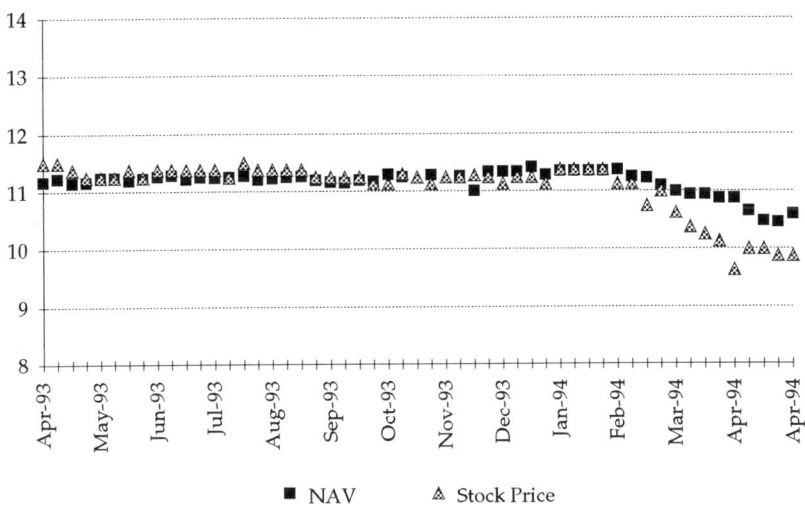

Premium/Discount Spread

■ NAV   △ Stock Price

Fund Outlook (KMM): Management believes that short-term interest rates will trend higher in the coming months and enable the fund to continue to earn a high level of income. This income should help offset the downward pressure on bond prices. Management is also positive on the high yield sector of the market. The fund is invested in an approximately equal weighting of high yield corporate bonds, foreign currency bonds and U.S. government securities.

Authors' Comments (KMM): One of the main benefits to be expected from a mutual fund, be it open- or closed-end, is active management. KMM delivers on this front. Over the last year, the fund has lowered its percentage of high yield securities to 30% of assets, down from over 50% a year ago, while increasing exposure to emerging country Brady Bond debt to over 20%. Management correctly felt that the Bradys were oversold, so stepped in, bought and then sold out most at a profit after about a month. The core holdings consist of high yield corporates, Treasuries, and European debt. A good fund for the aggressive income investor who desires a nimble, timing-oriented management style.

MFS Charter Income Trust

500 Boylston Street
Boston, MA 02116
(617) 954-5000

NYSE: MCR
Transfer Agent:
State Street Bank & Trust Co.
P.O. Box 8200
Boston, MA 02266-8200
(800) 637-2304

Income

Results

For 12-months Ending 4/29/94	Period End	Period Begin	Distributions	Yield Dist (%)	Total Return (%)
Share Price ($)	8.75	10.13	0.85	8.39	-5.23
NAV per Share ($)	10.04	10.58		8.03	2.93

Background: Initial public offering July 1989. Initial NAV was $11.16 per share.
Objective: Seeks current income by investing one third of its portfolio in each of the following sectors: U.S. Government securities, debt obligations of Foreign Governments and other foreign issuers, and high-yielding corporate fixed-income securities.
Portfolio: (3/1/94) U.S. Treasuries 22%, GNMAs 12%, High-Yield Corporates 30%, Foreign 34%. Country Exposure: Spain 3%, Sweden 5%, France 5%, Australia 5%, Ireland 4%, U.K. 2%, Denmark 2%.
Capitalization: (3/1/94) Common stock outstanding 86,060,639. No long-term debt.
Average Maturity (years): 7.6
Fee: 0.32% *Fund Manager:* Massachusetts Financial Ser. Co.
Income Distribution: Monthly *Capital Gains Distribution:* Annually
Reinvestment Plan: Yes *Shareholder Reports:* Semi-Annually

5 Year Performance

Fiscal Year Ending 11/30	1993	1992	1991	1990	1989
Net Assets ($mil)	919.50	898.80	923.30	864.30	977.90
Net Income Distribution ($)	0.72	0.90	1.06	1.22	0.38
Capital Gains Distribution ($)	0.23	0.15	0.00	0.07	0.00
Total Distribution ($)	0.95	1.05	1.06	1.29	0.38
Yield from Distribution (%)	9.62	9.65	11.61	11.73	-
Expense Ratio (%)	0.90	0.98	1.02	1.08	0.74
Portfolio Turnover (%)	397.00	198.00	416.00	184.00	480.00
NAV per Share ($)	10.68	10.23	10.59	9.93	11.00
Market Price per Share ($)	9.63	9.88	10.88	9.13	11.00
Premium (Discount) (%)	-9.88	-3.42	2.64	-8.01	0.00
Total Return, Stock Price (%)	7.09	0.46	30.78	-5.27	-

MFS Charter Income Trust

Premium/Discount Spread

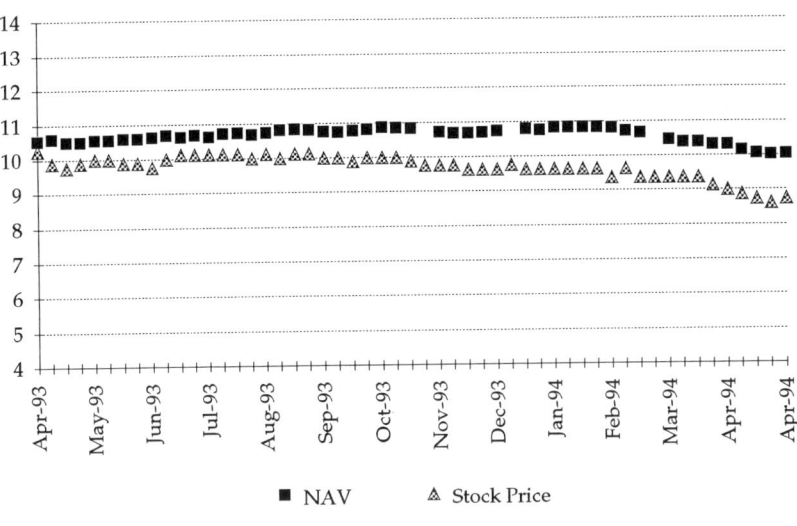

Fund Outlook (MCR): The international sector provides the brightest outlook for bond price appreciation. The fund has overweighted their holdings in Europe, which continues to be hard hit with economic recession. The weakness in Europe is much worse than many economists had predicted and interest rates are still unsustainably high. The fund's strategy is to continue to own those sovereign, European credits where real rates of interest are high on a relative basis and where nominal rates are also high relative to the depressed economic activity. As the European central banks lower interest rates to stimulate their economies, longer-term interest rates are likely to decline, resulting in increasing bond prices.

Authors' Comments (MCR): CMK is a conservatively managed multi-sector bond fund. The manager prefers to invest in developed economies rather than seek the higher and riskier yields available in the emerging economies. The portfolio mix is slightly weighted in the high yield sector which gives the dividend a nice boost. This is the authors' top pick for the conservative investor seeking comfortable diversification and solid management.

MFS Government Markets Income Trust   NYSE: MGF

500 Boylston Street
Boston, MA 02116-3741
(617) 954-5000

Transfer Agent:
State Street Bank & Trust Co.
P.O. Box 8201
Boston, MA 02266-8200
(800) 637-2304

Income

Results

For 12-months Ending 4/29/94	Period End	Period Begin	Distributions	Yield Dist (%)	Total Return (%)
Share Price ($)	6.31	7.50	0.58	7.73	-8.13
NAV per Share ($)	7.25	7.88		7.36	-0.63

Background: Initial public offering May 20, 1987 of 85,000,000 shares at $10 per share. Initial NAV was $9.40 per share.

Objective: Seeks high level of current income. Invests at least 65% in obligations issued or guaranteed by the U.S. Government and may engage in transactions involving related options. May invest up to 35% in obligations issued or guaranteed by Foreign Governments.

Portfolio: (3/1/94) U.S. Treasuries 24%, GNMAs 17%, FNMAs 2%, Other Agencies 16%. Foreign Investments: Spain 6%, Sweden 5%, Australia 6%, Denmark 5%, Mexico 5%, France 3%.

Capitalization: (3/1/94) Common stock outstanding 96,981,555. No long-term debt.

Average Maturity (years): 8.5
Fee: 0.32% *Fund Manager:* Massachusetts Financial Ser. Co.
Income Distribution: Monthly *Capital Gains Distribution:* Annually
Reinvestment Plan: Yes *Shareholder Reports:* Semi-Annually

5 Year Performance

Fiscal Year Ending 11/30	1993	1992	1991	1990	1989
Net Assets ($mil)	744.50	743.10	786.00	814.00	857.20
Net Income Distribution ($)	0.44	0.57	0.64	0.68	0.90
Capital Gains Distribution ($)	0.22	0.00	0.00	0.00	0.00
Total Distribution ($)	0.66	0.57	0.64	0.68	0.90
Yield from Distribution (%)	9.10	7.13	7.87	6.80	8.88
Expense Ratio (%)	0.93	1.03	1.04	1.05	1.08
Portfolio Turnover (%)	453.00	245.00	805.00	535.00	640.00
NAV per Share ($)	7.59	8.08	8.41	8.92	9.18
Market Price per Share ($)	7.13	7.25	8.00	8.13	10.00
Premium (Discount) (%)	-6.13	-4.48	-0.99	-3.33	12.11
Total Return, Stock Price (%)	7.45	-2.25	6.27	-11.90	7.60

MFS Government Markets Income Trust

Premium/Discount Spread

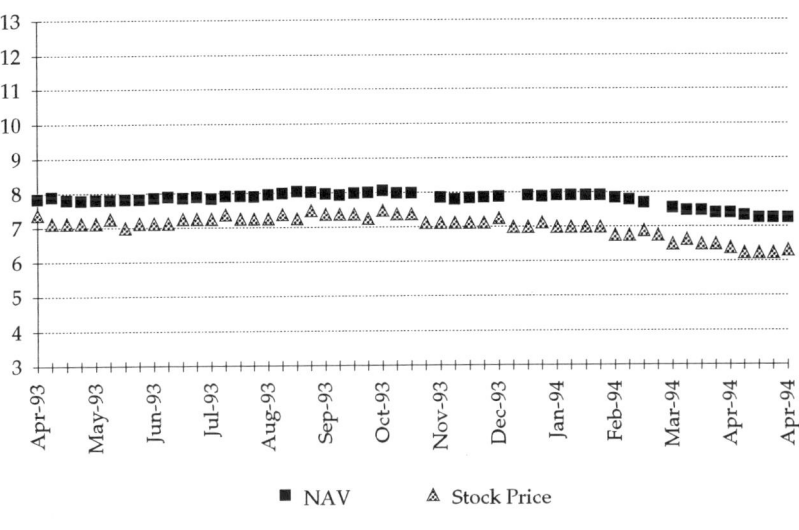

■ NAV △ Stock Price

Fund Outlook (MGF): The trust expects positive, fundamental trends in European bond markets to produce further gains in foreign holdings. Real (adjusted for inflation) interest rates are still high in Europe, putting downward pressure on economic activity and inflation. With growth and inflation remaining low or failing further, European bonds should produce attractive returns relative to the bond markets of other countries as the European central banks lower interest rates in an attempt to stimulate their economies. The trust also expects European currencies to weaken against the U.S. dollar, given the strength of the U.S. economy. As long as current conditions prevail, the trust expects to hedge the majority of their European exposure back into the dollar.

Authors' Comments (MGF): The foreign bond portfolio is concentrated in Europe, and is not hedged. Because of the large percentage of Treasuries held in the trust, the trust was particularly hard hit in February when the bond market collapsed, experiencing a decline in NAV. The trust recently reduced the average maturity to approximately 6.5 years by adding to one-, two-, three- and four-year Treasury notes with an off-set in mortgaged-backed securities to obtain additional yield. MGF is restricted from investing in junk. The 12-month trailing return is 0.20% which compares unfavorably with the performance of this group. However, the yield is appealing.

MFS Intermediate Income Trust

NYSE: MIN

500 Boylston Street
Boston, MA 02116-3741
(617) 954-5000

Transfer Agent:
State Street Bank & Trust Co.
P.O.Box 8202
Boston, MA 02266-8200
(800) 637-2304

Income

Results

For 12-months Ending 4/29/94	Period End	Period Begin	Distributions	Yield Dist (%)	Total Return (%)
Share Price ($)	6.63	7.63	0.61	7.99	-5.11
NAV per Share ($)	7.63	8.14		7.49	1.23

Background: Initial public offering March 11, 1988 of 200,000,000 shares at $10 per share. Initial NAV was $9.40 per share.

Objective: Seeks to preserve capital and provide high current income from investments in shorter-term U.S. Government securities and stable Foreign Governments. Maintains an average maturity between three and seven years.

Portfolio: (3/1/94) U.S. Treasuries 24%, GNMAs 18%, FNMAs 3%, Other Agencies 9%. Country Exposure: Spain 6%, Australia 7%, Sweden 3%, France 7%, Denmark 4%, U.K. 3%, Italy 7%.

Capitalization: (12/31/93) Common stock outstanding 196,808,716. No long-term debt.

Average Maturity (years): 5.7

Fee: 0.32%   **Fund Manager:** Massachussetts Financial Ser. Co.

Income Distribution: Monthly   **Capital Gains Distribution:** Annually

Reinvestment Plan: Yes   **Shareholder Reports:** Semi-Annually

5 Year Performance

Fiscal Year Ending 10/31	1993	1992	1991	1990	1989
Net Assets ($mil)	1596.60	1615.40	1643.70	1695.40	1790.70
Net Income Distribution ($)	0.52	0.60	0.62	0.63	0.92
Capital Gains Distribution ($)	0.16	0.00	0.00	0.00	0.00
Total Distribution ($)	0.68	0.60	0.62	0.63	0.92
Yield from Distribution (%)	8.50	7.50	8.27	7.20	9.81
Expense Ratio (%)	0.95	1.01	1.00	1.01	1.10
Portfolio Turnover (%)	270.00	401.00	1004.00	554.00	546.00
NAV per Share ($)	8.18	8.07	8.24	8.45	8.87
Market Price per Share ($)	7.63	8.00	8.00	7.50	8.75
Premium (Discount) (%)	-6.78	-0.87	-2.91	-11.24	-1.35
Total Return, Stock Price (%)	3.88	7.50	14.93	-7.09	3.09

MFS Intermediate Income Trust

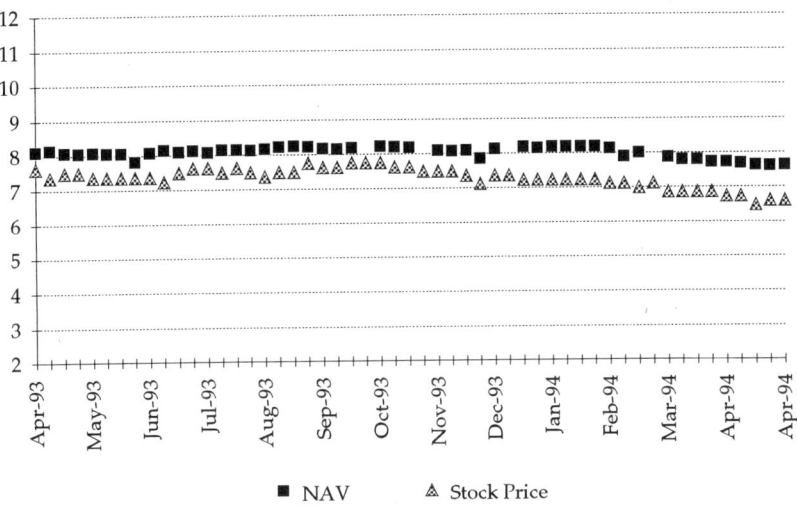

Premium/Discount Spread

■ NAV   △ Stock Price

Fund Outlook (MIN): The trust benefited from both declining interest rates and portfolio sector allocations. The trust's current outlook is biased toward more stable interest rates, continued outperformance of the U.S. Treasury sector over mortgage securities and a flattening of the yield curve. The trust expects the positive, fundamental trends in European bond markets to continue.

Authors' Comments (MIN): The foreign bond portfolio is concentrated in Europe where hedging strategies are utilized. The trust holds large positions of U.S. Treasuries on the premise that demand for Treasury securities will remain high and because of deficit reductions and the fact that new offerings will be reduced. In the past the trust has engaged in option writing to supplement income. However, recently this has been kept to a minimum. The 12-month trailing return is 1.73%.

MFS Multimarket Income Trust

500 Boylston Street
Boston, MA 02116-3741
(617) 954-5000

Income

NYSE: **MMT**
Transfer Agent:
State Street Bank & Trust Co.
P.O. Box 8203
Boston, MA 02266-8200
(800) 637-2304

Results

For 12-months Ending 4/29/94	Period End	Period Begin	Distributions	Yield Dist (%)	Total Return (%)
Share Price ($)	6.63	7.75	0.63	8.13	-6.32
NAV per Share ($)	7.28	7.77		8.11	1.80

Background: Initial public offering March 5, 1987 of 110,000,000 shares at $10 per share. Initial NAV was $9.40 per share.

Objective: Seeks high current income consistent with preservation of capital, with capital appreciation as a secondary consideration. The fund may invest in high-yielding corporate bonds, debt securities of non-U.S. Governments, U.S. Government securities, municipal securities, high-quality corporate obligations, cash equivalents, and, to the extent available, options and futures. Sector allocation is up to the discretion of the advisor.

Portfolio: (3/1/94) U.S. Government Securities 29% (U.S. Treasuries 18%, GNMAs 11%), Foreign 30%, High-Yield Corporates 32%, High-Grade Corporates 7%, Common Stocks 1%, Short-Term U.S. Obligations 1%. Country Exposure: Spain 4%, Sweden 5%, France 5%, Italy 5%, Australia 4%.

Capitalization: (3/1/94) Shares of beneficial interest outstanding 121,977,152. No long-term debt.

Average Maturity (years): 8.3

Fee: 0.34%   *Fund Manager:* Massachusetts Financial Ser. Co.
Income Distribution: Monthly   *Capital Gains Distribution:* Annually
Reinvestment Plan: Yes   *Shareholder Reports:* Quarterly

5 Year Performance

Fiscal Year Ending 10/31	1993	1992	1991	1990	1989
Net Assets ($mil)	947.30	947.30	929.40	917.50	1056.50
Net Income Distribution ($)	0.51	0.65	0.70	0.79	1.11
Capital Gains Distribution ($)	0.17	0.00	0.00	0.00	0.00
Total Distribution ($)	0.68	0.65	0.70	0.79	1.11
Yield from Distribution (%)	8.91	8.39	10.77	8.65	11.10
Expense Ratio (%)	1.03	1.11	1.11	1.19	1.23
Portfolio Turnover (%)	415.00	425.00	740.00	365.00	423.00
NAV per Share ($)	7.90	7.69	7.93	7.54	8.66
Market Price per Share ($)	7.38	7.63	7.75	6.50	9.13
Premium (Discount) (%)	-6.65	-0.91	-2.27	-13.79	5.31
Total Return, Stock Price (%)	5.64	6.84	30.00	-20.15	2.40

MFS Multimarket Income Trust

Pewmium/Discount Spread

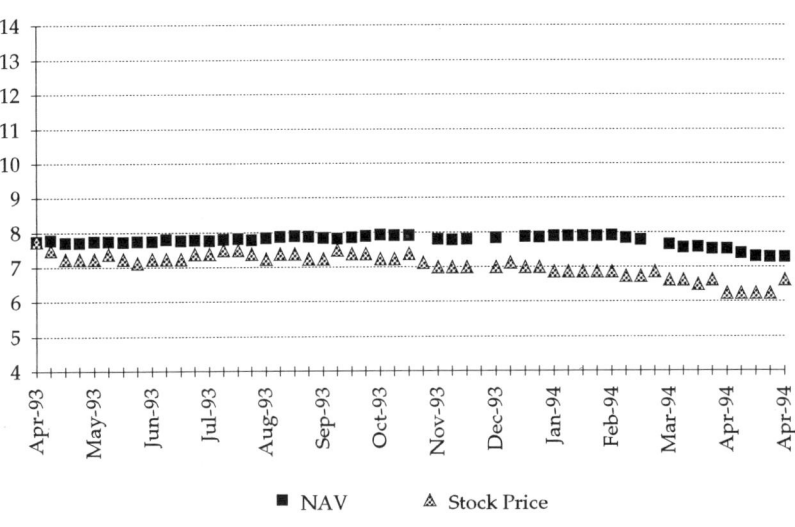

Fund Outlook (MMT): Many of the world's largest economies are exhibiting divergent trends. The major English-speaking countries (the U.S., U.K., Canada and Australia) are in various stages of economic recovery. Germany and Japan are in a recession, and most of continental Europe is in recession or showing very modest growth. However, growth remains strong in Southeast Asia and in much of Latin America, and the trust expects these regions will continue to show the strongest economic growth, based on continued strength in manufacturing, personal incomes and consumption.

Authors' Comments (MMT): The NAV 12-month trailing return of 2.36% is only slightly below the average return for this group of 2.42%. For a number of years, the trust maintained a stable dividend by supplementing income distributions with additional payments from capital. In May 1993 this policy was discontinued and as a result the dividend was reduced from $0.065 to the current rate of $0.047 per month. In the third quarter of 1993, the U.S. Government bond portfolio was reduced from 44% to the present 29% and foreign investments were increased. Foreign investment concentration is in Europe where the fund manager believes interest rates are unsustainably high. The corporate high-yield portion of the portfolio is expected to continue to perform well as the economy recovers and the issuers credit quality improves.

Putnam Master Income Trust

NYSE: PMT

One Post Office Square
Boston, MA 02109
(800) 225-1581

Transfer Agent:
Putnam Investor Services
P.O. Box 41203
Providence, RI 02940-1203
(800) 634-1587

Income

Results

For 12-months Ending 4/29/94	Period End	Period Begin	Distributions	Yield Dist (%)	Total Return (%)
Share Price ($)	8.38	9.13	0.86	9.42	1.20
NAV per Share ($)	8.99	9.39		9.16	4.90

Background: Initial public offering December 18, 1987 of 50,247,000 shares at $10 per share. Initial NAV was $9.30 per share.

Objective: Seeks high current income consistent with preservation of capital. Intends to diversify investments among three sectors of the fixed-income securities markets: U.S. Government and Agencies, high-yield corporate, and foreign issues. Debt securities will be rated A or better at the time of purchase.

Portfolio: (1/31/94) High-Yield 41%, Foreign 26%, U.S. Government Securities 33%. Sector Weightings: Retail & Container 8%, Manufacturing & Industrial 7%, Media & Communications 6%, Hotel & Recreation 4%. Top Holdings: GNMA, U.S. Treasury Notes, Government of Netherlands 7.5%.

Capitalization: (10/31/92) Common stock outstanding 53,375,649. No long-term debt.

Average Maturity (years): 12.6
Fee: 0.75%
Income Distribution: Monthly
Reinvestment Plan: Yes
Fund Manager: Putnam Management Co., Inc.
Capital Gains Distribution: Annually
Shareholder Reports: Quarterly

5 Year Performance

Fiscal Year Ending 10/31	1993	1992	1991	1990	1989
Net Assets ($mil)	513.30	488.30	468.20	429.00	482.50
Net Income Distribution ($)	0.73	0.77	0.82	0.84	0.96
Capital Gains Distribution ($)	0.00	0.10	0.00	0.01	0.19
Total Distribution ($)	0.73	0.87	0.82	0.85	1.15
Yield from Distribution (%)	8.71	10.38	11.71	10.14	12.78
Expense Ratio (%)	0.92	0.95	1.08	1.08	1.06
Portfolio Turnover (%)	132.24	221.30	323.27	125.33	323.44
NAV per Share ($)	9.62	9.15	8.80	8.01	8.86
Market Price per Share ($)	8.88	8.38	8.38	7.00	8.38
Premium (Discount) (%)	-7.74	-8.42	-4.77	-12.61	-5.53
Total Return, Stock Price (%)	14.68	10.38	31.43	-6.32	5.89

Putnam Master Income Trust

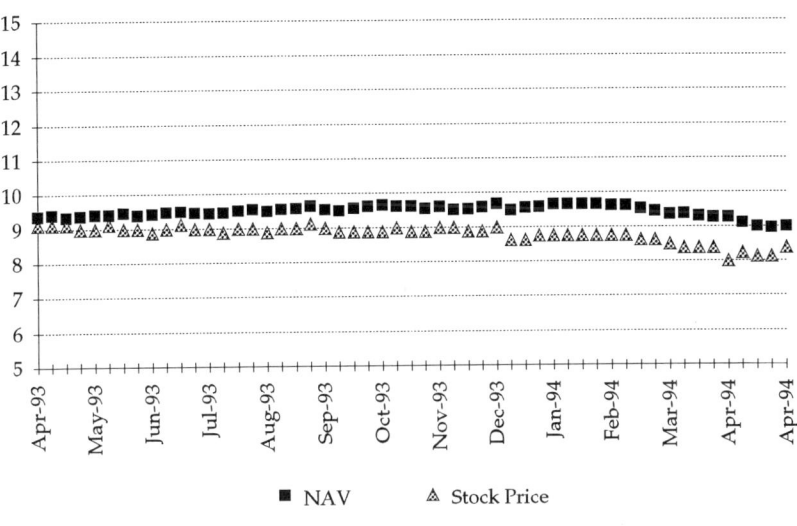

Fund Outlook (PMT): The same trends that helped high-yield bonds prosper—economic vigor and healthier corporate profits—helped keep performance in the U.S. Government securities sector lagging. Investors who feared increased inflation and believed government securities could not keep pace avoided this sector. Good news, however, was in mortgage-backed securities, which performed well through the recent rise in short-term interest rates. The trust believes that U.S. interest rates are now past their nadir. In anticipation of rising short-term rates, the trust expects to reduce holdings of U.S. government securities. This should help protect the value of the portfolio. Looking ahead, the trust believes that any weakening in this sector should be balanced by strength in the high-yield sector, enabling the trust to deliver attractive returns.

Authors' Comments (PMT): The dividend yield is attractive. The high-yield bond sector has been the strongest investment area for the trust for a second year in a row. In February the portfolio manager reduced the total position of the portfolio by 20%, selling equal amounts from each of the sectors, and subsequently reinvesting the funds shortly thereafter in the high-yield sector, increasing the latter. Foreign investments are diversified and include holdings in Japan, Denmark, Italy, U.K. and Australia, as well as the emerging markets of Argentina. The 12-month trailing return is 5.30%, outperforming its peer group.

Putnam Master Intermediate Income Trust

One Post Office Square
Boston, MA 02109
(800) 225-1581

Income

NYSE: PIM
Transfer Agent:
Putnam Investors Services, Inc.
P.O. Box 41204
Providence, RI 02940-1203
(800) 634-1587

Results

For 12-months Ending 4/29/94	Period End	Period Begin	Distributions	Yield Dist (%)	Total Return (%)
Share Price ($)	7.88	8.50	0.70	8.24	0.94
NAV per Share ($)	8.48	8.51		8.23	7.87

Background: Initial public offering April 29, 1988 of 40,000,000 shares at $10 per share. Initial NAV was $9.30 per share.

Objective: Seeks high current income with relative stability of NAV. Invests in U.S. Government securities, high-yield and international fixed-income securities having a dollar-weighted average maturity of more than five years but not more than ten years.

Portfolio: (12/31/93) Corporate Bonds & Notes 38%, U.S. Government & Agencies 32%, Foreign 26%, Short-Term & Other 4%. Country Exposure: Japan 6%, France 5%, U.K. 4%, Italy 3%, Denmark 2%, Australia 2%.

Capitalization: (12/31/93) Common stock outstanding 39,005,338. No long-term debt.

Average Maturity (years): 10.2
Fee: 0.75%
Income Distribution: Monthly
Reinvestment Plan: Yes
Fund Manager: Putnam Management Co., Inc.
Capital Gains Distribution: Annually
Shareholder Reports: Quarterly

5 Year Performance

Fiscal Year Ending 9/30	1993	1992	1991	1990	1989
Net Assets ($mil)	347.60	339.90	317.70	301.60	301.60
Net Income Distribution ($)	0.68	0.74	0.76	0.85	0.99
Capital Gains Distribution ($)	0.00	0.00	0.00	0.08	0.08
Total Distribution ($)	0.68	0.74	0.76	0.93	1.07
Yield from Distribution (%)	8.00	9.55	11.69	11.10	10.83
Expense Ratio (%)	0.96	0.98	1.08	1.04	1.04
Portfolio Turnover (%)	237.63	134.43	204.31	211.22	202.47
NAV per Share ($)	8.91	8.71	8.16	7.60	8.62
Market Price per Share ($)	8.38	8.50	7.75	6.50	8.38
Premium (Discount) (%)	-6.00	-2.41	-5.02	-14.47	-2.90
Total Return, Stock Price (%)	6.59	19.23	30.92	-11.34	-4.35

Putnam Master Intermediate Income Trust

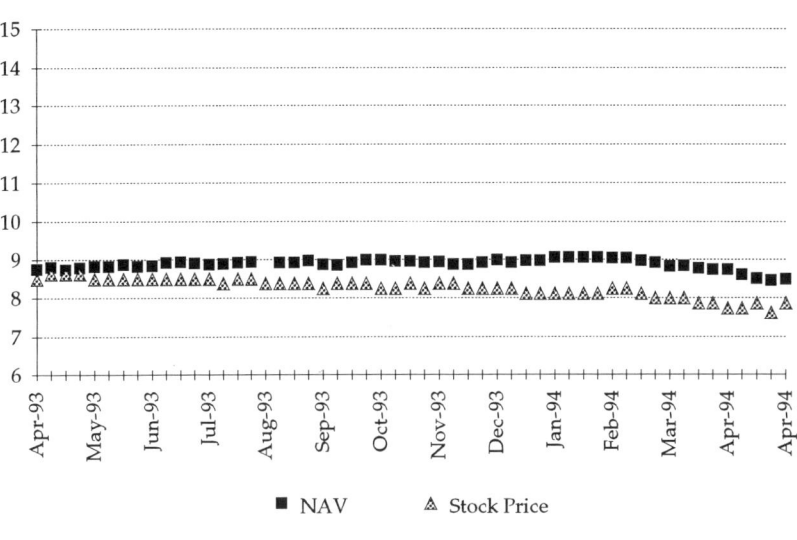

Premium/Discount Spread

■ NAV △ Stock Price

Fund Outlook (PIM): The trust's U.S. government holdings were affected by the drop in bond prices. A shift from a portfolio of bonds with maturities concentrated in the four- to five-year maturity range to bonds with maturities grouped around each end of the overall maturity spectrum is expected. On the international front, the trust continued to rely heavily on hedging strategies to protect the foreign holdings against unfavorable currency shifts. In coming months, the trust will closely monitor conditions in emerging markets and will seek additional opportunities in Latin America as well as Asia, Africa and Eastern Europe.

Authors' Comments (PIM): The 12-month trailing return is 4.78%. In the second and third quarters of 1993, holdings in mortgaged-backed securities were reduced in order to reduce pre-payment risk. The remainder of the government sector was equally divided between three- and ten-year maturities. Because of the average maturities in this trust, the total return will be less. However, there should be a lower level of volatility inasmuch as the shorter-term maturities are less vulnerable to changes in interest rates. Foreign investments are diversified and include holdings in Europe, Australia, Japan and Canada.

Putnam Premier Income Trust

NYSE: PPT

One Post Office Square
Boston, MA 02109
(800) 225-1581

Transfer Agent:
Putnam Investor Services, Inc.
P.O. Box 41203
Providence, RI 02940-1203
(800) 648-7410

Income

Results

For 12-months Ending 4/29/94	Period End	Period Begin	Distributions	Yield Dist (%)	Total Return (%)
Share Price ($)	7.75	8.38	0.73	8.71	1.19
NAV per Share ($)	8.47	8.81		8.29	4.43

Background: Initial public offering February 26, 1988 of 140,000,000 shares at $10 per share. Initial NAV was $9.30 per share.

Objective: Seeks high current income. Investments are allocated among three sectors of the fixed-income securities market: U.S. Government, high-yield, and international. Capital appreciation is incidental. Generally, the fund invests a portion of its assets in each sector, but at times it may only be in one.

Portfolio: (1/31/94) Corporate Bonds & Notes 39%, U.S. Government & Agencies 32%, Foreign 25%. Country Exposure: U.K. 4%, France 4%, Japan 4%, Netherlands 2%, Italy 2%, Argentina 2%.

Capitalization: (1/31/94) Shares of beneficial interest outstanding 140,759,960. No long-term debt.

Average Maturity (years): 13.6

Fee: 0.75% **Fund Manager:** Putnam Management Co., Inc.

Income Distribution: Monthly **Capital Gains Distribution:** Annually

Reinvestment Plan: Yes **Shareholder Reports:** Quarterly

5 Year Performance

Fiscal Year Ending 7/31	1993	1992	1991	1990	1989
Net Assets ($mil)	1249.20	1195.00	1106.80	1169.00	1279.00
Net Income Distribution ($)	0.71	0.75	0.75	0.75	0.88
Capital Gains Distribution ($)	0.00	0.00	0.00	0.02	0.27
Total Distribution ($)	0.71	0.75	0.75	0.77	1.15
Yield from Distribution (%)	8.00	9.68	10.52	8.11	11.94
Expense Ratio (%)	0.84	0.88	1.06	1.02	0.99
Portfolio Turnover (%)	250.65	203.27	350.45	165.97	249.07
NAV per Share ($)	8.87	8.51	7.90	8.20	8.98
Market Price per Share ($)	8.25	8.88	7.75	7.13	9.50
Premium (Discount) (%)	-6.99	4.23	-1.90	-13.17	5.79
Total Return, Stock Price (%)	0.90	24.26	19.21	-16.84	10.59

Putnam Premier Income Trust

Premium/Discount Spread

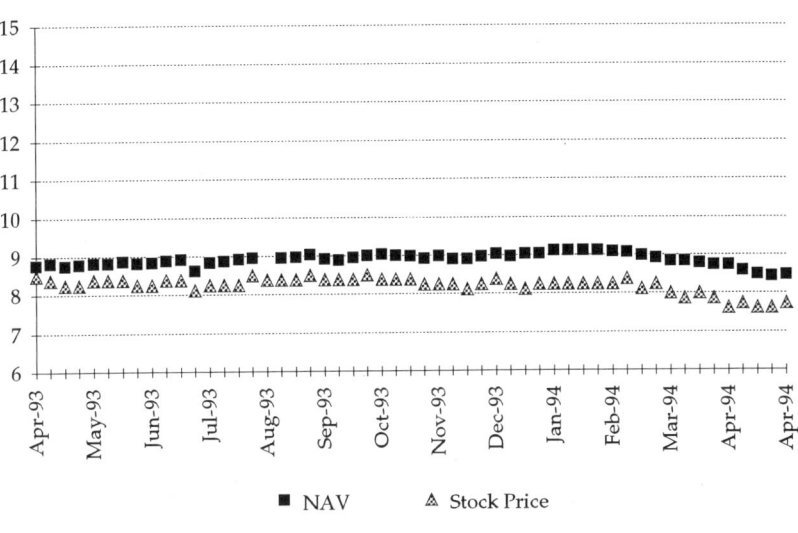

■ NAV   △ Stock Price

Fund Outlook (PPT): In all, the trust believes the outlook for its multi-sector strategy is bright. The trust expects higher-yielding corporate bonds in the U.S. to make the most of renewed economic strength and will maintain an overweighted position there. At the same time, the trust expects mortgages to provide a competitive edge against Treasuries in an environment of stable or rising rates. Overseas, the trust will look to concentrate assets in the smaller European countries which it feels are en route to economic recovery and will maintain a cautious stance with respect to the trust's holdings in Japan.

Authors' Comments (PPT): The 12-month trailing return is 4.87%. The outstanding performance of this trust can be attributed to the overweighting of the high-yield sector, which has been the strongest performer and, in an improving economy, will continue to perform well. The international bond portfolio is well diversified and includes investments in Europe, Japan, Argentina and Mexico. Currency hedging strategies are used.

Appendix

Sources of Additional Information

The following reference list of financial publications, newsletters, books, and associations is provided to assist the reader in locating additional information on closed-end funds.

The American Association of Individual Investors
625 North Michigan Avenue, Suite 1900
Chicago, IL 60611
(312) 280-0170 / FAX (312) 280-9883

A 16-year-old association with over 150,000 members that assists individuals in becoming effective managers of their own assets through programs of education, information, and research. A one-year membership includes the monthly *AAII Journal*, the comprehensive book, *The Individual Investor's Guide to Low-Load Mutual Funds*, an annual year-end tax planning guide, membership in local chapter groups, and discounts on investment publications, software, and videocourses.

SOURCE: The Complete Guide to Investment Information (How to Find It and How to Use It) by Jae K. Shim, Ph.D. and Joel G. Siegel, Ph.D.
International Publishing Corporation, Inc.
625 N. Michigan Avenue, Suite 1920
Chicago, IL 60611
(312) 943-7354 / (800) 488-4149 / FAX (312) 642-0679

This comprehensive investment information handbook shows where to find investment information and gives advice on how to read and interpret the various data sources. Includes large numbers of illustrations and examples, handy formulas for investment decision making, an investment quick-reference matrix, a glossary of essential investment terms, and a meticulously compiled index for ease of use.

Frank Cappiello's Closed-End Fund Digest
1224 Coast Village Circle, Suite 11
Santa Barbara, CA 93108
(805) 565-5651/ FAX (805) 565-3433

An 8-page monthly newsletter devoted exclusively to closed-end funds, featuring four model portfolios: balanced, global, income (tax-free), income (taxable);

monthly performance data, including buy/sell recommendations, on all equity and bond closed-end funds (see Figure 1.2 of this book); Editorial Comments and Analyst's Comments. Subscribers to the newsletter receive a copy of *99 Best Closed-End Funds to Own Now*.

The Investor's Guide to Closed-End Mutual Funds
Thomas Herzfeld
P.O. Box 161465
Miami, FL 31116
(305) 271-1900 / FAX (305) 270-1040

A monthly newsletter on closed-end funds features buy/sell recommendations, performance figures, and one model portfolio.

The Scott Letter: Closed-End Fund Report
Cole Publishing
318 William Street
Fredericksburg, VA 22401
(800) 356-3508 / (804) 741-8707

A monthly newsletter featuring model portfolios, manager interviews, and commentary.

Morningstar Closed-End Funds
225 West Wacker Drive
Chicago, IL 60606
(800) 876-5005 / (312) 427-1985 / FAX (312) 427-9215

A comprehensive source of closed-end fund data updated every two weeks.

Mutual Fund Forecaster
The Institute of Econometric Research
3471 North Federal Highway
Fort Lauderdale, FL 33306
(800) 327-6720 / (305) 563-9000 / FAX (305) 563-9003

Mutual fund selection and market predictions. Covers some 60 closed-end funds.

Lipper Closed-End Bond and Closed-End Equity Funds Analysis
Lipper Analytical Services, Inc.
1380 Lawrence Street, Suite 950
Denver, CO 80204
(303) 534-3472 / FAX (303) 573-5702

Exhaustive data for the professional investor.

Investment Company Institute
1600 M Street N.W., Suite 600
Washington, DC 20036
(202) 293-7700 / FAX (202) 955-6230

The trade association for the investment company industry.

Standard & Poor's Stock Reports
Standard & Poor's Corporation
25 Broadway
New York, NY 10004
(212) 208-8000 / FAX (212) 509-8994

Reports include statistics on companies traded on NYSE, AMEX, and OTC markets. Each report is a succinct profile of the company's activities and financial position, supported by extensive statistics that facilitate quick year-to-year comparisons.

Value Line Investment Survey
Value Line, Inc.
711 Third Avenue
New York, NY 10017
(212) 687-3965 / (800) 634-3583 / FAX (212) 338-9623

Weekly publication with in-depth descriptions on a multitude of stocks and closed-end funds. Gives ratings and opinions.

CDA Wiesenberger Companies Service
1355 Piccard Drive
Rockville, MA 20850
(800) 232-2285 / (301) 975-9600 / FAX (301) 590-1389

Publishes quarterly and annual reports which provide performance results on selected closed-end funds.

FINANCIAL PRESS

Barron's
Dow Jones & Company
200 Liberty Street
New York, NY 10281
(212) 416-2700 / FAX (212) 416-2829

Publishes both equity and bond figures for closed-end funds. Has weekly feature on mutual funds and often contains articles concerning closed-end funds.

The New York Times
229 W. 43rd Street
New York, NY 10036
(212) 556-1234

Closed-end fund equity figures appear in the Saturday edition and bond figures appear in the Wednesday edition.

The Wall Street Journal
200 Liberty Street
New York, NY 10281
(212) 416-2000 / FAX (212) 416-2658

Closed-end equity fund figures for the preceding Friday (NAV, market price, discount/premium) are published in the Monday edition under the heading "Publicly Traded Funds".

BROKERAGE HOUSES

The following brokerage houses offer periodic closed-end fund research reports. Contact your local branch for their latest reports:

A.G. Edwards & Sons, Inc.
PaineWebber Securities
Prudential Bache Securities
Smith Barney Harris Upham & Co., Inc.
Shearson Lehman
Merrill Lynch
Kidder Peabody

Index

ACM Managed Multi-Market Trust, 242-43
Adams Express Company, 8, 52, 53, 58-59
Alliance Global Environment Fund, 118-19
American Capital Income Trust, 258-59
American Municipal Term Trust, Inc., 154-55
Argentina Fund, 78-79
Austria Fund (The), 80-81
Baker, Fentress & Company, 60-61
BlackRock Advantage Term Trust, Inc., 230-31
BlackRock Target Term Trust, Inc., 232-33
Central Securities Corporation, 62-63
Chile Fund, Inc. (The), 82-83
Clemente Global Growth Fund, Inc., 120-21
Colonial Intermarket Income Trust I, 260-61
Colonial Intermediate High Income Securities, 188-89
Current Income Shares, Inc., 206-7
Dean Witter Government Income Trust, 220-21
Dreyfus Strategic Governments Income, Inc., 262-63
Emerging Germany Fund, Inc., 84-85
Emerging Mexico Fund, 86-87
Fidelity Advisor Emerging Asia, 122-23
First Australia Fund, 88-89
First Commonwealth, 244-45
First Iberian Fund, Inc., 90-91

First Philippine Fund, Inc., 92-93
France Growth Fund, Inc. (The), 194-95
General American Investors, 29, 64-65
Global Governments Plus Fund, Inc., 246-47
Global Health Sciences, 124-25
Global Yield Fund, Inc. (The), 248-249
Growth Fund of Spain, 96-97
H & Q Life Sciences Investors, 66-67
High Income Advantage Trust, 190-91
High Income Advantage Trust II, 192-93
High Income Advantage Trust III, 194-95
Hyperion 1999 Term Trust, Inc., 234-35
Income Opportunities Fund 1999, 236-37
India Growth Fund, Inc., 98-99
Irish Investment Funds, 100-1
Italy Fund, Inc. (The), 102-3
John Hancock Income Securities Trust, 208-9
Kemper Intermediate Government Trust, 222-23
Kemper Multi-Market Income Trust, 264-65
Kemper Municipal Income Trust, 156-57
Kleinwort Benson Australian Income Fund, Inc., 250-51
Latin America Discovery Fund, 126-27
Liberty Term Trust 1999, 238-39
Lincoln National Convertible Securities, 198-99

Malaysia Fund, Inc. (The), 104-5
Mentor Income Fund, 224-25
Mexico Fund, Inc., 106-7
MFS Charter Income Trust, 266-67
MFS Government Markets Income Trust, 268-69
MFS Intermediate Income Trust, 270-71
MFS Multimarket Income Trust, 272-73
Minnesota Municipal Term Trust, 132-33
Montgomery Street Income Securities, 210-11
Morgan Grenfell SMALLCap Fund, Inc., 68-69
Municipal High Income Fund, 178-79
Municipal Premium Income Trust, 158-59
MuniEnhanced Fund, Inc., 160-61
MuniInsured Fund Inc., 180-81
MuniYield Fund, 162-63
Nuveen California Investment Quality Municipal Fund, 134-35
Nuveen Florida Investment Quality Municipal Fund, 136-37
Nuveen Florida Quality Income Municipal Fund, 138-39
Nuveen Municipal Market Opportunity Fund, 164-65
Nuveen Municipal Value Fund, Inc., 182-83
Nuveen New Jersey Quality Income Municipal Fund, 140-41
Nuveen New York Investment Quality Municipal Fund, 142-43
Nuveen Pennsylvania Investment Quality Municipal Fund, 144-45
Petroleum & Resources Corporation, 128-29
Pilgrim Prime Rate Trust, 212-13
Portugal Fund, Inc., 108-9
Putnam High Income Convertible & Bond Fund, 200-1
Putnam Intermediate Government Income Trust, 226-27

Putnam Investment Grade Municipal Trust, 166-67
Putnam Master Income Trust, 274-75
Putnam Master Intermediate Income Trust, 276-77
Putnam Premier Income Trust, 278-79
ROC Taiwan Fund, Inc., 110-11
Royce Value Trust, Inc., 70-71
Salomon Brothers Fund, 72-73
Seligman Select Municipal Fund, 168-69
Smith Barney Intermediate Municipal Fund, 184-85
State Mutual Securities Trust, 214-15
Strategic Global Income, 252-53
Swiss Helvetia Fund, Inc., 112-13
Taurus MuniCalifornia Holdings, Inc., 146-47
TCW Convertible Securities Fund, Inc., 202-3
Templeton Global Income Fund, Inc., 254-55
Tri-Continental Corporation, 74-75
United Kingdom Fund, Inc., 114-15
USLife Income Fund, Inc., 216-17
Van Kampen Merritt Advantage Municipal Income Trust, 170-71
Van Kampen Merritt Municipal Opportunity Trust, 172-73
Van Kampen Merritt Municipal Trust, 174-75
Van Kampen Merritt New York Quality Municipal Trust, 148-49
Van Kampen Merritt Pennsylvania Quality Municipal, 150-51

Earn Higher Investment Returns with Lower Costs

Now in its second edition, revised, and made even more practical than before, *Value Averaging: The Safe and Easy Strategy for Higher Investment Returns:*
- shows you how to make the buying and selling of investments nearly automatic, relieving you of emotional anxiety and the need for market-timing and stock picking skills;
- recommends investments best suited for value averaging;
- tells you how to build real wealth easily and consistently over time;
- demonstrates in detail how to use both dollar cost averaging and value averaging for specific investment goals, such as college tuition for your children or your own retirement.

Here's what reviewers said about the last edition:

"The latest wrinkle in automatic investing . . . Compared over time with dollar cost averaging, value averaging will always lower your total cost per share, and it will typically provide a rate of return that's about one percentage point higher . . . "
Kiplinger's Personal Finance Magazine

" 'Today's Best Way to Invest' The smartest strategy today is not to shun stock—but to add money a little at a time. . . . The most familiar such technique is dollar cost averaging. . . . But a lesser-known version called value averaging can get better results by forcing you to make an extra investment in a month when stocks are down and to invest less—or actually a little less—when stocks advance."
Money Magazine

"Value averaging takes dollar cost averaging one step further. Besides buying low, you sell shares when the markets soar." *The New York Times*

- -

Please send me _____ copies of *Value Averaging: The Safe and Easy Strategy for Higher Investment Returns,* 2nd ed., revised, by Michael E. Edleson, PH.D., at $22.95 for each copy.

Name_____

Address_____

City / State / Zip Code_____

Here is my check made payable to International Publishing Corporation. I have added $2.00 for each book to cover postage and handling. (In Illinois, I have added 8.75% sales tax.)

Payment $_____, or charge my VISA/Master Card #_____ Exp. date _____

Signature_____

MAIL TO: International Publishing Corp., Inc., 625 N. Michigan Ave., Suite 1920, Chicago, IL 60611 or call 1-800-488-4149 for faster service.

- -

One-of-a-Kind Investment Information Guide

It took a seasoned financial planner a mere five minutes of leafing through this book's 400-plus pages to recognize its enormous potential value for both financial beginners and old pro's.

For her client, an admitted neophyte, *SOURCE: The Complete Guide to Investment Information, Where to Find It and How to Use It* provides a painless education in how to discover the most pertinent investment information and how to employ it—not to mention how to better understand what the financial planner and her stockbroker are talking about. For more experienced investors, it offers the one-stop convenience of up-to-date source information; as such, it's a first-of-its-kind tool.

SOURCE is an investment information handbook designed for students of finance and investments as well as for practical investors. *SOURCE* shows where to find information and advice on different types of investment instruments and how to read and interpret those sources. *SOURCE* breaks down the information into an overview, a look at how to choose the right type of security in each investment category, how to read related information given for each source. From the most common and accessible daily newspaper or radio report to the most sophisticated and often costly investment newsletter, no information source is overlooked.

SOURCE, by Jae K. Shim and Joel G. Siegel, who also co-authored the best-selling *The Vest Pocket MBA*, is an invaluable one-of-a-kind investment decision making tool for both beginning and experienced investors.

Send me _____ copies of *SOURCE: The Complete Guide to Investment Information, Where to Find It and How to Use It*, by Jae K. Shim and Joel G. Siegel at $29.95 each (hardcover).

Name_____

Address_____

City / State / Zip _____

Here is my check made payable to International Publishing Corporation. I have added $2.00 for each book to cover postage and handling. (In Illinois, I have also added 8.75% sales tax.)

Payment $ _____, or charge my VISA/Master Card # _____ Exp. date____

Signature_____

MAIL TO: International Publishing Corp., Inc., 625 N. Michigan Ave., Suite 1920, Chicago, IL 60611 or call 1-800-488-4149 for faster service.